Shojo Beat

VAMPIRE KNIGHT

MEMORIES

VOLUME

5

STORY & ART BY
Matsuri Hino

The Story of VAMPIRE KNIGHT

Previously...

Vampire Knight is the story of Yuki Kuran, a pureblood vampire princess who was brought up as a human.

A moment of peace has arrived after a fierce battle between humans and vampires. But Kaname Kuran, whose heart became the Ancestor Metal for weapons capable of killing vampires, continues to sleep within the coffin of ice. A thousand years later, Yuki gives Kaname her heart, and he is revived as a human. Yuki and Kaname's daughter, Ai, begins to tell him about the days that have passed...

The bombings by the "Vampire King" have ceased thanks to the work of Yuki and her friends, but the identities of those responsible remain a mystery. A summit held by the mayor triggers a riot. Headmaster Cross intervenes and loses his life. Ren is born into a world in greater turmoil...

CHARACTERS

YUKI KURAN (CROSS)

The adopted daughter of the headmaster of Cross Academy. She is a pureblood vampire and the princess of the noble Kuran family. She has always adored Kaname, even when she did not have her memory.

KANAME KURAN

A pureblood vampire and the progenitor of the Kurans. He is Yuki's fiancé and was raised as her sibling. He knows Yuki's true identity and cares for her...

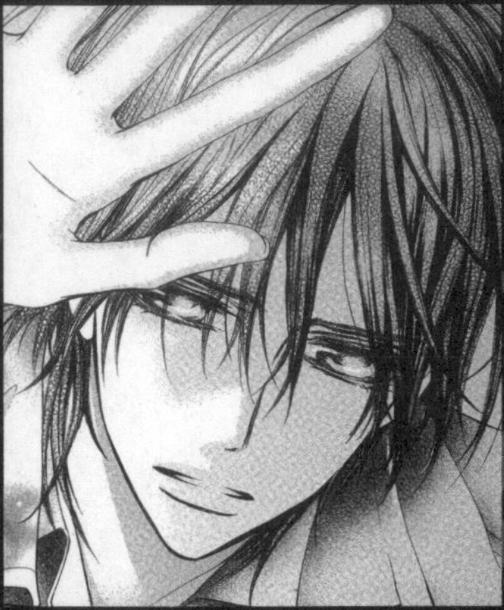

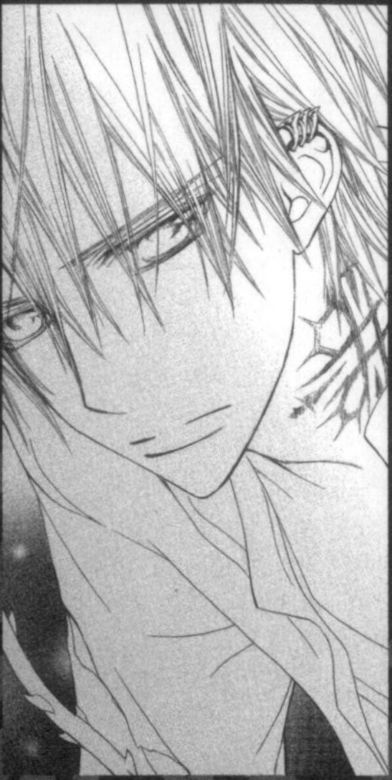

ZERO KIRYU

He was born into a family of vampire hunters and later was turned into a vampire. His parents were killed by a pureblood. He has agonized over his feelings for Yuki and his role as a vampire hunter.

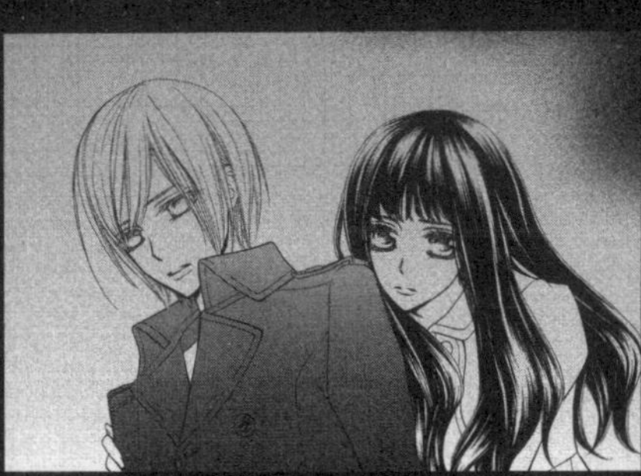

REN AND AI

Yuki's children

HANABUSA AIDO

He was an upperclassman in the Night Class. He is working to create a medicine that will turn vampires into humans...

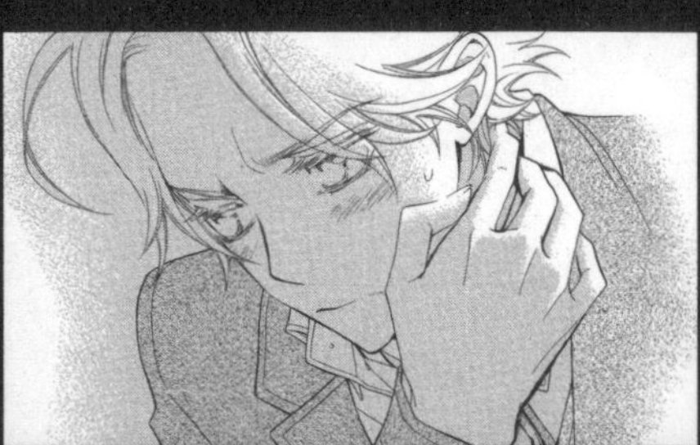

VAMPIRE KNIGHT
MEMORIES

CONTENTS

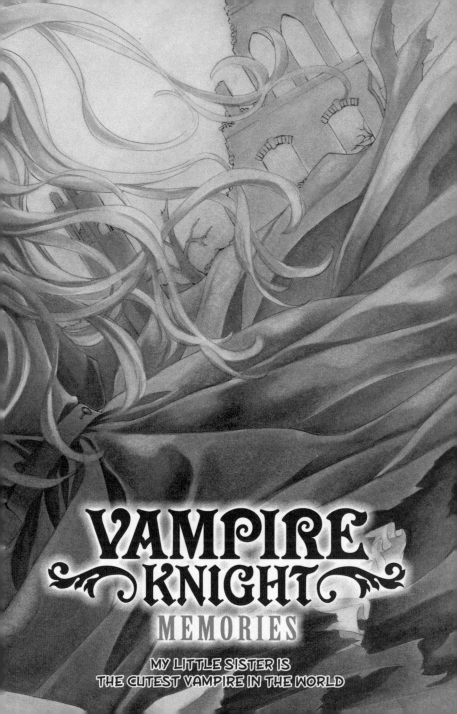

VAMPIRE KNIGHT
MEMORIES

MY LITTLE SISTER IS
THE CUTEST VAMPIRE IN THE WORLD

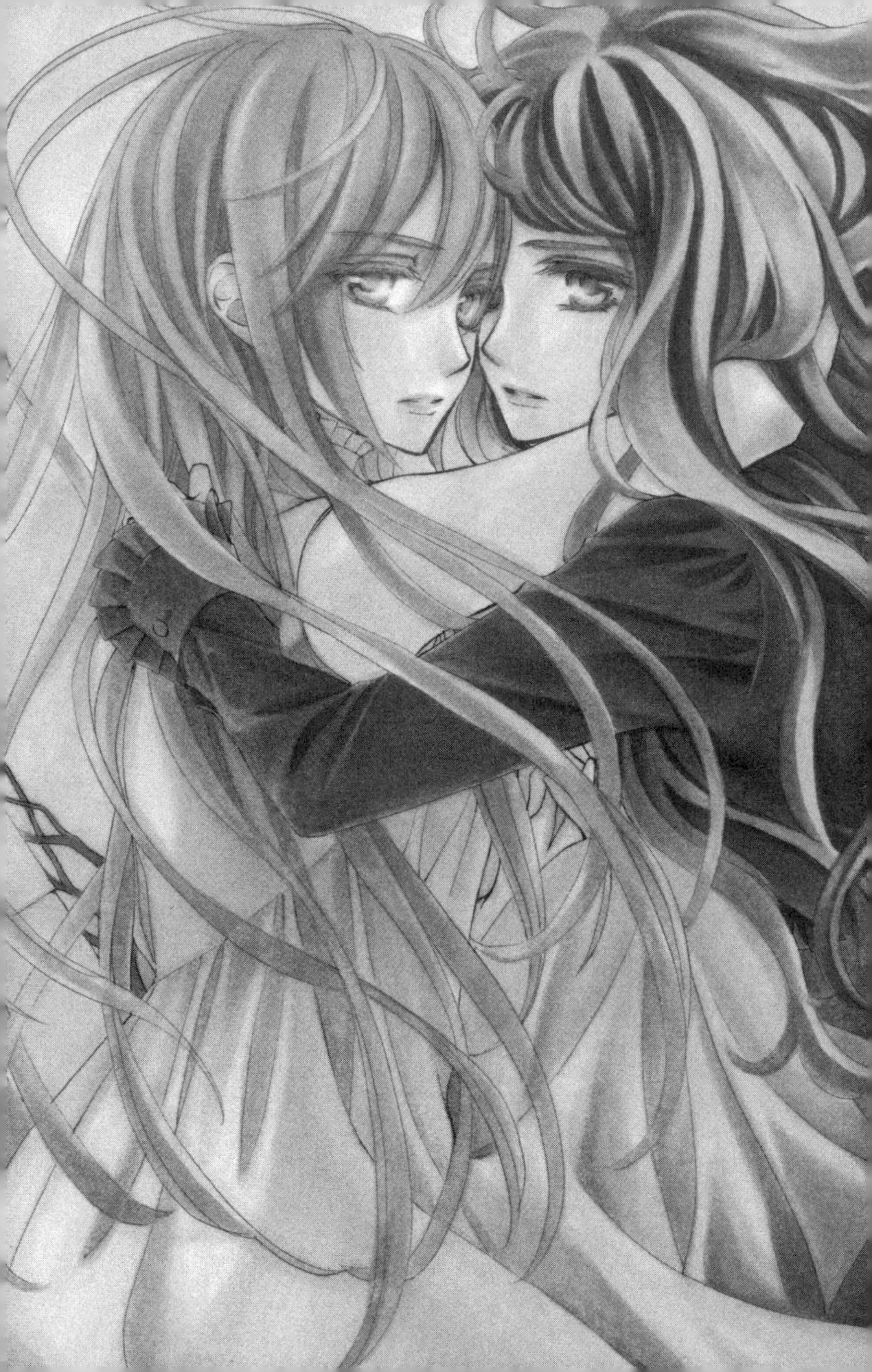

By the time this volume comes out in Japan, Hino (the person writing this) will have entered her 25th year as a professional mangaka. The reason I've been able to continue for so long is thanks to all the people who read my work and support me. It's also thanks to all my past editors who gave me advice, the various people affiliated with my work and the people around me, including my assistants, who work together to meet deadlines. Thank you very much to everyone!!

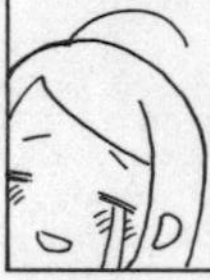

An exhibit of my original work commemorating my 25th year will be held in 2019. Thank you very much. It is such an honor for me. This is truly thanks to everyone.

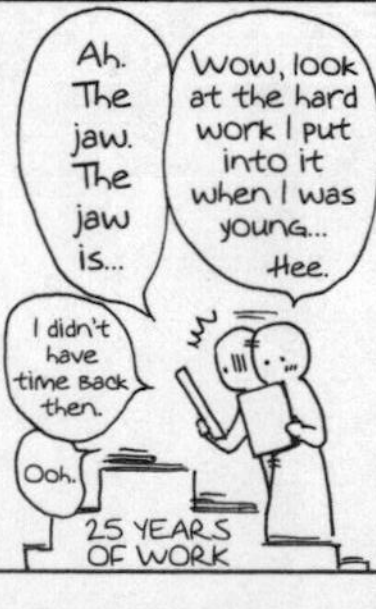
Wow, look at the hard work I put into it when I was young... Hee.
Ah. The jaw. The jaw is...
I didn't have time back then.
Ooh.
25 YEARS OF WORK

Most of my colored illustrations and selected final drafts of manga will be exhibited. Goods and illustration books will be sold too.

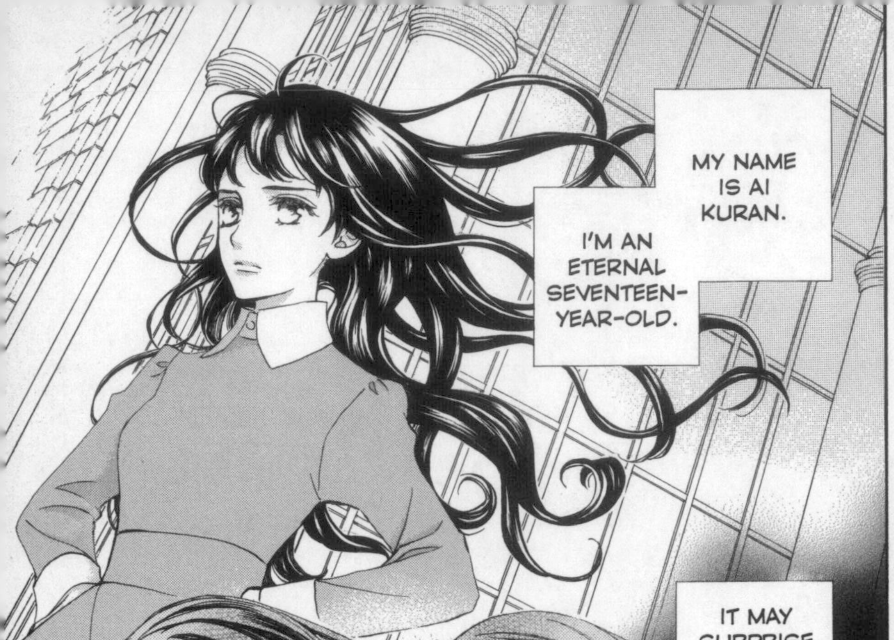
MY NAME IS AI KURAN.
I'M AN ETERNAL SEVENTEEN-YEAR-OLD.
IT MAY SURPRISE YOU, BUT MY PARENTS ARE VAMPIRES.
PREEMINENT PUREBLOOD VAMPIRES OF NOBLE ANCESTRY.
HAVING BEEN BORN FROM THOSE TWO, I REMAIN...
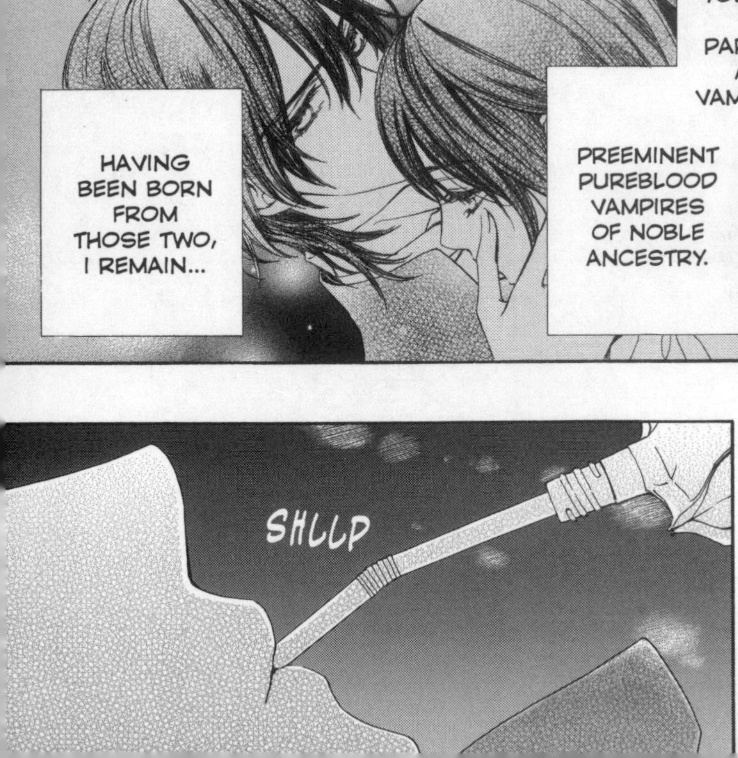
SHLLP

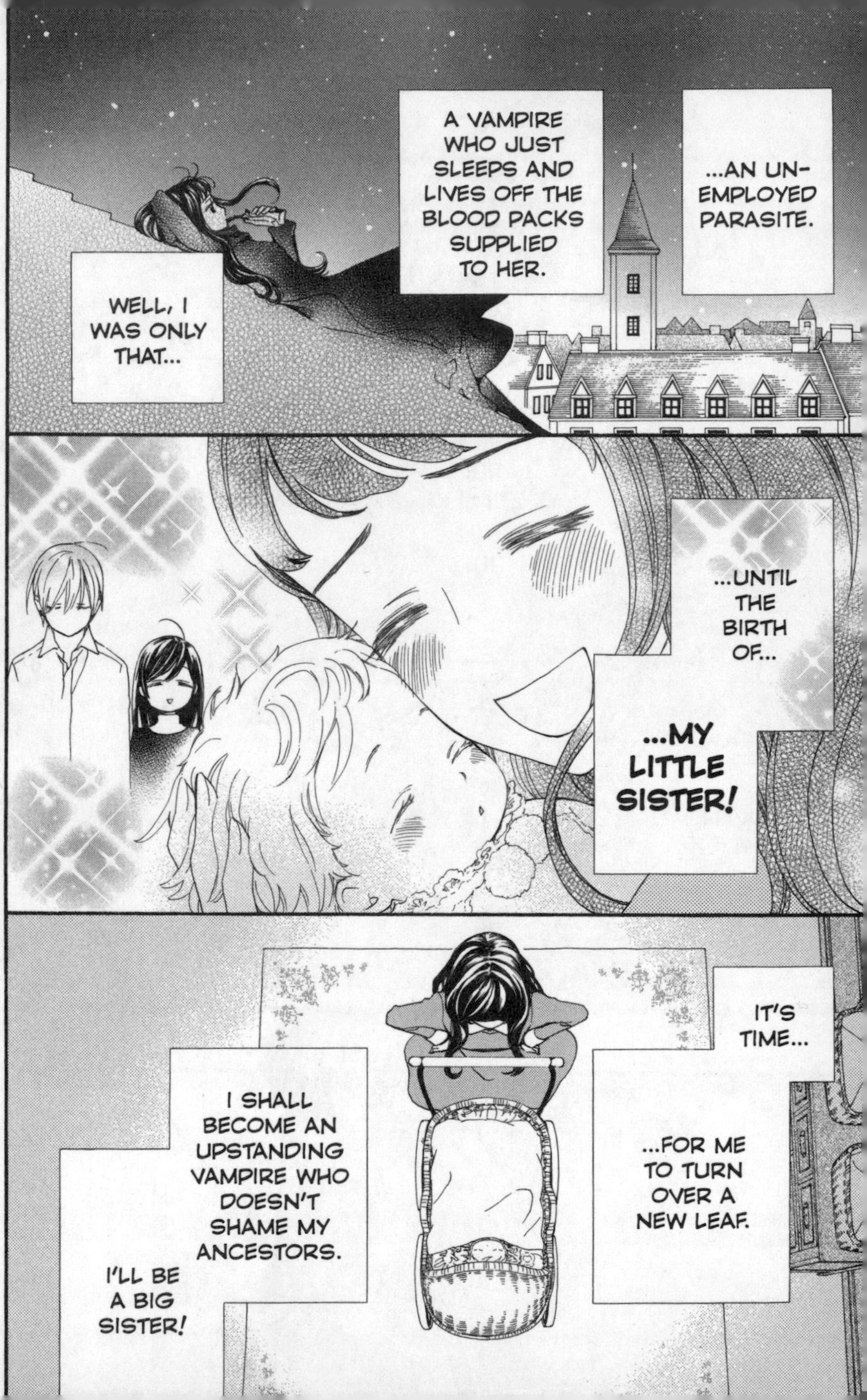
...AN UN-EMPLOYED PARASITE.
A VAMPIRE WHO JUST SLEEPS AND LIVES OFF THE BLOOD PACKS SUPPLIED TO HER.
WELL, I WAS ONLY THAT...
...UNTIL THE BIRTH OF...
...MY LITTLE SISTER!
IT'S TIME...
...FOR ME TO TURN OVER A NEW LEAF.
I SHALL BECOME AN UPSTANDING VAMPIRE WHO DOESN'T SHAME MY ANCESTORS.
I'LL BE A BIG SISTER!

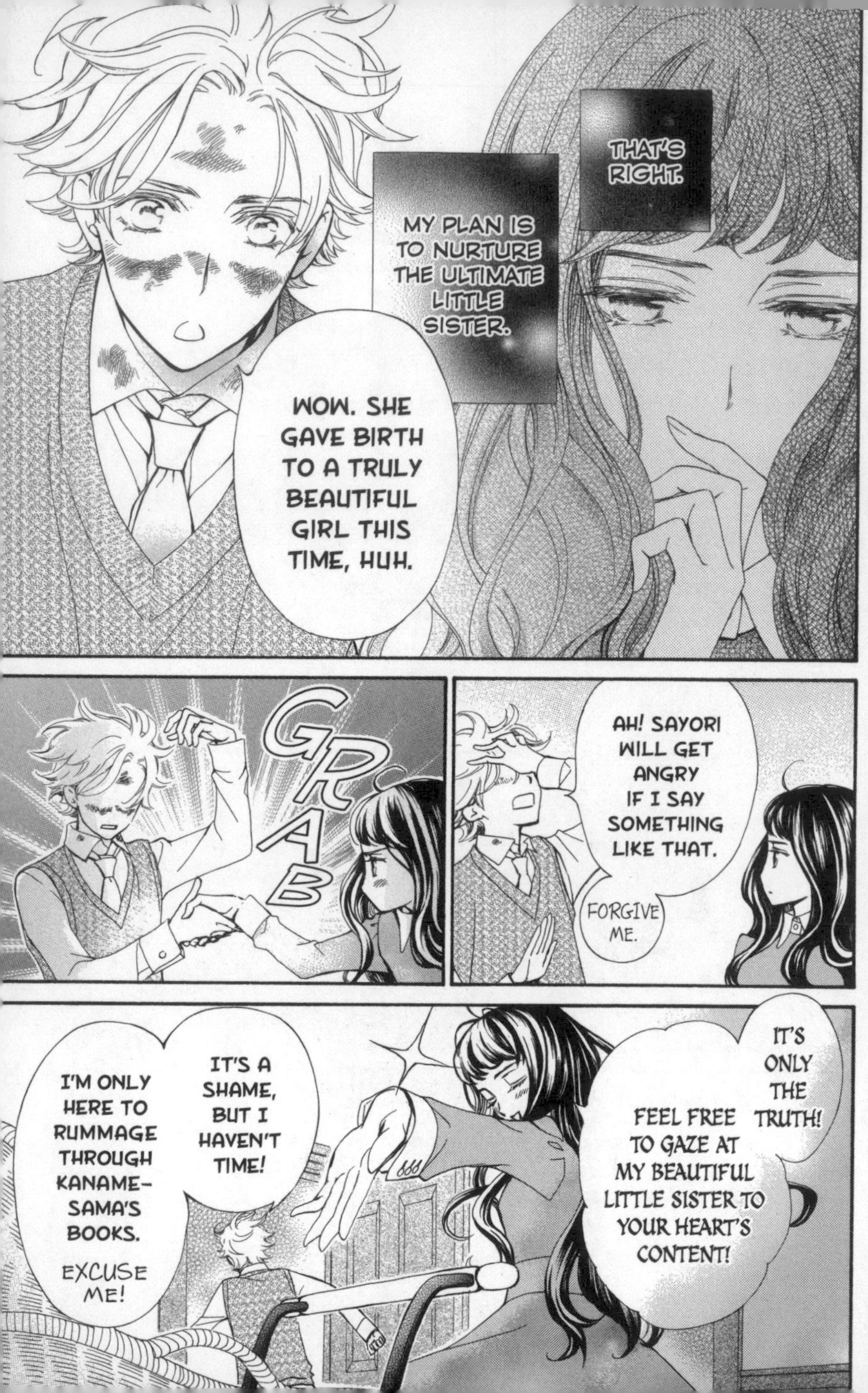
THAT'S RIGHT.
MY PLAN IS TO NURTURE THE ULTIMATE LITTLE SISTER.
WOW. SHE GAVE BIRTH TO A TRULY BEAUTIFUL GIRL THIS TIME, HUH.
AH! SAYORI WILL GET ANGRY IF I SAY SOMETHING LIKE THAT.
FORGIVE ME.
GRAB
IT'S ONLY THE TRUTH!
FEEL FREE TO GAZE AT MY BEAUTIFUL LITTLE SISTER TO YOUR HEART'S CONTENT!
IT'S A SHAME, BUT I HAVEN'T TIME!
I'M ONLY HERE TO RUMMAGE THROUGH KANAME-SAMA'S BOOKS.
EXCUSE ME!

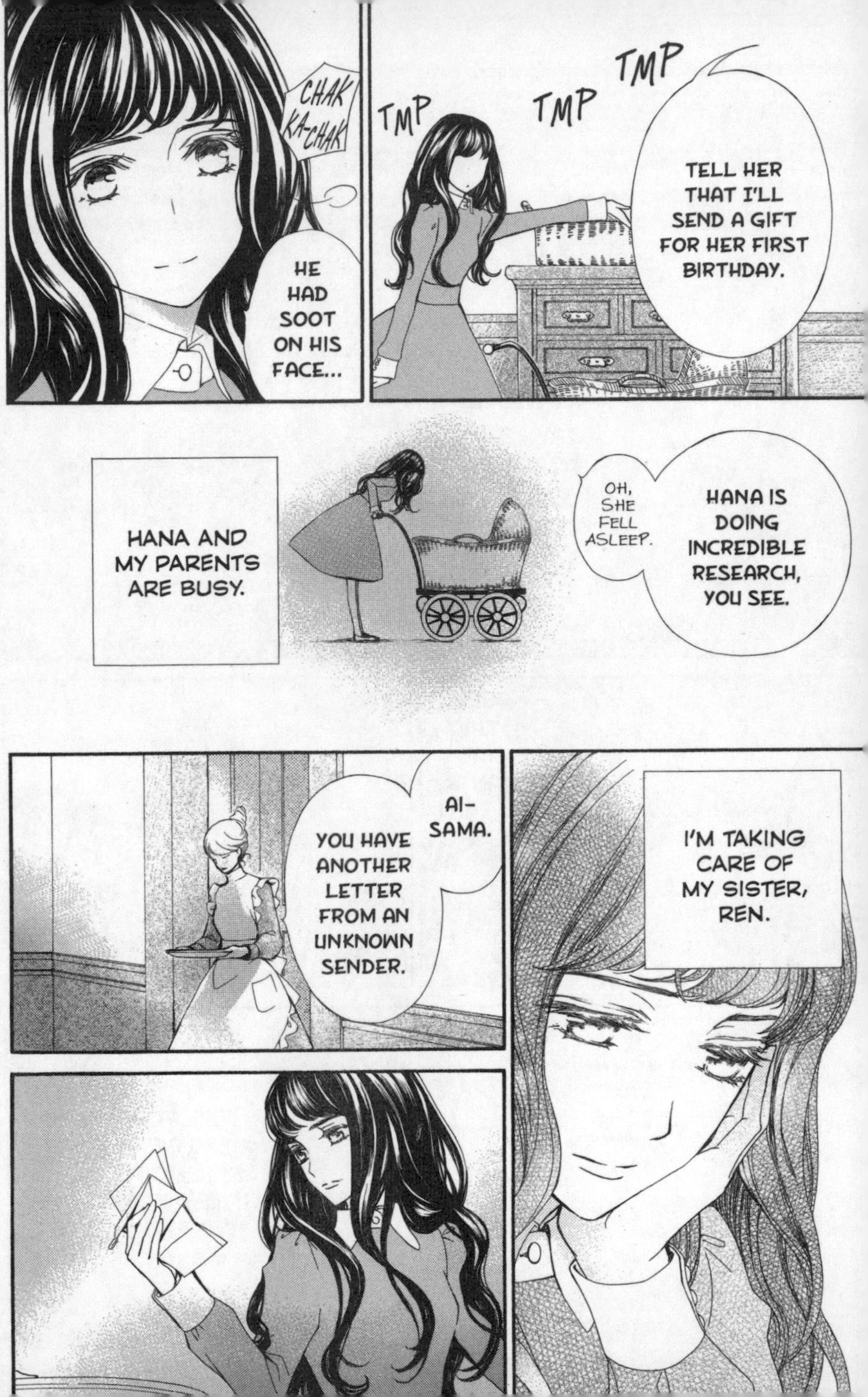
TMP
TMP
TMP
TELL HER THAT I'LL SEND A GIFT FOR HER FIRST BIRTHDAY.
CHAK KA-CHAK
HE HAD SOOT ON HIS FACE...
HANA IS DOING INCREDIBLE RESEARCH, YOU SEE.
OH, SHE FELL ASLEEP.
HANA AND MY PARENTS ARE BUSY.
I'M TAKING CARE OF MY SISTER, REN.
AI-SAMA.
YOU HAVE ANOTHER LETTER FROM AN UNKNOWN SENDER.

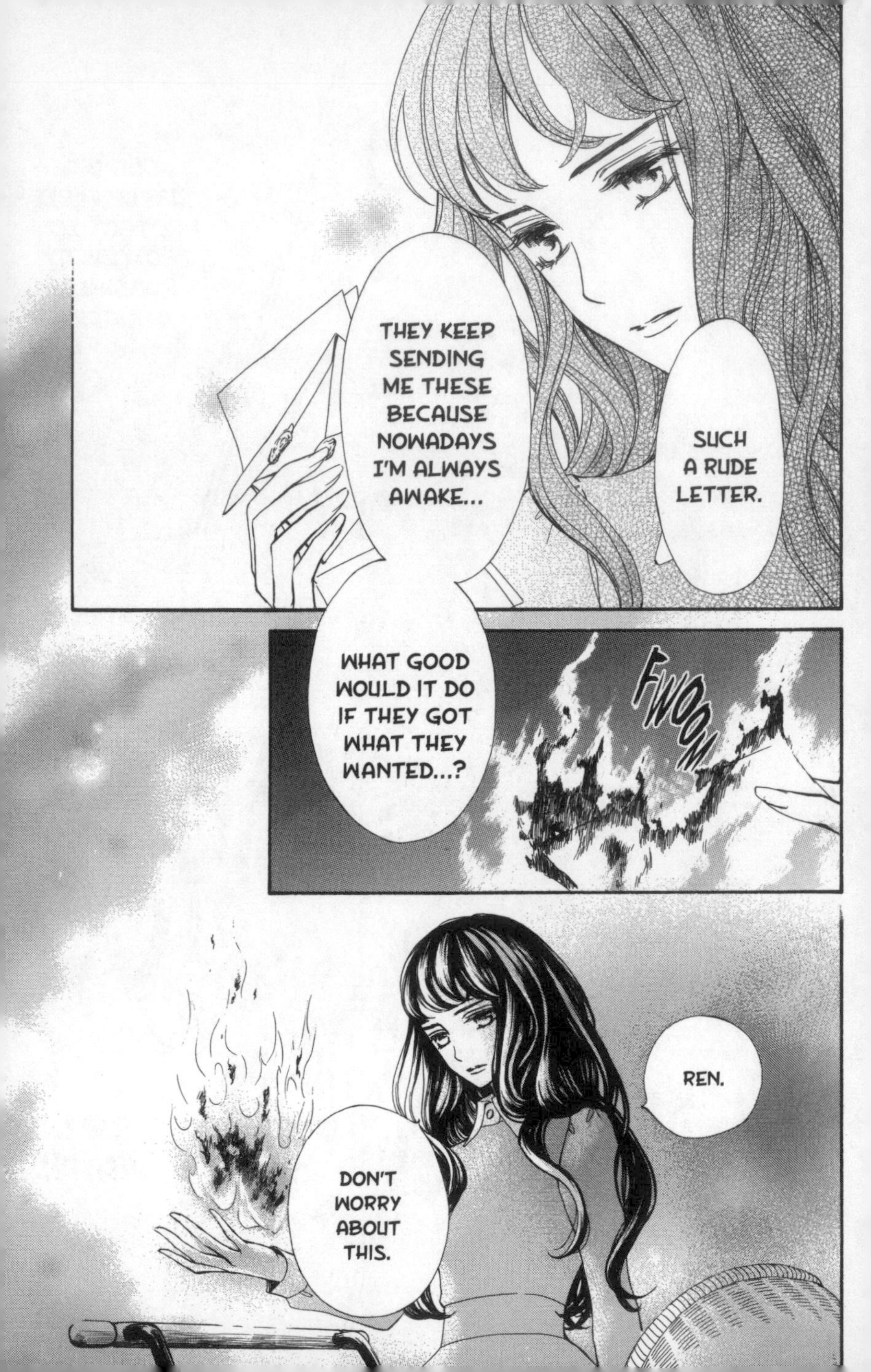
SUCH A RUDE LETTER.
THEY KEEP SENDING ME THESE BECAUSE NOWADAYS I'M ALWAYS AWAKE...
WHAT GOOD WOULD IT DO IF THEY GOT WHAT THEY WANTED...?
FWOOM
REN.
DON'T WORRY ABOUT THIS.

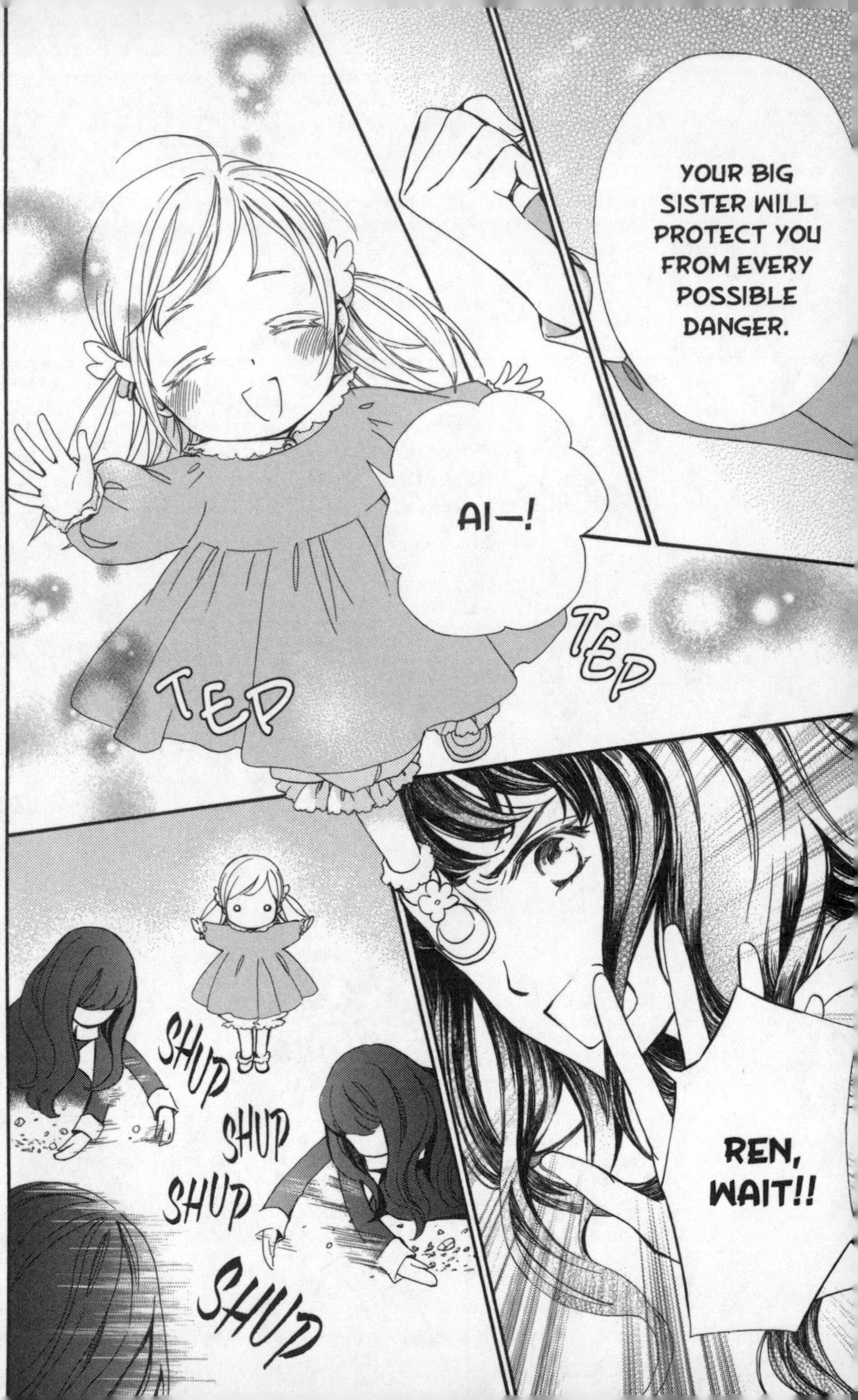
YOUR BIG SISTER WILL PROTECT YOU FROM EVERY POSSIBLE DANGER.
AI—!
TEP
TEP
REN, WAIT!!
SHUP
SHUP
SHUP
SHUP

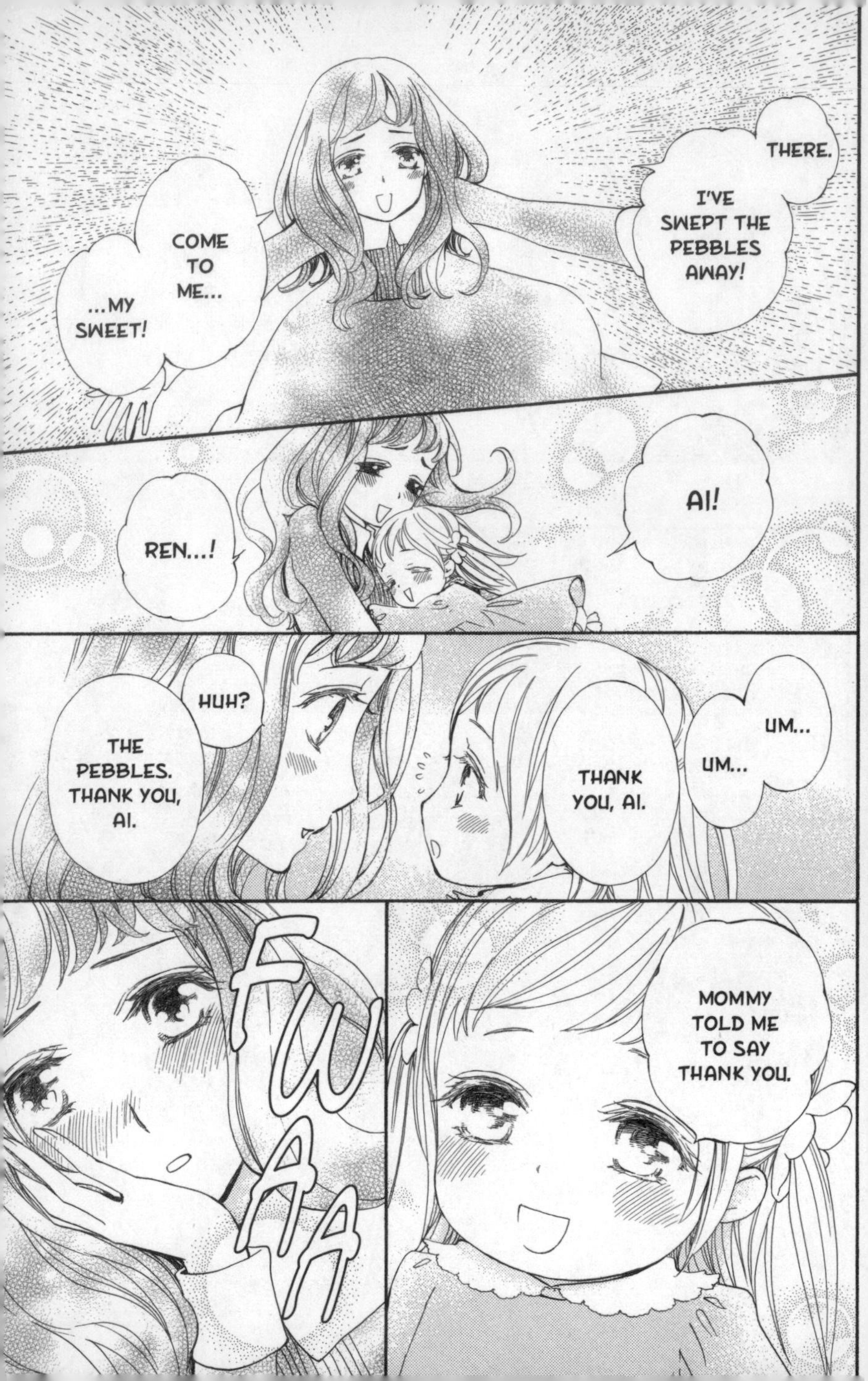
THERE.
I'VE SWEPT THE PEBBLES AWAY!
COME TO ME...
...MY SWEET!
AI!
REN...!
UM...
UM...
THANK YOU, AI.
HUH?
THE PEBBLES. THANK YOU, AI.
MOMMY TOLD ME TO SAY THANK YOU.
FWAA

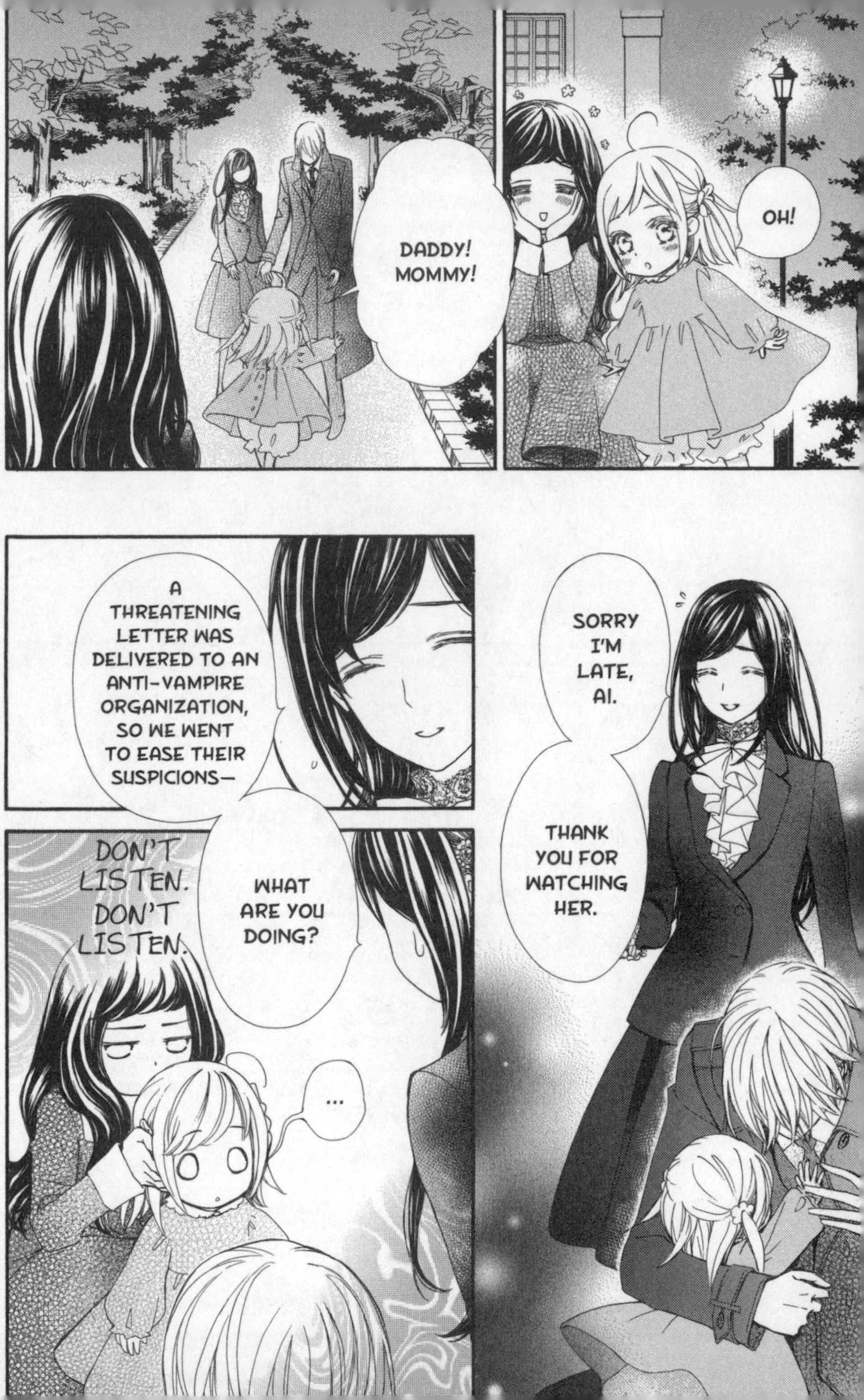
OH!
DADDY! MOMMY!
SORRY I'M LATE, AI.
THANK YOU FOR WATCHING HER.
A THREATENING LETTER WAS DELIVERED TO AN ANTI-VAMPIRE ORGANIZATION, SO WE WENT TO EASE THEIR SUSPICIONS—
WHAT ARE YOU DOING?
DON'T LISTEN. DON'T LISTEN.
...

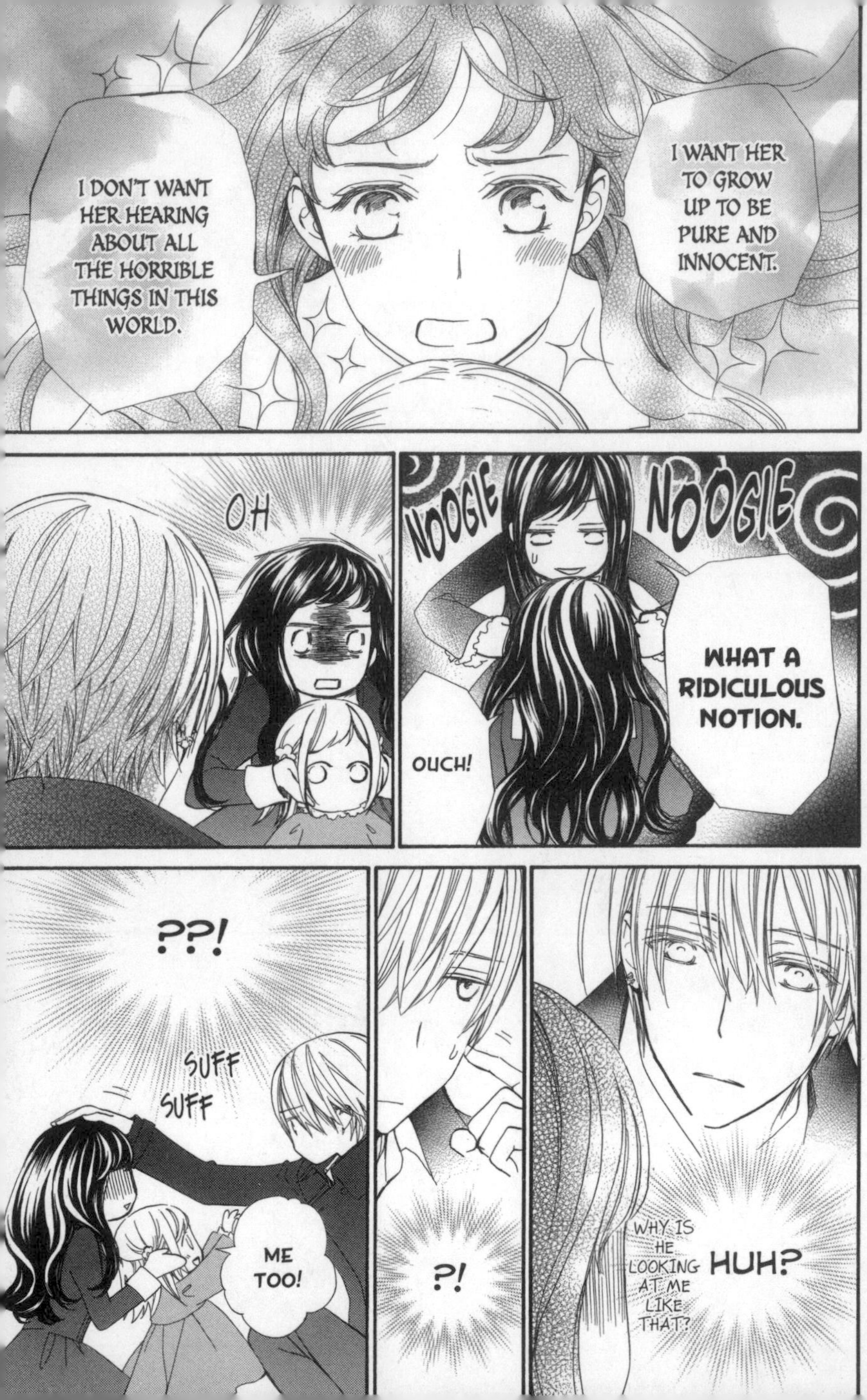
I WANT HER TO GROW UP TO BE PURE AND INNOCENT.
I DON'T WANT HER HEARING ABOUT ALL THE HORRIBLE THINGS IN THIS WORLD.
NOOGIE
NOOGIE
WHAT A RIDICULOUS NOTION.
OUCH!
OH
HUH?
WHY IS HE LOOKING AT ME LIKE THAT?
?!
??!
SUFF
SUFF
ME TOO!

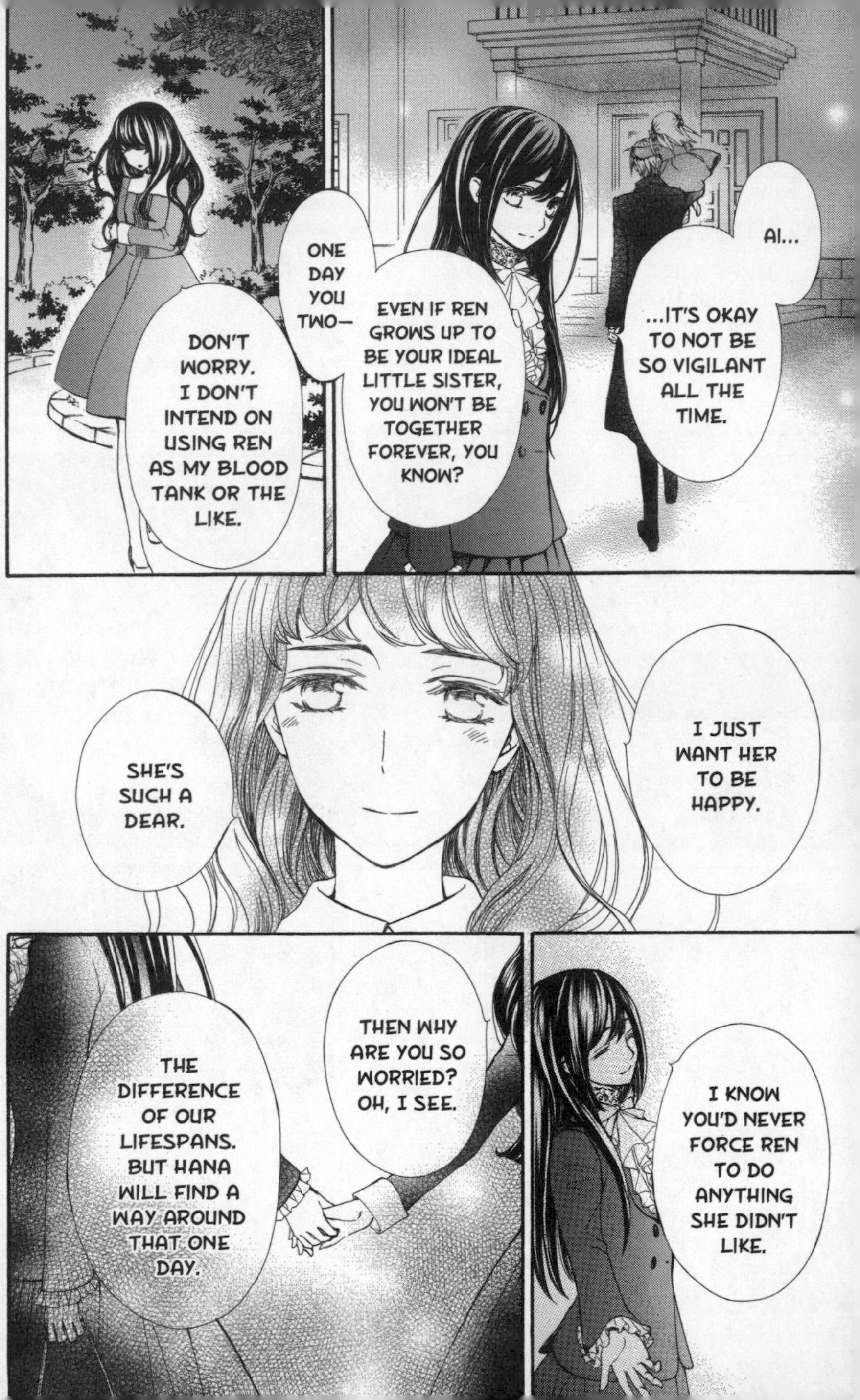
AI...
...IT'S OKAY TO NOT BE SO VIGILANT ALL THE TIME.
EVEN IF REN GROWS UP TO BE YOUR IDEAL LITTLE SISTER, YOU WON'T BE TOGETHER FOREVER, YOU KNOW?
ONE DAY YOU TWO—
DON'T WORRY. I DON'T INTEND ON USING REN AS MY BLOOD TANK OR THE LIKE.
I JUST WANT HER TO BE HAPPY.
SHE'S SUCH A DEAR.
I KNOW YOU'D NEVER FORCE REN TO DO ANYTHING SHE DIDN'T LIKE.
THEN WHY ARE YOU SO WORRIED? OH, I SEE.
THE DIFFERENCE OF OUR LIFESPANS. BUT HANA WILL FIND A WAY AROUND THAT ONE DAY.

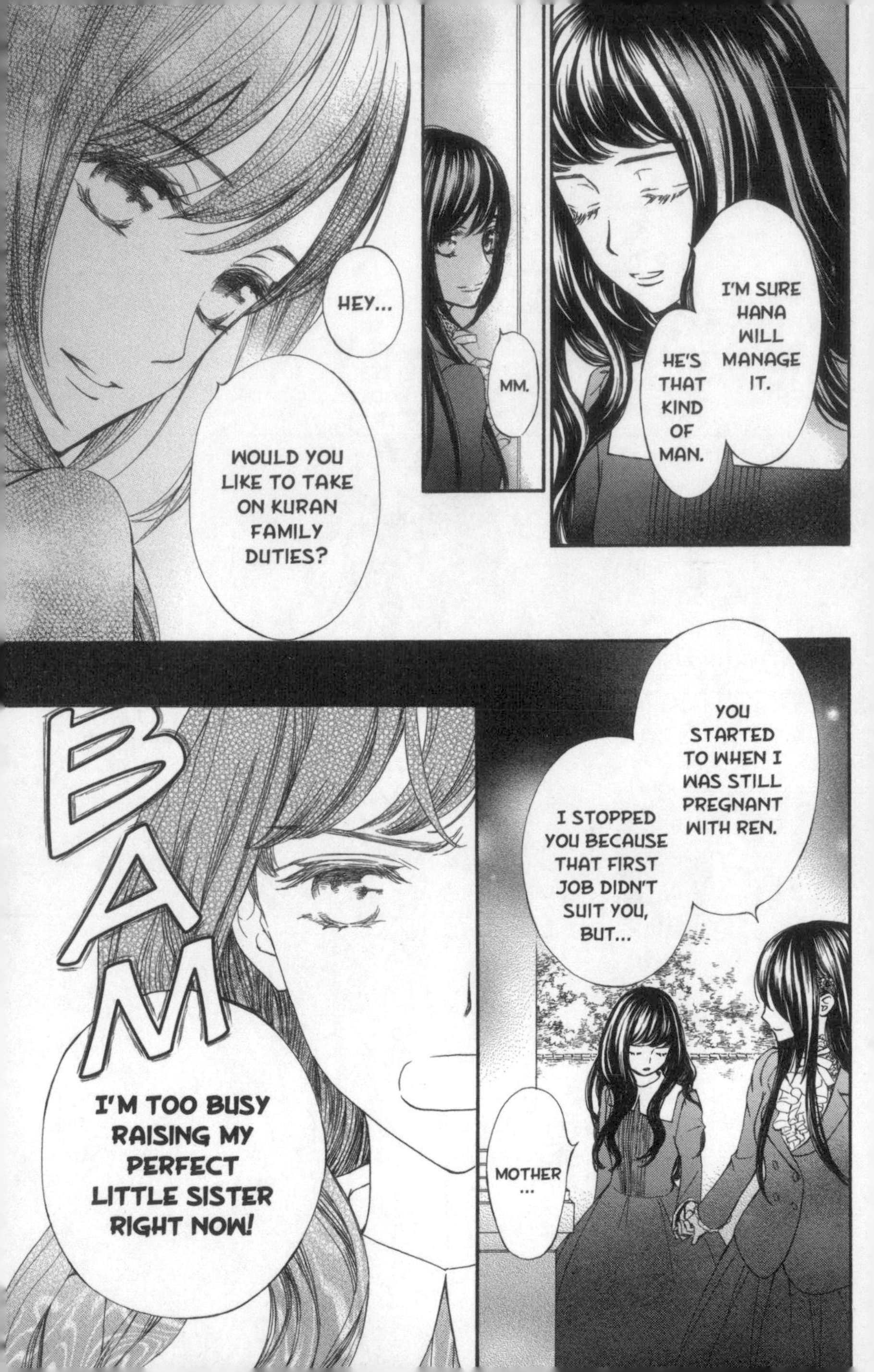

I'M SURE HANA WILL MANAGE IT.
HE'S THAT KIND OF MAN.
MM.
HEY...
WOULD YOU LIKE TO TAKE ON KURAN FAMILY DUTIES?
YOU STARTED TO WHEN I WAS STILL PREGNANT WITH REN.
I STOPPED YOU BECAUSE THAT FIRST JOB DIDN'T SUIT YOU, BUT...
MOTHER...
BAM
I'M TOO BUSY RAISING MY PERFECT LITTLE SISTER RIGHT NOW!

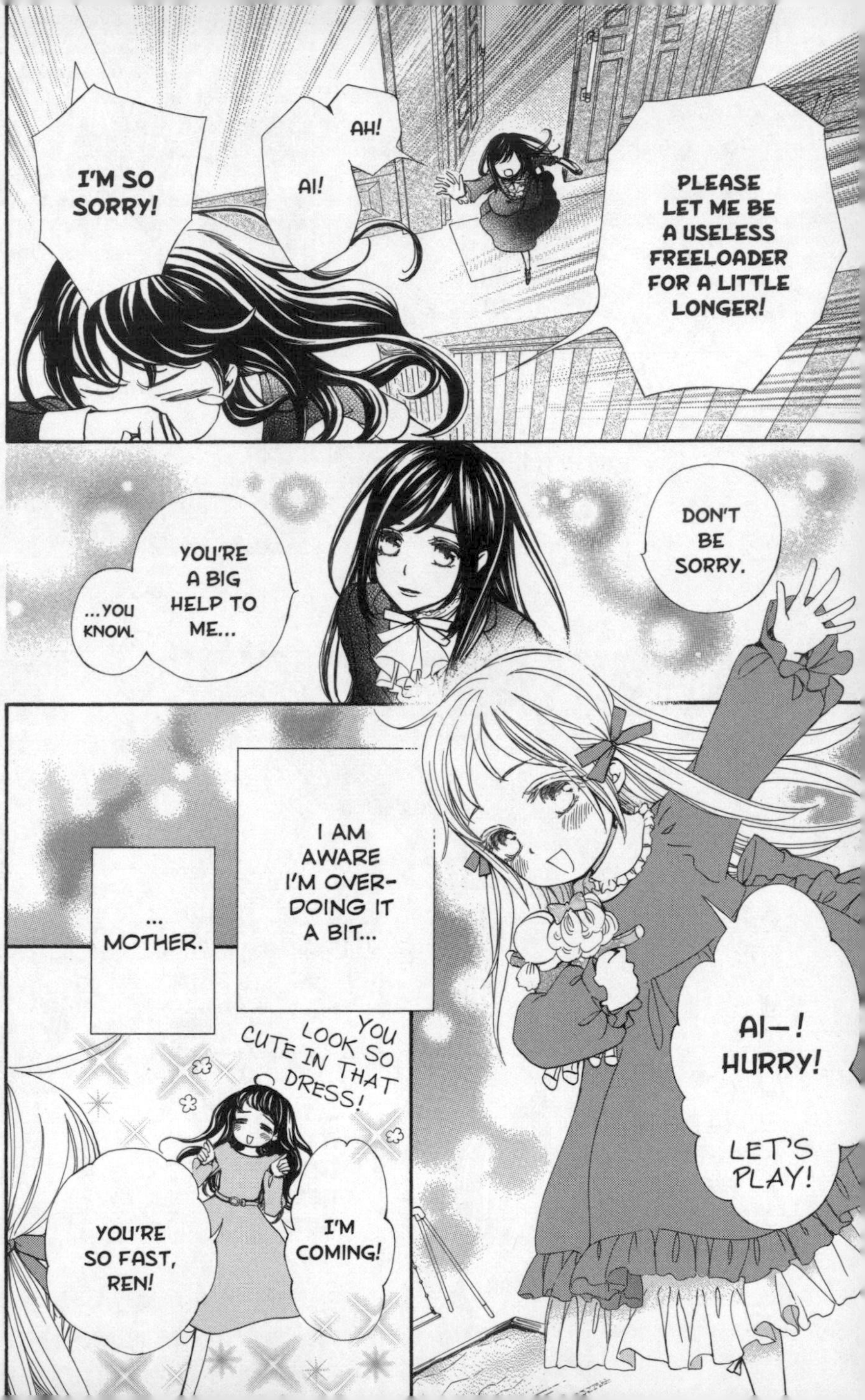
PLEASE LET ME BE A USELESS FREELOADER FOR A LITTLE LONGER!
AH!
AI!
I'M SO SORRY!
DON'T BE SORRY.
YOU'RE A BIG HELP TO ME...
...YOU KNOW.
AI—! HURRY!
LET'S PLAY!
I AM AWARE I'M OVER-DOING IT A BIT...
... MOTHER.
YOU LOOK SO CUTE IN THAT DRESS!
I'M COMING!
YOU'RE SO FAST, REN!

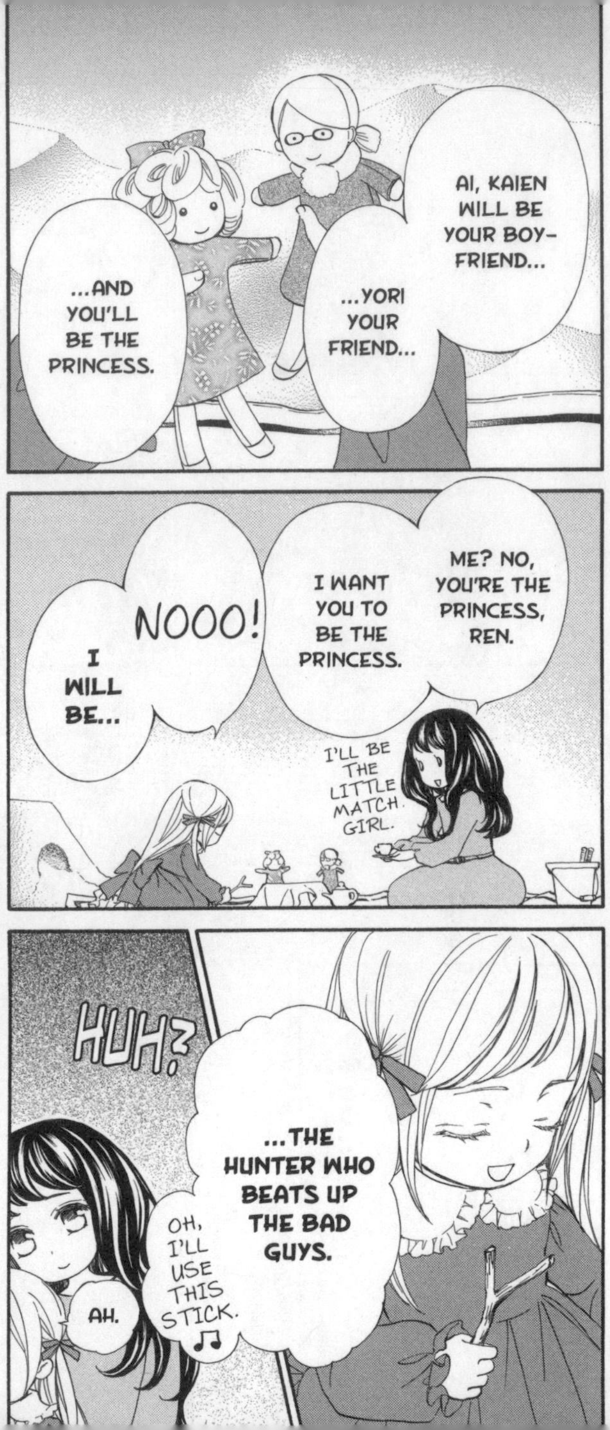
AI, KAIEN WILL BE YOUR BOY-FRIEND...
...YORI YOUR FRIEND...
...AND YOU'LL BE THE PRINCESS.
ME? NO, YOU'RE THE PRINCESS, REN.
I WANT YOU TO BE THE PRINCESS.
NOOO!
I WILL BE...
I'LL BE THE LITTLE MATCH GIRL.
...THE HUNTER WHO BEATS UP THE BAD GUYS.
OH, I'LL USE THIS STICK. ♫
HUH?
AH.

I bring to you *Vampire Knight: Memories* volume 5. Thank you very much for your continued support. This doesn't really feel like a story about what happened during the 1,000 years of the original *Vampire Knight* series, but I'm still going to write it because I need it as a prelude for upcoming chapters! I hope you enjoy it. The story will take a rather large turn in the next volume, but I won't forget to include the romantic moments too... I will do my best to keep working on the series. Please look forward to volume 6.

樋野まつり
Matsuri Hino

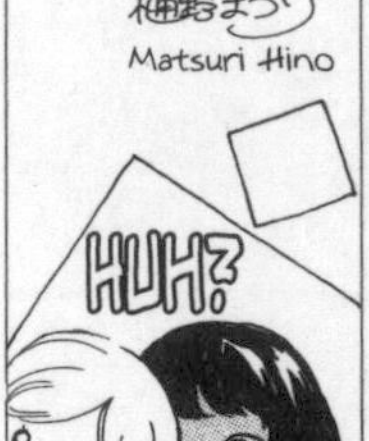
HUH?

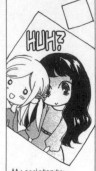

My assistants:
O. Mio-sama
K. Midori-sama
A. Ichiya-sama
Thank you very much!

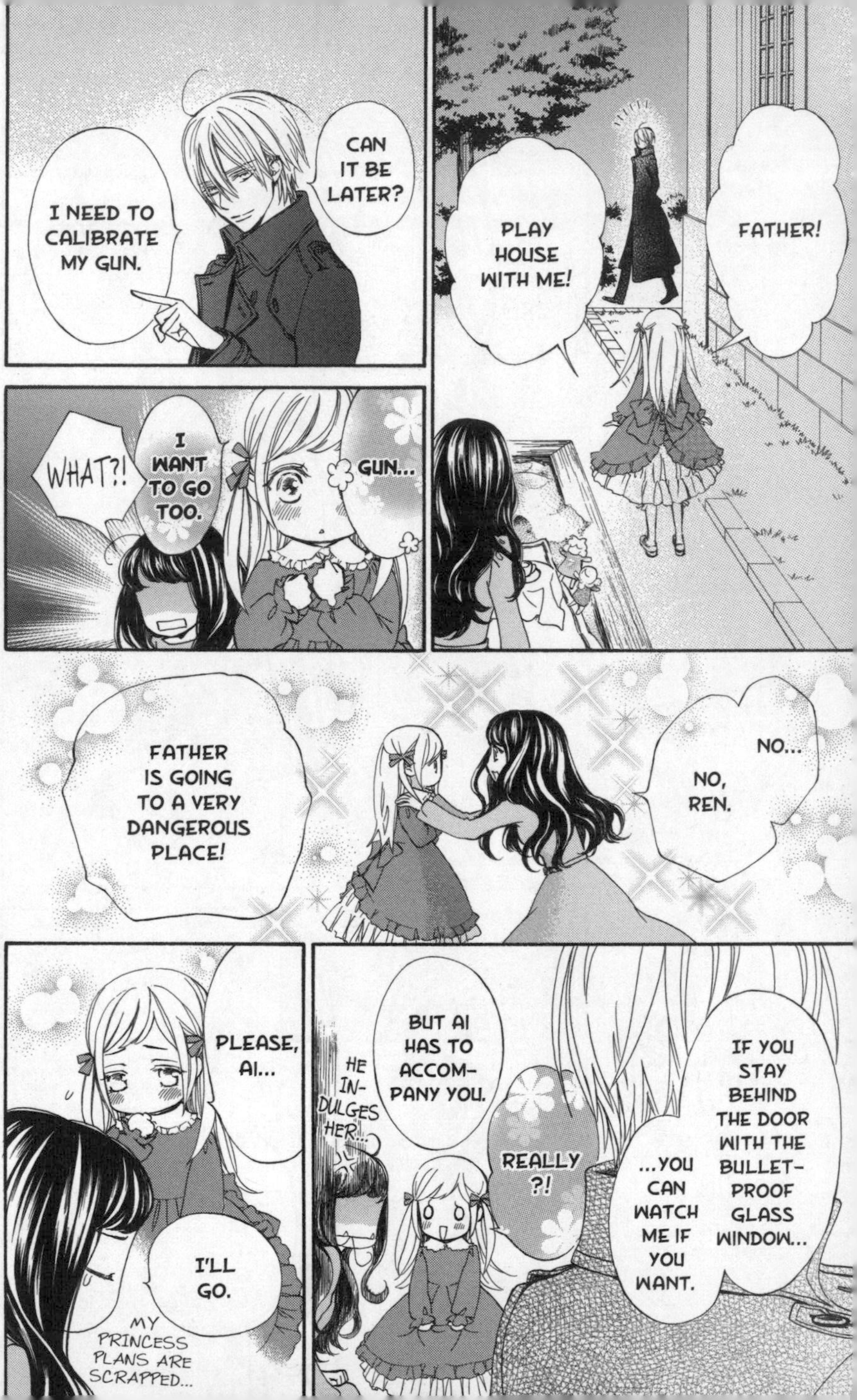
FATHER!
PLAY HOUSE WITH ME!
CAN IT BE LATER?
I NEED TO CALIBRATE MY GUN.
GUN...
I WANT TO GO TOO.
WHAT?!
NO...
NO, REN.
FATHER IS GOING TO A VERY DANGEROUS PLACE!
IF YOU STAY BEHIND THE DOOR WITH THE BULLET-PROOF GLASS WINDOW...
...YOU CAN WATCH ME IF YOU WANT.
REALLY?!
BUT AI HAS TO ACCOMPANY YOU.
HE INDULGES HER...
PLEASE, AI...
I'LL GO.
MY PRINCESS PLANS ARE SCRAPPED...

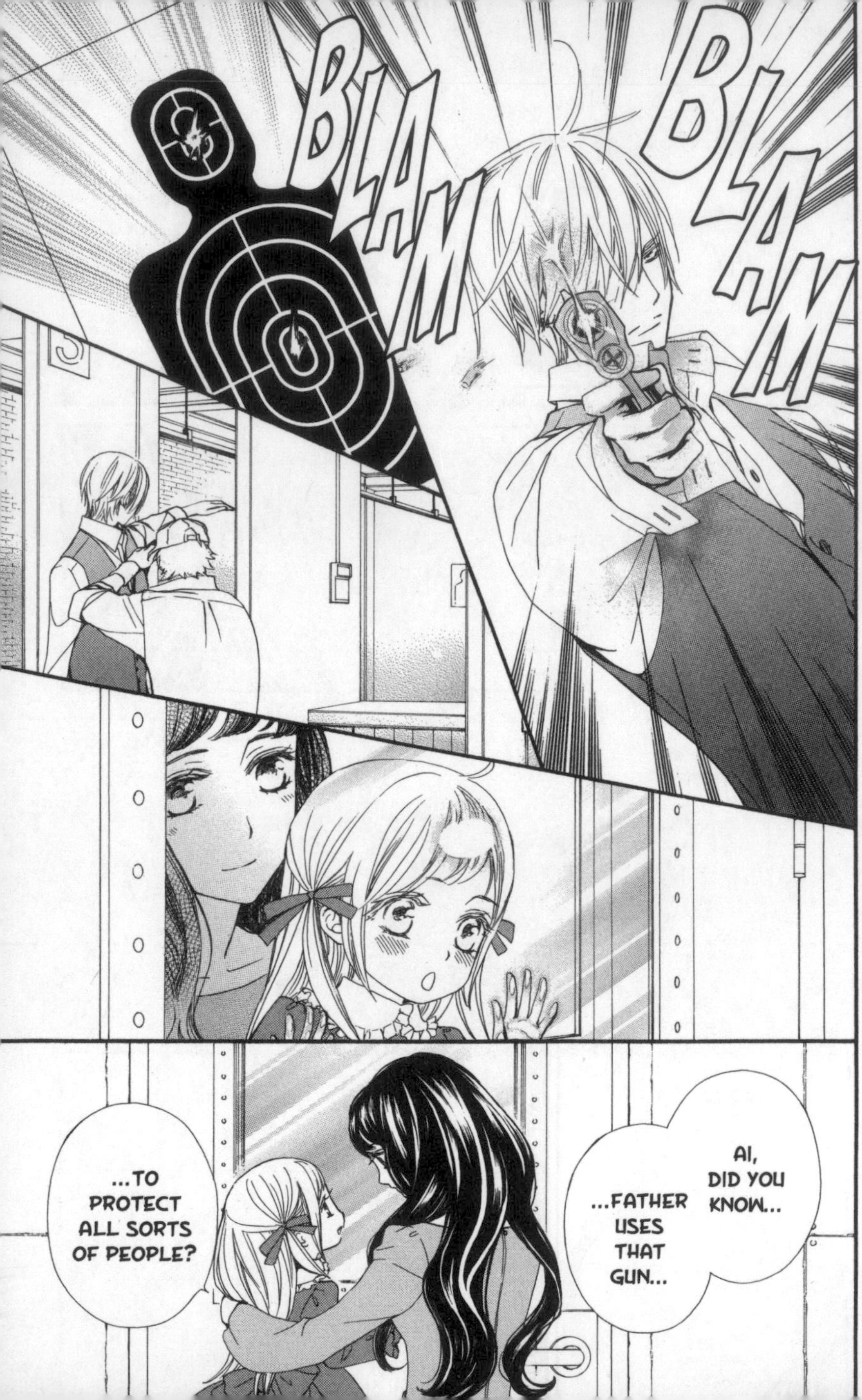
BLAM
BLAM
AI, DID YOU KNOW...
...FATHER USES THAT GUN...
...TO PROTECT ALL SORTS OF PEOPLE?

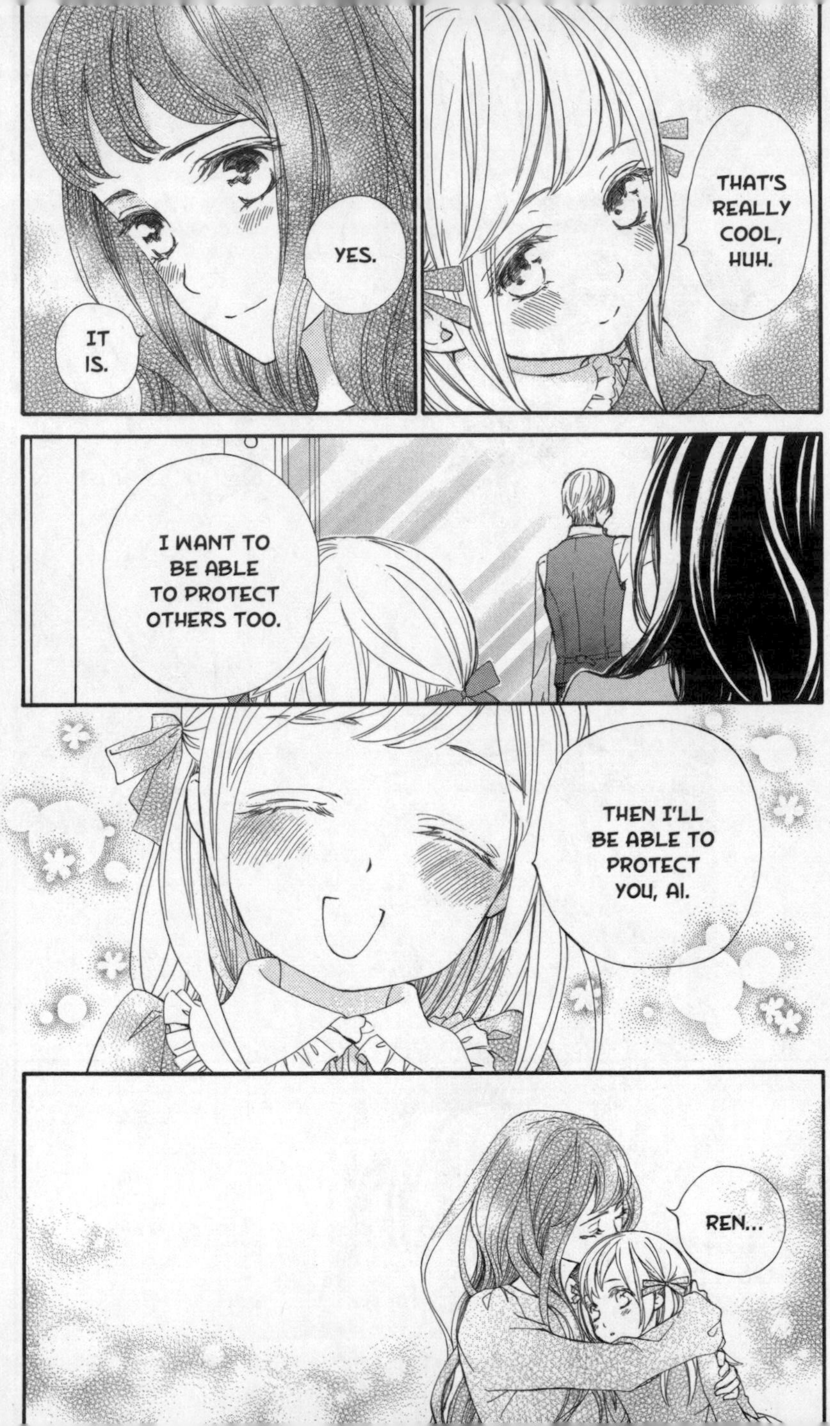
THAT'S REALLY COOL, HUH.
YES.
IT IS.
I WANT TO BE ABLE TO PROTECT OTHERS TOO.
THEN I'LL BE ABLE TO PROTECT YOU, AI.
REN...

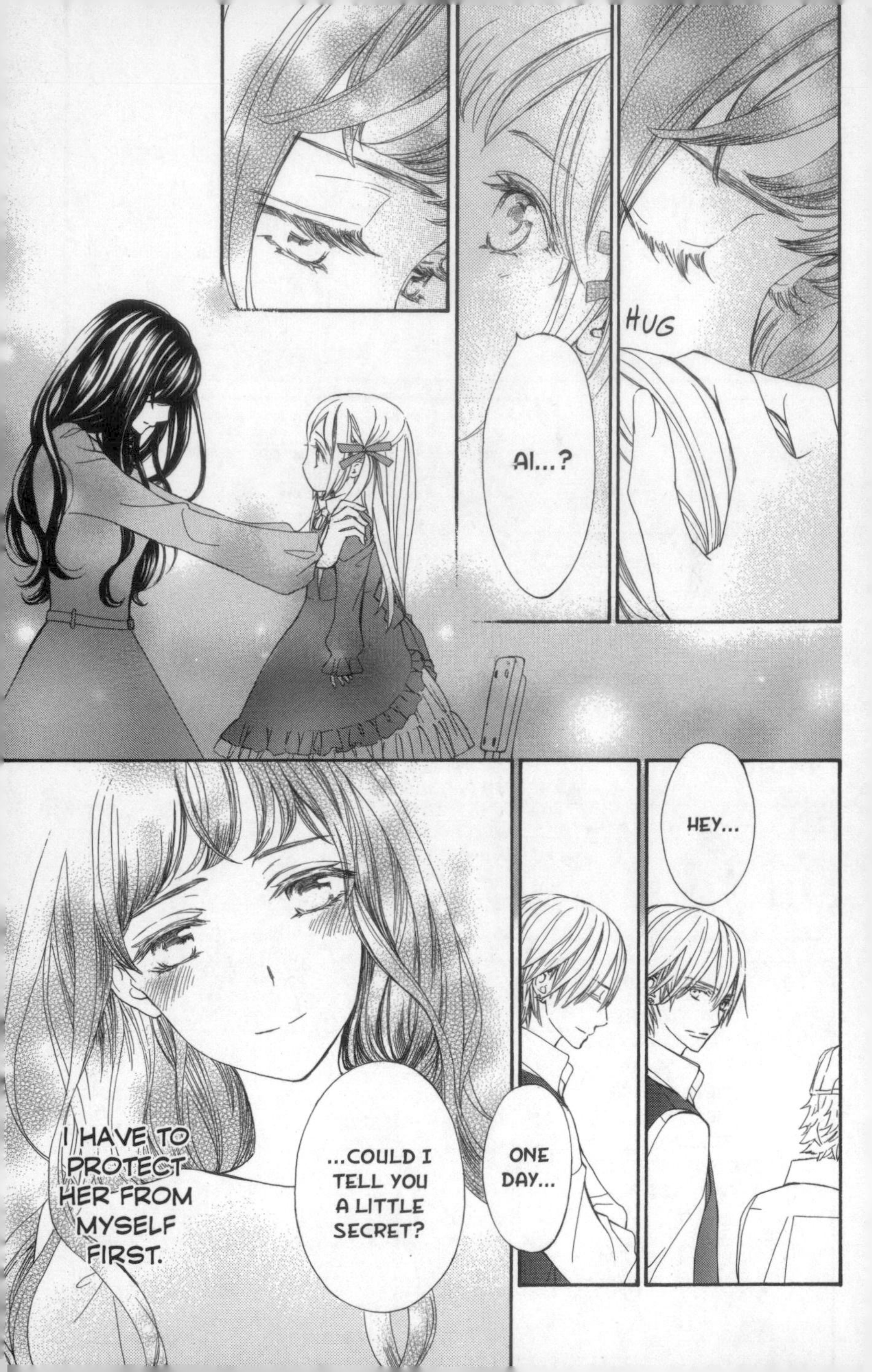
HUG
AI...?
HEY...
ONE DAY...
...COULD I TELL YOU A LITTLE SECRET?
I HAVE TO PROTECT HER FROM MYSELF FIRST.

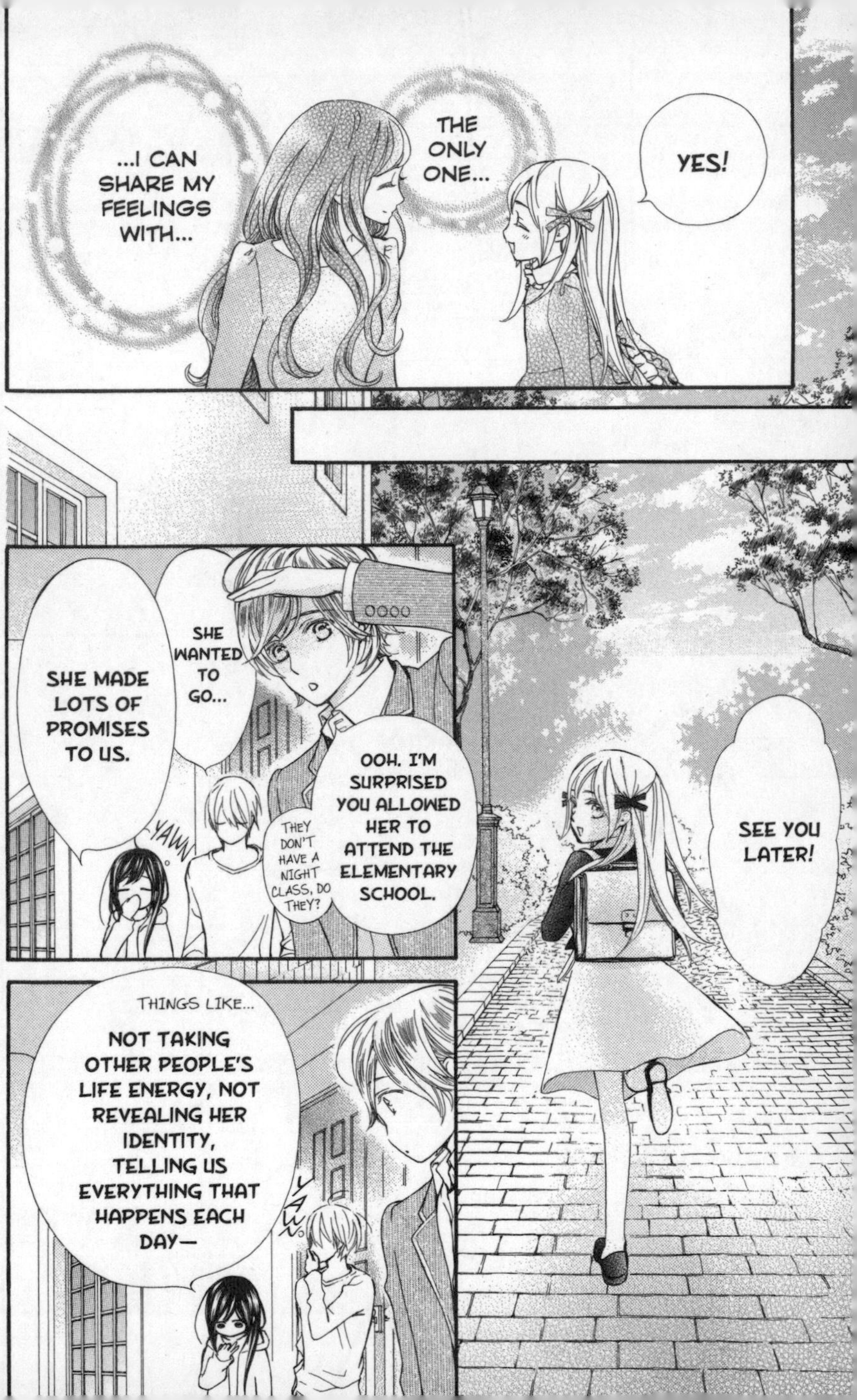
YES!
THE ONLY ONE...
...I CAN SHARE MY FEELINGS WITH...
SEE YOU LATER!
OOH. I'M SURPRISED YOU ALLOWED HER TO ATTEND THE ELEMENTARY SCHOOL.
THEY DON'T HAVE A NIGHT CLASS, DO THEY?
SHE WANTED TO GO...
SHE MADE LOTS OF PROMISES TO US.
YAWN
THINGS LIKE...
NOT TAKING OTHER PEOPLE'S LIFE ENERGY, NOT REVEALING HER IDENTITY, TELLING US EVERYTHING THAT HAPPENS EACH DAY—
YAWN

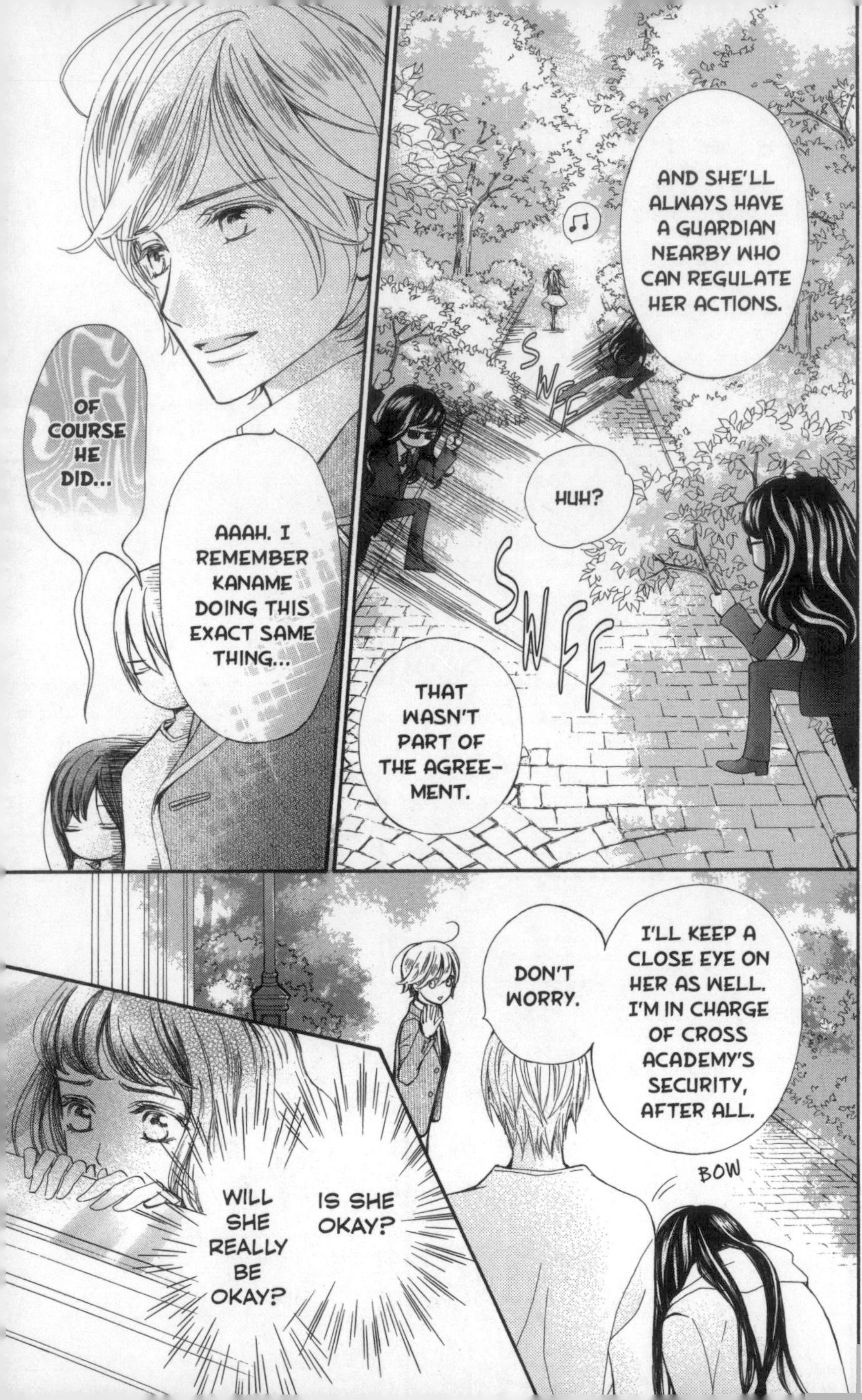
AND SHE'LL ALWAYS HAVE A GUARDIAN NEARBY WHO CAN REGULATE HER ACTIONS.
♫
SWFF
HUH?
SWFF
THAT WASN'T PART OF THE AGREE-MENT.
AAAH. I REMEMBER KANAME DOING THIS EXACT SAME THING...
OF COURSE HE DID...
I'LL KEEP A CLOSE EYE ON HER AS WELL. I'M IN CHARGE OF CROSS ACADEMY'S SECURITY, AFTER ALL.
DON'T WORRY.
BOW
IS SHE OKAY?
WILL SHE REALLY BE OKAY?

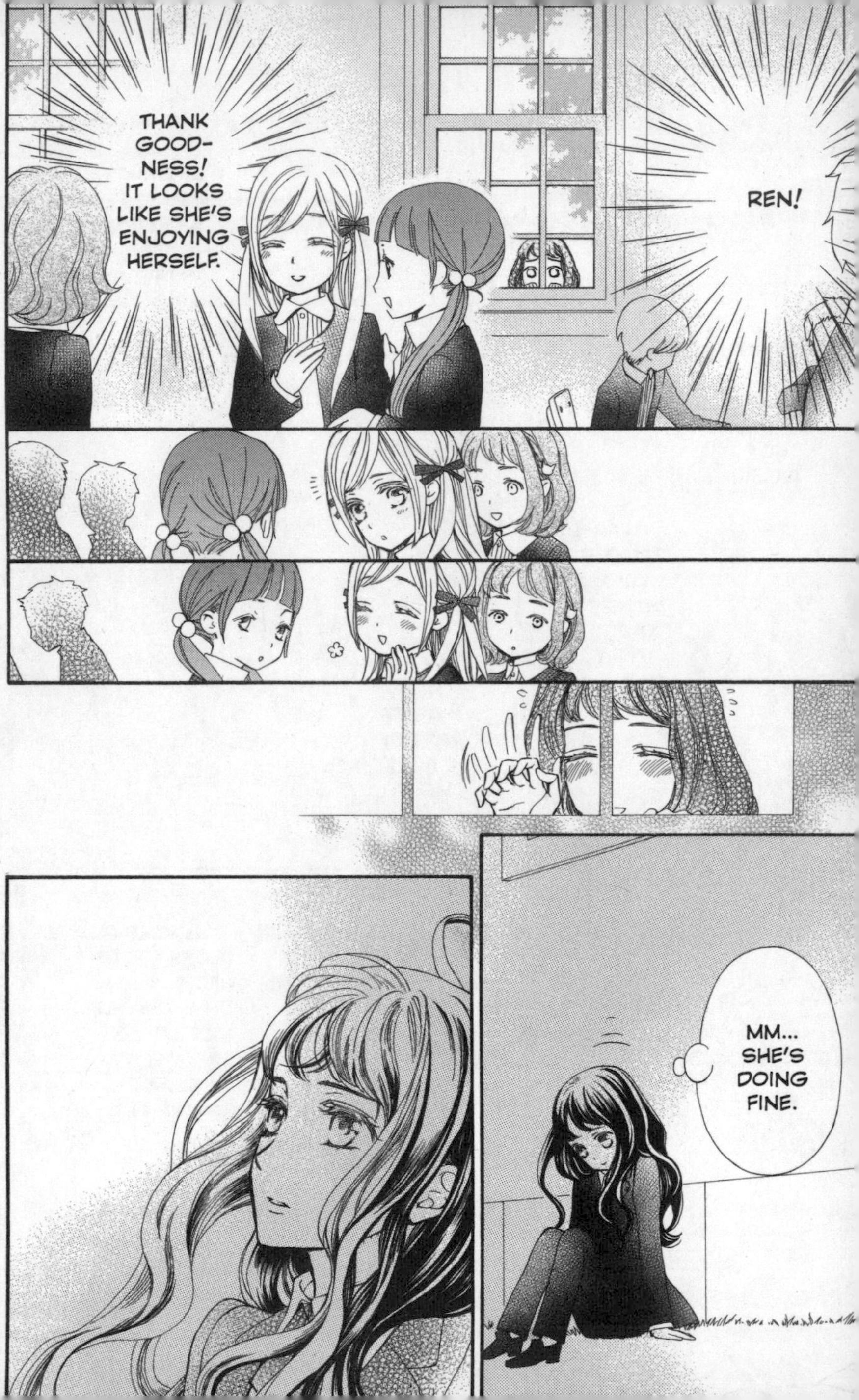
REN!
THANK GOODNESS! IT LOOKS LIKE SHE'S ENJOYING HERSELF.
MM... SHE'S DOING FINE.

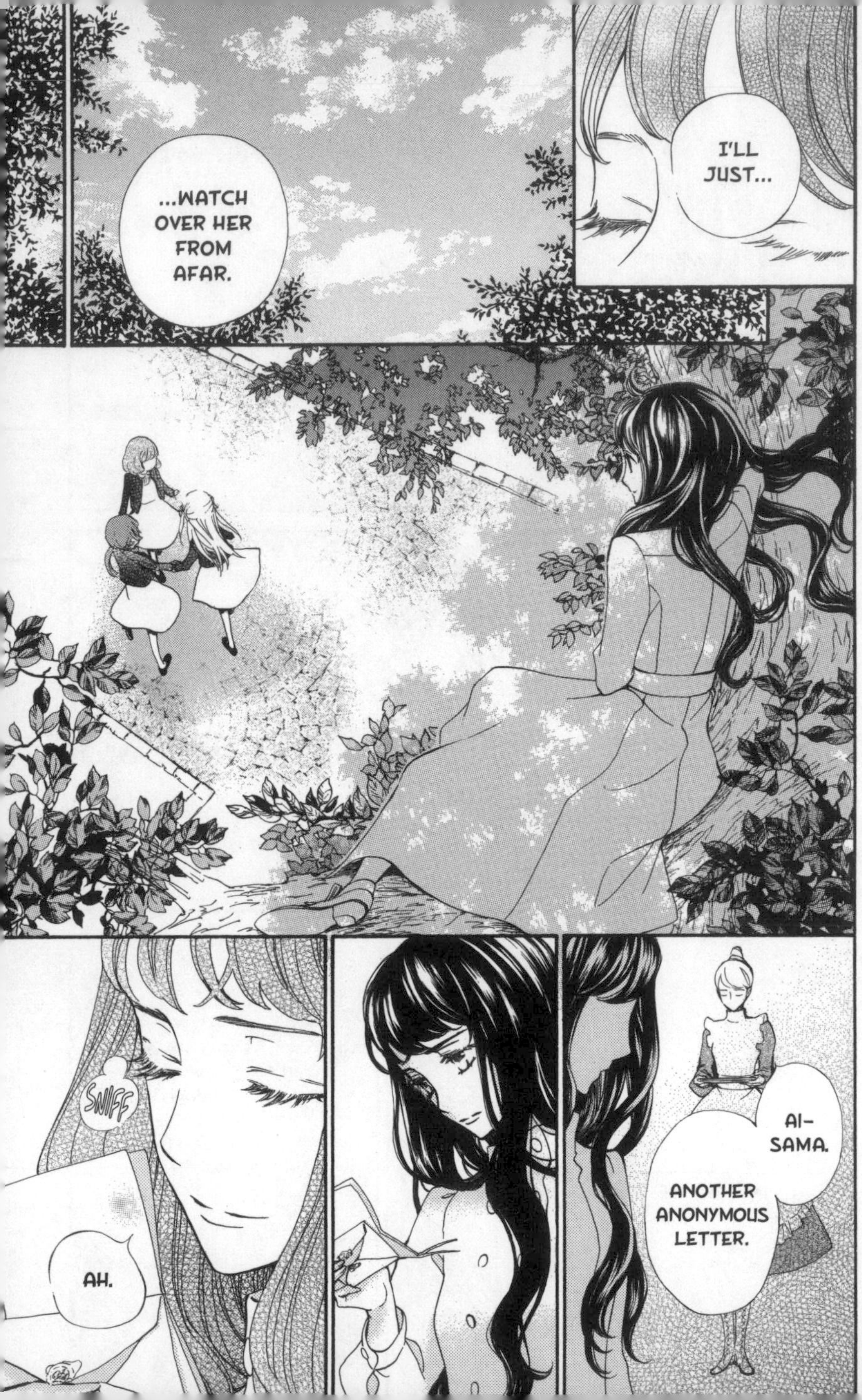
I'LL JUST...
...WATCH OVER HER FROM AFAR.
AI-SAMA.
ANOTHER ANONYMOUS LETTER.
SNIFF
AH.

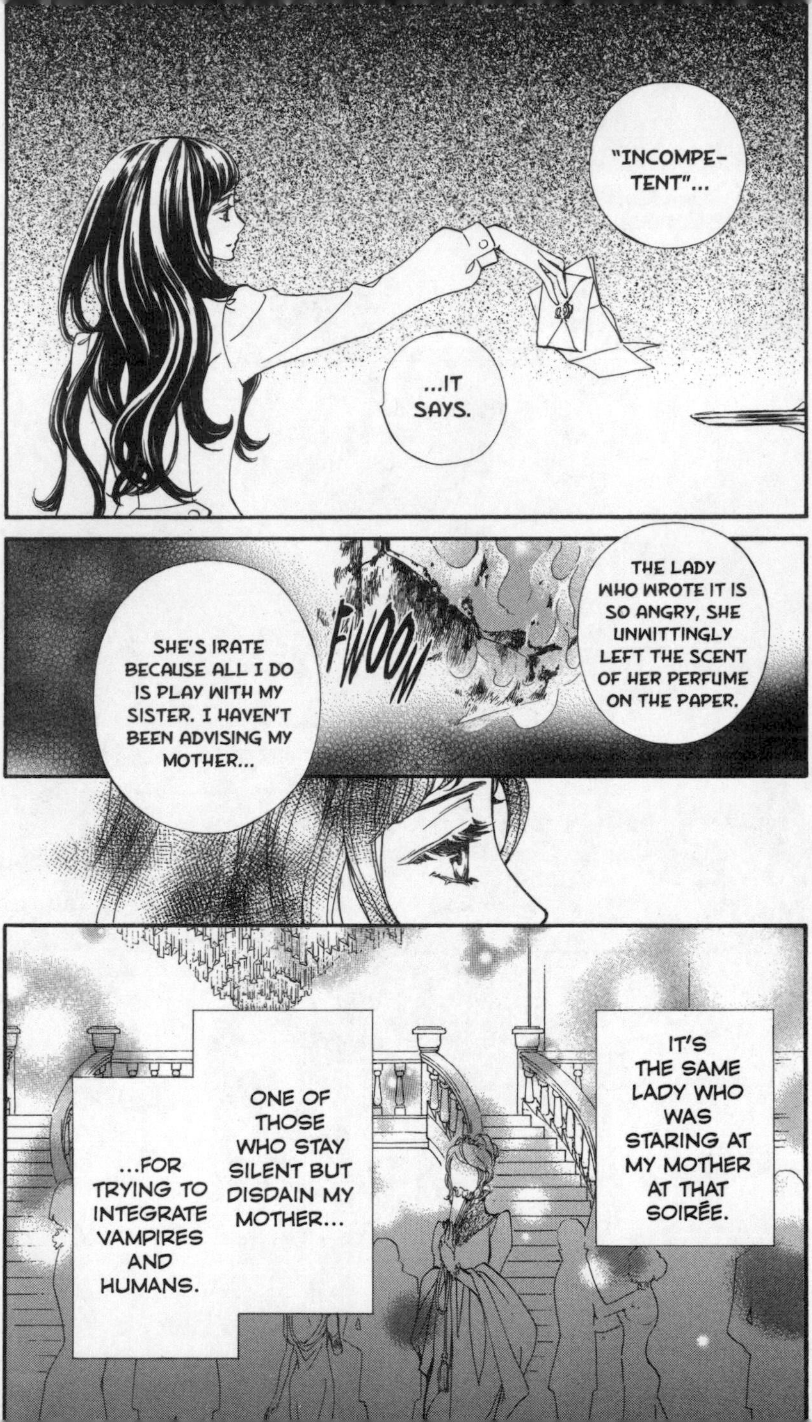
"INCOMPE-TENT"...
...IT SAYS.
THE LADY WHO WROTE IT IS SO ANGRY, SHE UNWITTINGLY LEFT THE SCENT OF HER PERFUME ON THE PAPER.
FWOOM
SHE'S IRATE BECAUSE ALL I DO IS PLAY WITH MY SISTER. I HAVEN'T BEEN ADVISING MY MOTHER...
IT'S THE SAME LADY WHO WAS STARING AT MY MOTHER AT THAT SOIRÉE.
ONE OF THOSE WHO STAY SILENT BUT DISDAIN MY MOTHER...
...FOR TRYING TO INTEGRATE VAMPIRES AND HUMANS.

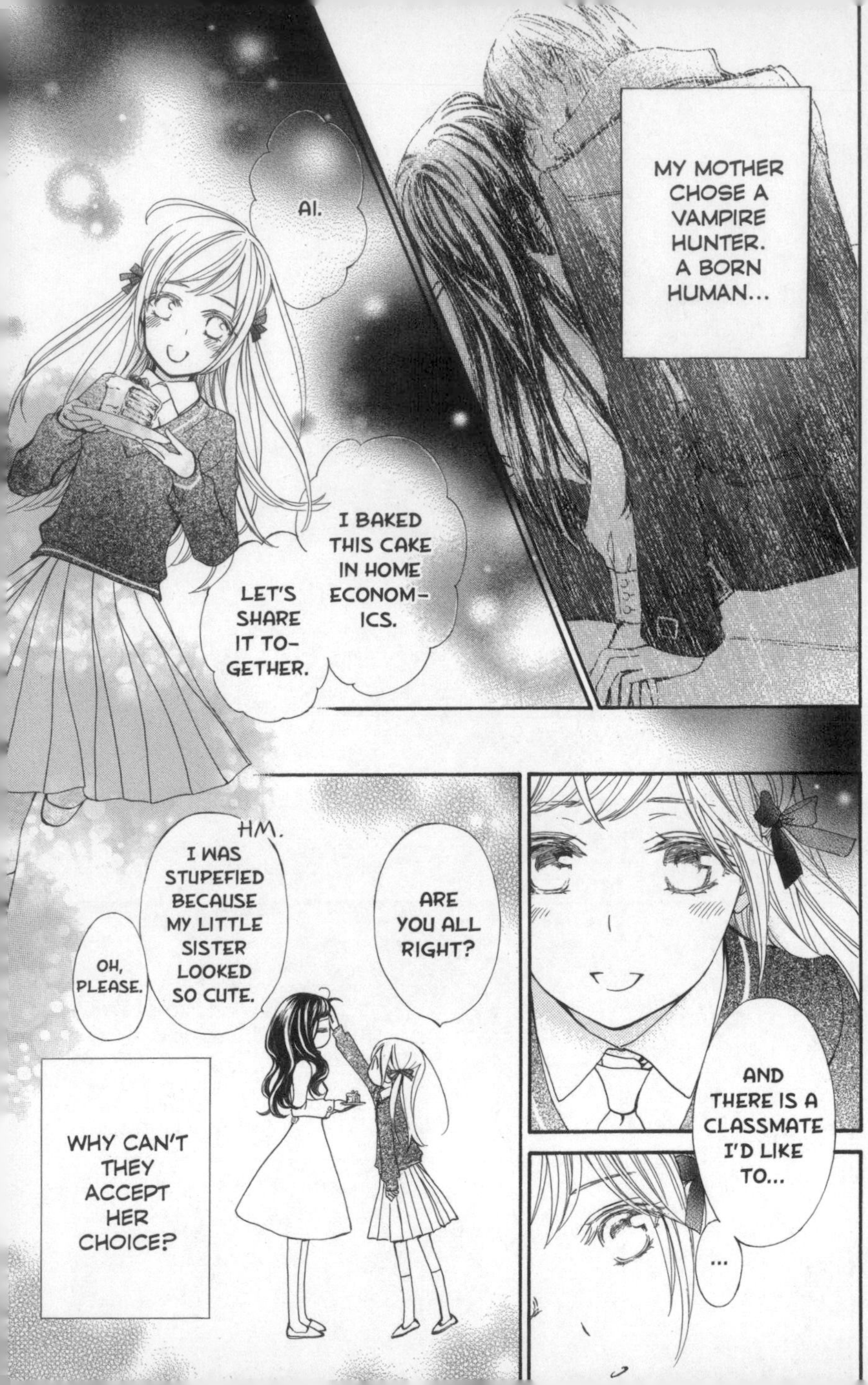
MY MOTHER CHOSE A VAMPIRE HUNTER. A BORN HUMAN...
AI.
I BAKED THIS CAKE IN HOME ECONOMICS.
LET'S SHARE IT TOGETHER.
AND THERE IS A CLASSMATE I'D LIKE TO...
...
ARE YOU ALL RIGHT?
HM.
I WAS STUPEFIED BECAUSE MY LITTLE SISTER LOOKED SO CUTE.
OH, PLEASE.
WHY CAN'T THEY ACCEPT HER CHOICE?

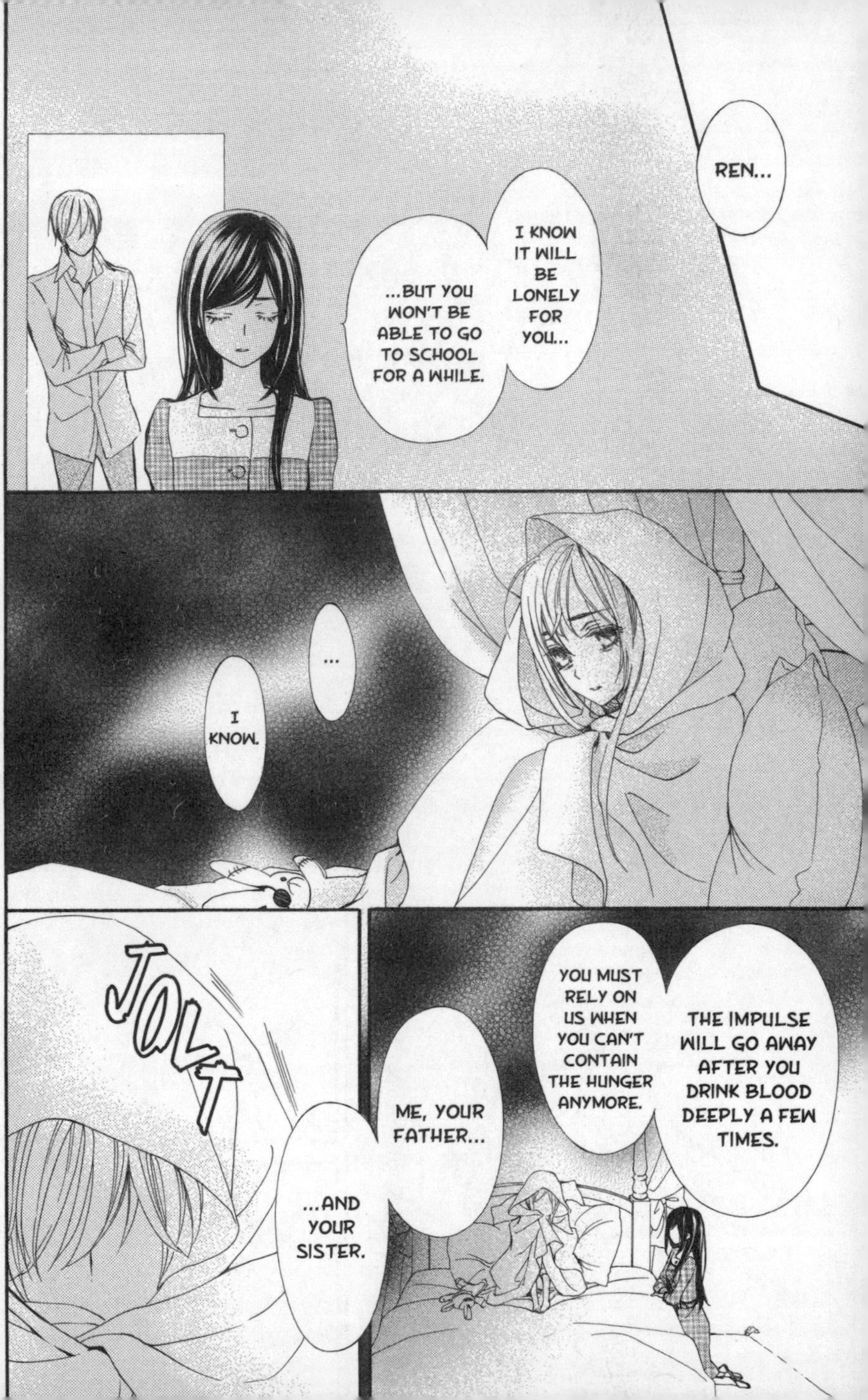
REN...
I KNOW IT WILL BE LONELY FOR YOU...
...BUT YOU WON'T BE ABLE TO GO TO SCHOOL FOR A WHILE.
...
I KNOW.
THE IMPULSE WILL GO AWAY AFTER YOU DRINK BLOOD DEEPLY A FEW TIMES.
YOU MUST RELY ON US WHEN YOU CAN'T CONTAIN THE HUNGER ANYMORE.
ME, YOUR FATHER...
...AND YOUR SISTER.
JOLT

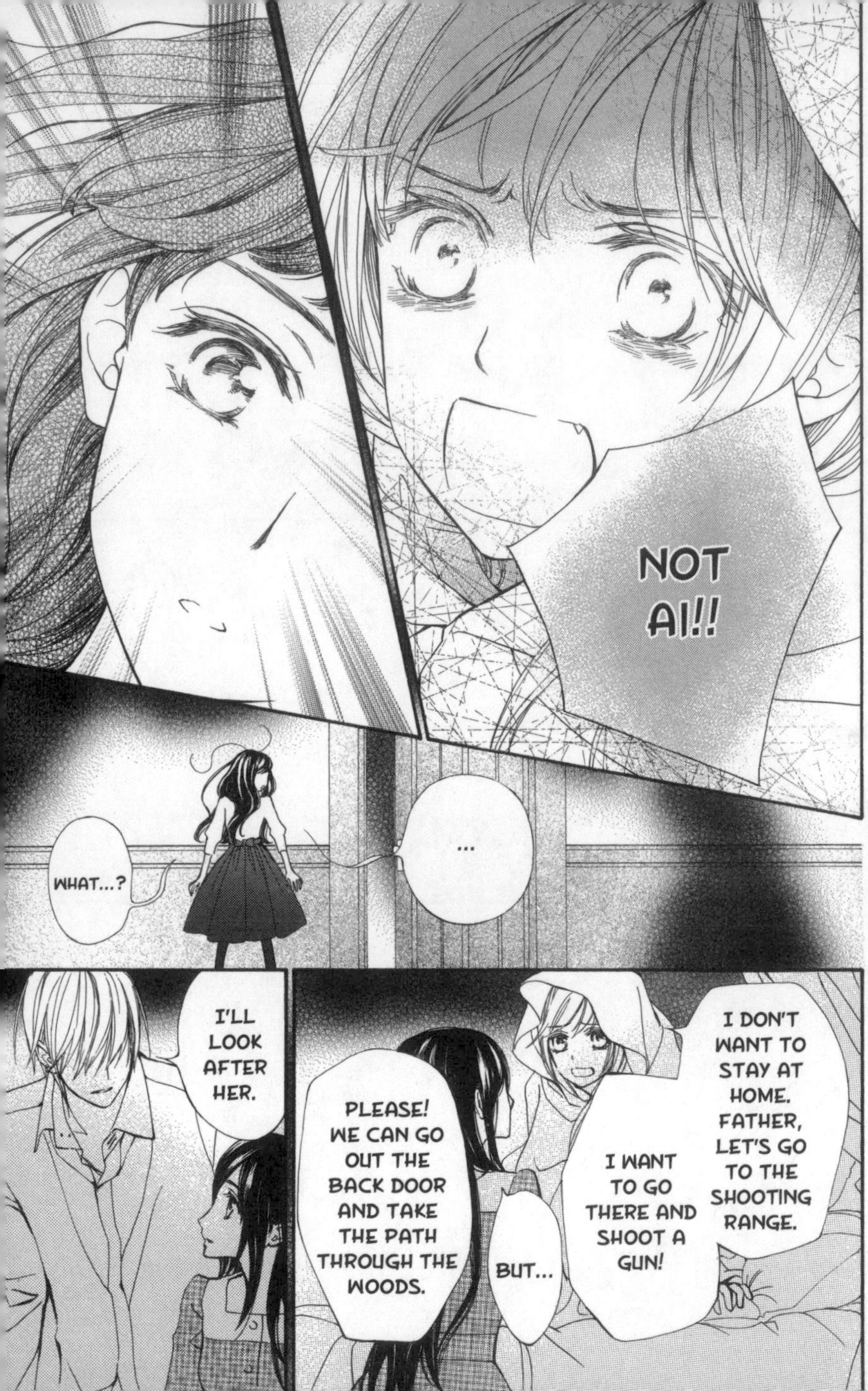
NOT AI!!
...
WHAT...?
I DON'T WANT TO STAY AT HOME. FATHER, LET'S GO TO THE SHOOTING RANGE.
I WANT TO GO THERE AND SHOOT A GUN!
BUT...
PLEASE! WE CAN GO OUT THE BACK DOOR AND TAKE THE PATH THROUGH THE WOODS.
I'LL LOOK AFTER HER.

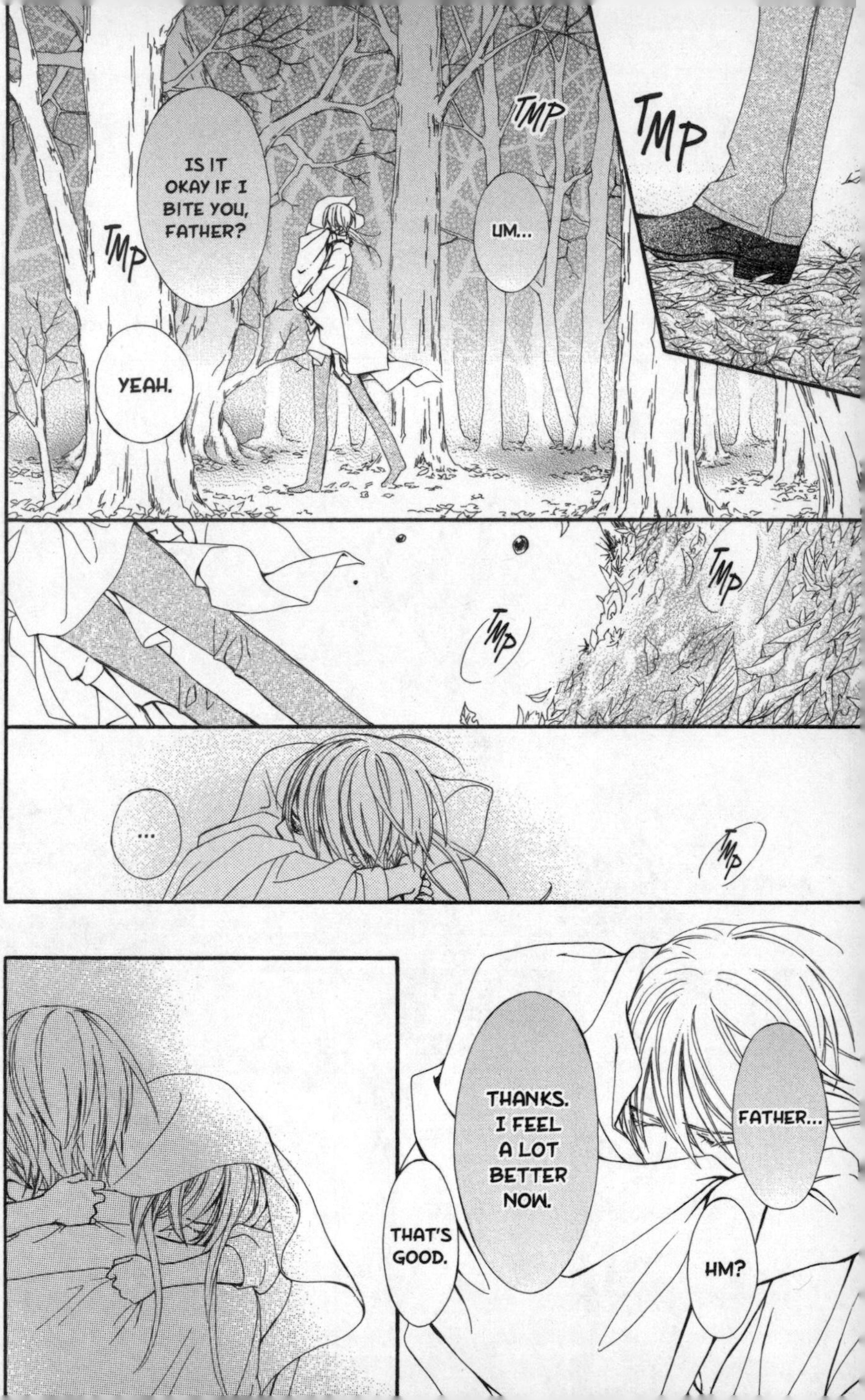
TMP
TMP
UM...
IS IT OKAY IF I BITE YOU, FATHER?
TMP
YEAH.
TMP
TMP
TMP
...
FATHER...
HM?
THANKS. I FEEL A LOT BETTER NOW.
THAT'S GOOD.

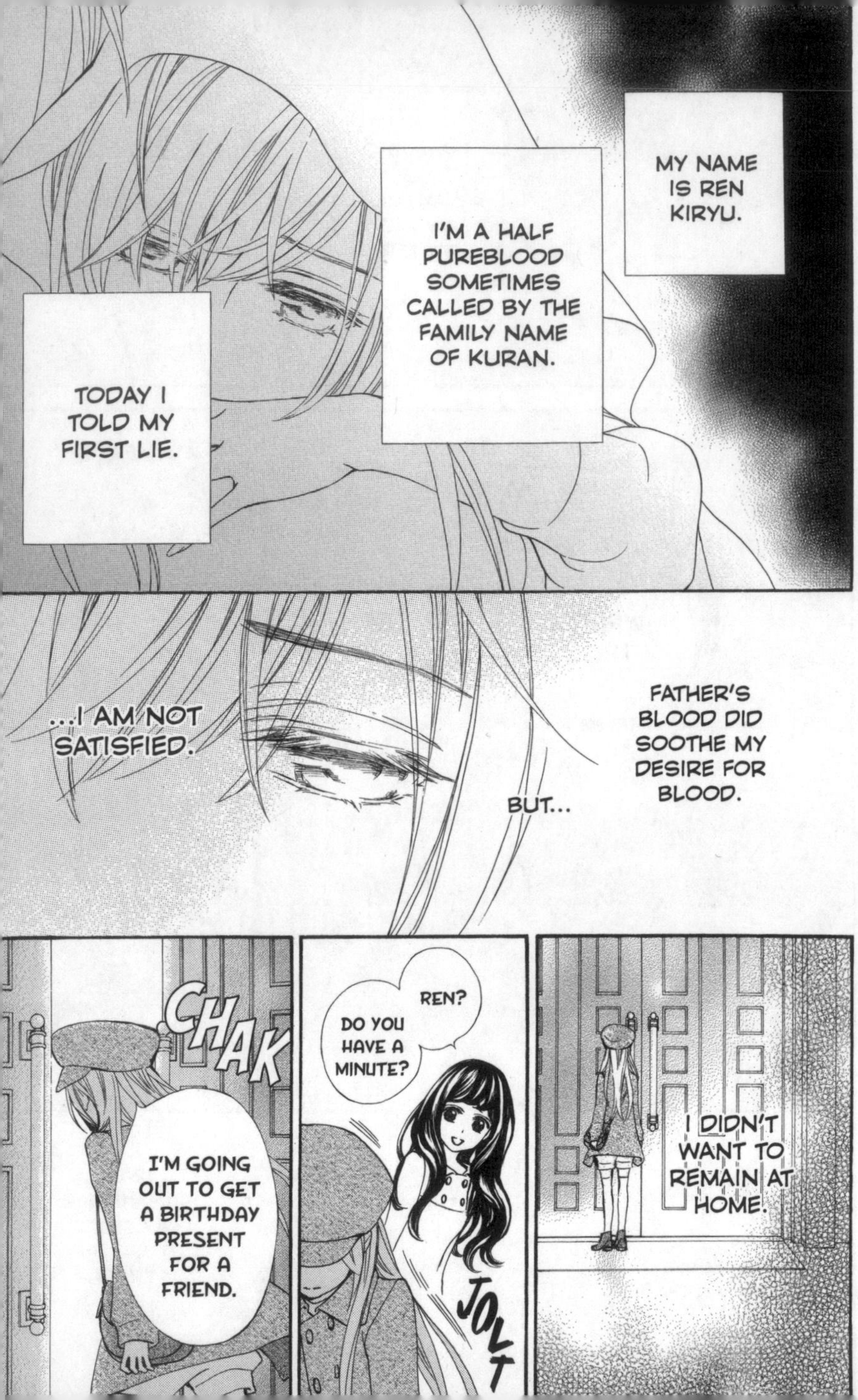
MY NAME IS REN KIRYU.
I'M A HALF PUREBLOOD SOMETIMES CALLED BY THE FAMILY NAME OF KURAN.
TODAY I TOLD MY FIRST LIE.
FATHER'S BLOOD DID SOOTHE MY DESIRE FOR BLOOD.
BUT...
...I AM NOT SATISFIED.
I DIDN'T WANT TO REMAIN AT HOME.
REN?
DO YOU HAVE A MINUTE?
JOLT
CHAK
I'M GOING OUT TO GET A BIRTHDAY PRESENT FOR A FRIEND.

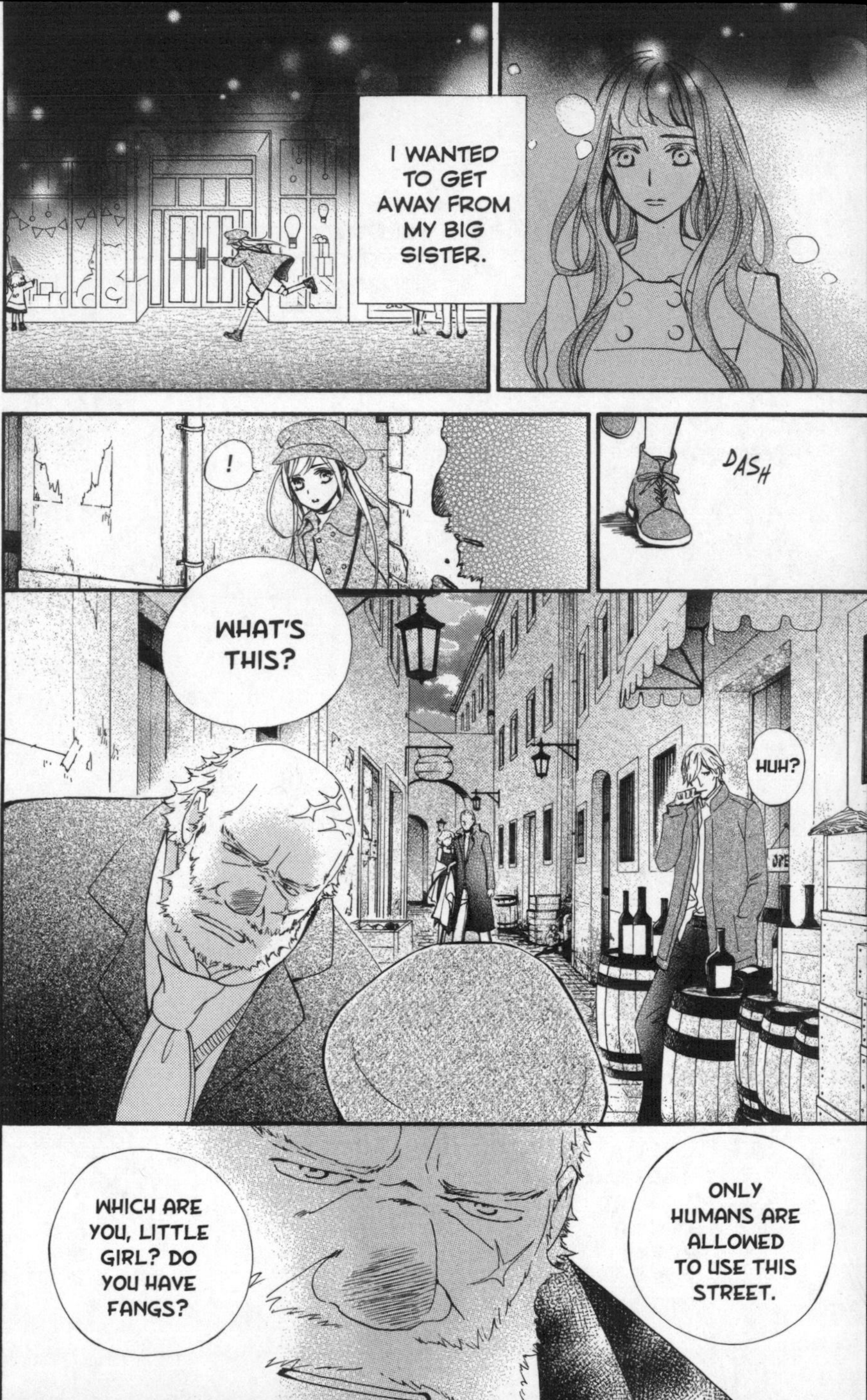
I WANTED TO GET AWAY FROM MY BIG SISTER.
DASH
!
WHAT'S THIS?
HUH?
ONLY HUMANS ARE ALLOWED TO USE THIS STREET.
WHICH ARE YOU, LITTLE GIRL? DO YOU HAVE FANGS?

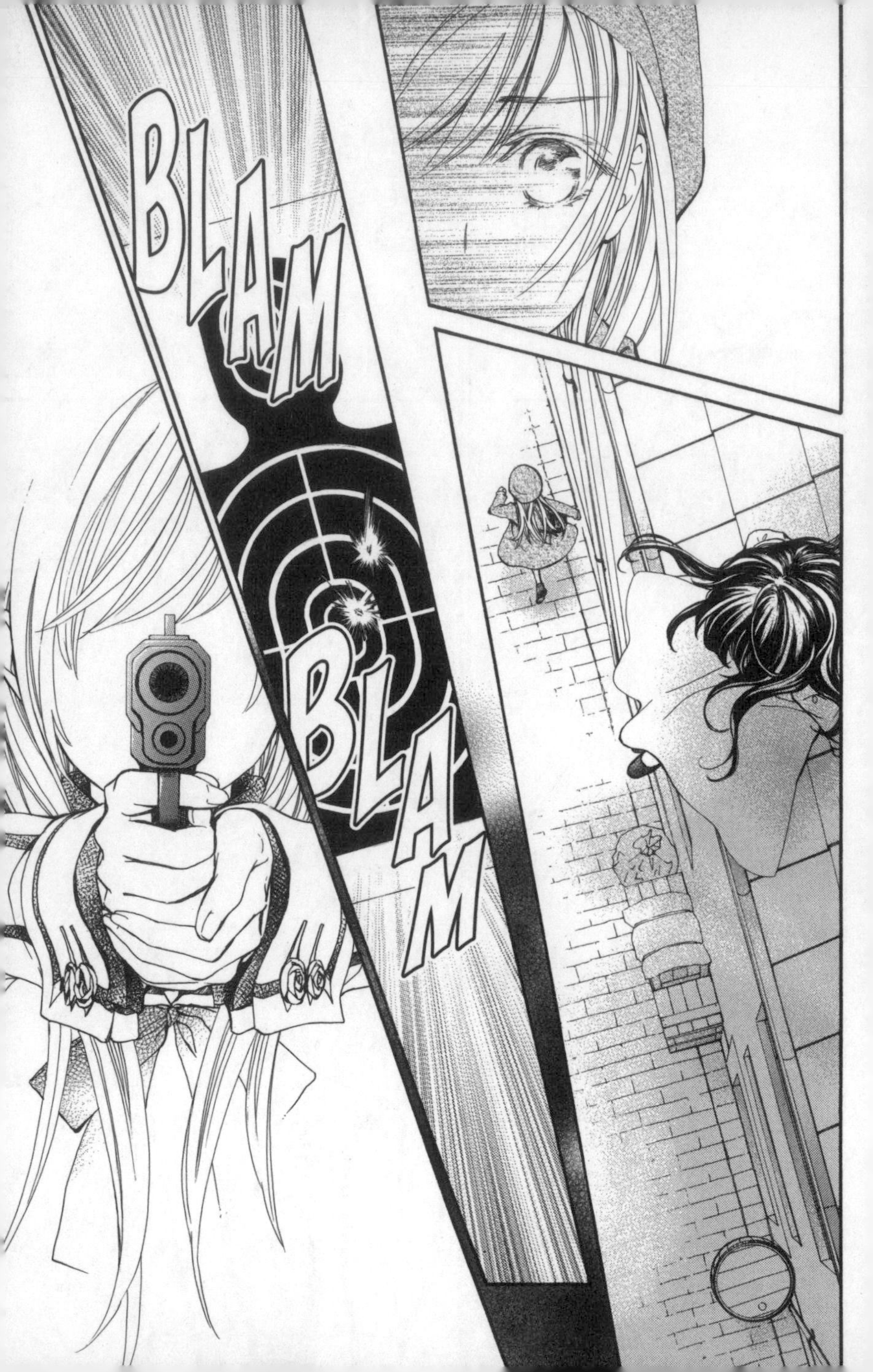
BLAM
BLAM

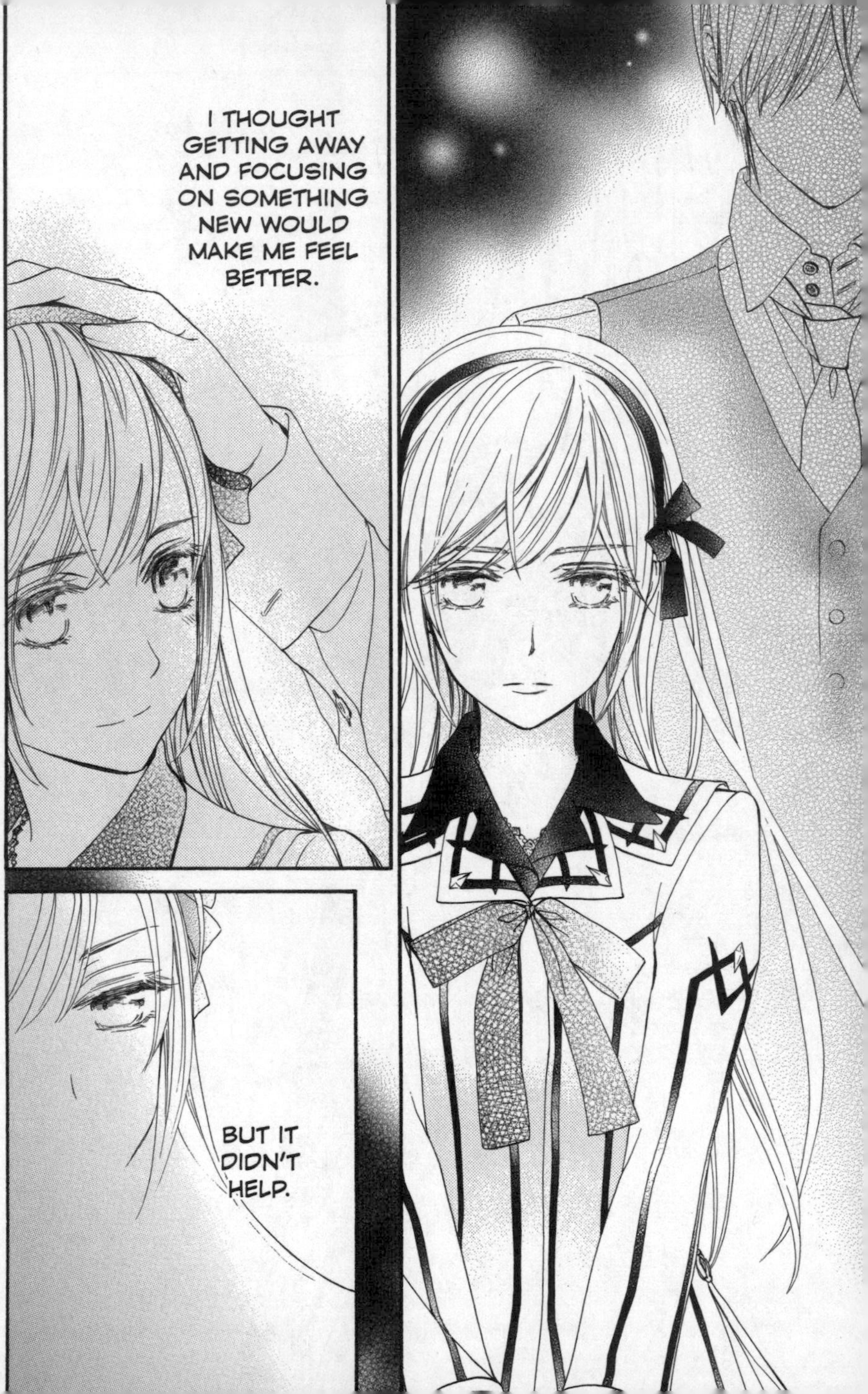
I THOUGHT GETTING AWAY AND FOCUSING ON SOMETHING NEW WOULD MAKE ME FEEL BETTER.
BUT IT DIDN'T HELP.

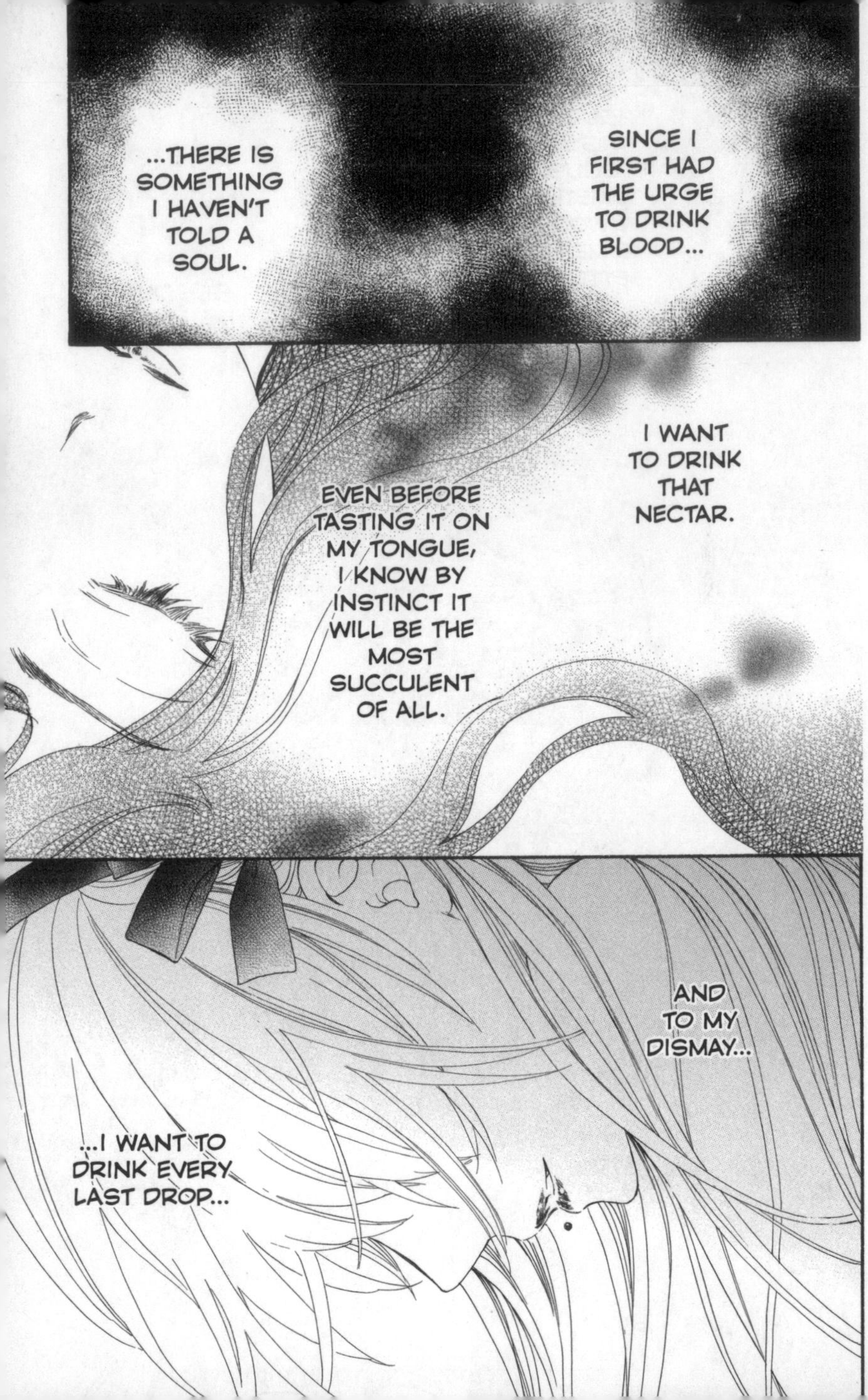
SINCE I FIRST HAD THE URGE TO DRINK BLOOD...
...THERE IS SOMETHING I HAVEN'T TOLD A SOUL.
I WANT TO DRINK THAT NECTAR.
EVEN BEFORE TASTING IT ON MY TONGUE, I KNOW BY INSTINCT IT WILL BE THE MOST SUCCULENT OF ALL.
AND TO MY DISMAY...
...I WANT TO DRINK EVERY LAST DROP...

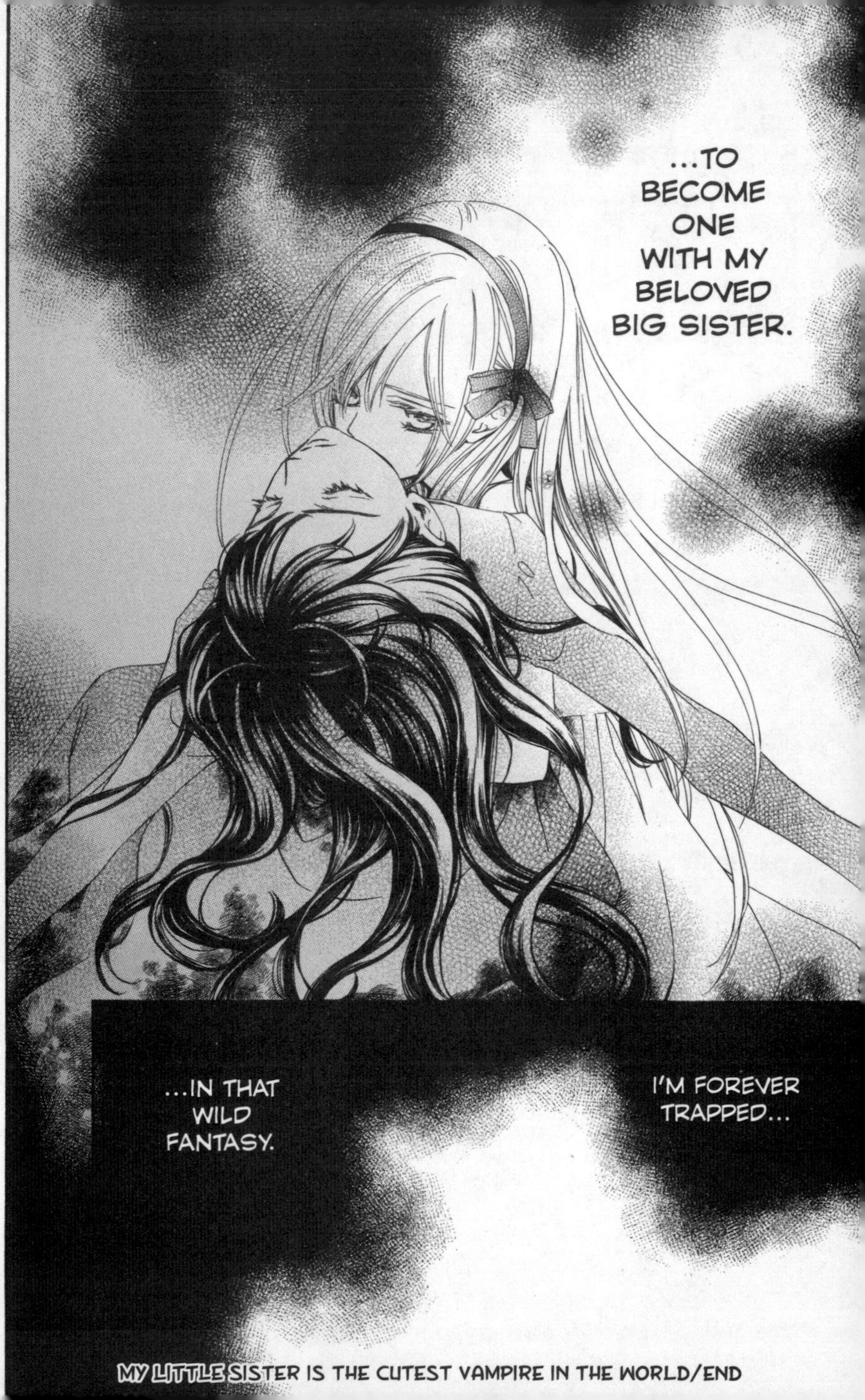
...TO BECOME ONE WITH MY BELOVED BIG SISTER.
I'M FOREVER TRAPPED...
...IN THAT WILD FANTASY.
MY LITTLE SISTER IS THE CUTEST VAMPIRE IN THE WORLD/END

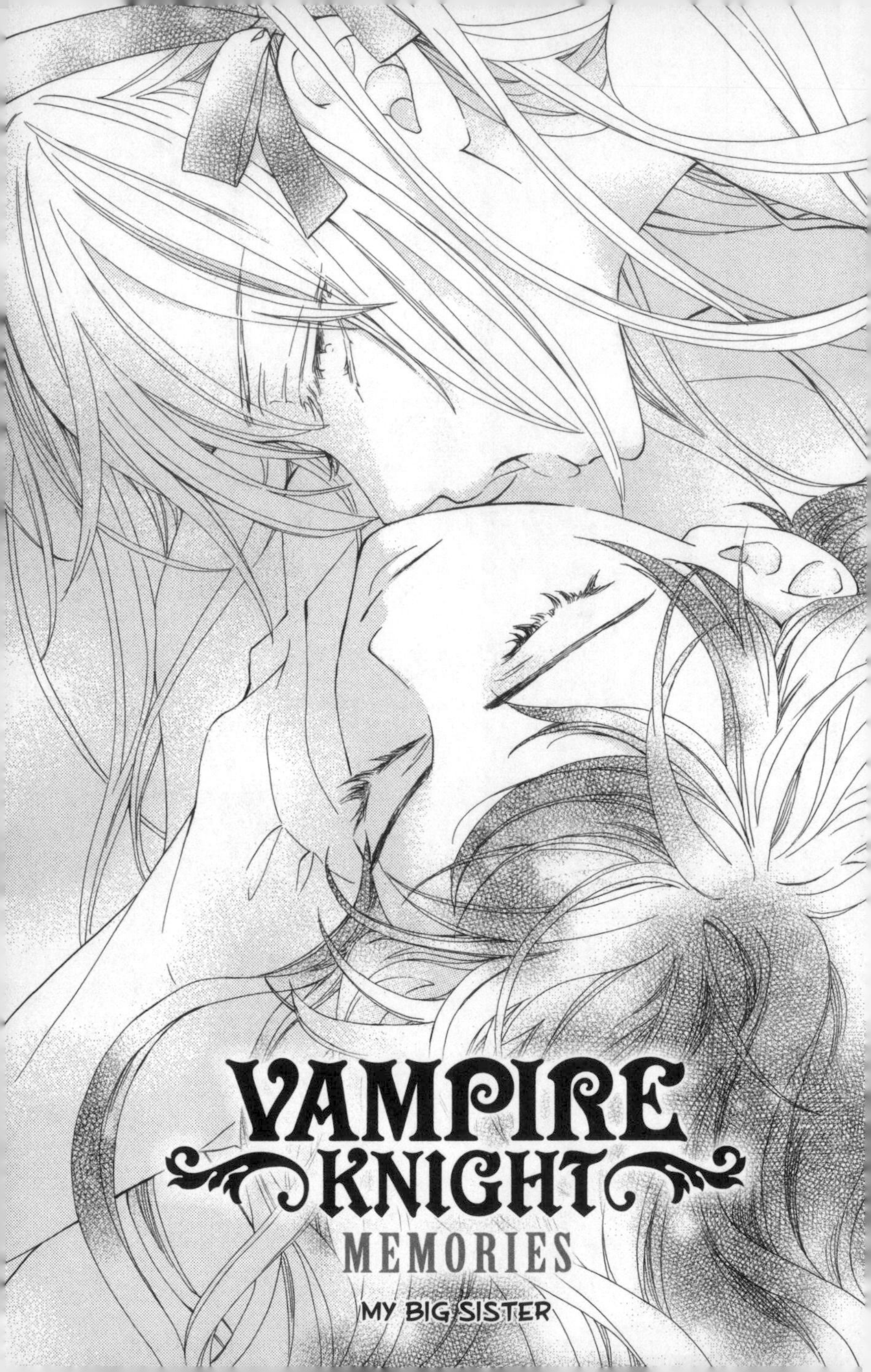
VAMPIRE KNIGHT
MEMORIES
MY BIG SISTER

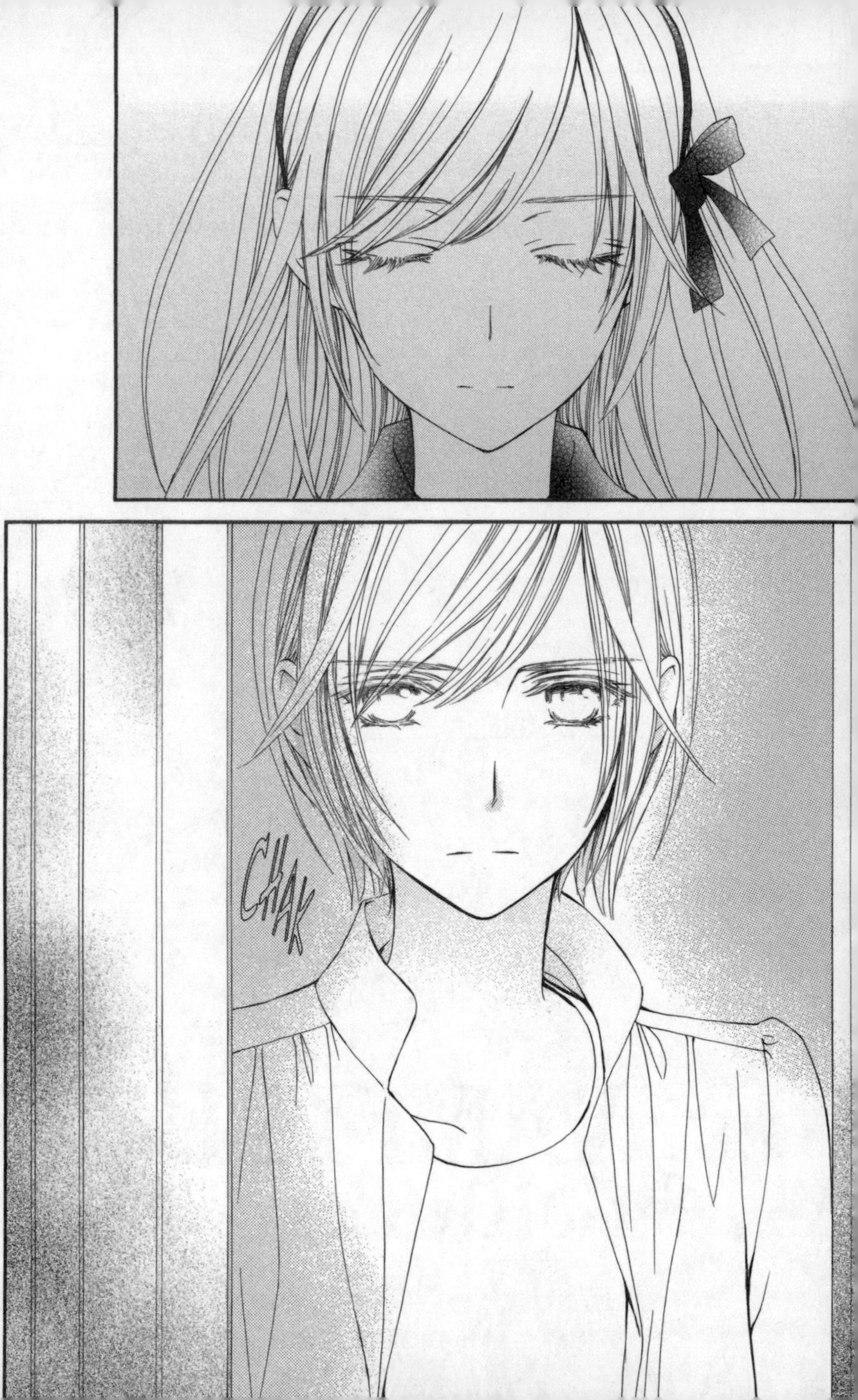
CHAK

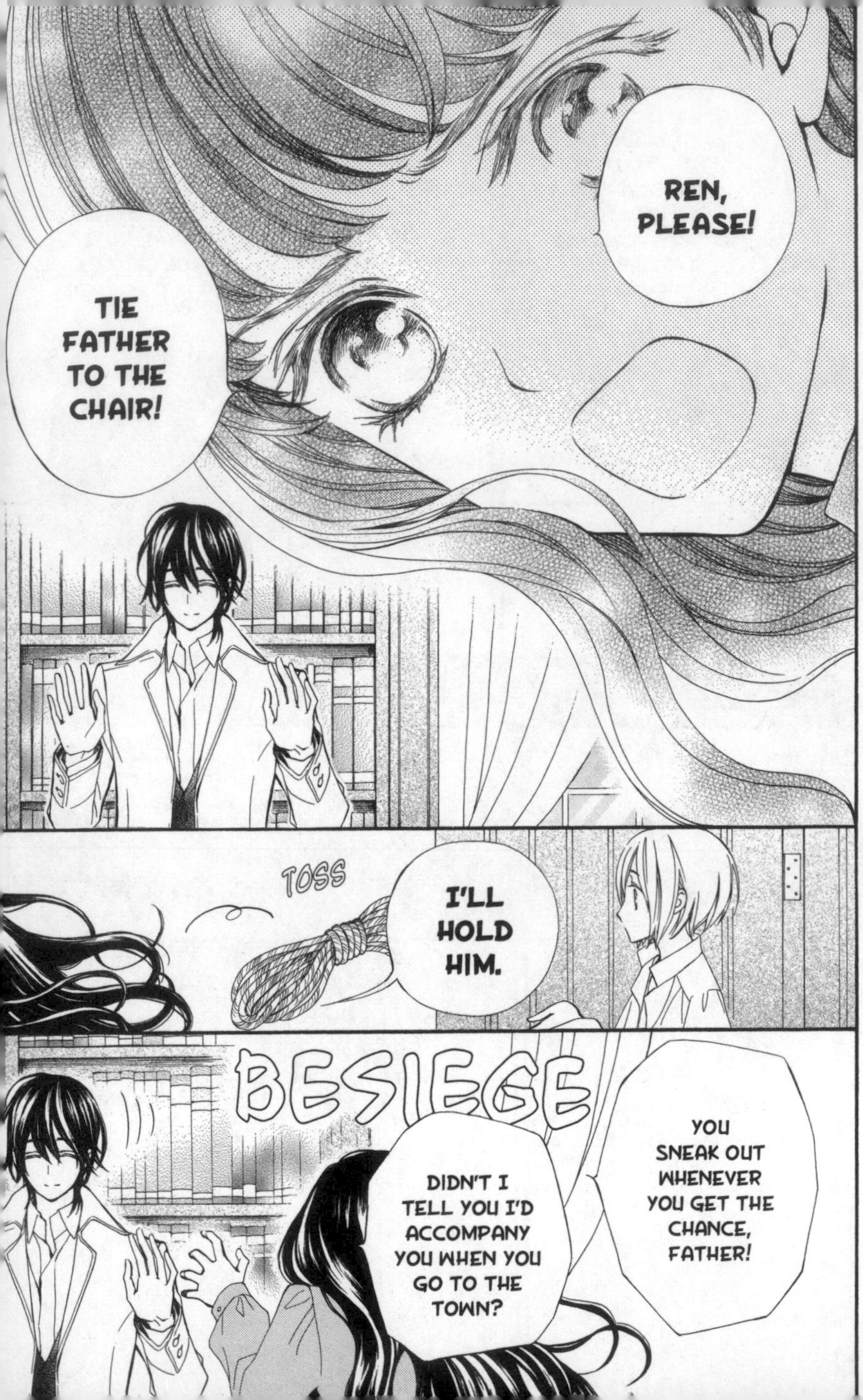

REN, PLEASE!
TIE FATHER TO THE CHAIR!
I'LL HOLD HIM.
TOSS
YOU SNEAK OUT WHENEVER YOU GET THE CHANCE, FATHER!
DIDN'T I TELL YOU I'D ACCOMPANY YOU WHEN YOU GO TO THE TOWN?
BESIEGE

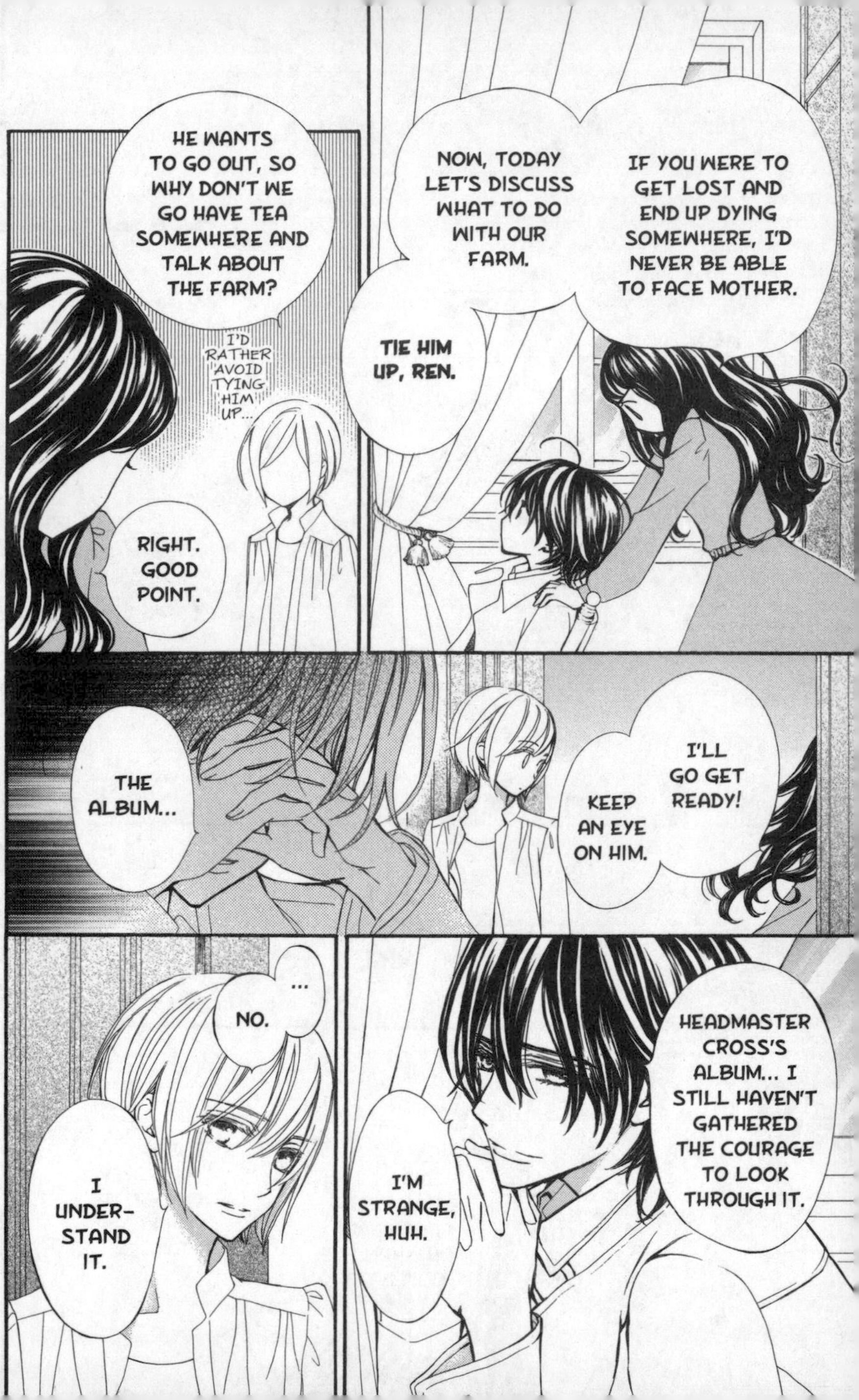
IF YOU WERE TO GET LOST AND END UP DYING SOMEWHERE, I'D NEVER BE ABLE TO FACE MOTHER.
NOW, TODAY LET'S DISCUSS WHAT TO DO WITH OUR FARM.
TIE HIM UP, REN.
HE WANTS TO GO OUT, SO WHY DON'T WE GO HAVE TEA SOMEWHERE AND TALK ABOUT THE FARM?
I'D RATHER AVOID TYING HIM UP...
RIGHT. GOOD POINT.
I'LL GO GET READY!
KEEP AN EYE ON HIM.
THE ALBUM...
HEADMASTER CROSS'S ALBUM... I STILL HAVEN'T GATHERED THE COURAGE TO LOOK THROUGH IT.
I'M STRANGE, HUH.
...
NO.
I UNDER-STAND IT.

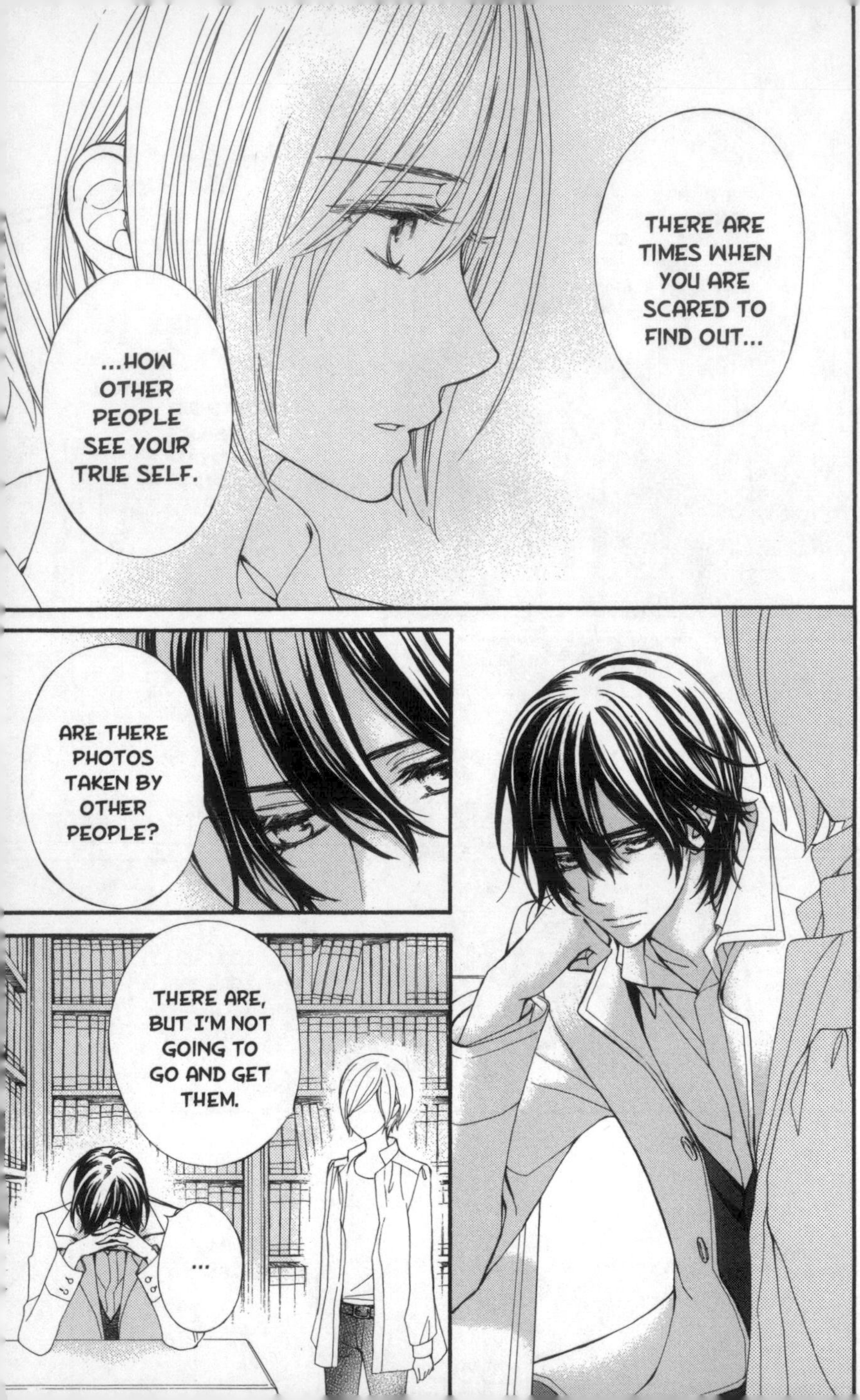
THERE ARE TIMES WHEN YOU ARE SCARED TO FIND OUT...
...HOW OTHER PEOPLE SEE YOUR TRUE SELF.
ARE THERE PHOTOS TAKEN BY OTHER PEOPLE?
THERE ARE, BUT I'M NOT GOING TO GO AND GET THEM.
...

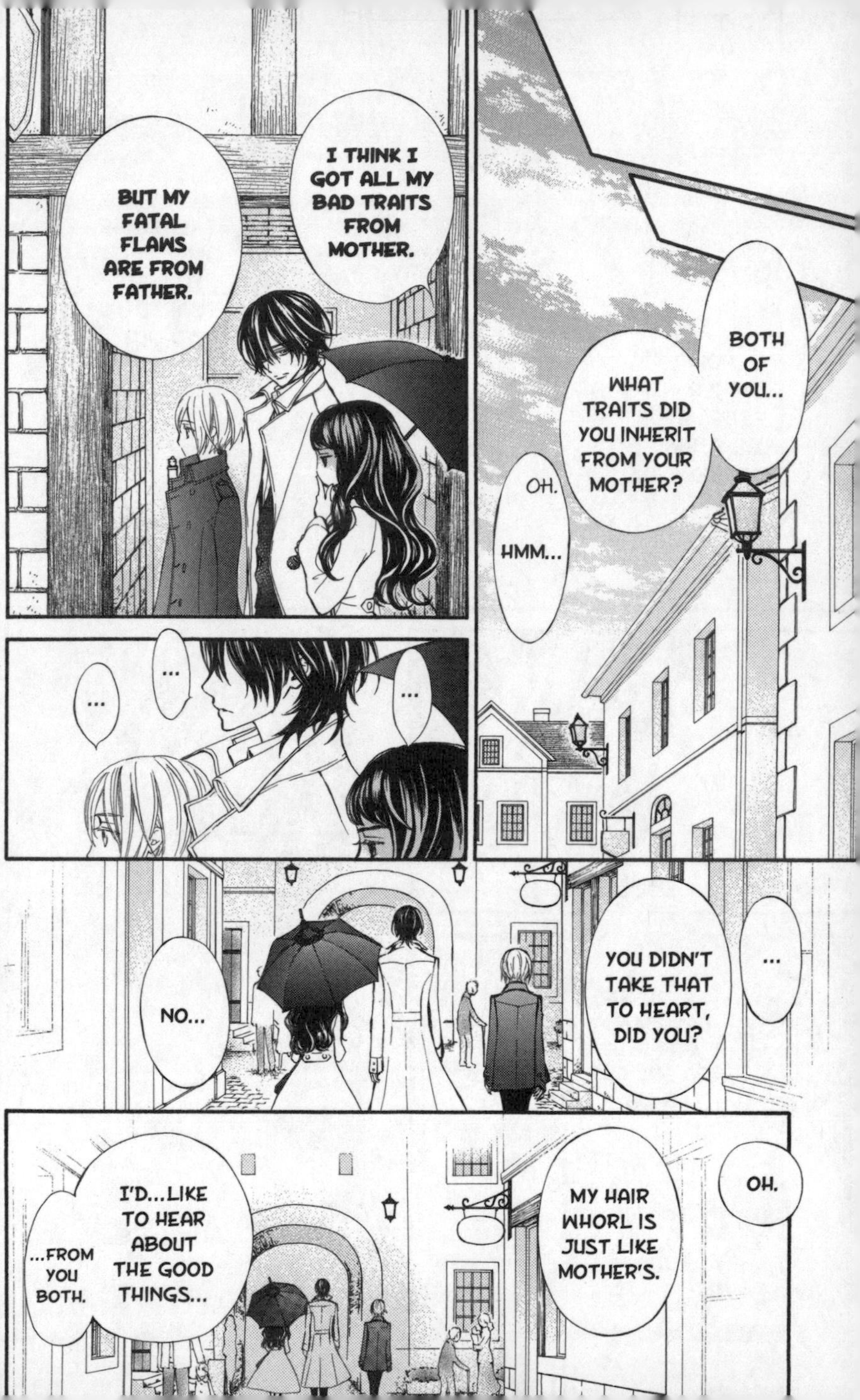

BOTH OF YOU...
WHAT TRAITS DID YOU INHERIT FROM YOUR MOTHER?
OH.
HMM...
I THINK I GOT ALL MY BAD TRAITS FROM MOTHER.
BUT MY FATAL FLAWS ARE FROM FATHER.
...
...
...
...
YOU DIDN'T TAKE THAT TO HEART, DID YOU?
NO...
OH.
MY HAIR WHORL IS JUST LIKE MOTHER'S.
I'D...LIKE TO HEAR ABOUT THE GOOD THINGS...
...FROM YOU BOTH.

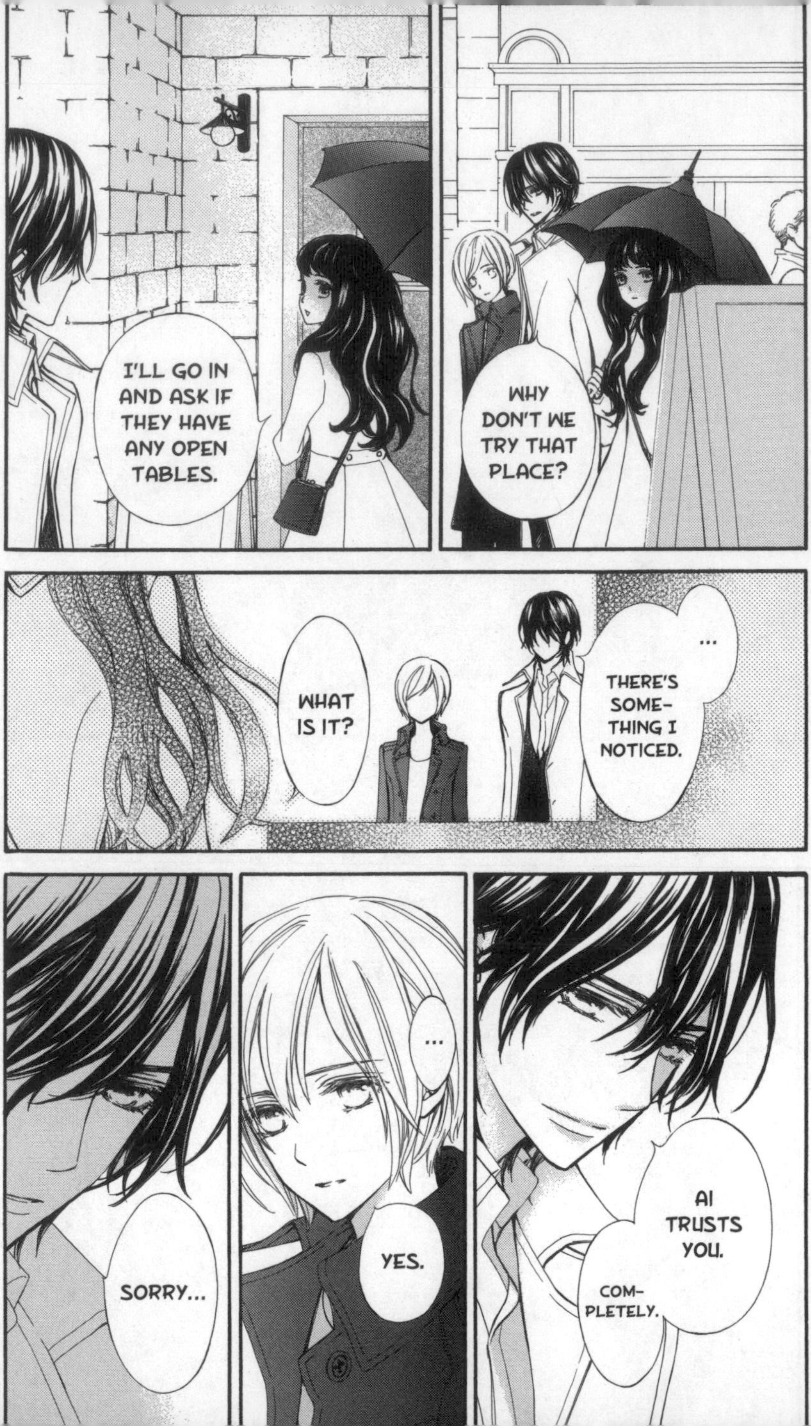
WHY DON'T WE TRY THAT PLACE?
I'LL GO IN AND ASK IF THEY HAVE ANY OPEN TABLES.
...
THERE'S SOME-THING I NOTICED.
WHAT IS IT?
AI TRUSTS YOU.
COM-PLETELY.
...
YES.
SORRY...

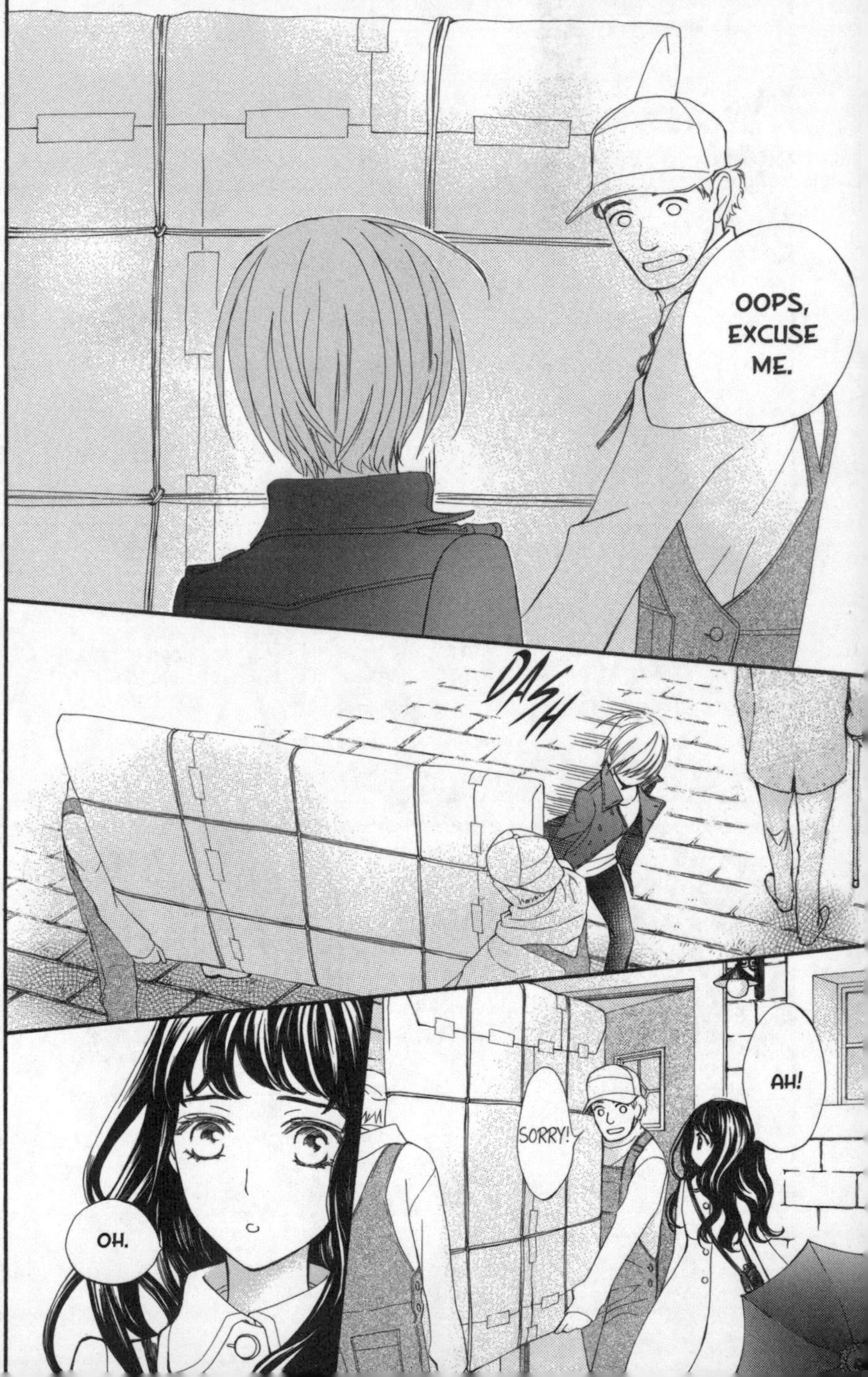
OOPS, EXCUSE ME.
DASH
AH!
SORRY!
OH.

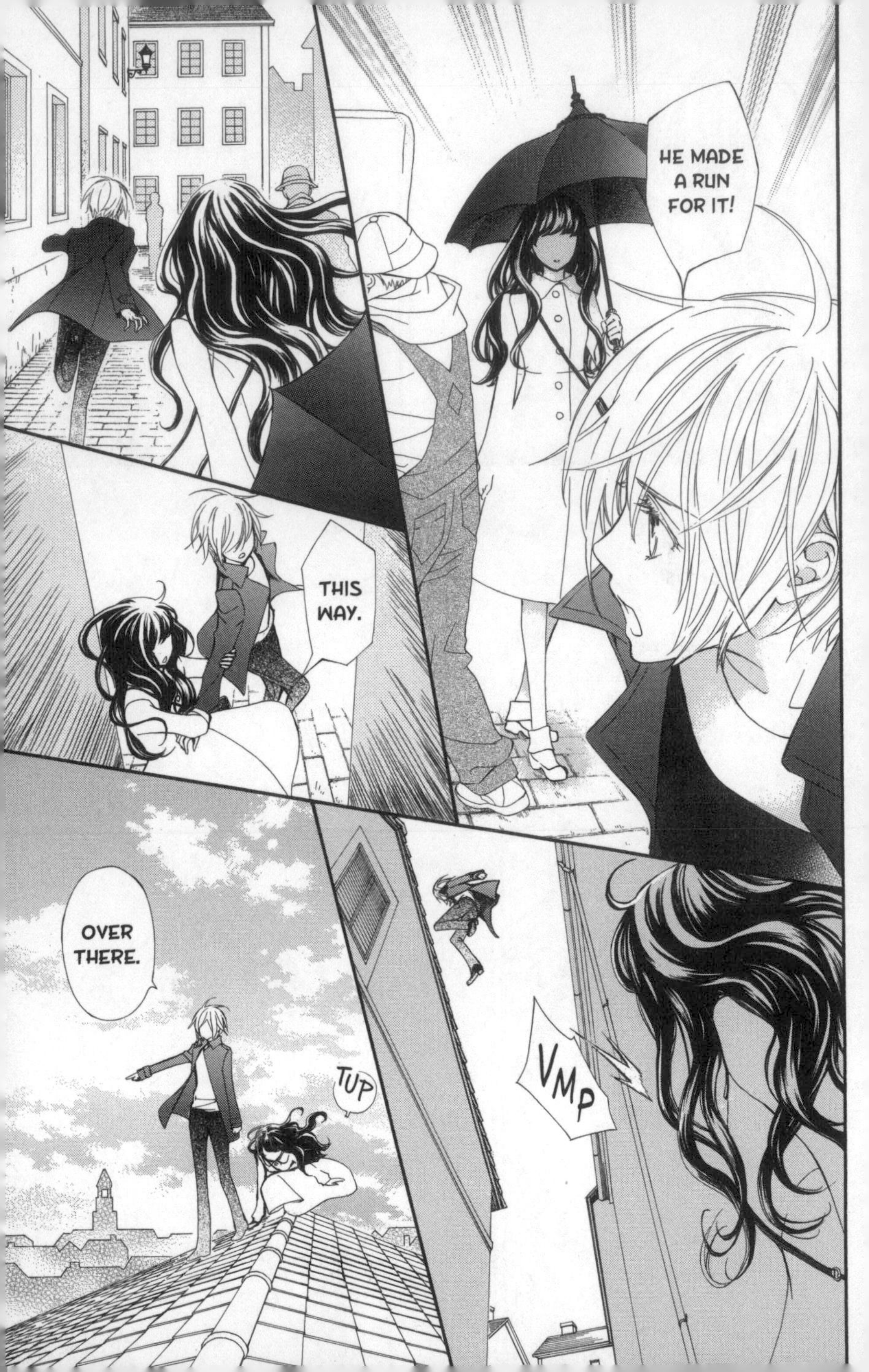
HE MADE A RUN FOR IT!
THIS WAY.
VMP
OVER THERE.
TUP

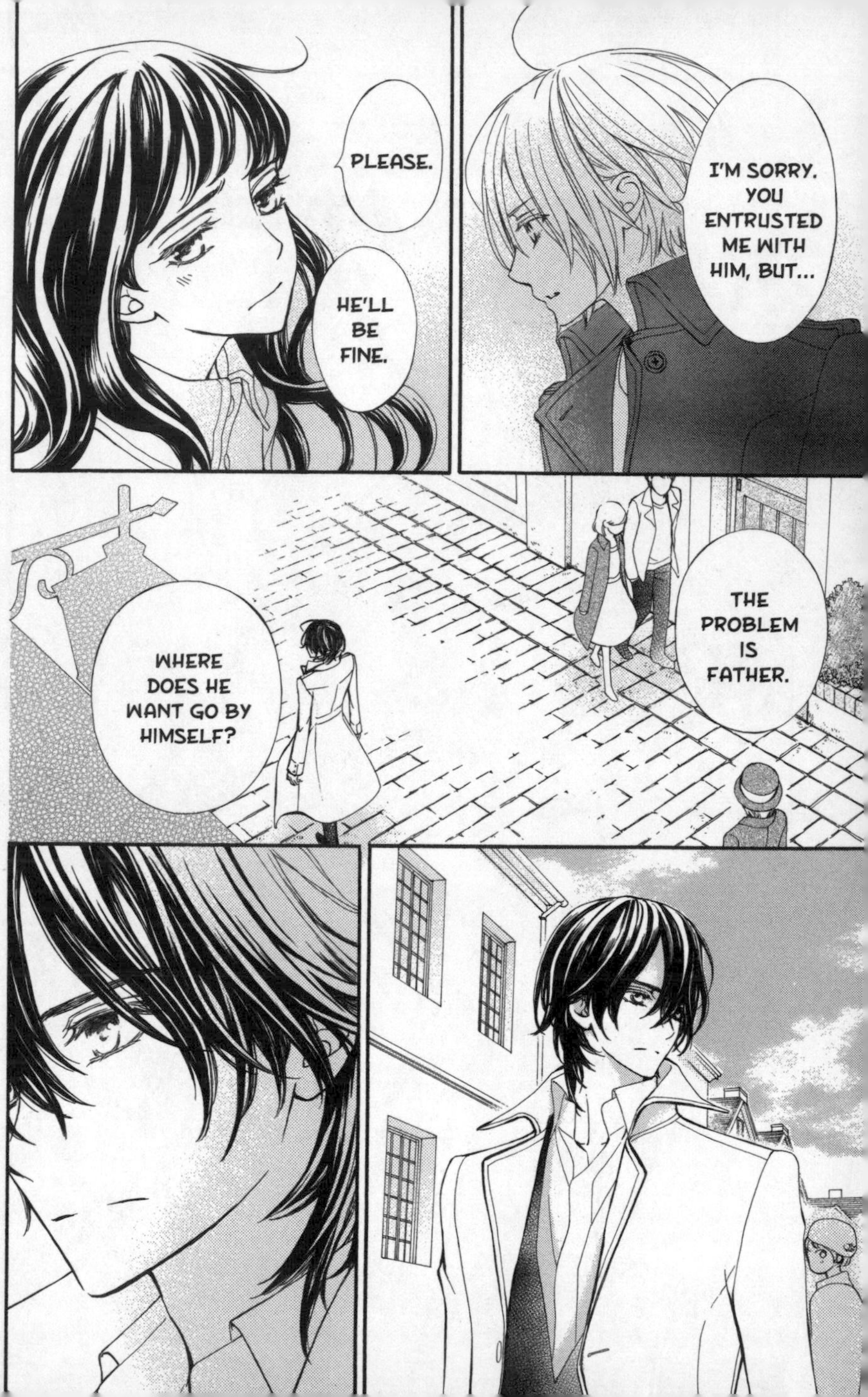
I'M SORRY. YOU ENTRUSTED ME WITH HIM, BUT...
PLEASE.
HE'LL BE FINE.
THE PROBLEM IS FATHER.
WHERE DOES HE WANT GO BY HIMSELF?

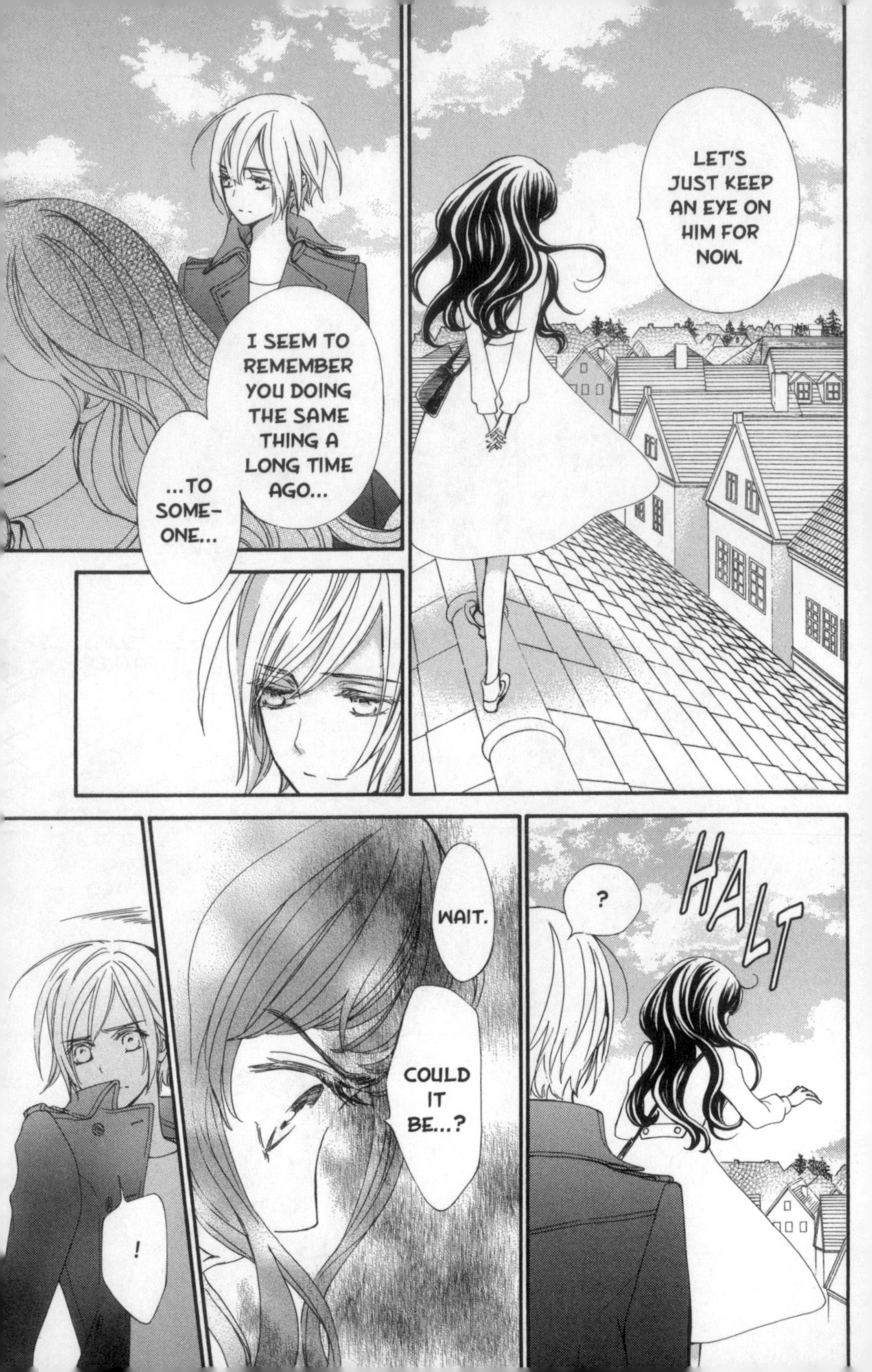
LET'S JUST KEEP AN EYE ON HIM FOR NOW.
I SEEM TO REMEMBER YOU DOING THE SAME THING A LONG TIME AGO...
...TO SOME-ONE...
HALT
?
WAIT.
COULD IT BE...?
!

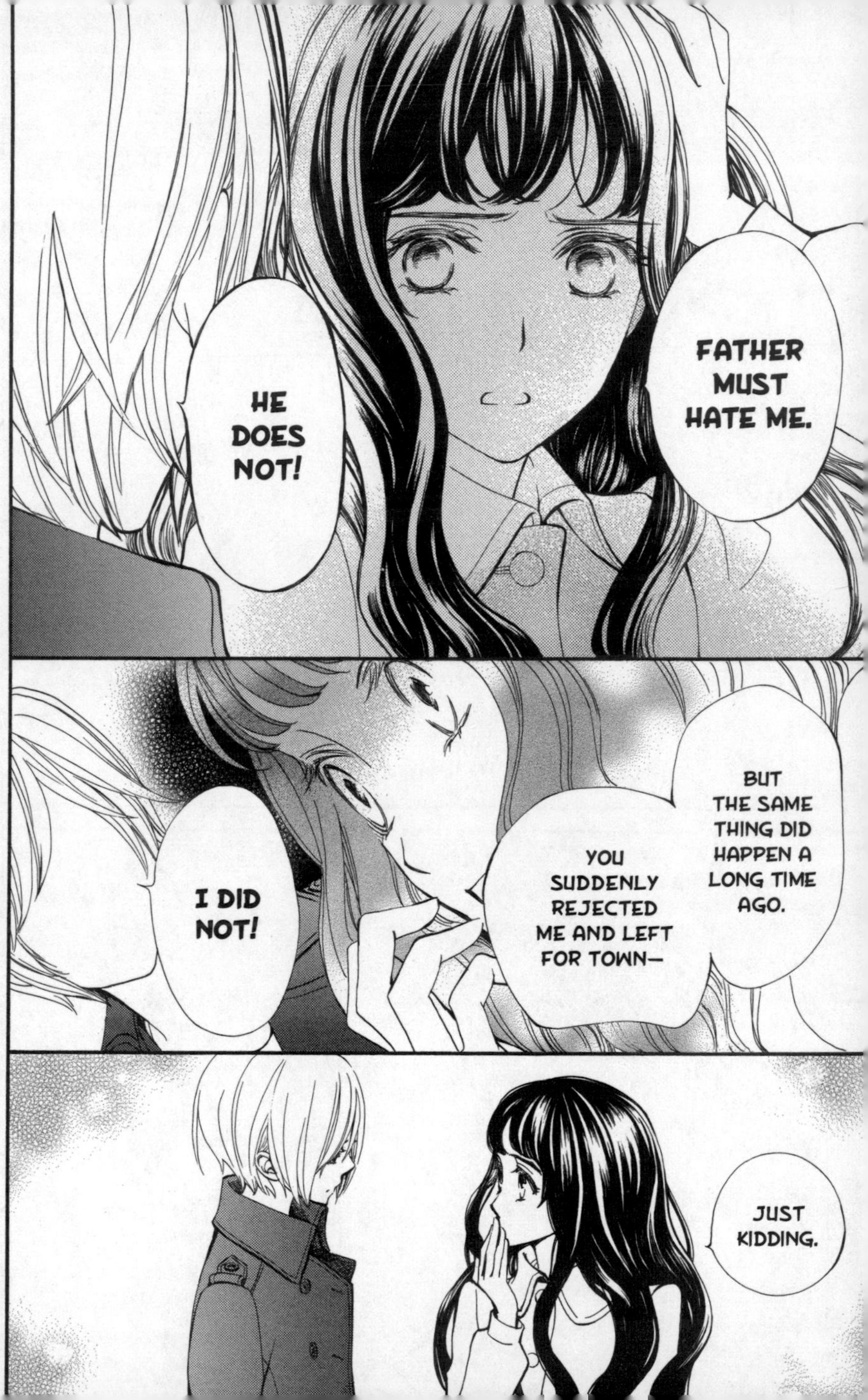
FATHER MUST HATE ME.
HE DOES NOT!
BUT THE SAME THING DID HAPPEN A LONG TIME AGO.
YOU SUDDENLY REJECTED ME AND LEFT FOR TOWN—
I DID NOT!
JUST KIDDING.

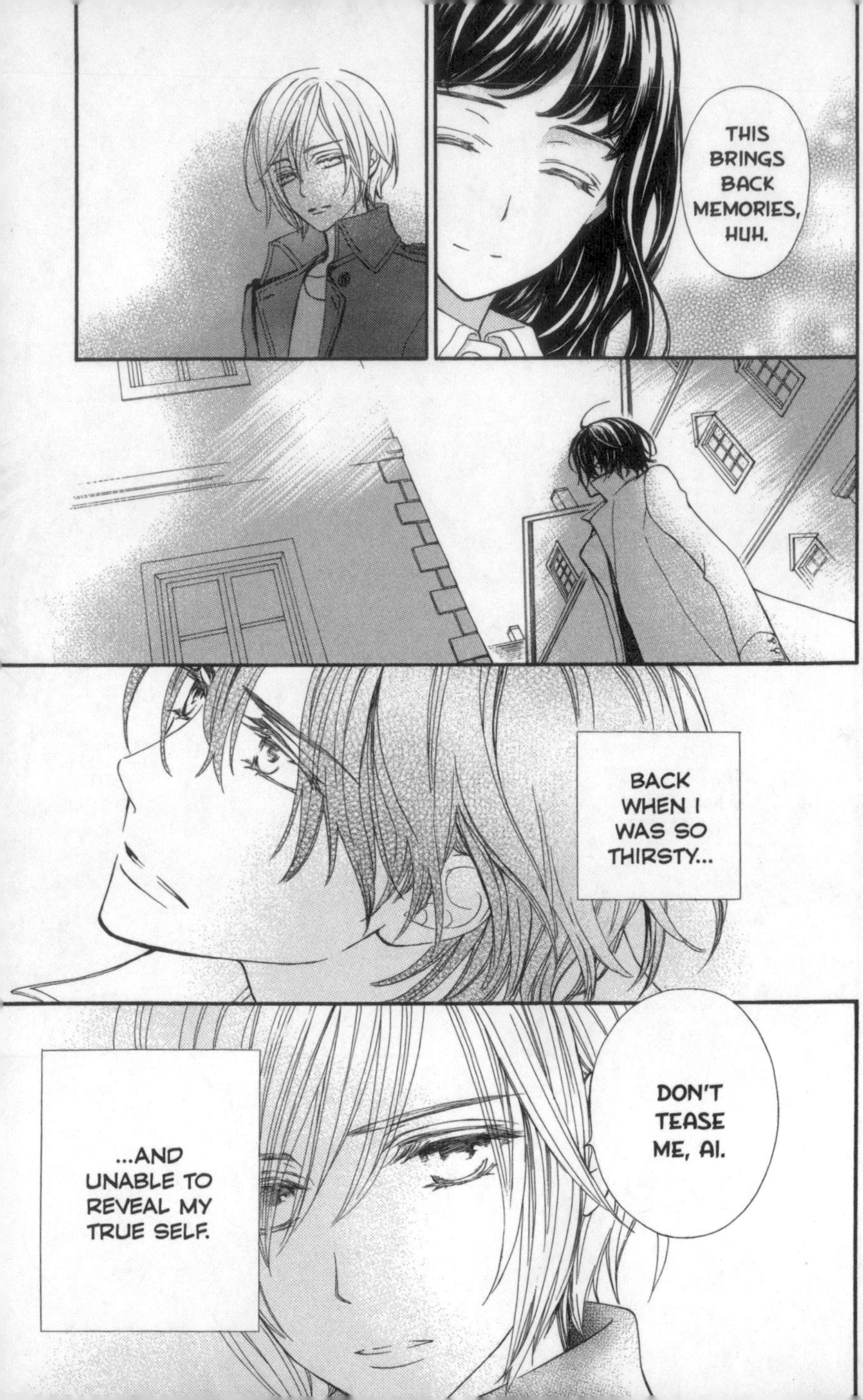
THIS BRINGS BACK MEMORIES, HUH.
BACK WHEN I WAS SO THIRSTY...
DON'T TEASE ME, AI.
...AND UNABLE TO REVEAL MY TRUE SELF.

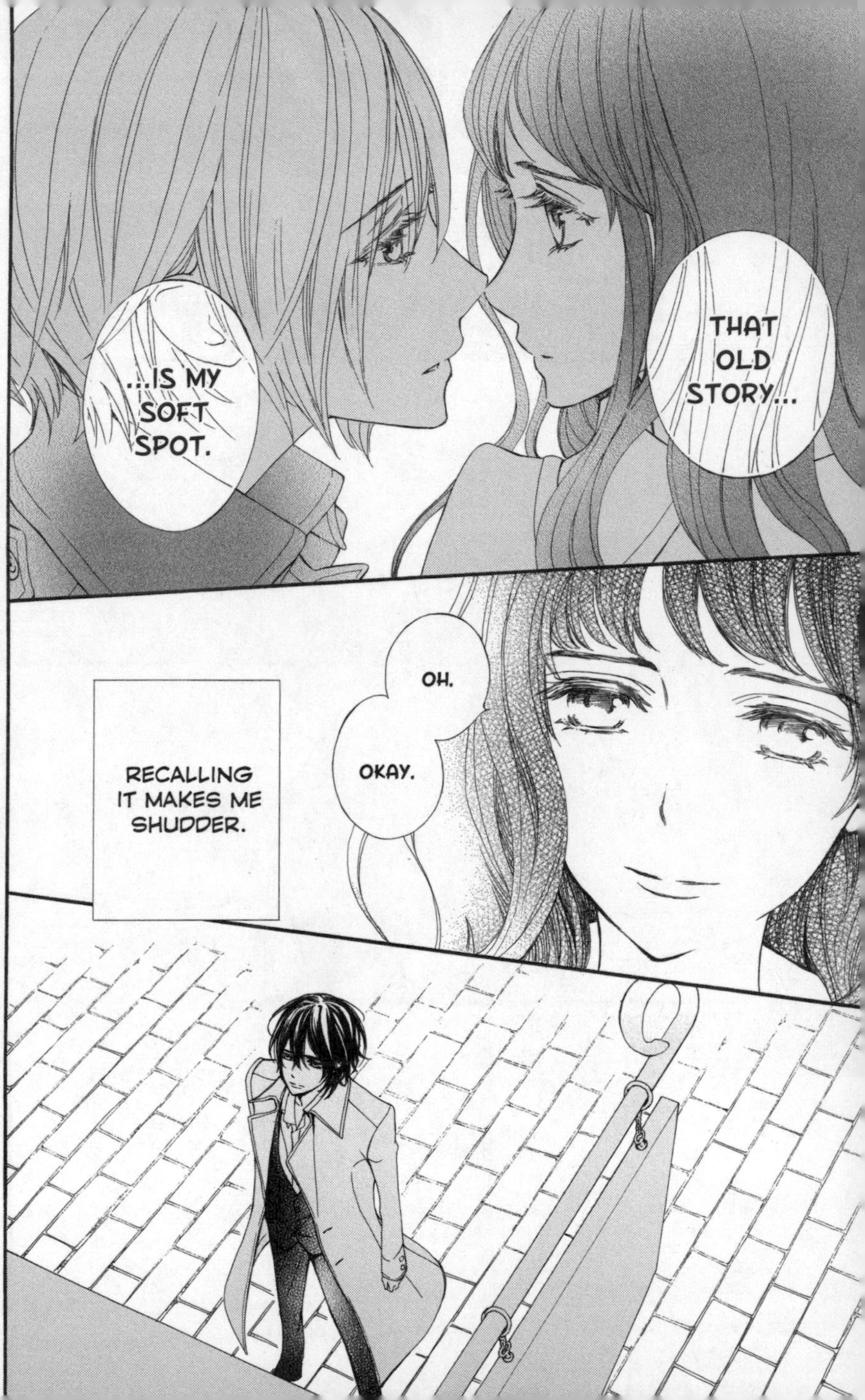
THAT OLD STORY...
...IS MY SOFT SPOT.
OH.
OKAY.
RECALLING IT MAKES ME SHUDDER.

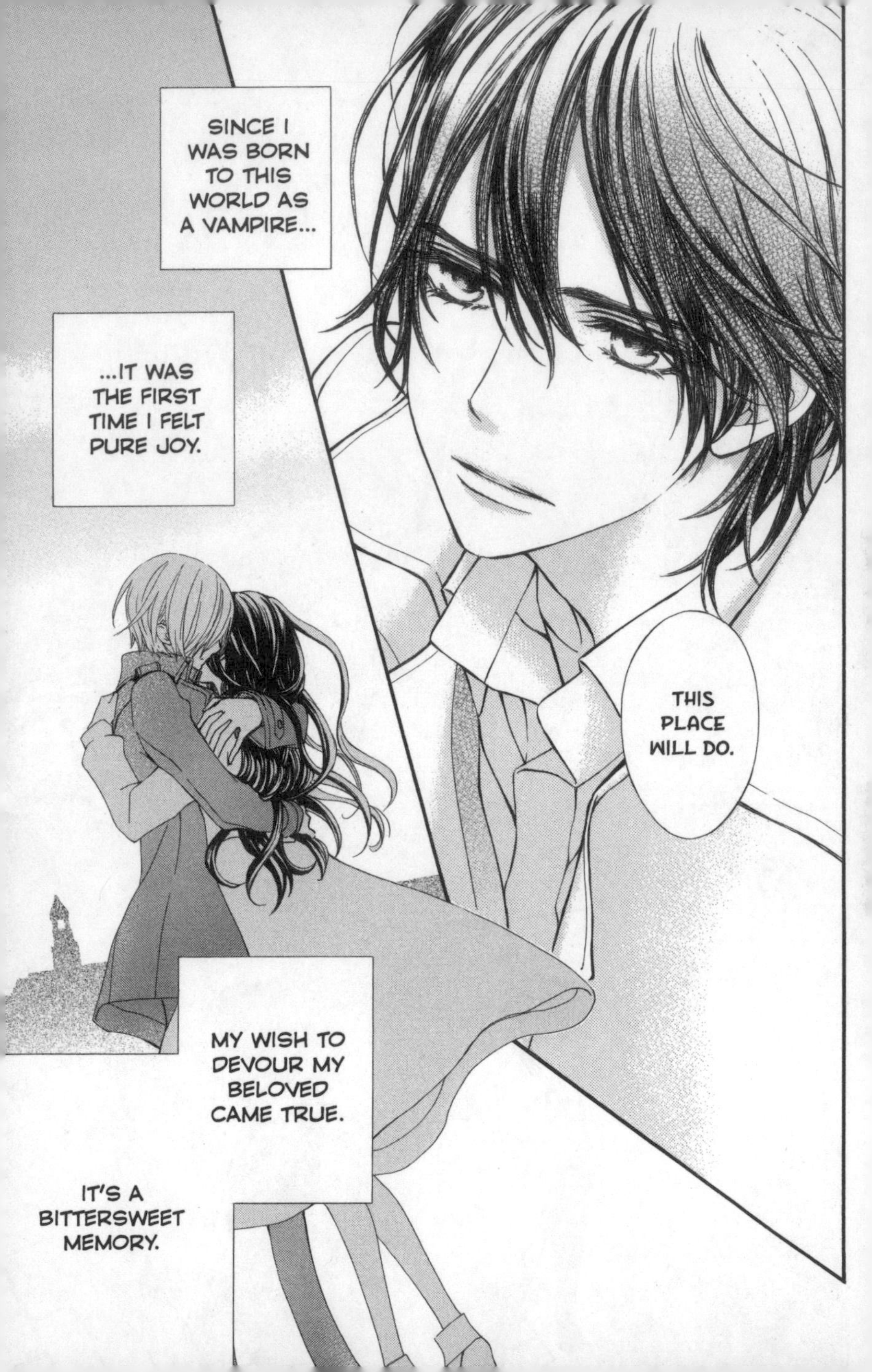
THIS PLACE WILL DO.
SINCE I WAS BORN TO THIS WORLD AS A VAMPIRE...
...IT WAS THE FIRST TIME I FELT PURE JOY.
MY WISH TO DEVOUR MY BELOVED CAME TRUE.
IT'S A BITTERSWEET MEMORY.

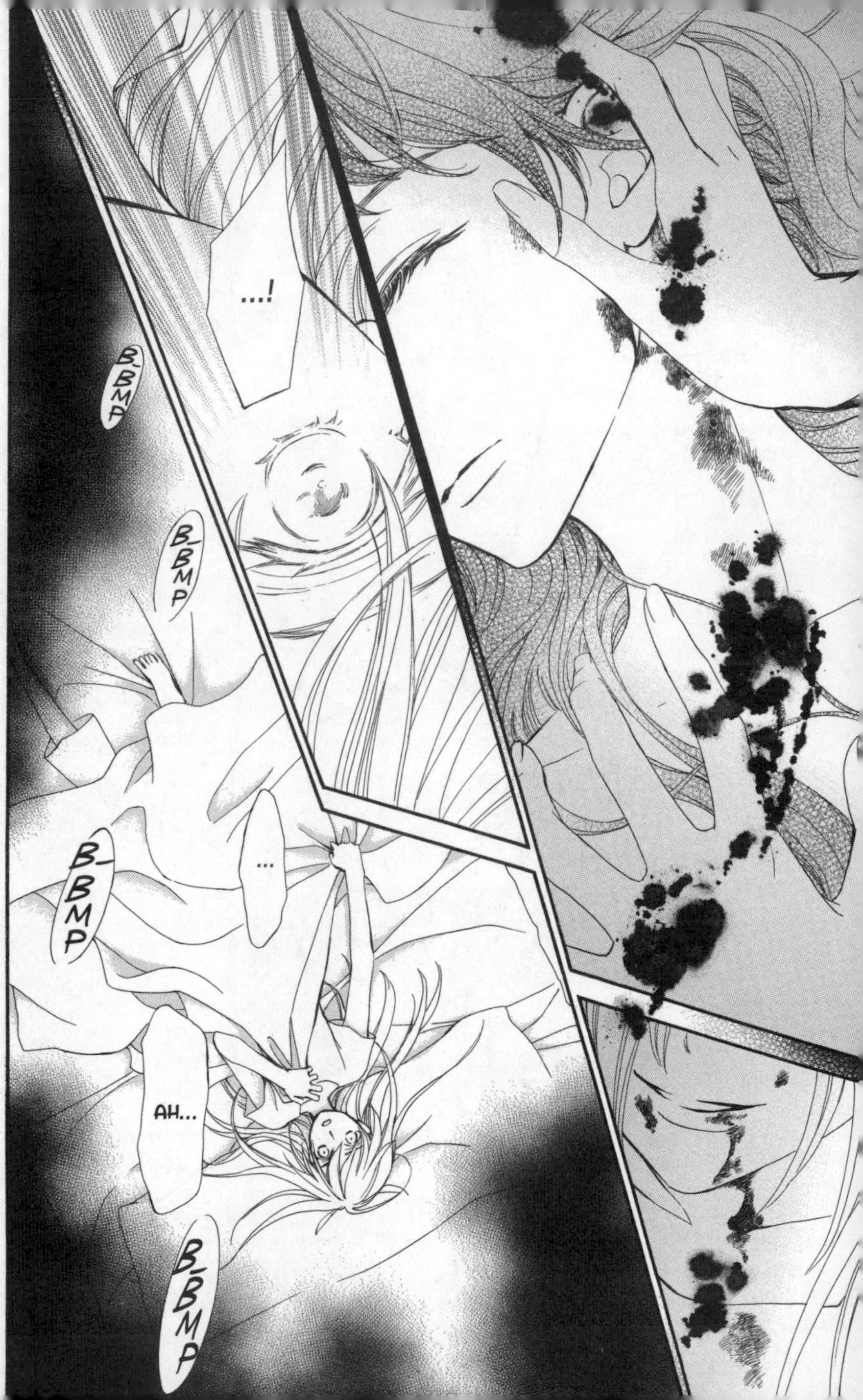
...!
...
B-BMP
B-BMP
B-BMP
AH...
B-BMP

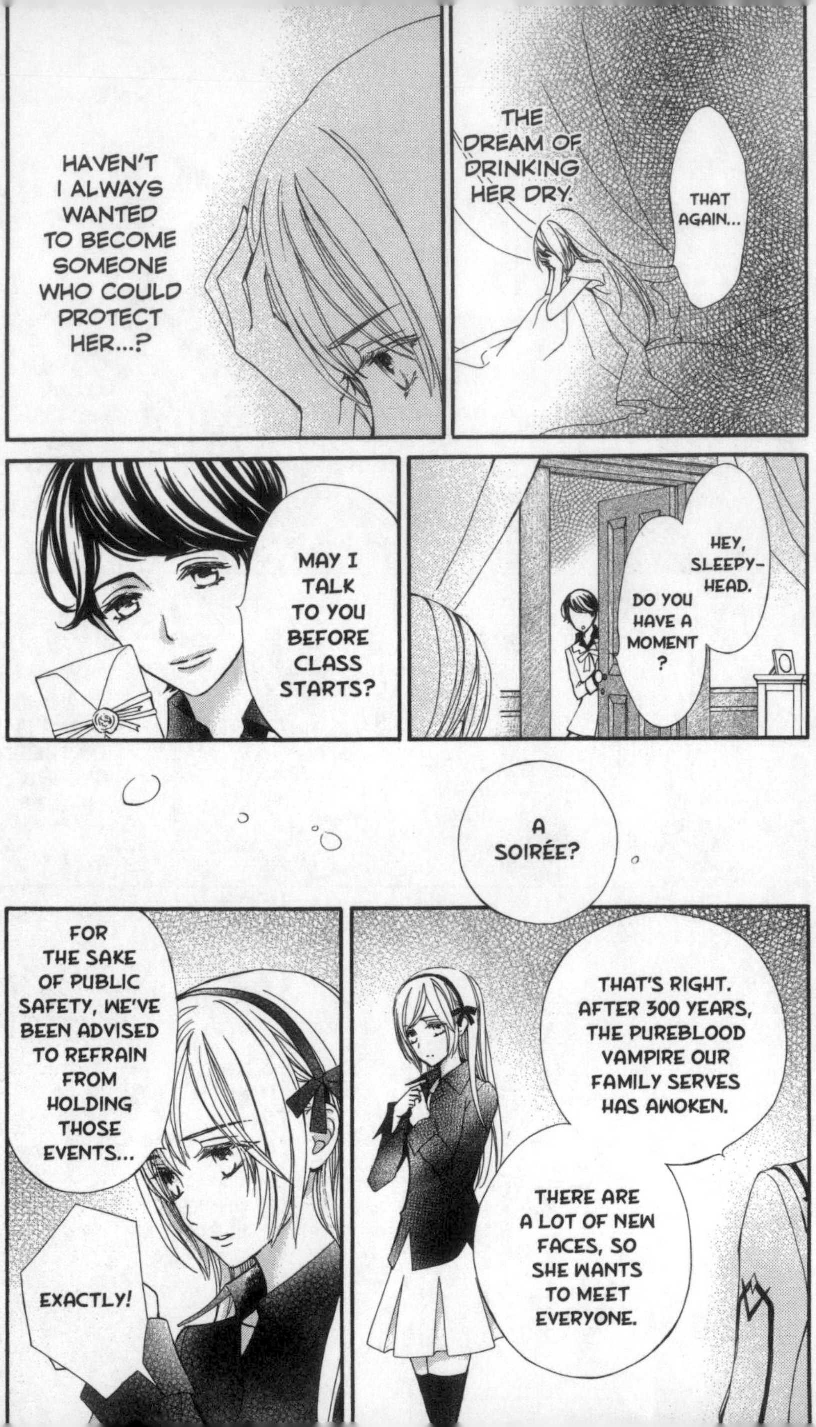
THAT AGAIN...
THE DREAM OF DRINKING HER DRY.
HAVEN'T I ALWAYS WANTED TO BECOME SOMEONE WHO COULD PROTECT HER...?
HEY, SLEEPY-HEAD.
DO YOU HAVE A MOMENT?
MAY I TALK TO YOU BEFORE CLASS STARTS?
A SOIRÉE?
THAT'S RIGHT. AFTER 300 YEARS, THE PUREBLOOD VAMPIRE OUR FAMILY SERVES HAS AWOKEN.
THERE ARE A LOT OF NEW FACES, SO SHE WANTS TO MEET EVERYONE.
FOR THE SAKE OF PUBLIC SAFETY, WE'VE BEEN ADVISED TO REFRAIN FROM HOLDING THOSE EVENTS...
EXACTLY!

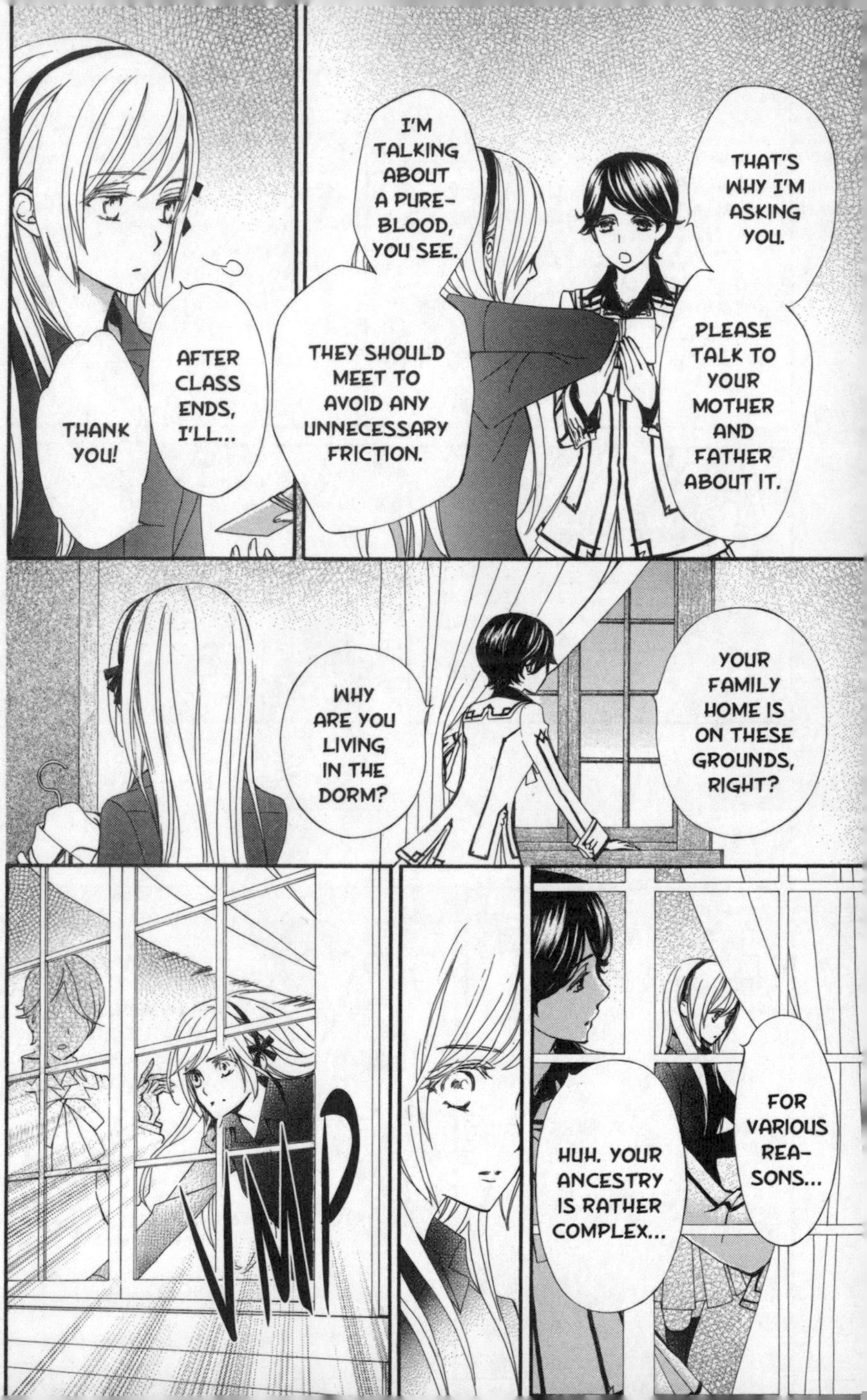
THAT'S WHY I'M ASKING YOU.
I'M TALKING ABOUT A PURE-BLOOD, YOU SEE.
PLEASE TALK TO YOUR MOTHER AND FATHER ABOUT IT.
THEY SHOULD MEET TO AVOID ANY UNNECESSARY FRICTION.
AFTER CLASS ENDS, I'LL...
THANK YOU!
YOUR FAMILY HOME IS ON THESE GROUNDS, RIGHT?
WHY ARE YOU LIVING IN THE DORM?
FOR VARIOUS REA-SONS...
HUH. YOUR ANCESTRY IS RATHER COMPLEX...
VMP

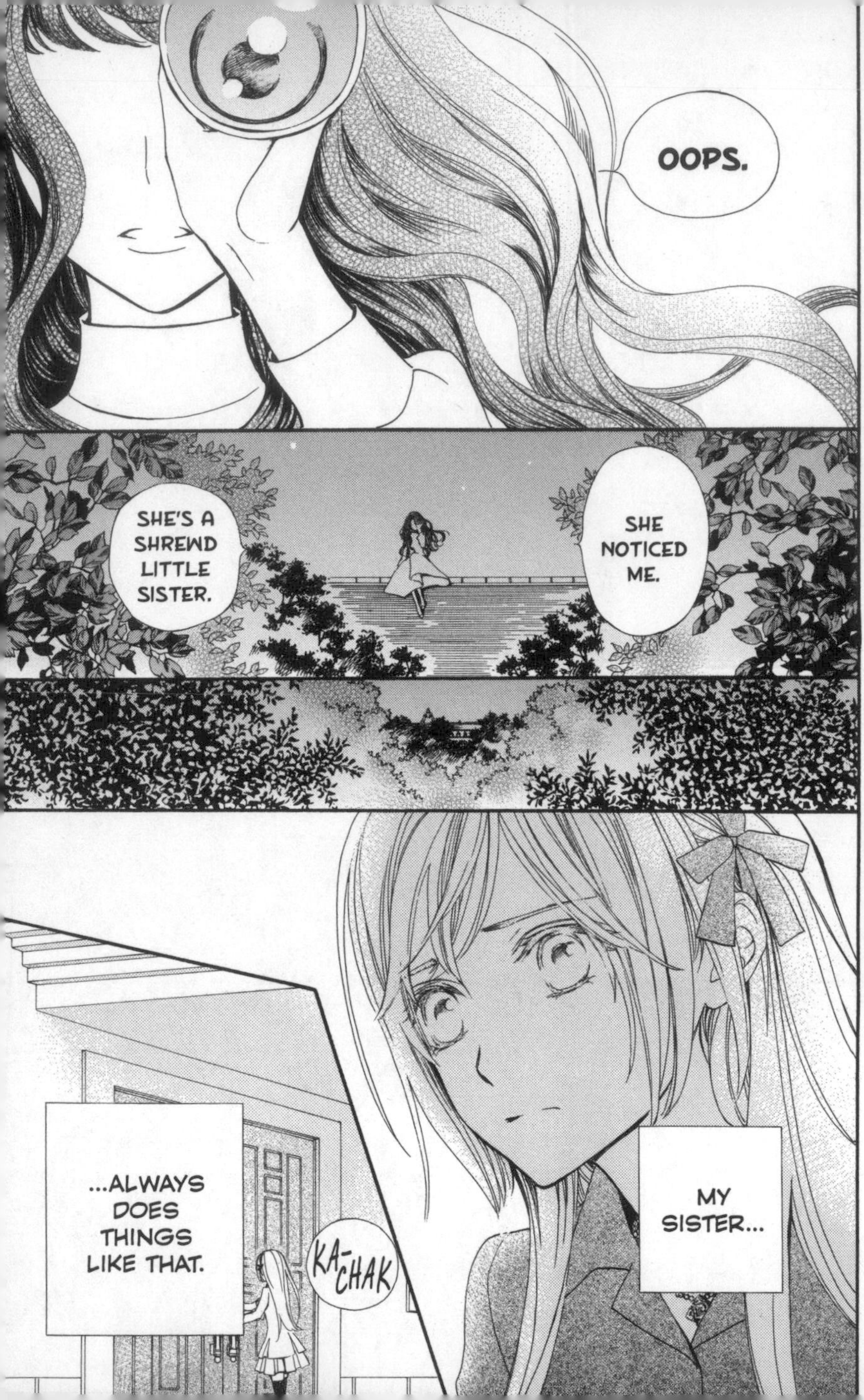
OOPS.
SHE NOTICED ME.
SHE'S A SHREWD LITTLE SISTER.
MY SISTER...
...ALWAYS DOES THINGS LIKE THAT.
KA-CHAK

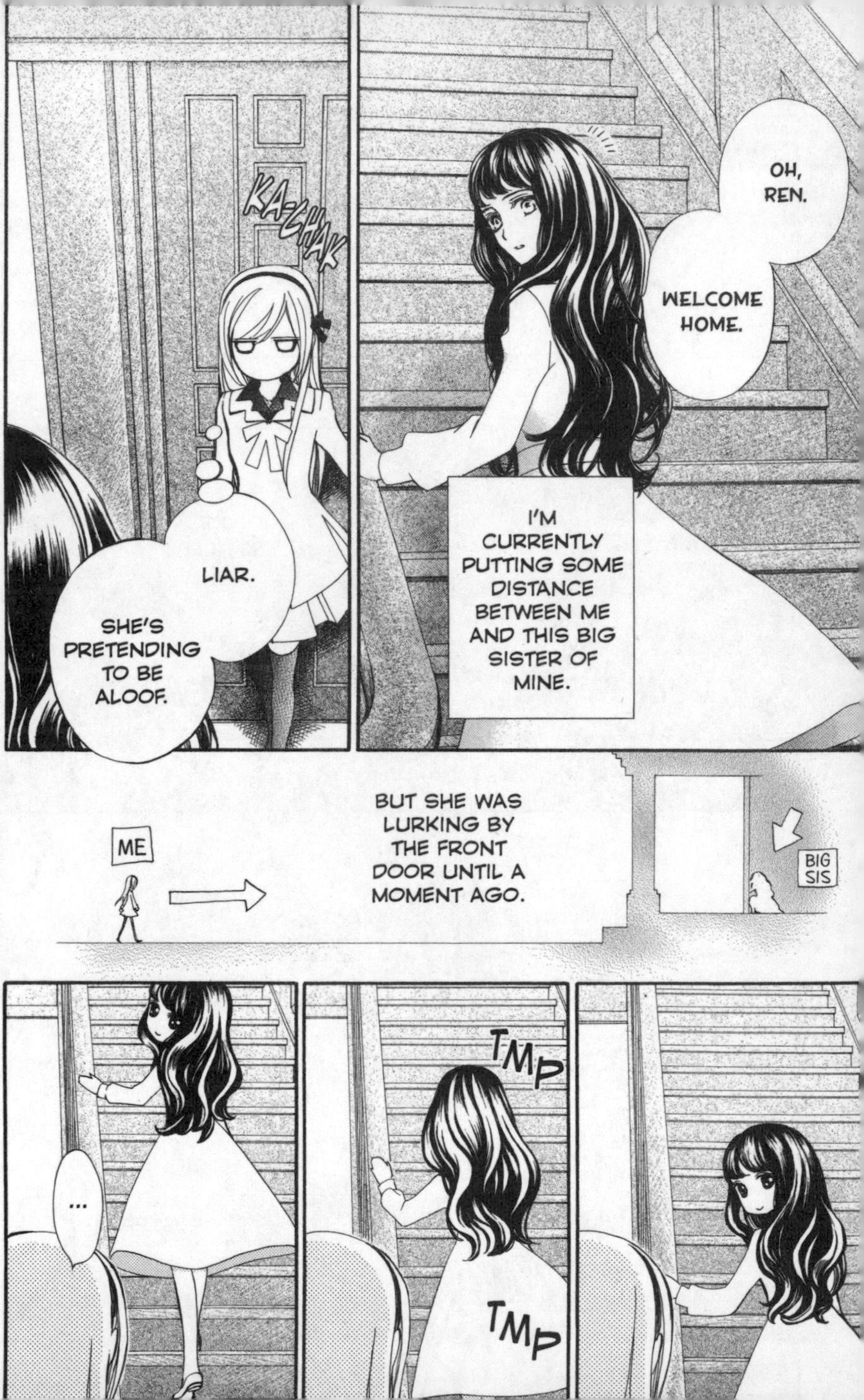
OH, REN.
WELCOME HOME.
I'M CURRENTLY PUTTING SOME DISTANCE BETWEEN ME AND THIS BIG SISTER OF MINE.
KA-CHAK
LIAR.
SHE'S PRETENDING TO BE ALOOF.
BIG SIS
BUT SHE WAS LURKING BY THE FRONT DOOR UNTIL A MOMENT AGO.
ME
TMP
TMP
...

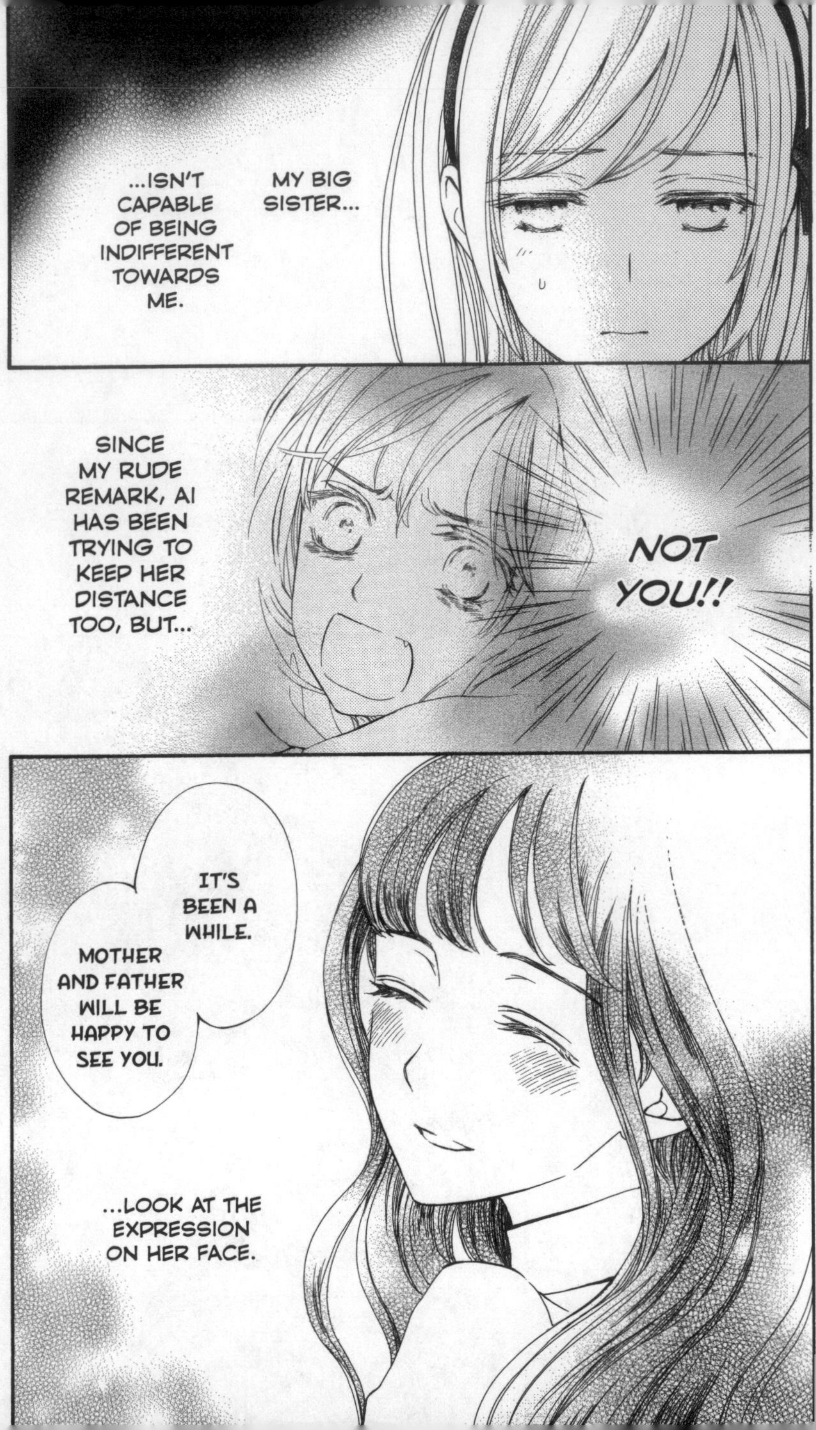
MY BIG SISTER...
...ISN'T CAPABLE OF BEING INDIFFERENT TOWARDS ME.
NOT YOU!!
SINCE MY RUDE REMARK, AI HAS BEEN TRYING TO KEEP HER DISTANCE TOO, BUT...
IT'S BEEN A WHILE. MOTHER AND FATHER WILL BE HAPPY TO SEE YOU.
...LOOK AT THE EXPRESSION ON HER FACE.

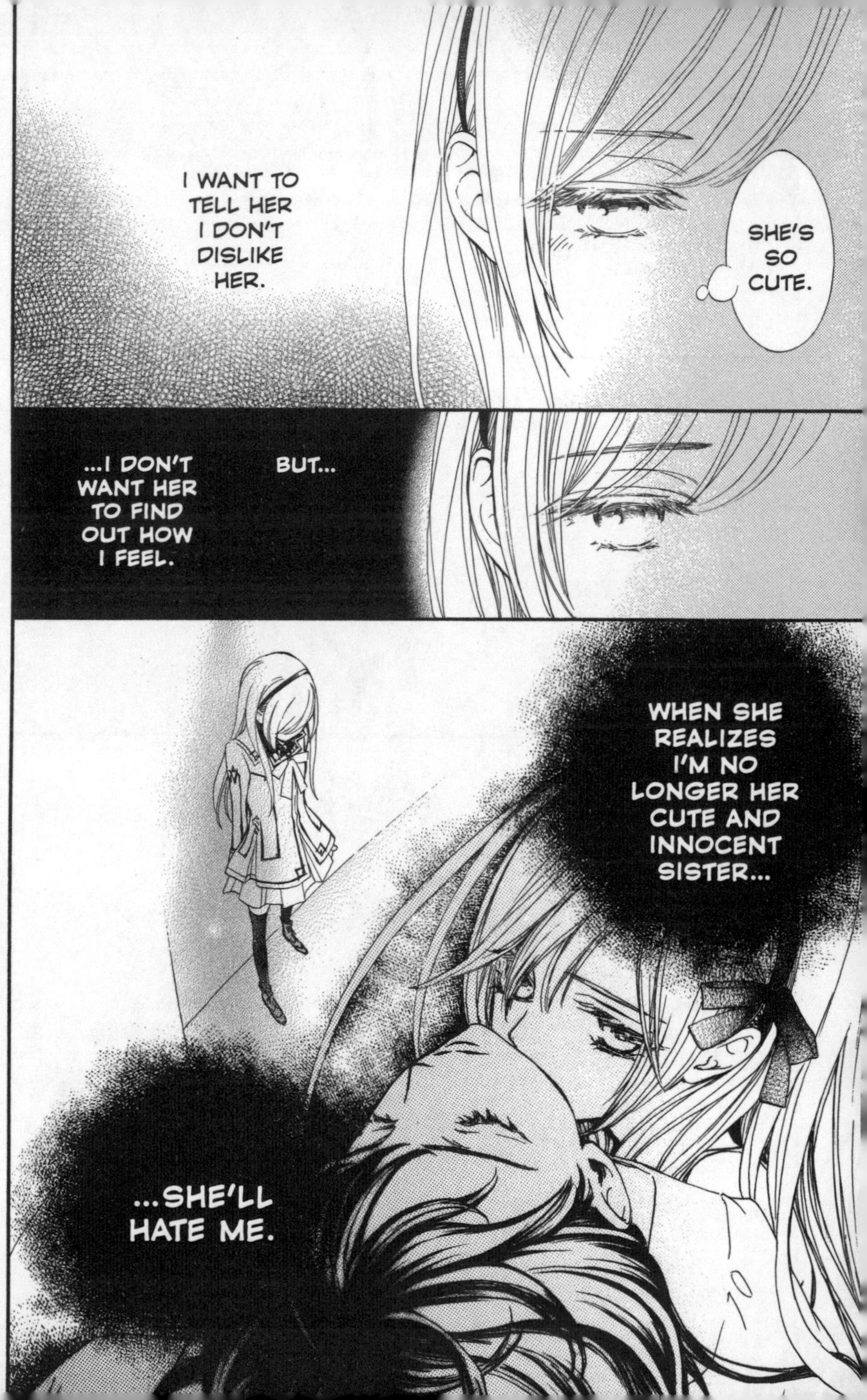
SHE'S SO CUTE.
I WANT TO TELL HER I DON'T DISLIKE HER.
BUT...
...I DON'T WANT HER TO FIND OUT HOW I FEEL.
WHEN SHE REALIZES I'M NO LONGER HER CUTE AND INNOCENT SISTER...
...SHE'LL HATE ME.

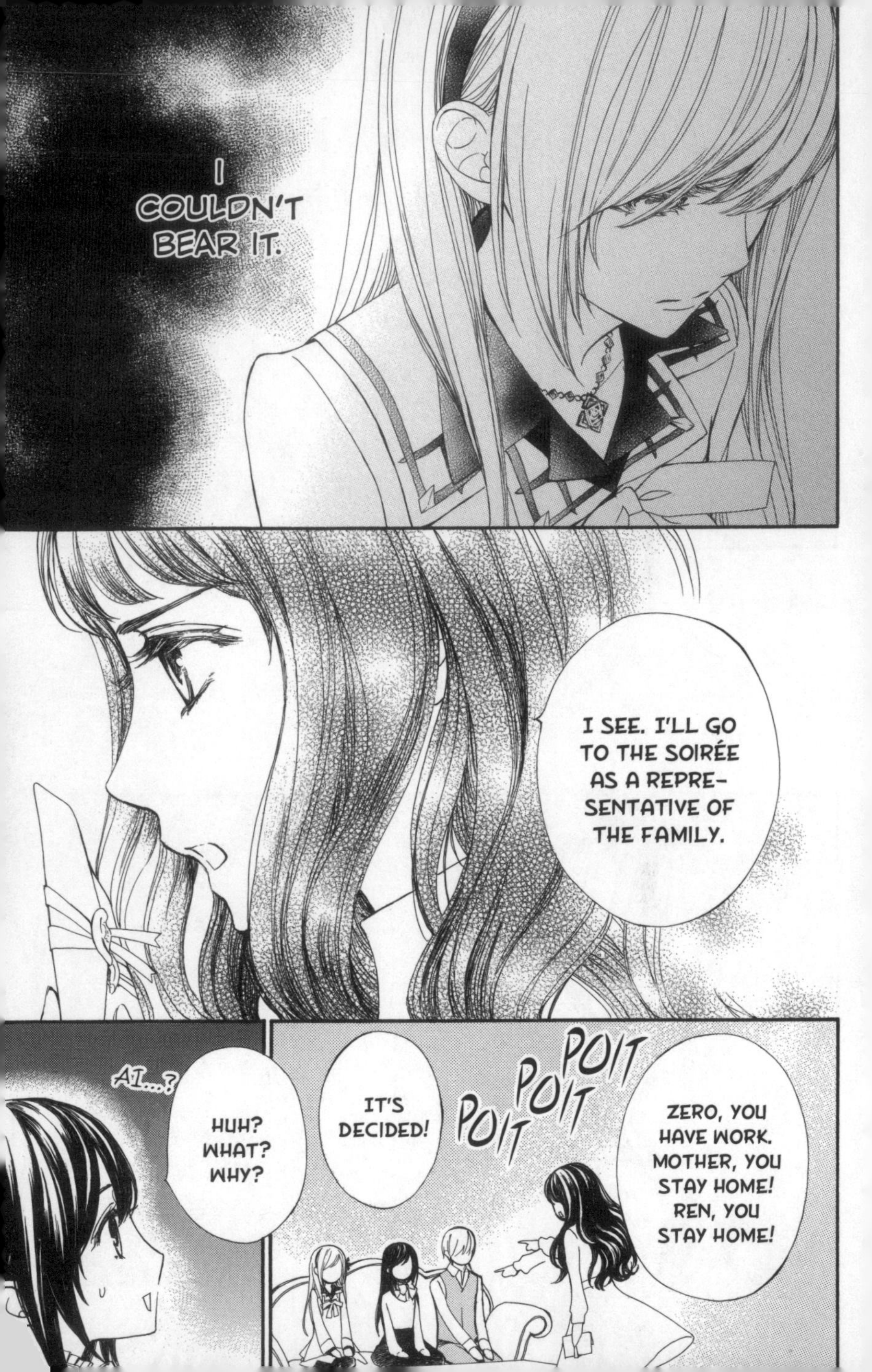
I COULDN'T BEAR IT.
I SEE. I'LL GO TO THE SOIRÉE AS A REPRE-SENTATIVE OF THE FAMILY.
POIT POIT POIT
ZERO, YOU HAVE WORK. MOTHER, YOU STAY HOME! REN, YOU STAY HOME!
IT'S DECIDED!
HUH? WHAT? WHY?
AI...?

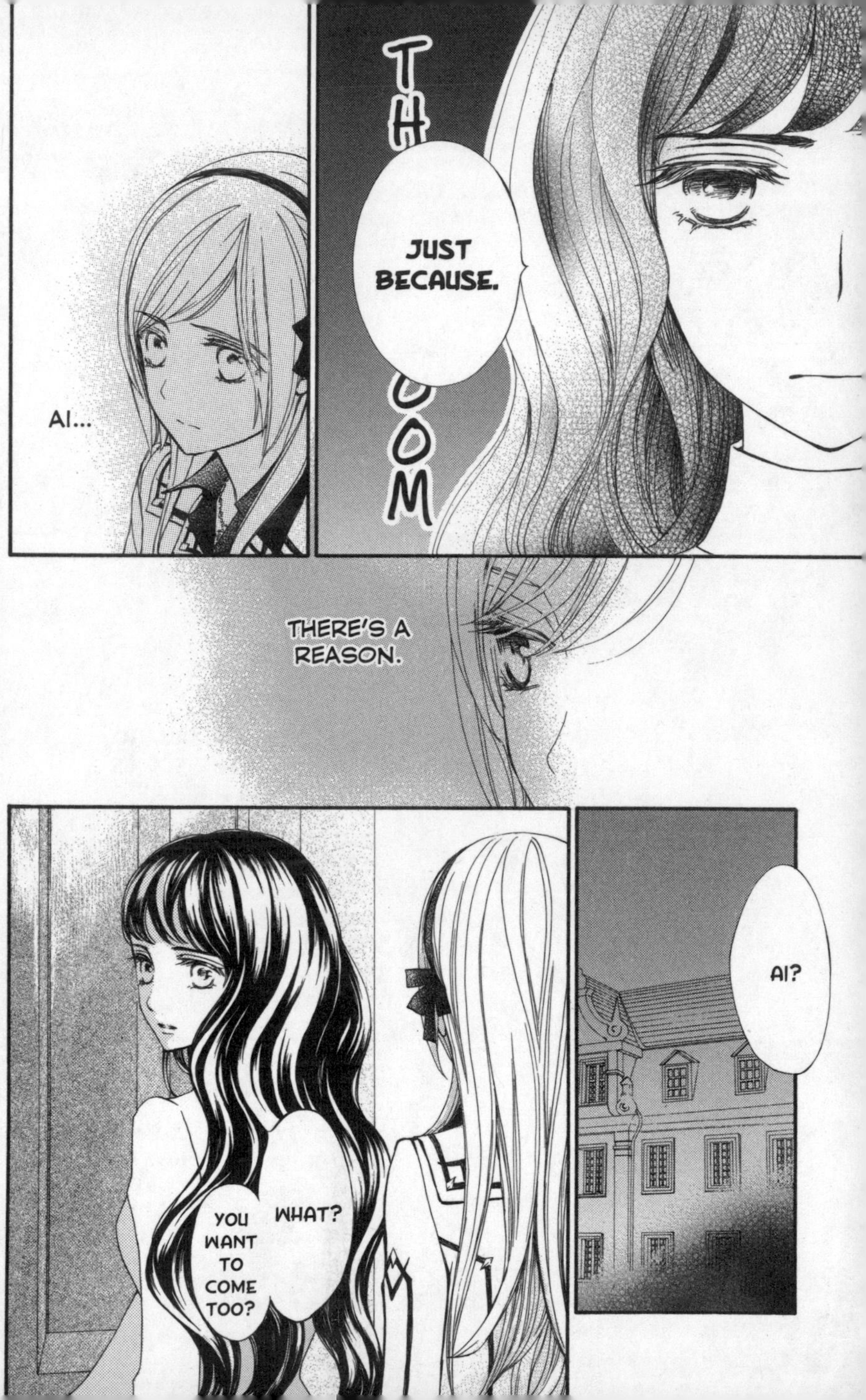
THOOM
JUST BECAUSE.
AI...
THERE'S A REASON.
AI?
WHAT?
YOU WANT TO COME TOO?

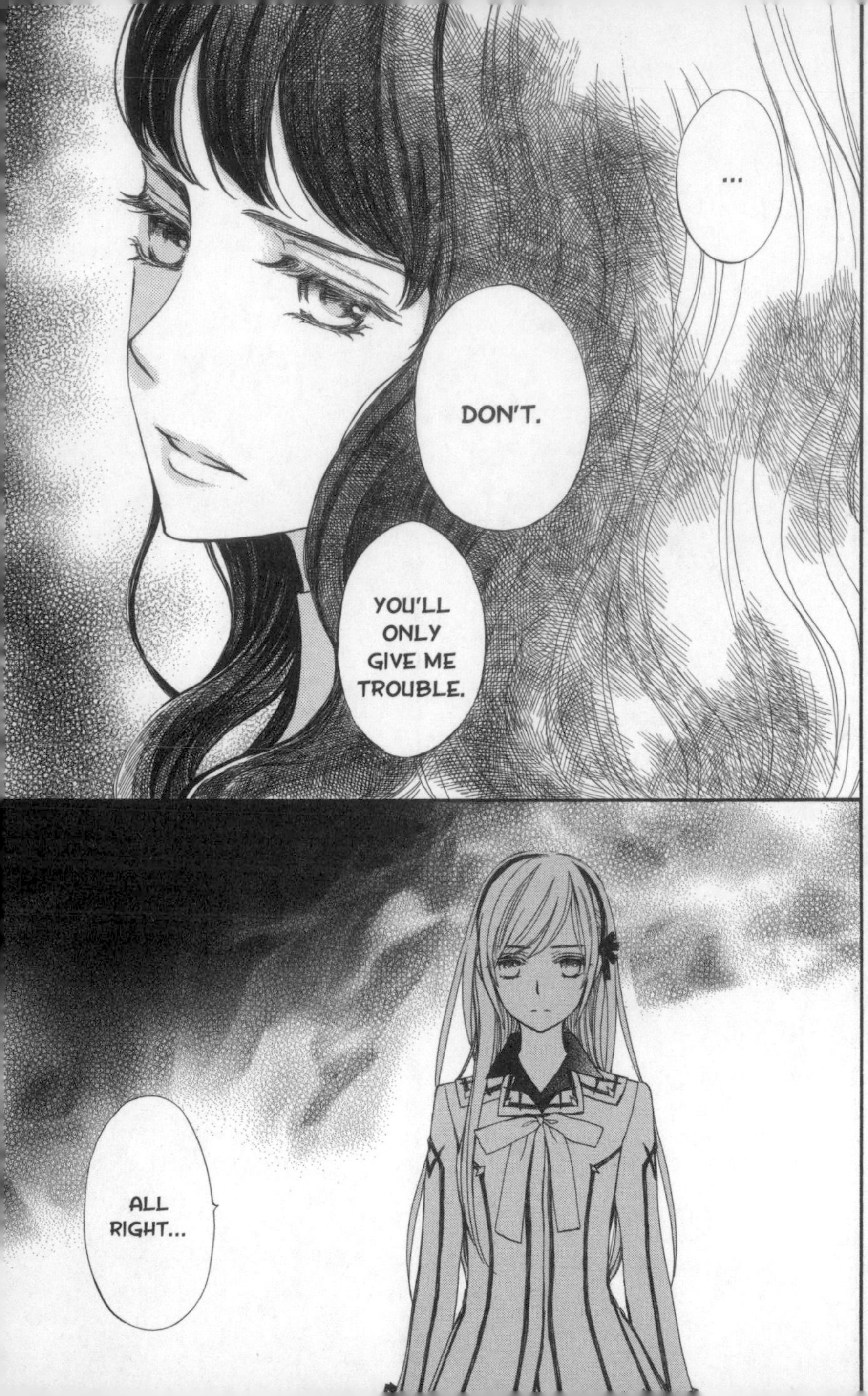
...
DON'T.
YOU'LL ONLY GIVE ME TROUBLE.
ALL RIGHT...

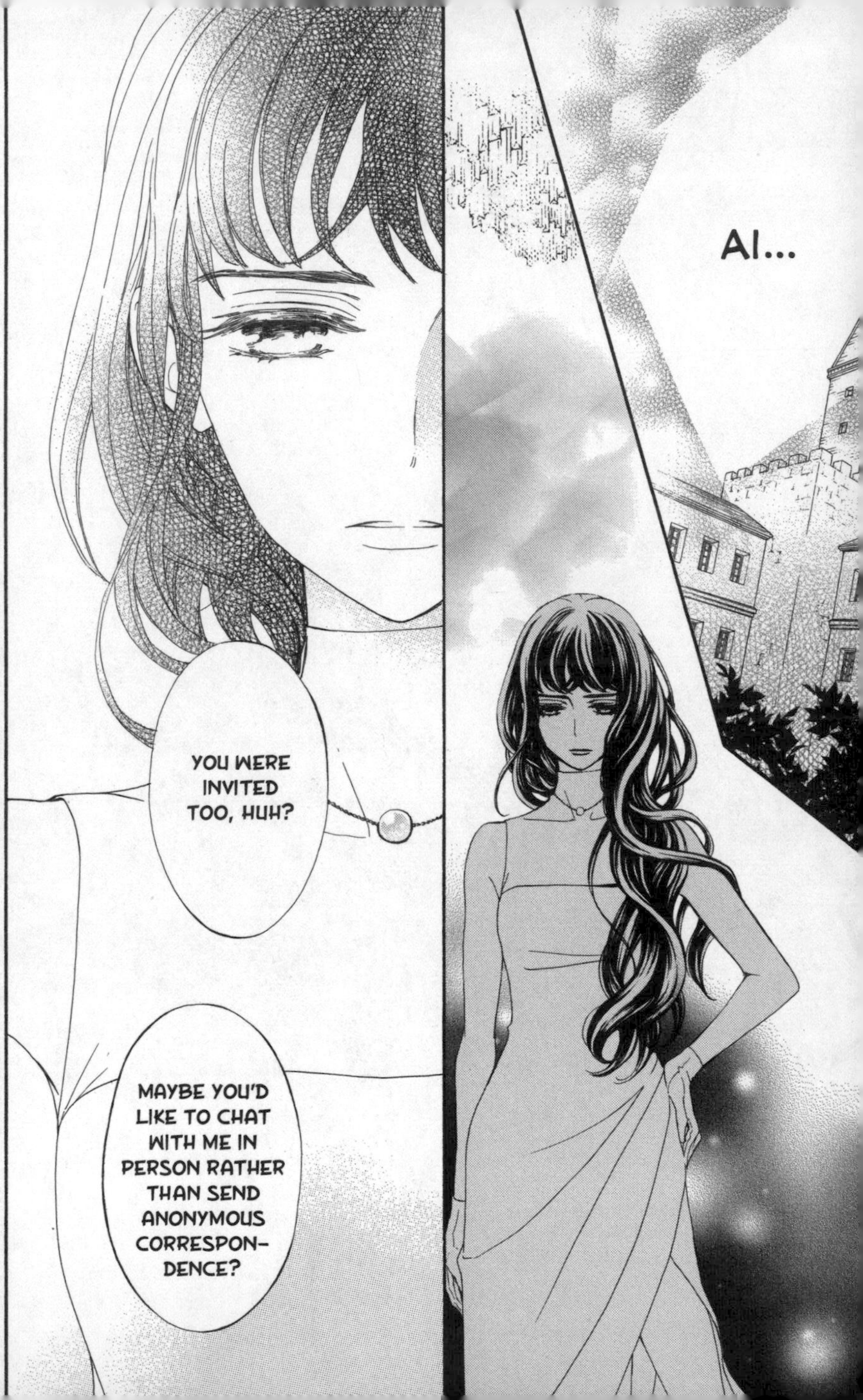
AI...
YOU WERE INVITED TOO, HUH?
MAYBE YOU'D LIKE TO CHAT WITH ME IN PERSON RATHER THAN SEND ANONYMOUS CORRESPON-DENCE?

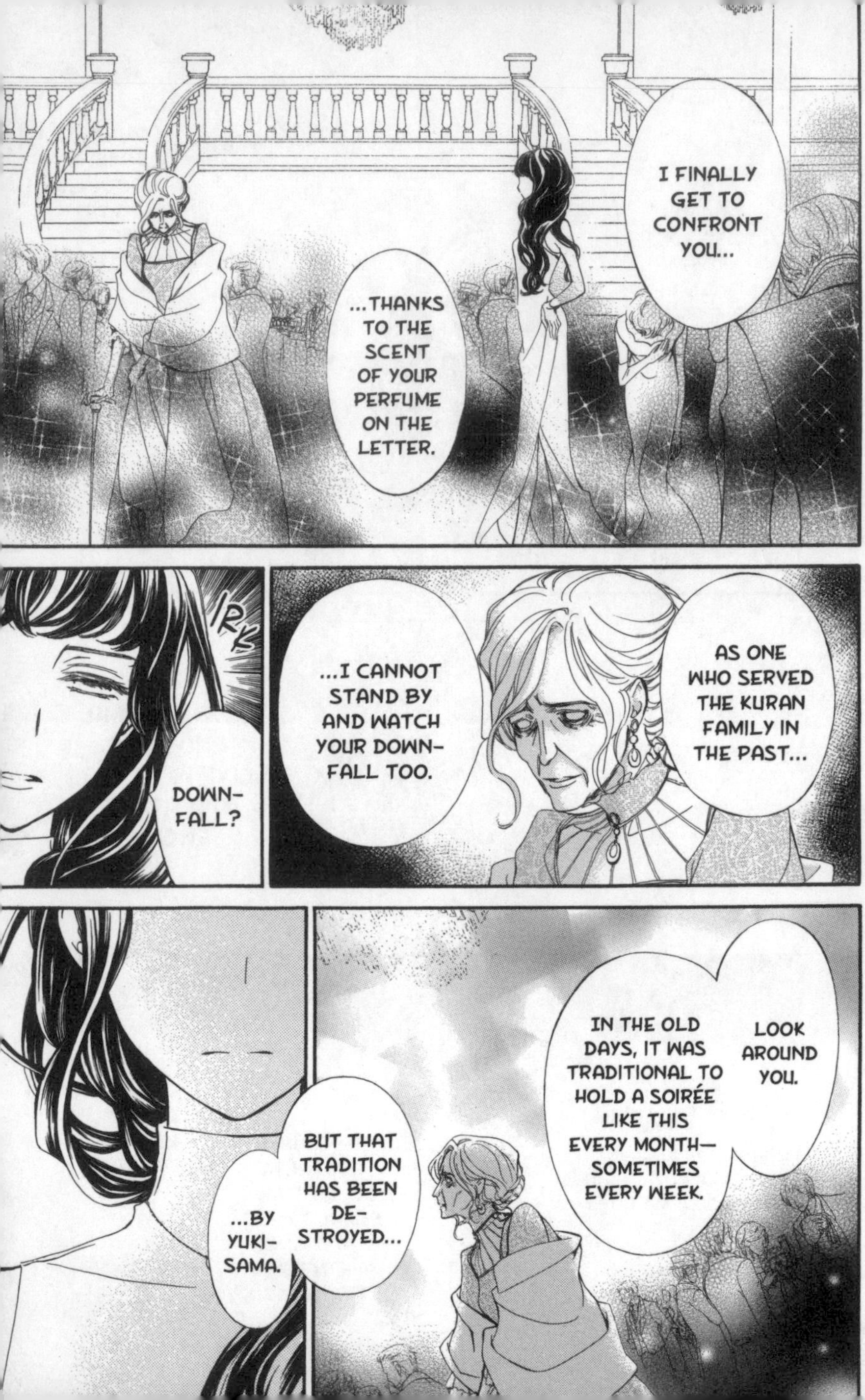
I FINALLY GET TO CONFRONT YOU...
...THANKS TO THE SCENT OF YOUR PERFUME ON THE LETTER.
AS ONE WHO SERVED THE KURAN FAMILY IN THE PAST...
...I CANNOT STAND BY AND WATCH YOUR DOWN-FALL TOO.
IRK
DOWN-FALL?
LOOK AROUND YOU.
IN THE OLD DAYS, IT WAS TRADITIONAL TO HOLD A SOIRÉE LIKE THIS EVERY MONTH—SOMETIMES EVERY WEEK.
BUT THAT TRADITION HAS BEEN DE-STROYED...
...BY YUKI-SAMA.

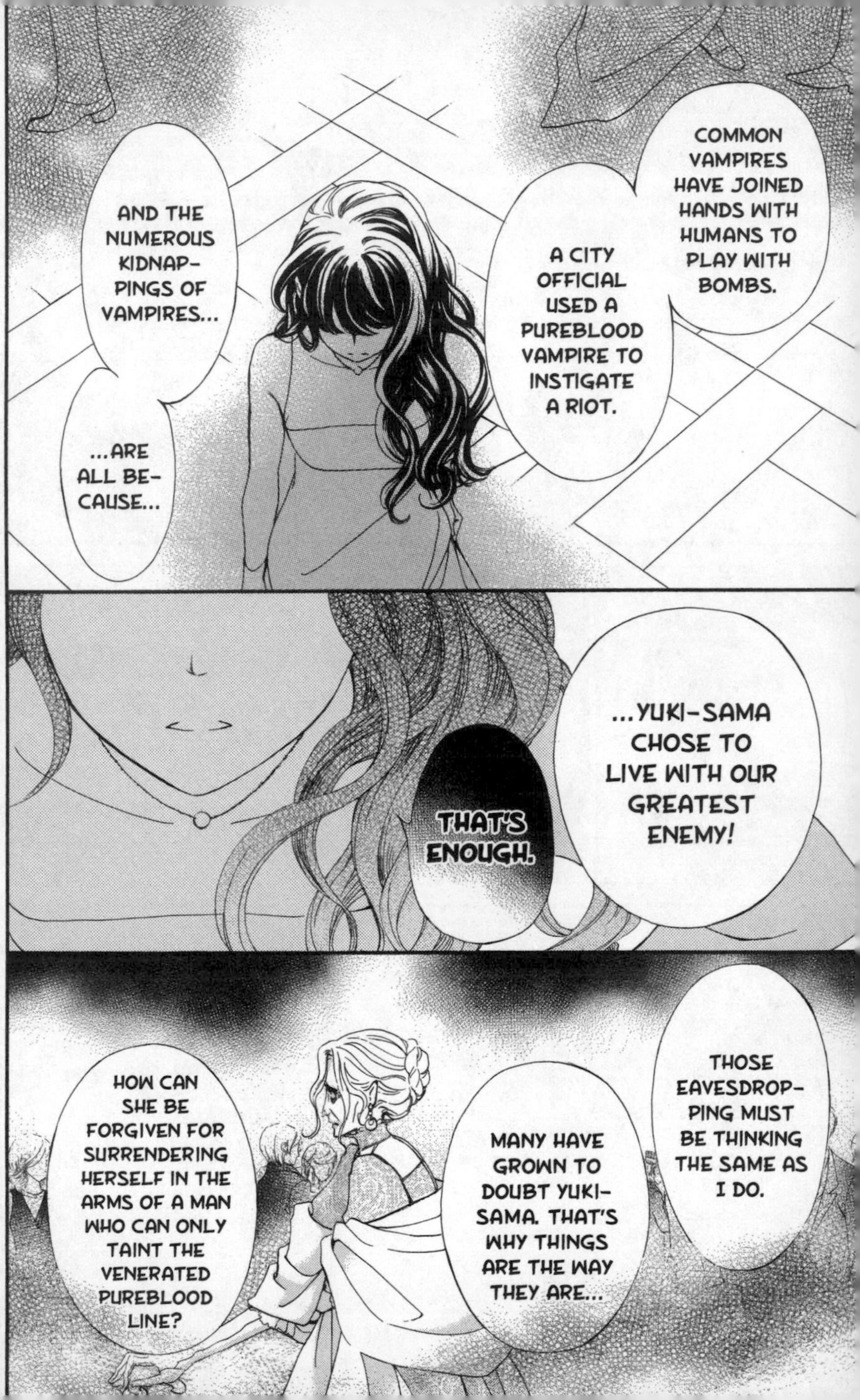
COMMON VAMPIRES HAVE JOINED HANDS WITH HUMANS TO PLAY WITH BOMBS.
A CITY OFFICIAL USED A PUREBLOOD VAMPIRE TO INSTIGATE A RIOT.
AND THE NUMEROUS KIDNAPPINGS OF VAMPIRES...
...ARE ALL BECAUSE...
...YUKI-SAMA CHOSE TO LIVE WITH OUR GREATEST ENEMY!
THAT'S ENOUGH.
THOSE EAVESDROPPING MUST BE THINKING THE SAME AS I DO.
MANY HAVE GROWN TO DOUBT YUKI-SAMA. THAT'S WHY THINGS ARE THE WAY THEY ARE...
HOW CAN SHE BE FORGIVEN FOR SURRENDERING HERSELF IN THE ARMS OF A MAN WHO CAN ONLY TAINT THE VENERATED PUREBLOOD LINE?

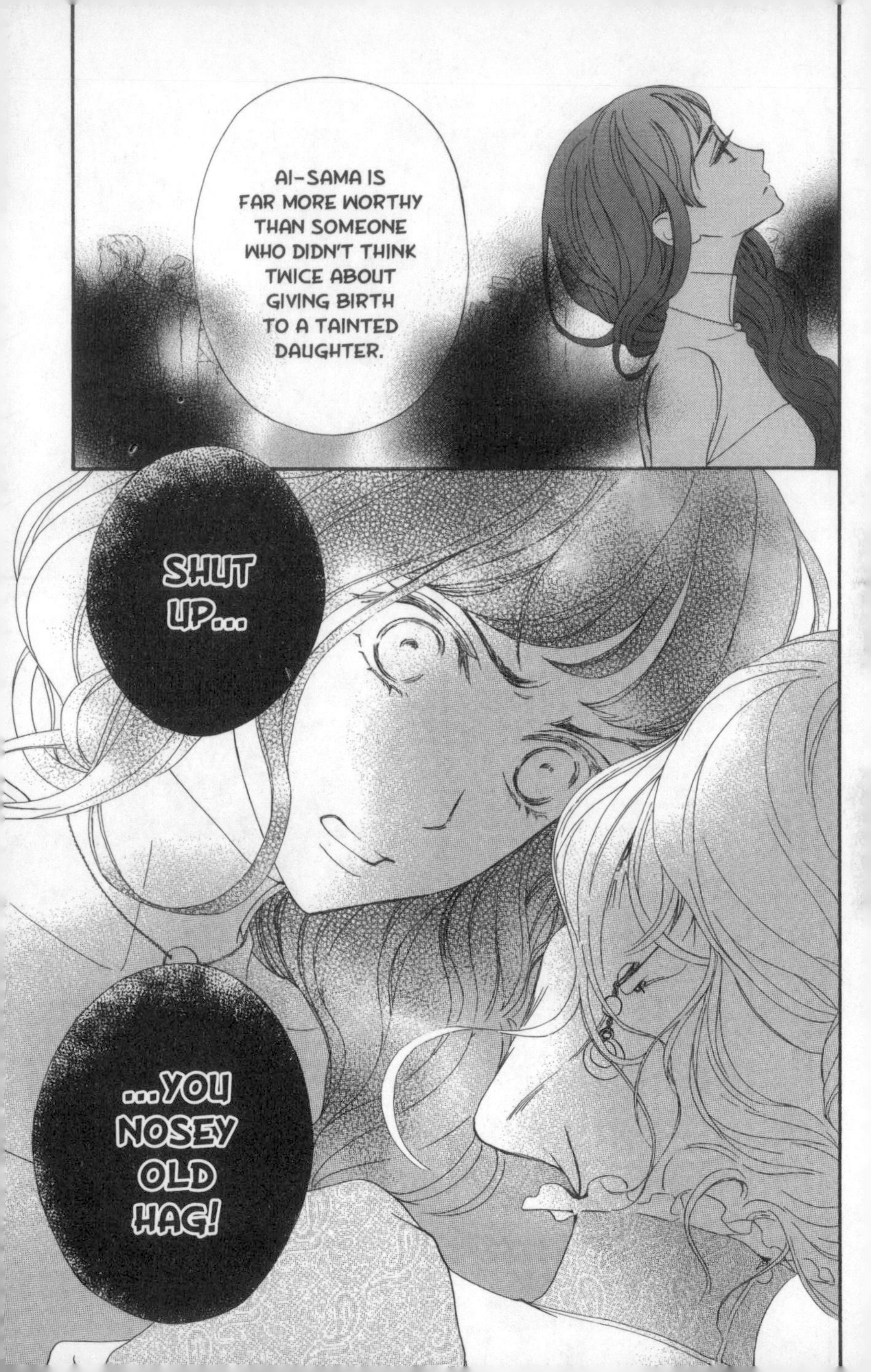
AI-SAMA IS FAR MORE WORTHY THAN SOMEONE WHO DIDN'T THINK TWICE ABOUT GIVING BIRTH TO A TAINTED DAUGHTER.
SHUT UP...
...YOU NOSEY OLD HAG!

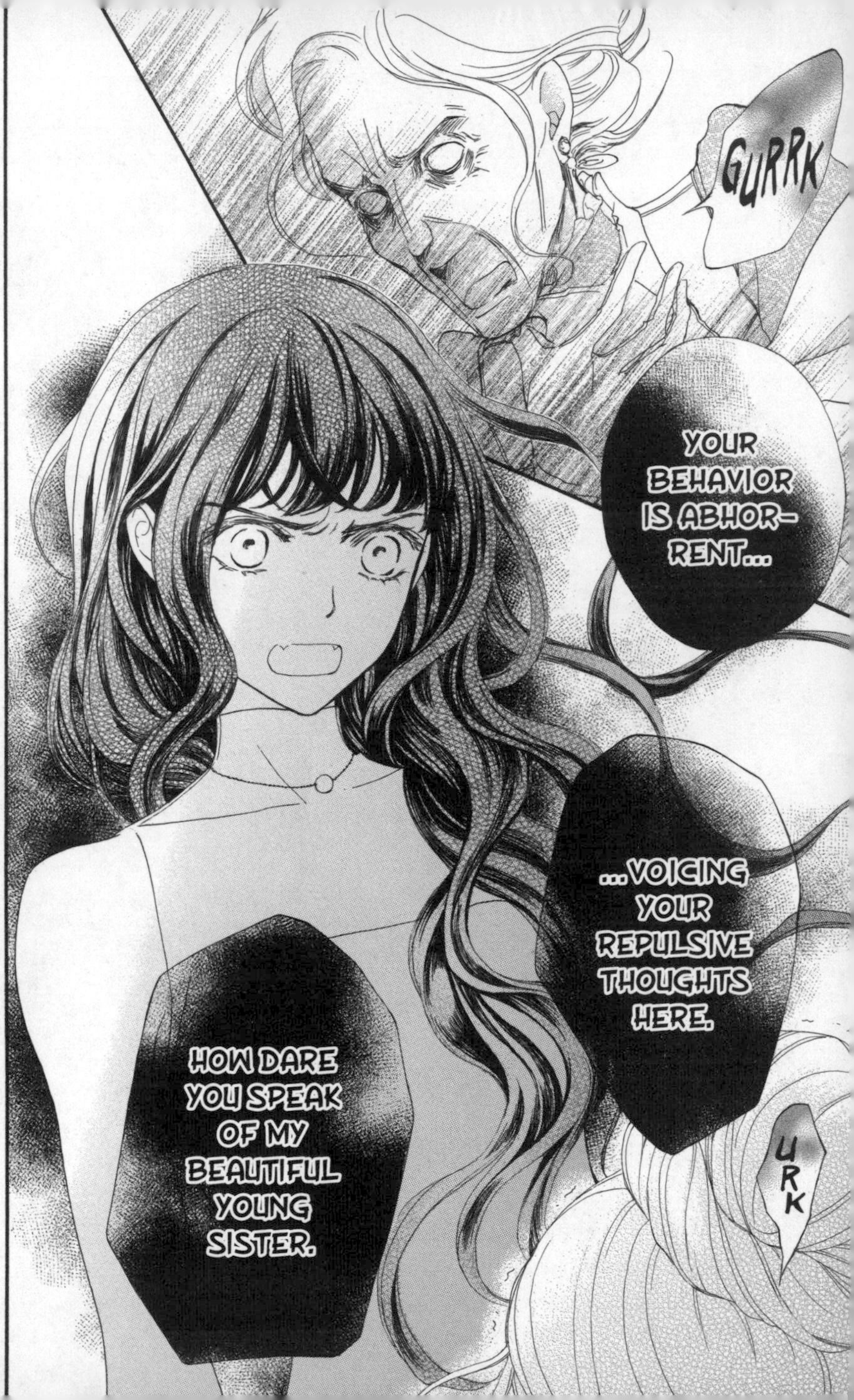
GURRK
YOUR BEHAVIOR IS ABHOR-RENT...
...VOICING YOUR REPULSIVE THOUGHTS HERE.
URK
HOW DARE YOU SPEAK OF MY BEAUTIFUL YOUNG SISTER.

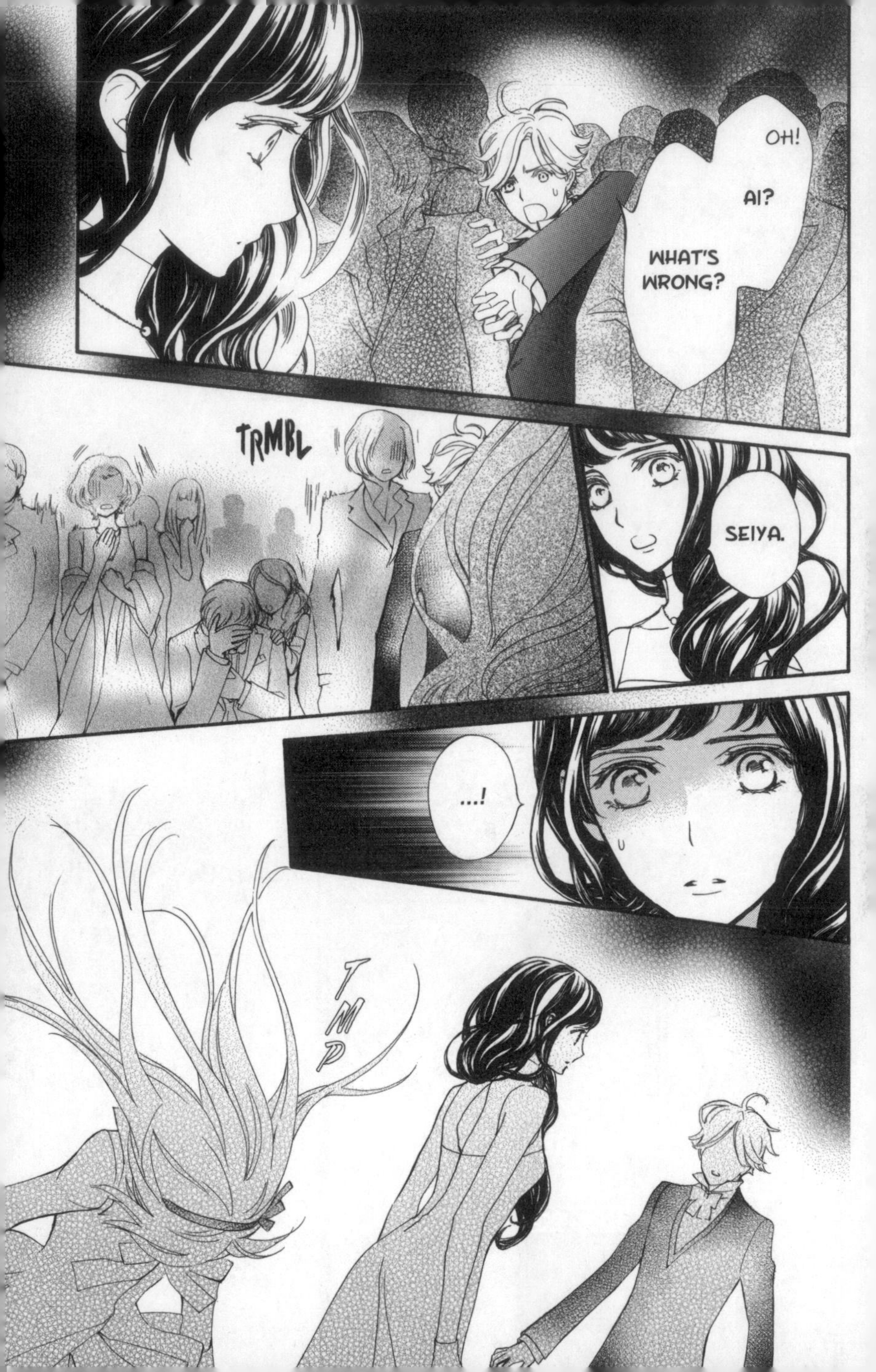
OH!
AI?
WHAT'S WRONG?
SEIYA.
TRMBL
...!
TMP

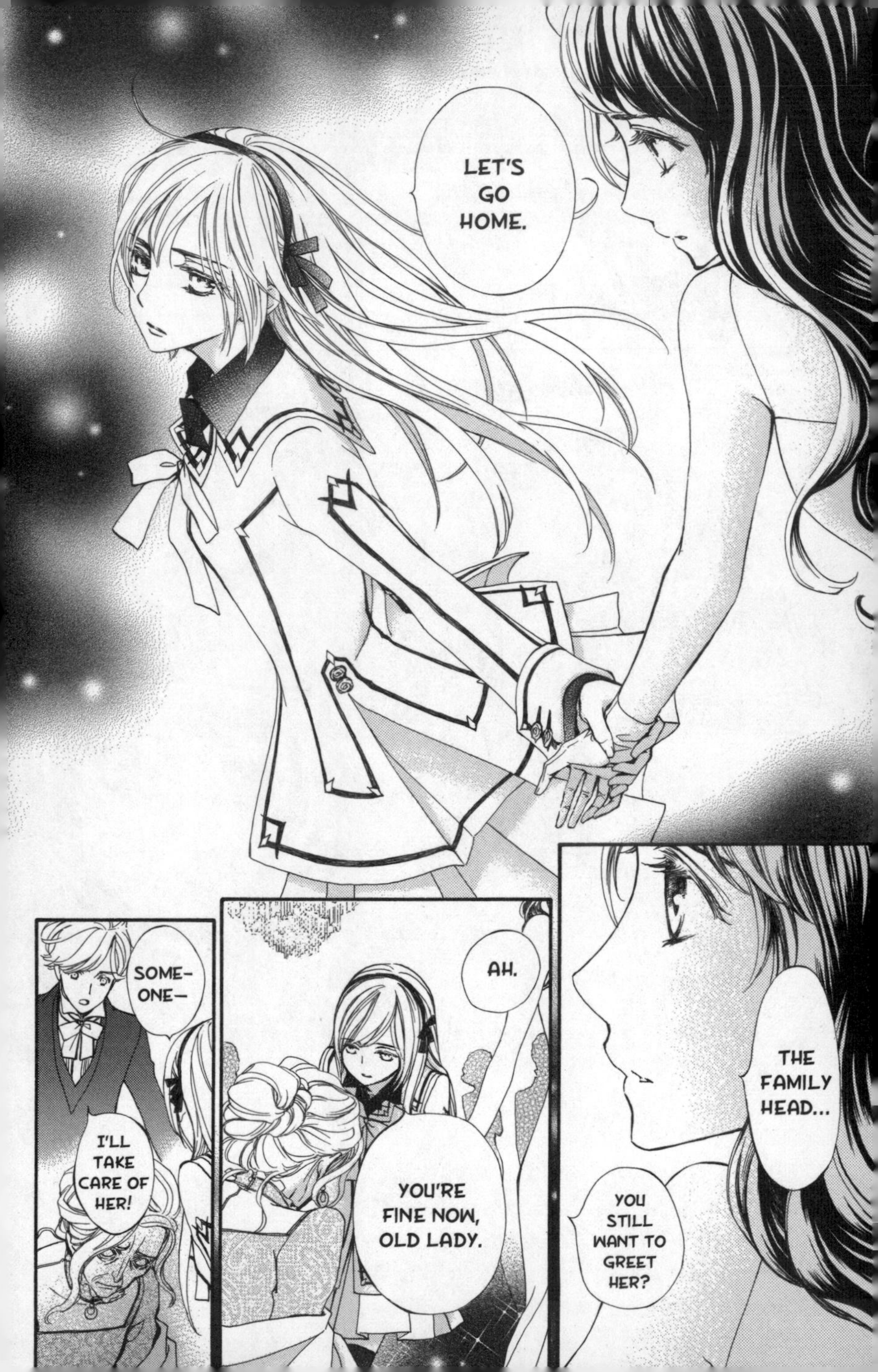
LET'S GO HOME.
THE FAMILY HEAD...
YOU STILL WANT TO GREET HER?
AH.
YOU'RE FINE NOW, OLD LADY.
SOME-ONE—
I'LL TAKE CARE OF HER!

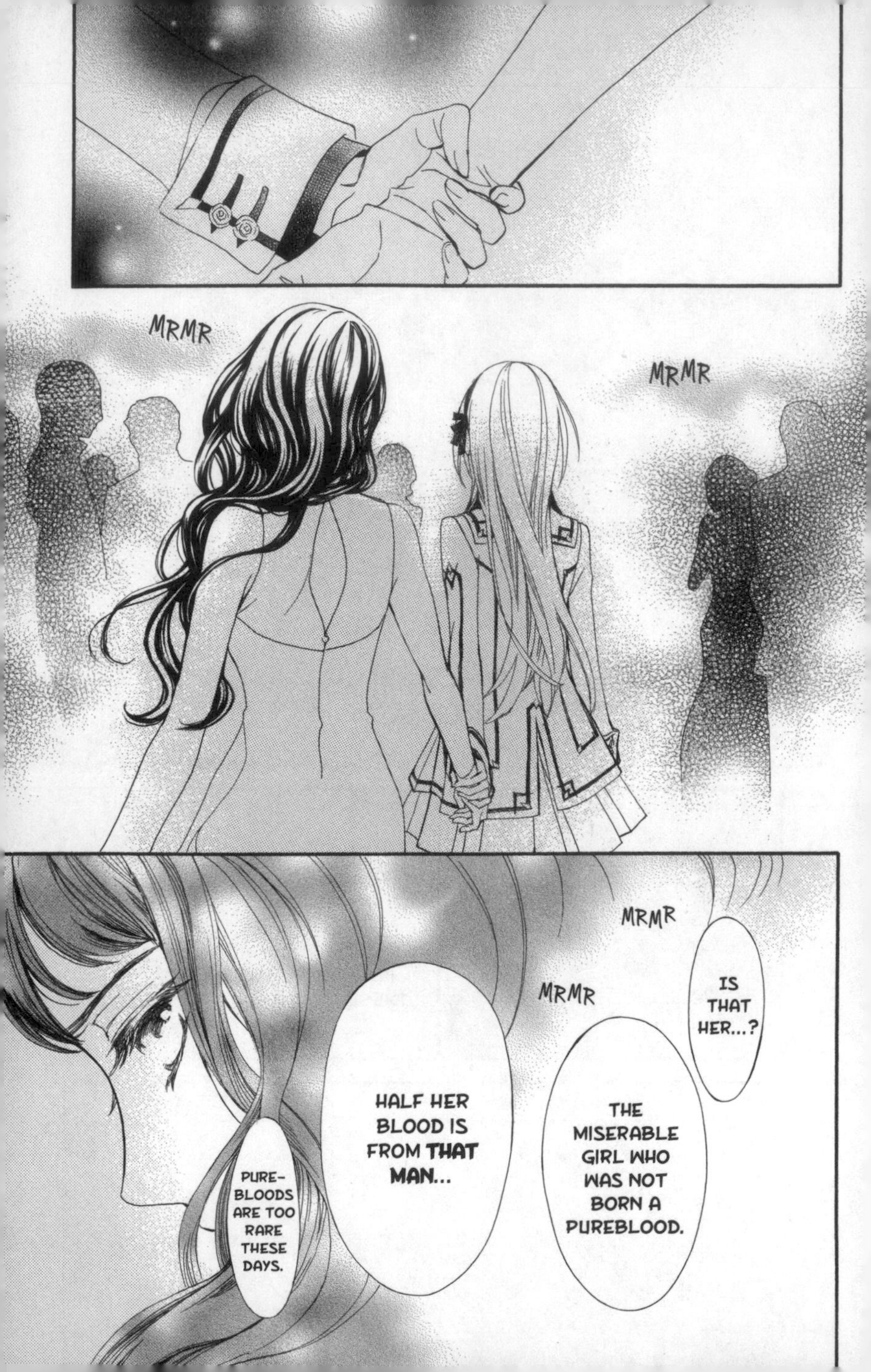
MRMR
MRMR
MRMR
IS THAT HER...?
MRMR
THE MISERABLE GIRL WHO WAS NOT BORN A PUREBLOOD.
HALF HER BLOOD IS FROM **THAT MAN**...
PURE-BLOODS ARE TOO RARE THESE DAYS.

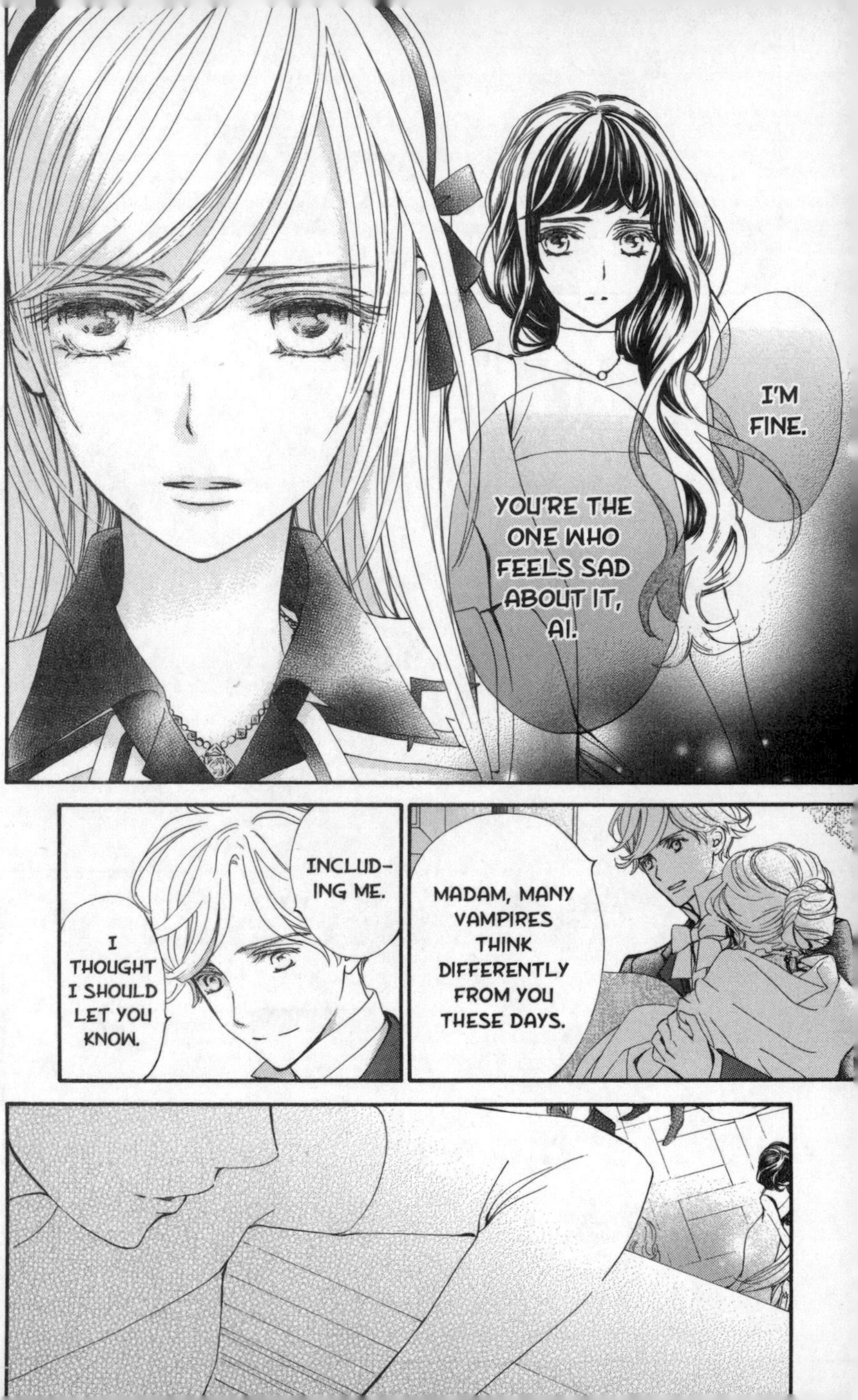
I'M FINE.
YOU'RE THE ONE WHO FEELS SAD ABOUT IT, AI.
MADAM, MANY VAMPIRES THINK DIFFERENTLY FROM YOU THESE DAYS.
INCLUD-ING ME.
I THOUGHT I SHOULD LET YOU KNOW.

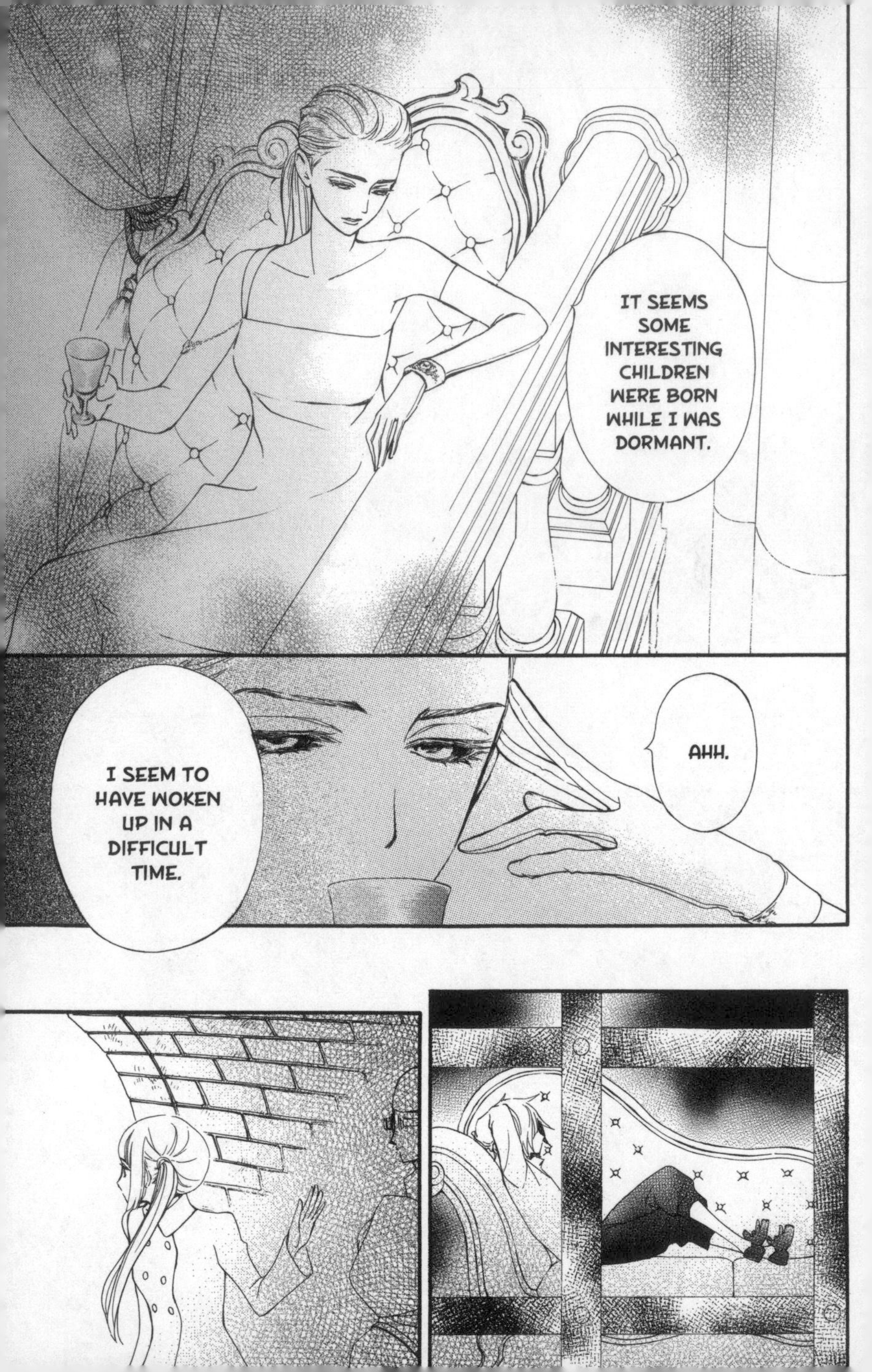
IT SEEMS SOME INTERESTING CHILDREN WERE BORN WHILE I WAS DORMANT.
AHH.
I SEEM TO HAVE WOKEN UP IN A DIFFICULT TIME.

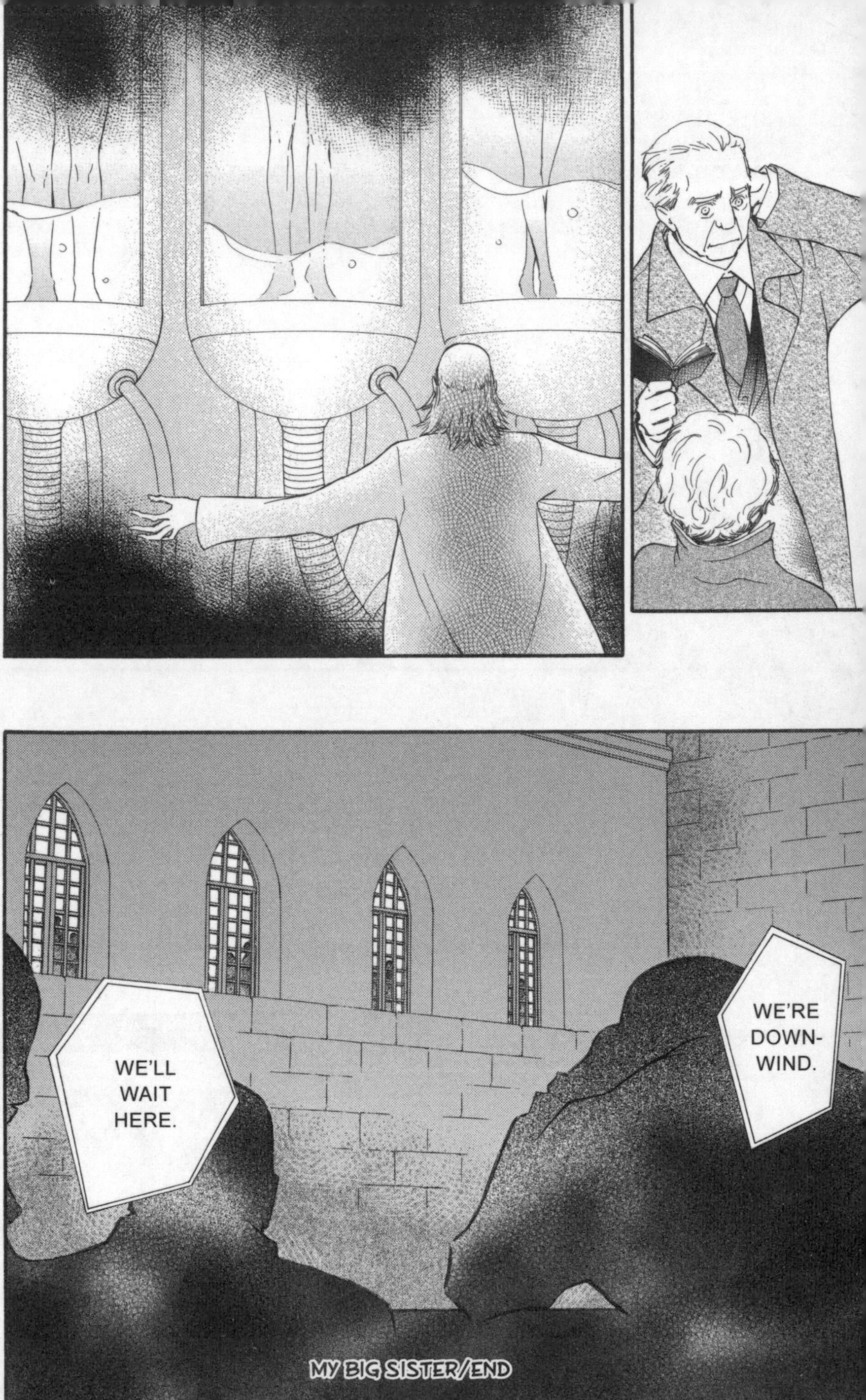
WE'RE DOWN-WIND.
WE'LL WAIT HERE.
MY BIG SISTER/END

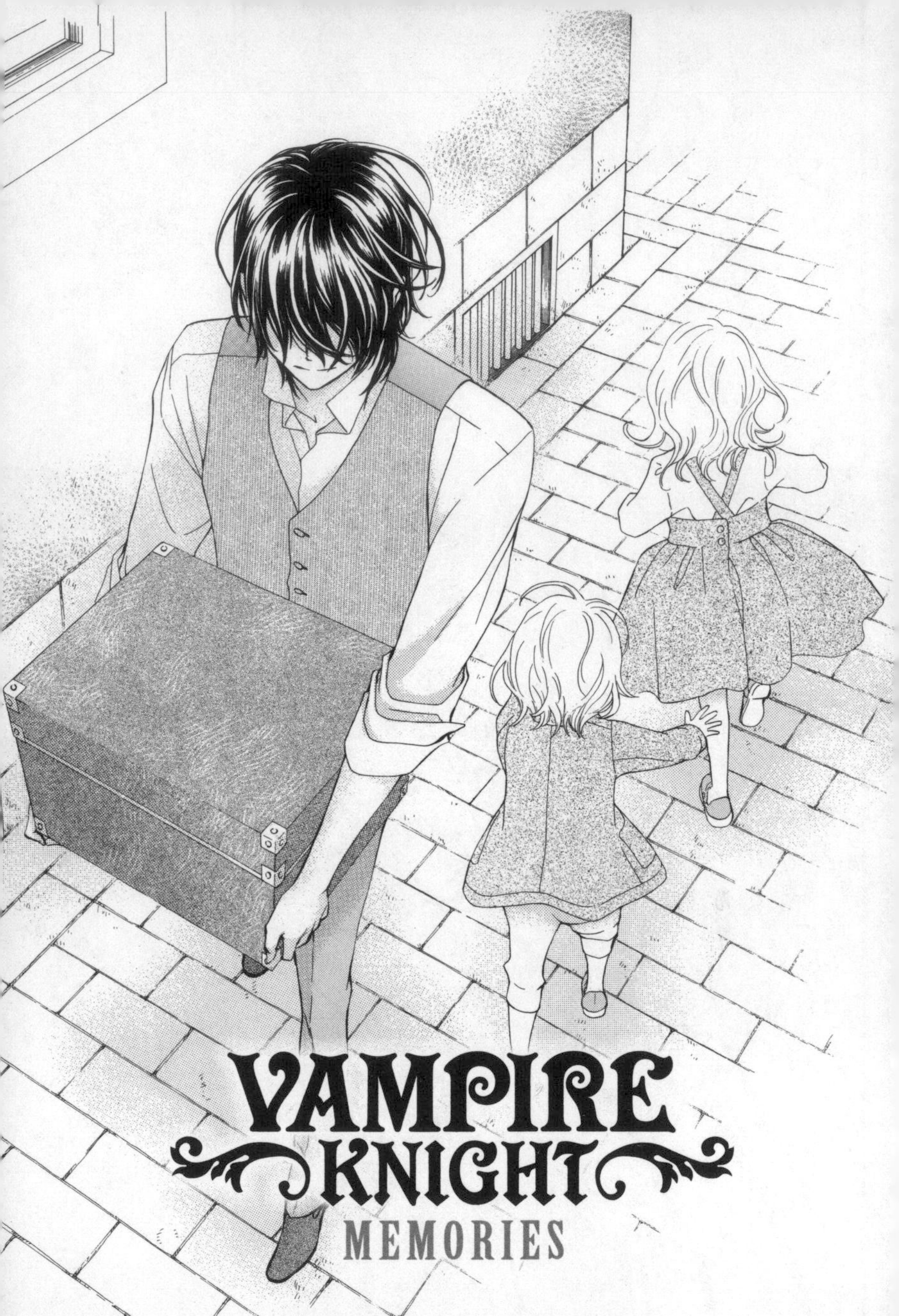
VAMPIRE KNIGHT
MEMORIES

BEING LOVED IS NOT ENOUGH

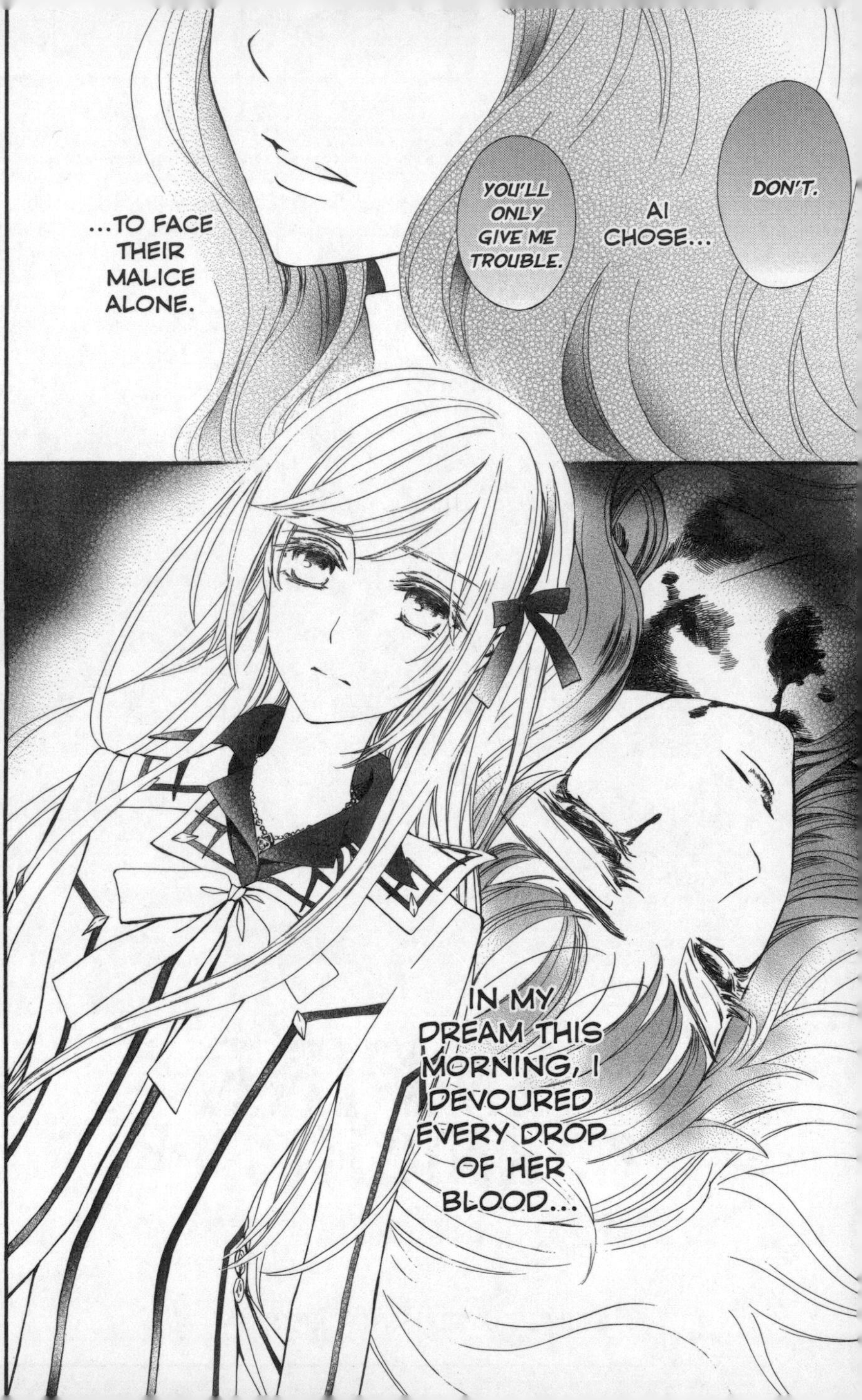
DON'T.
AI CHOSE...
YOU'LL ONLY GIVE ME TROUBLE.
...TO FACE THEIR MALICE ALONE.
IN MY DREAM THIS MORNING, I DEVOURED EVERY DROP OF HER BLOOD...

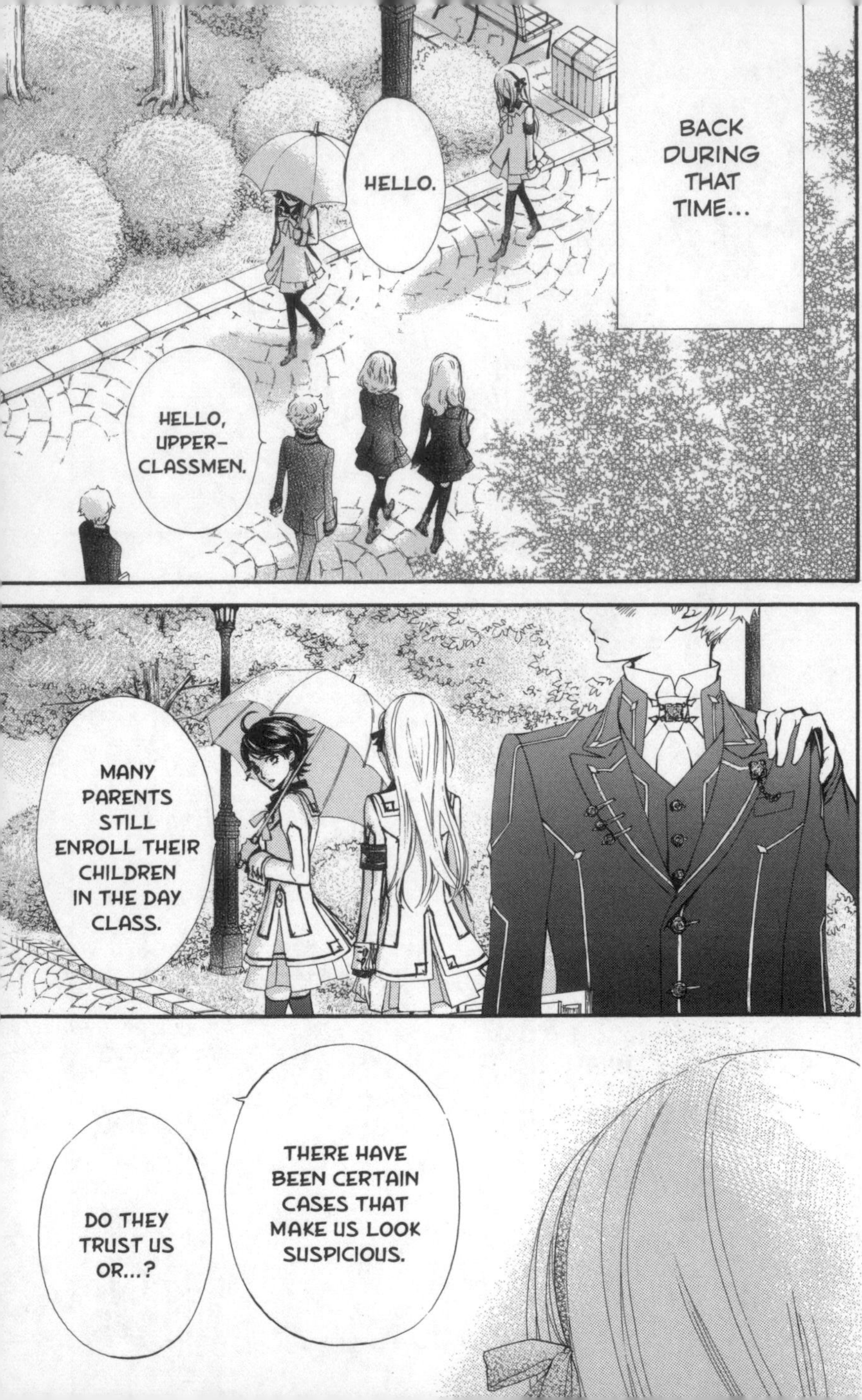
BACK DURING THAT TIME...
HELLO.
HELLO, UPPER-CLASSMEN.
MANY PARENTS STILL ENROLL THEIR CHILDREN IN THE DAY CLASS.
THERE HAVE BEEN CERTAIN CASES THAT MAKE US LOOK SUSPICIOUS.
DO THEY TRUST US OR...?

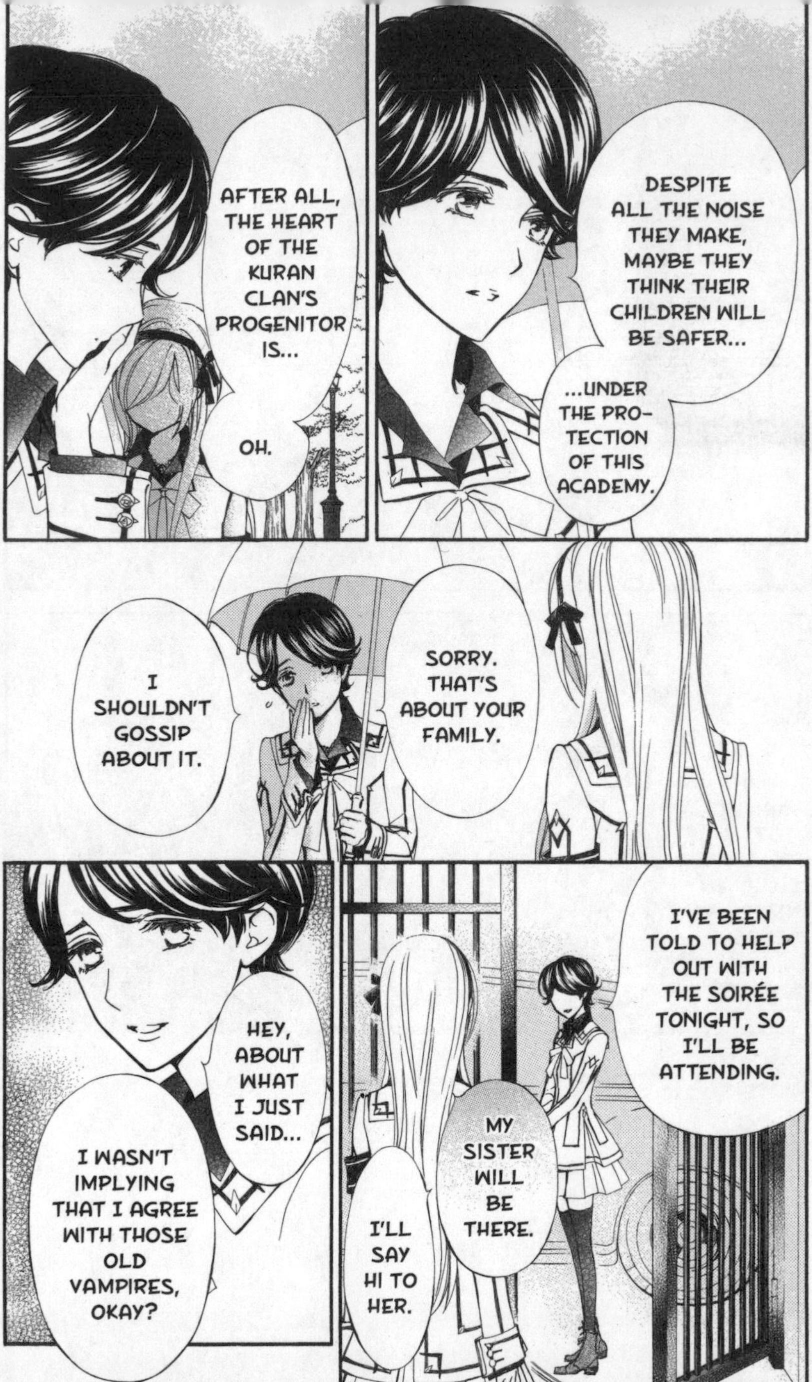
DESPITE ALL THE NOISE THEY MAKE, MAYBE THEY THINK THEIR CHILDREN WILL BE SAFER...
...UNDER THE PROTECTION OF THIS ACADEMY.
AFTER ALL, THE HEART OF THE KURAN CLAN'S PROGENITOR IS...
OH.
SORRY. THAT'S ABOUT YOUR FAMILY.
I SHOULDN'T GOSSIP ABOUT IT.
I'VE BEEN TOLD TO HELP OUT WITH THE SOIRÉE TONIGHT, SO I'LL BE ATTENDING.
MY SISTER WILL BE THERE.
I'LL SAY HI TO HER.
HEY, ABOUT WHAT I JUST SAID...
I WASN'T IMPLYING THAT I AGREE WITH THOSE OLD VAMPIRES, OKAY?

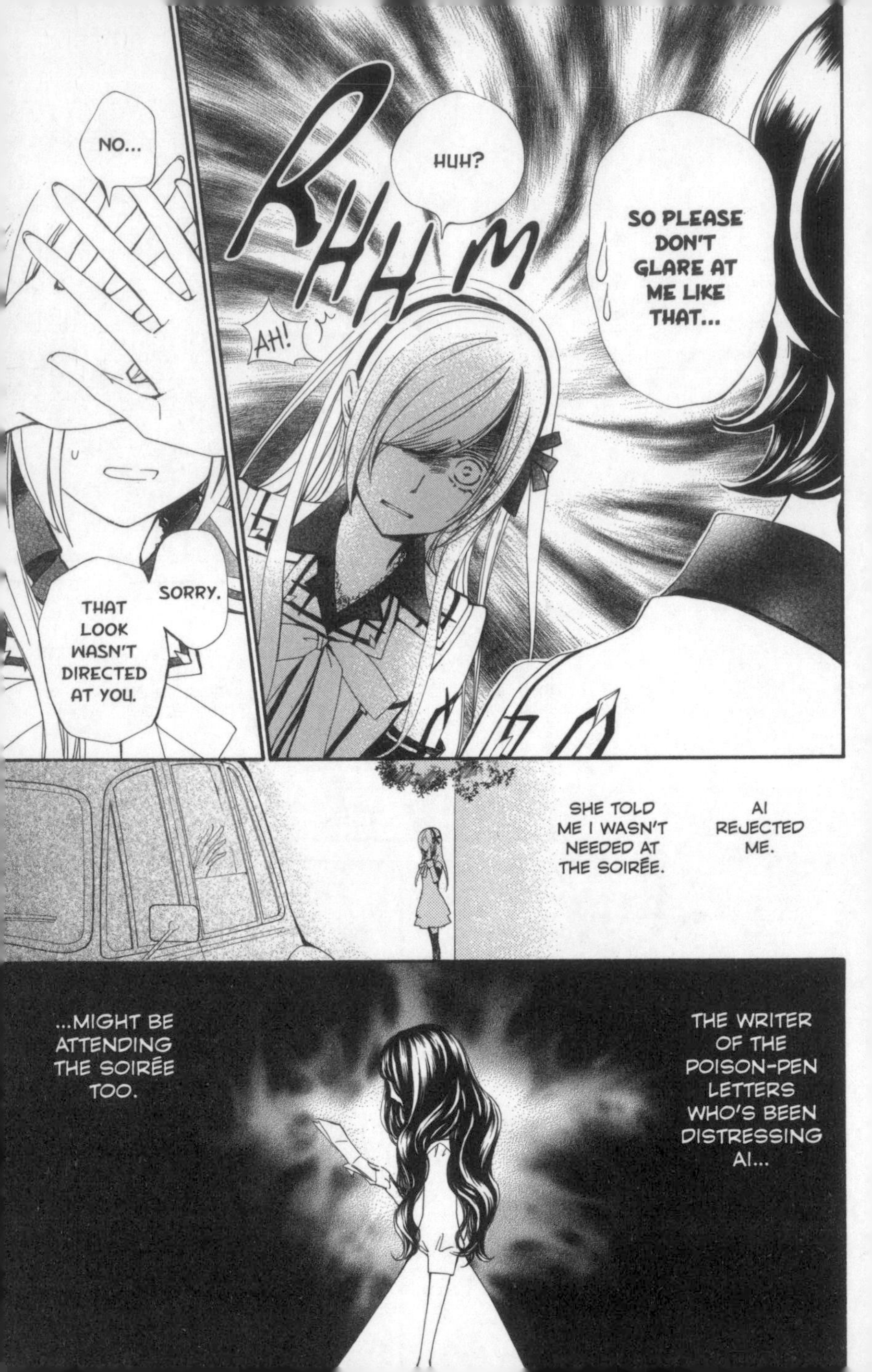
SO PLEASE DON'T GLARE AT ME LIKE THAT...
HUH?
RHHM
AH!
NO...
SORRY.
THAT LOOK WASN'T DIRECTED AT YOU.
AI REJECTED ME.
SHE TOLD ME I WASN'T NEEDED AT THE SOIRÉE.
THE WRITER OF THE POISON-PEN LETTERS WHO'S BEEN DISTRESSING AI...
...MIGHT BE ATTENDING THE SOIRÉE TOO.

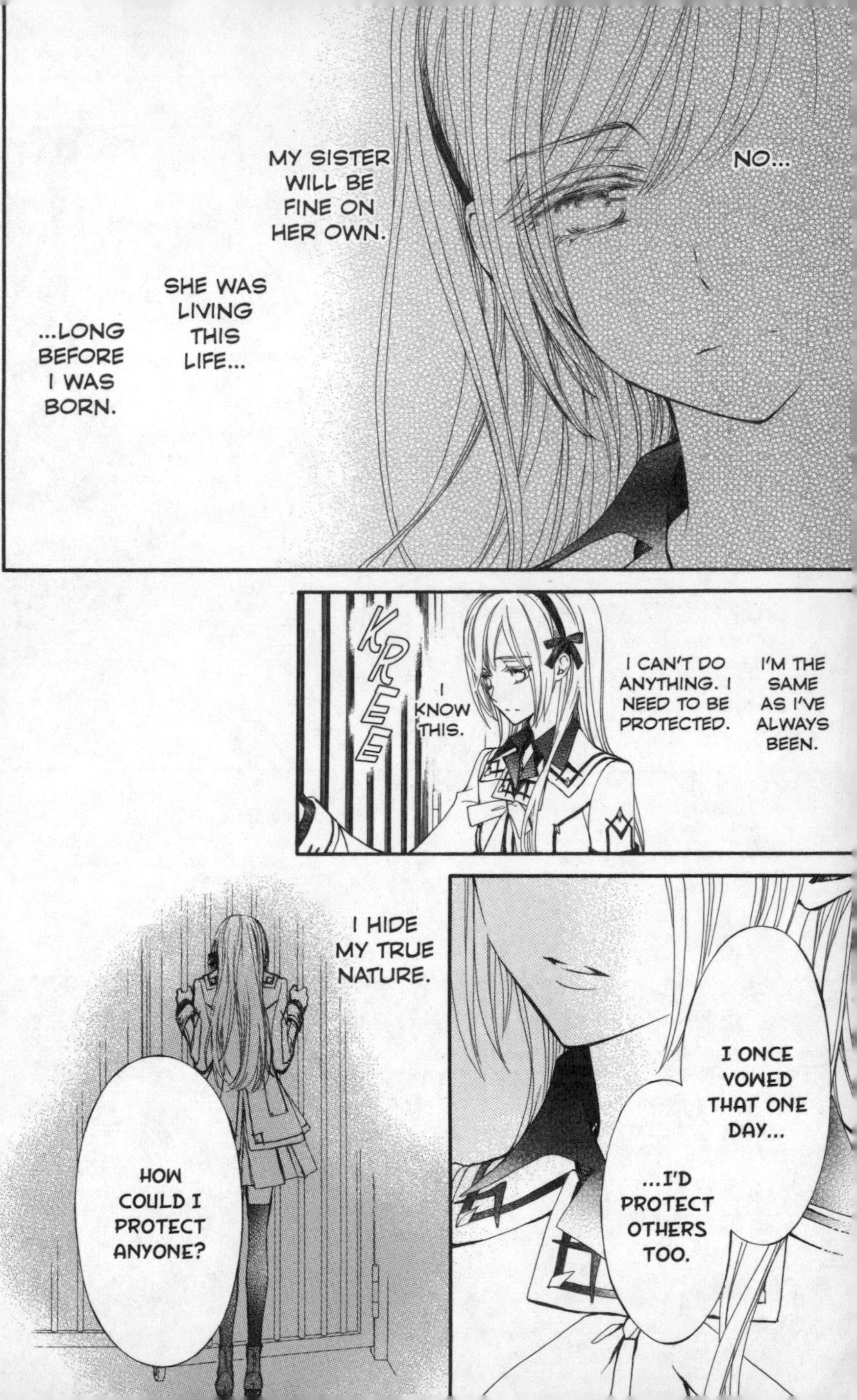
NO...
MY SISTER WILL BE FINE ON HER OWN.
SHE WAS LIVING THIS LIFE...
...LONG BEFORE I WAS BORN.
I'M THE SAME AS I'VE ALWAYS BEEN.
I CAN'T DO ANYTHING. I NEED TO BE PROTECTED.
I KNOW THIS.
KREE
I ONCE VOWED THAT ONE DAY...
...I'D PROTECT OTHERS TOO.
I HIDE MY TRUE NATURE.
HOW COULD I PROTECT ANYONE?

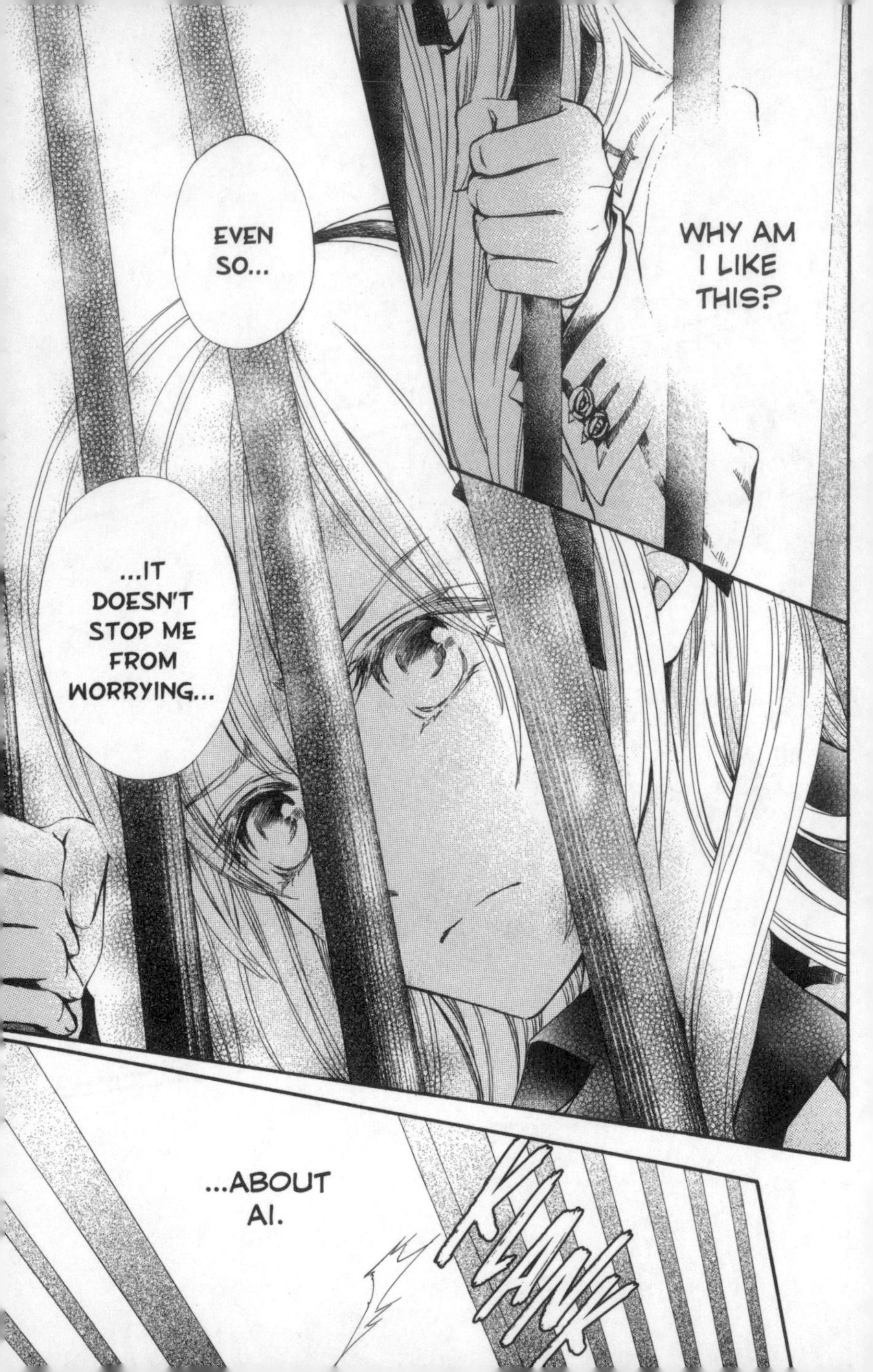
WHY AM I LIKE THIS?
EVEN SO...
...IT DOESN'T STOP ME FROM WORRYING...
...ABOUT AI.
KLANK

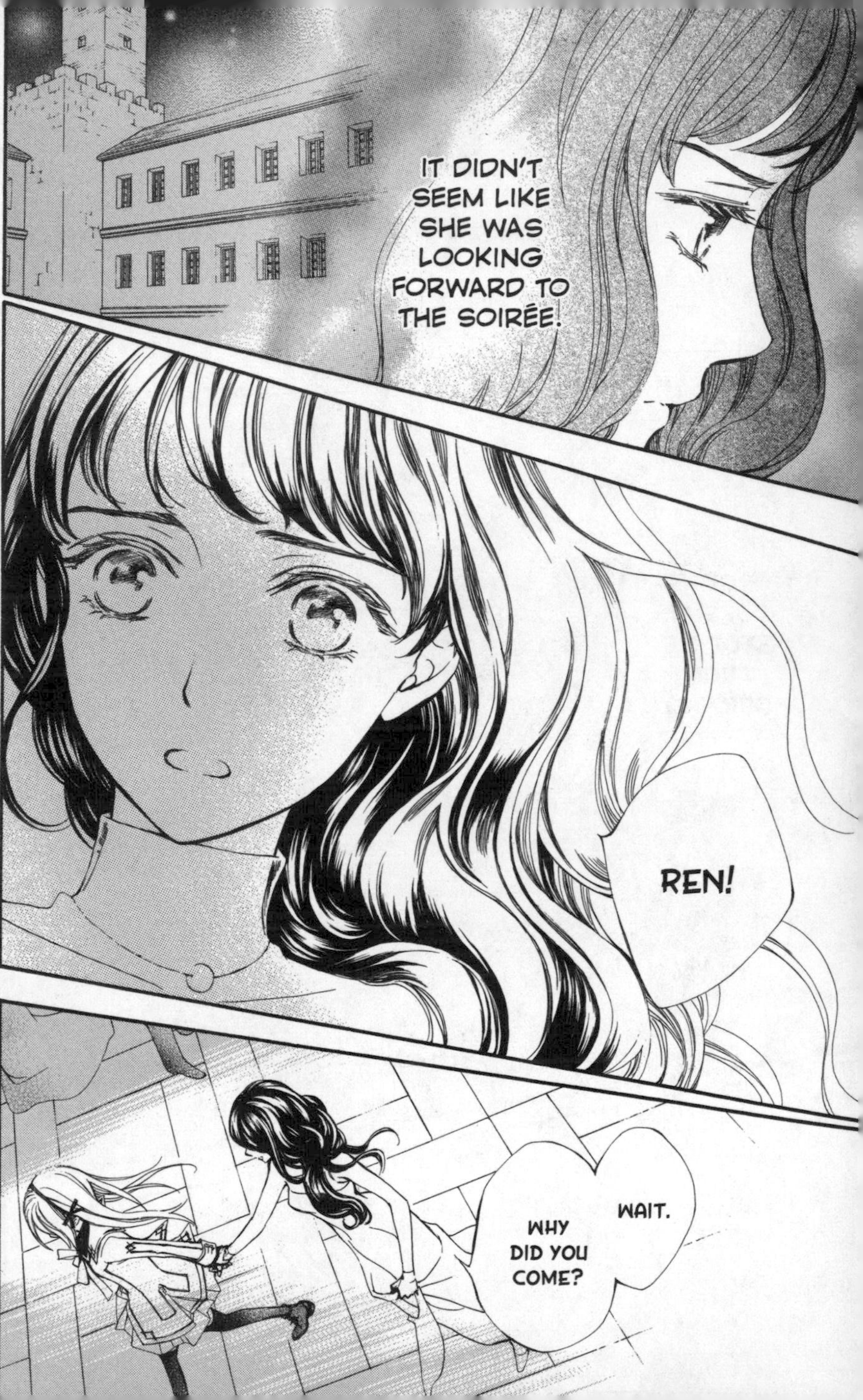
IT DIDN'T SEEM LIKE SHE WAS LOOKING FORWARD TO THE SOIRÉE.
REN!
WAIT.
WHY DID YOU COME?

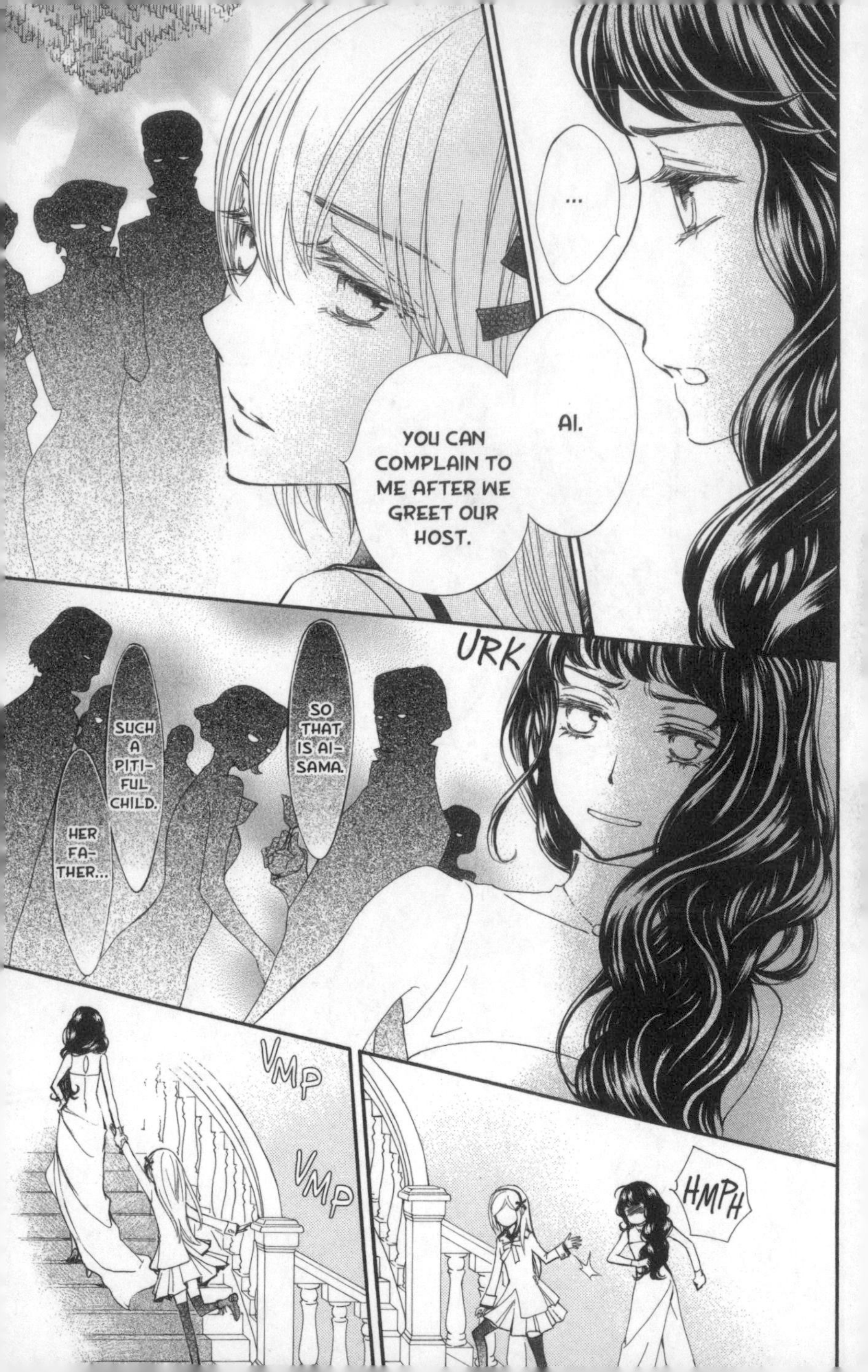
...
AI.
YOU CAN COMPLAIN TO ME AFTER WE GREET OUR HOST.
URK
SO THAT IS AI-SAMA.
SUCH A PITIFUL CHILD.
HER FATHER...
HMPH
VMP
VMP

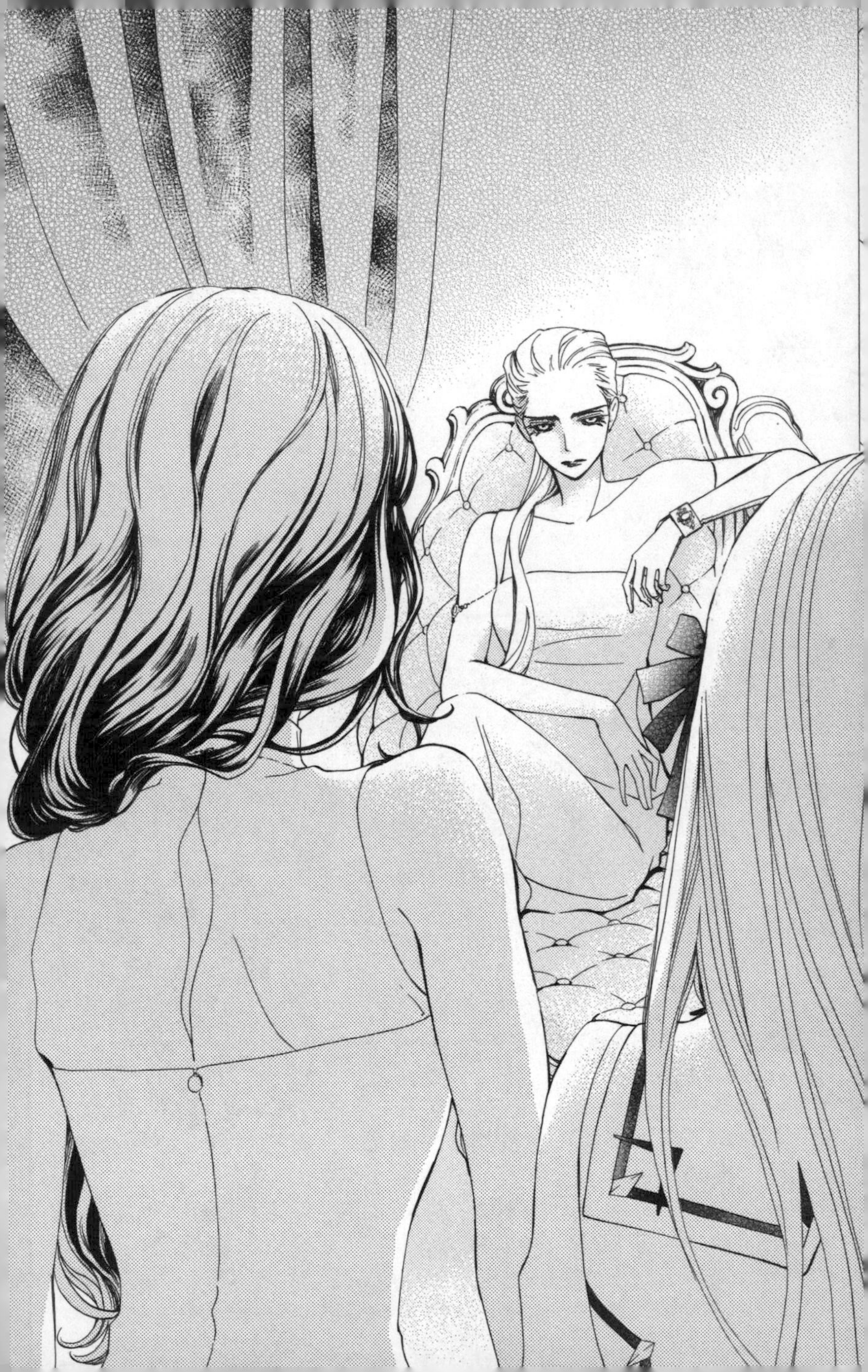

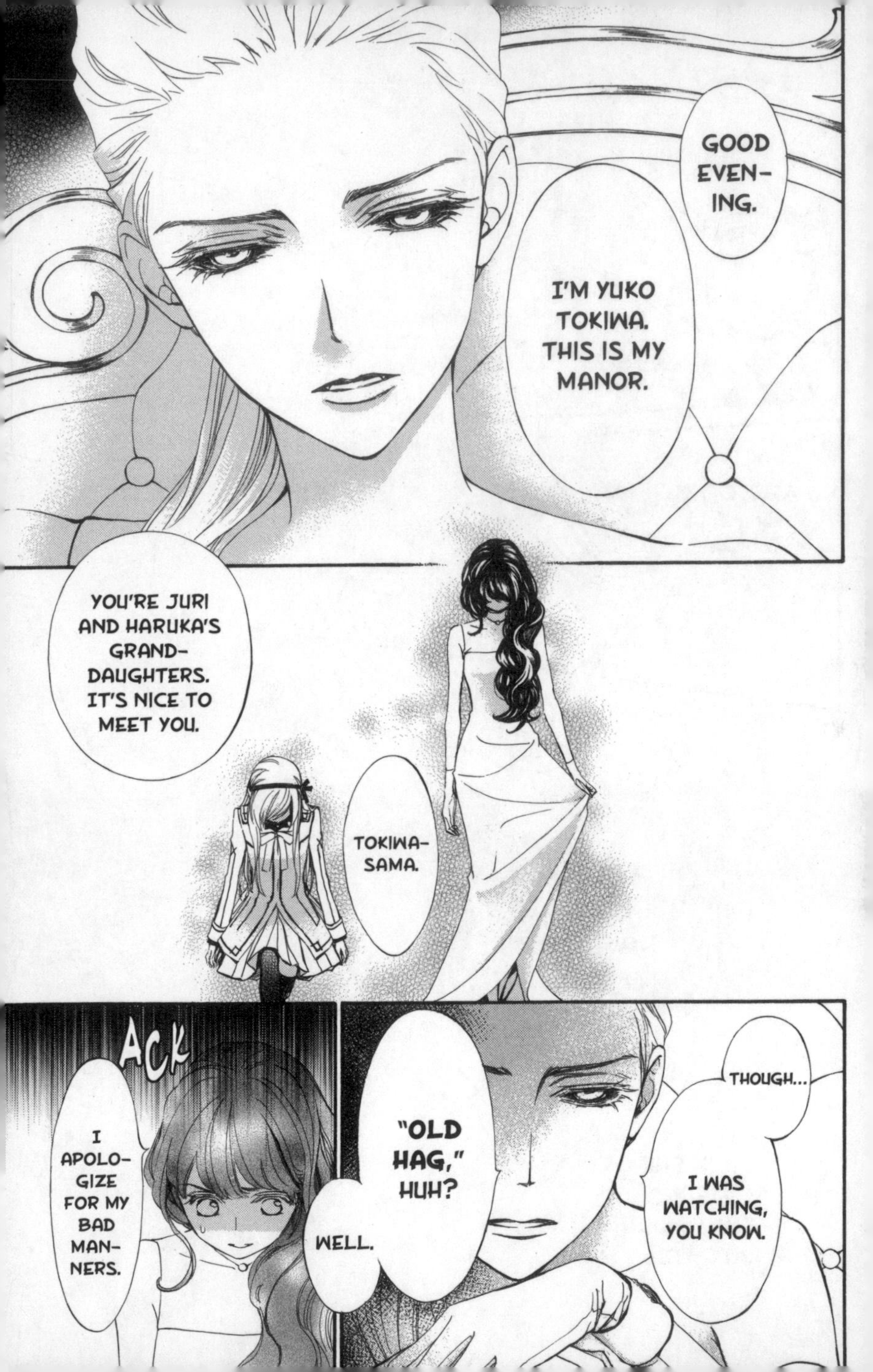
GOOD EVENING.
I'M YUKO TOKIWA. THIS IS MY MANOR.
YOU'RE JURI AND HARUKA'S GRAND-DAUGHTERS. IT'S NICE TO MEET YOU.
TOKIWA-SAMA.
THOUGH...
I WAS WATCHING, YOU KNOW.
"OLD HAG," HUH?
WELL.
ACK
I APOLO-GIZE FOR MY BAD MAN-NERS.

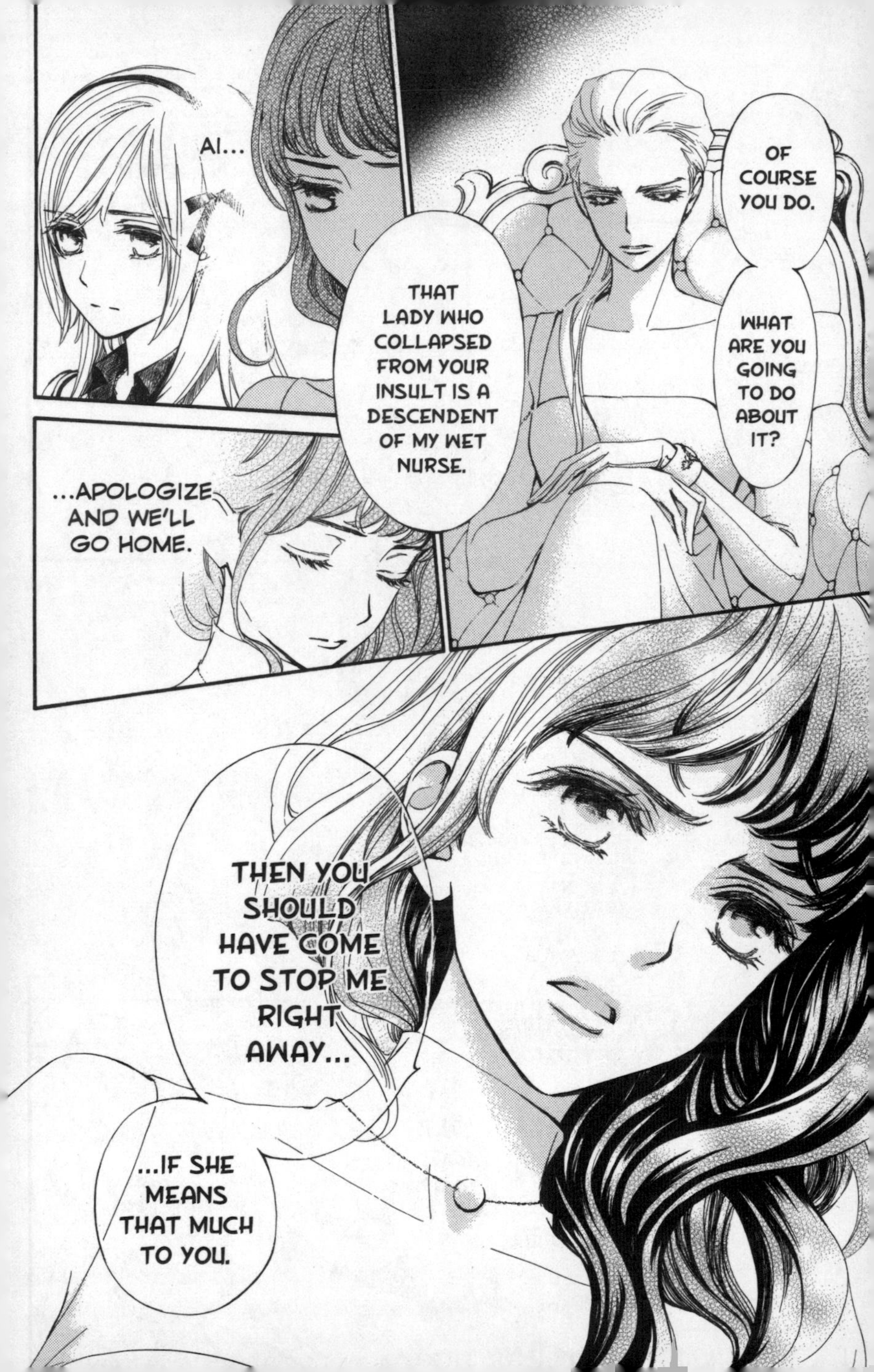
OF COURSE YOU DO.
WHAT ARE YOU GOING TO DO ABOUT IT?
THAT LADY WHO COLLAPSED FROM YOUR INSULT IS A DESCENDENT OF MY WET NURSE.
AI...
...APOLOGIZE AND WE'LL GO HOME.
THEN YOU SHOULD HAVE COME TO STOP ME RIGHT AWAY...
...IF SHE MEANS THAT MUCH TO YOU.

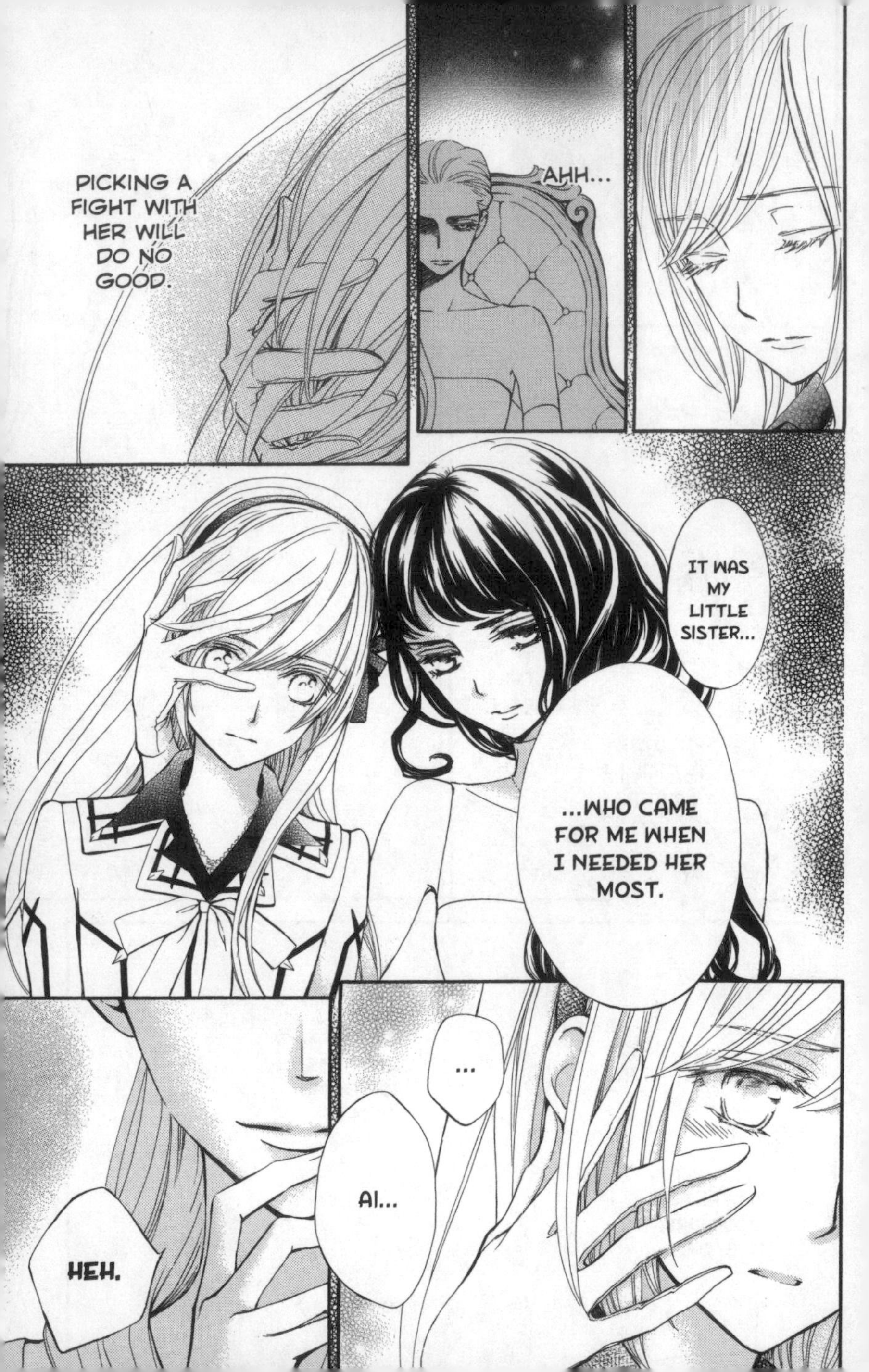
AHH...
PICKING A FIGHT WITH HER WILL DO NO GOOD.
IT WAS MY LITTLE SISTER...
...WHO CAME FOR ME WHEN I NEEDED HER MOST.
...
AI...
HEH.

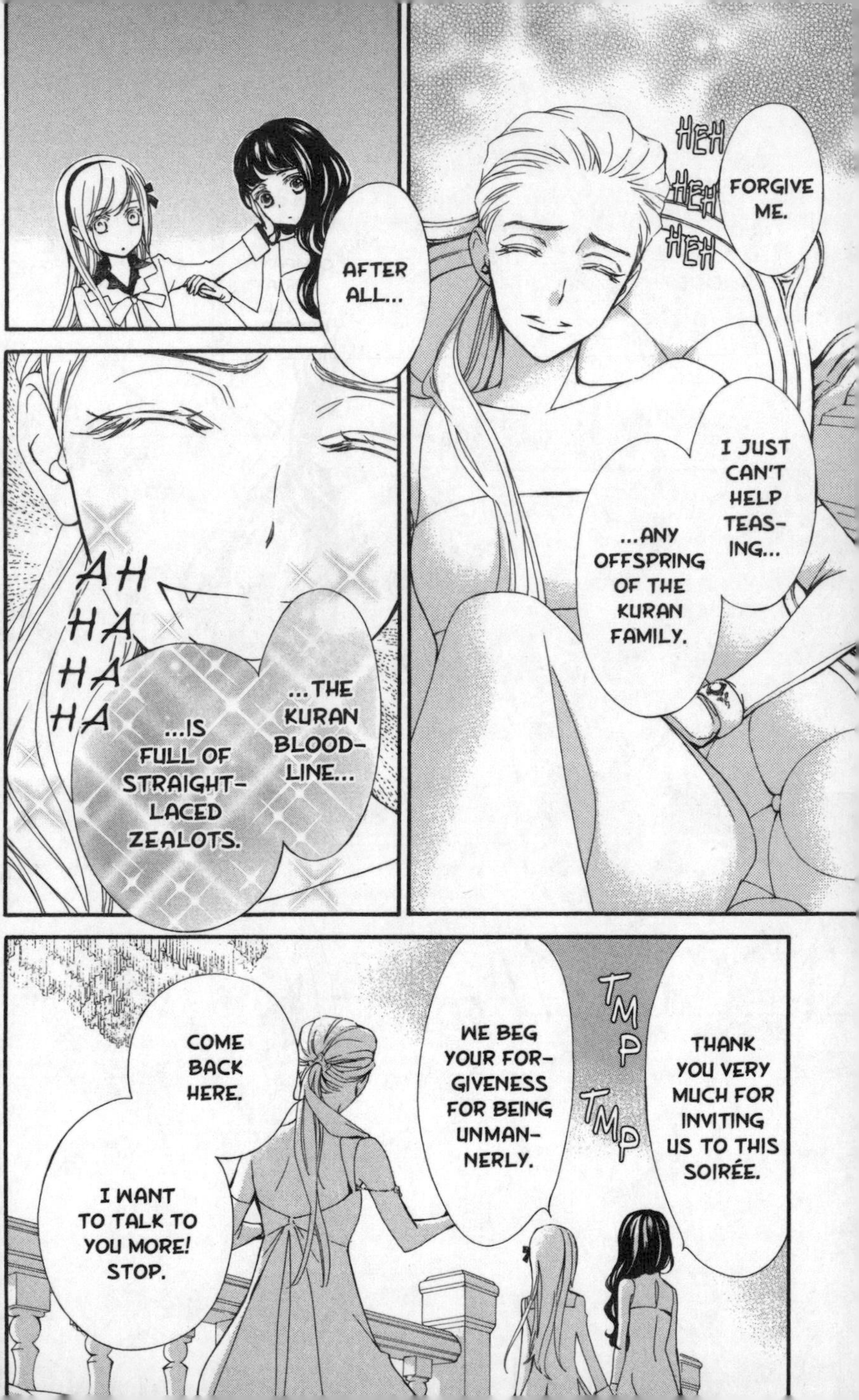
HEH HEH HEH
FORGIVE ME.
I JUST CAN'T HELP TEAS-ING...
...ANY OFFSPRING OF THE KURAN FAMILY.
AFTER ALL...
AH HA HA HA
...THE KURAN BLOOD-LINE...
...IS FULL OF STRAIGHT-LACED ZEALOTS.
THANK YOU VERY MUCH FOR INVITING US TO THIS SOIRÉE.
TMP TMP
WE BEG YOUR FOR-GIVENESS FOR BEING UNMAN-NERLY.
COME BACK HERE.
I WANT TO TALK TO YOU MORE! STOP.

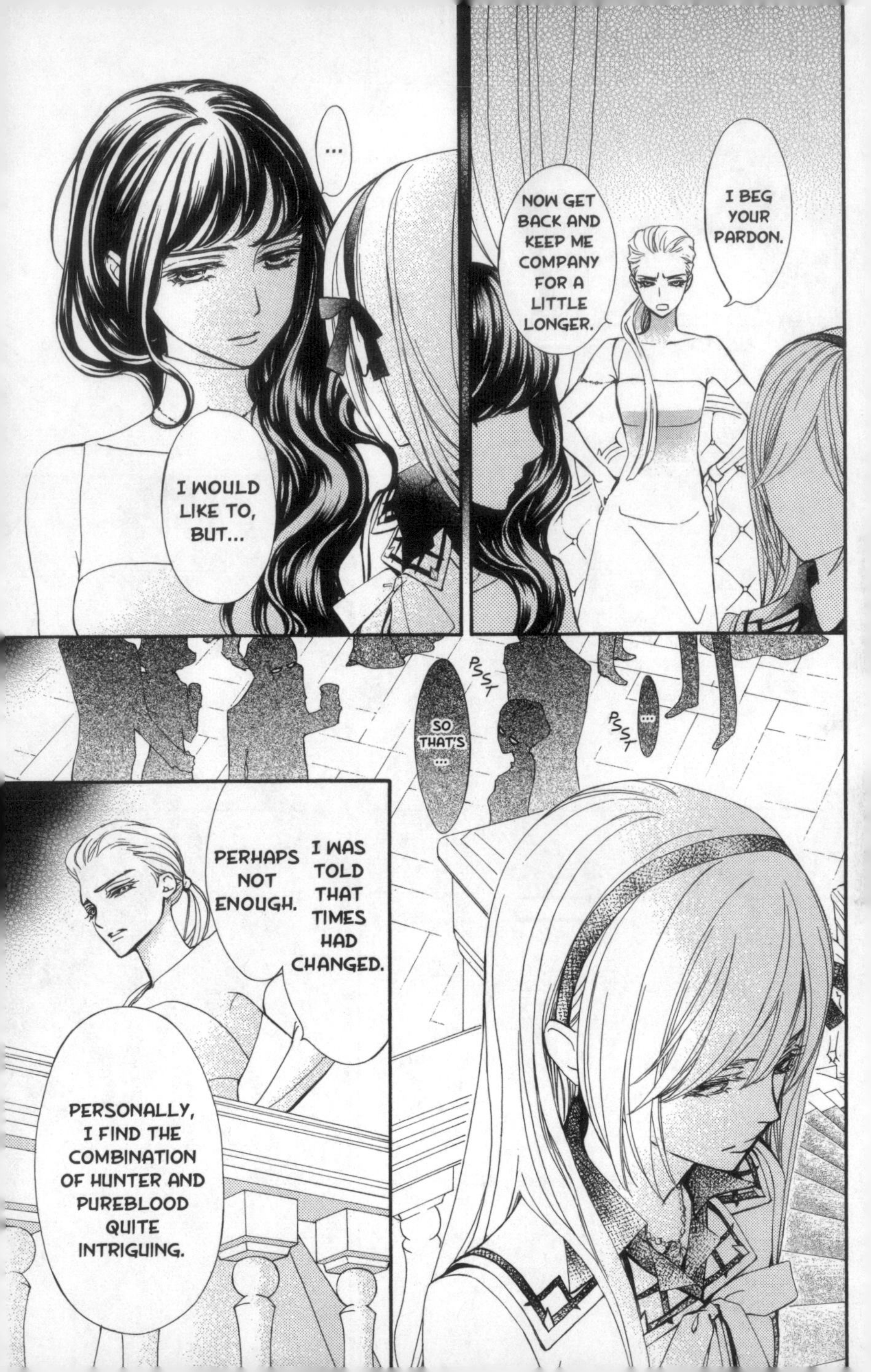
I BEG YOUR PARDON.
NOW GET BACK AND KEEP ME COMPANY FOR A LITTLE LONGER.
...
I WOULD LIKE TO, BUT...
...
PSST
PSST
SO THAT'S...
I WAS TOLD THAT TIMES HAD CHANGED.
PERHAPS NOT ENOUGH.
PERSONALLY, I FIND THE COMBINATION OF HUNTER AND PUREBLOOD QUITE INTRIGUING.

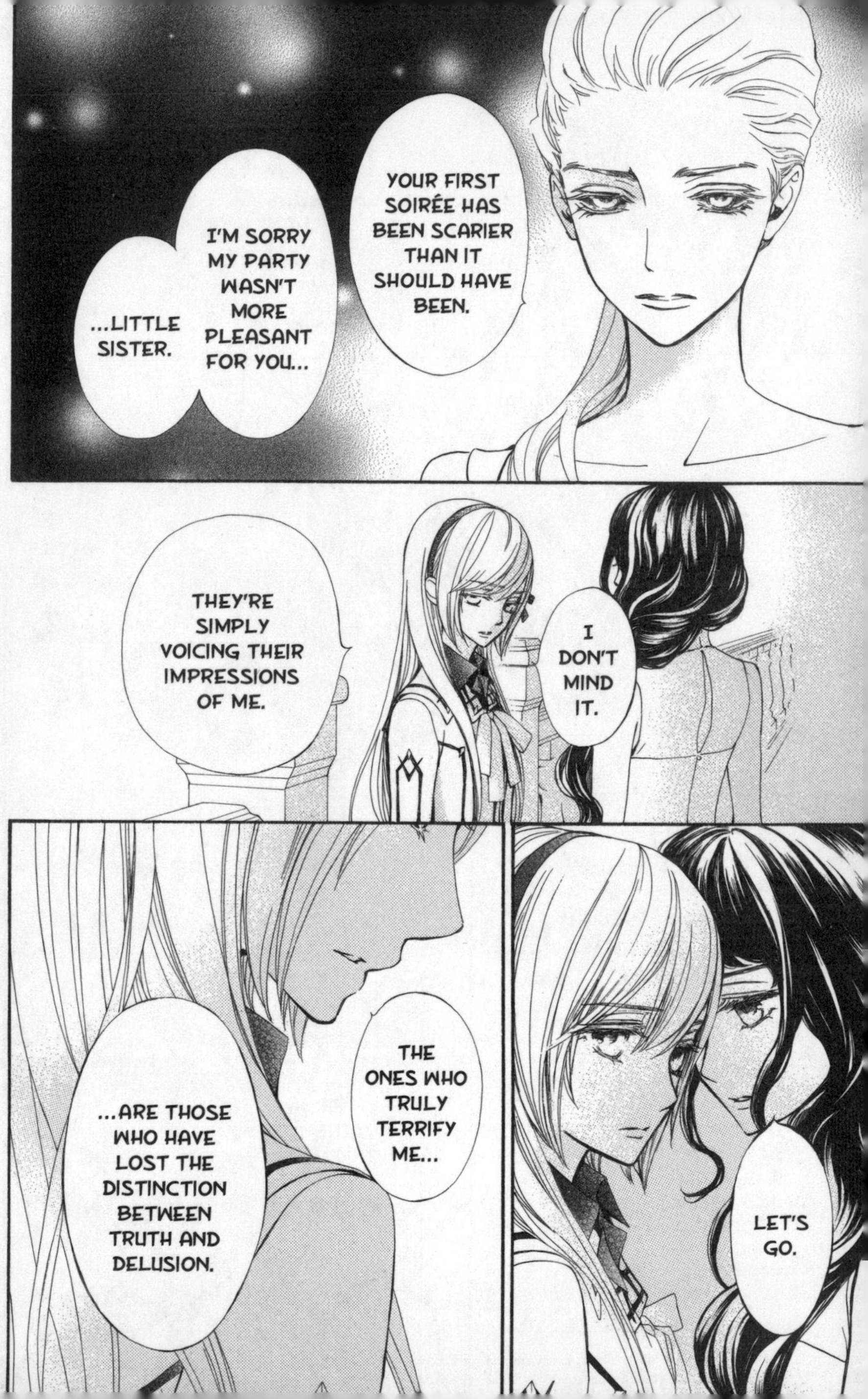
YOUR FIRST SOIRÉE HAS BEEN SCARIER THAN IT SHOULD HAVE BEEN.
I'M SORRY MY PARTY WASN'T MORE PLEASANT FOR YOU...
...LITTLE SISTER.
I DON'T MIND IT.
THEY'RE SIMPLY VOICING THEIR IMPRESSIONS OF ME.
LET'S GO.
THE ONES WHO TRULY TERRIFY ME...
...ARE THOSE WHO HAVE LOST THE DISTINCTION BETWEEN TRUTH AND DELUSION.

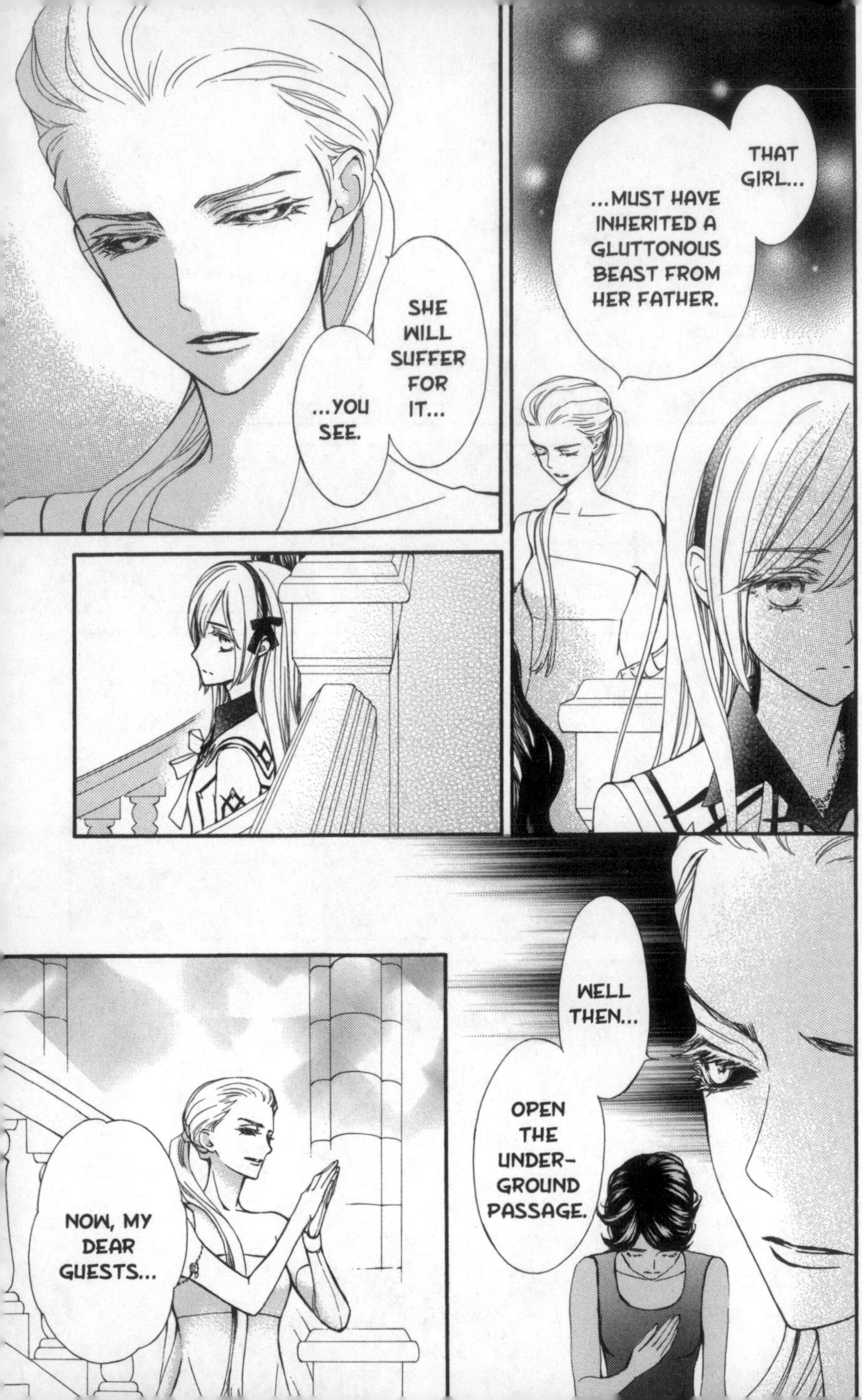
THAT GIRL...
...MUST HAVE INHERITED A GLUTTONOUS BEAST FROM HER FATHER.
SHE WILL SUFFER FOR IT...
...YOU SEE.
WELL THEN...
OPEN THE UNDER-GROUND PASSAGE.
NOW, MY DEAR GUESTS...

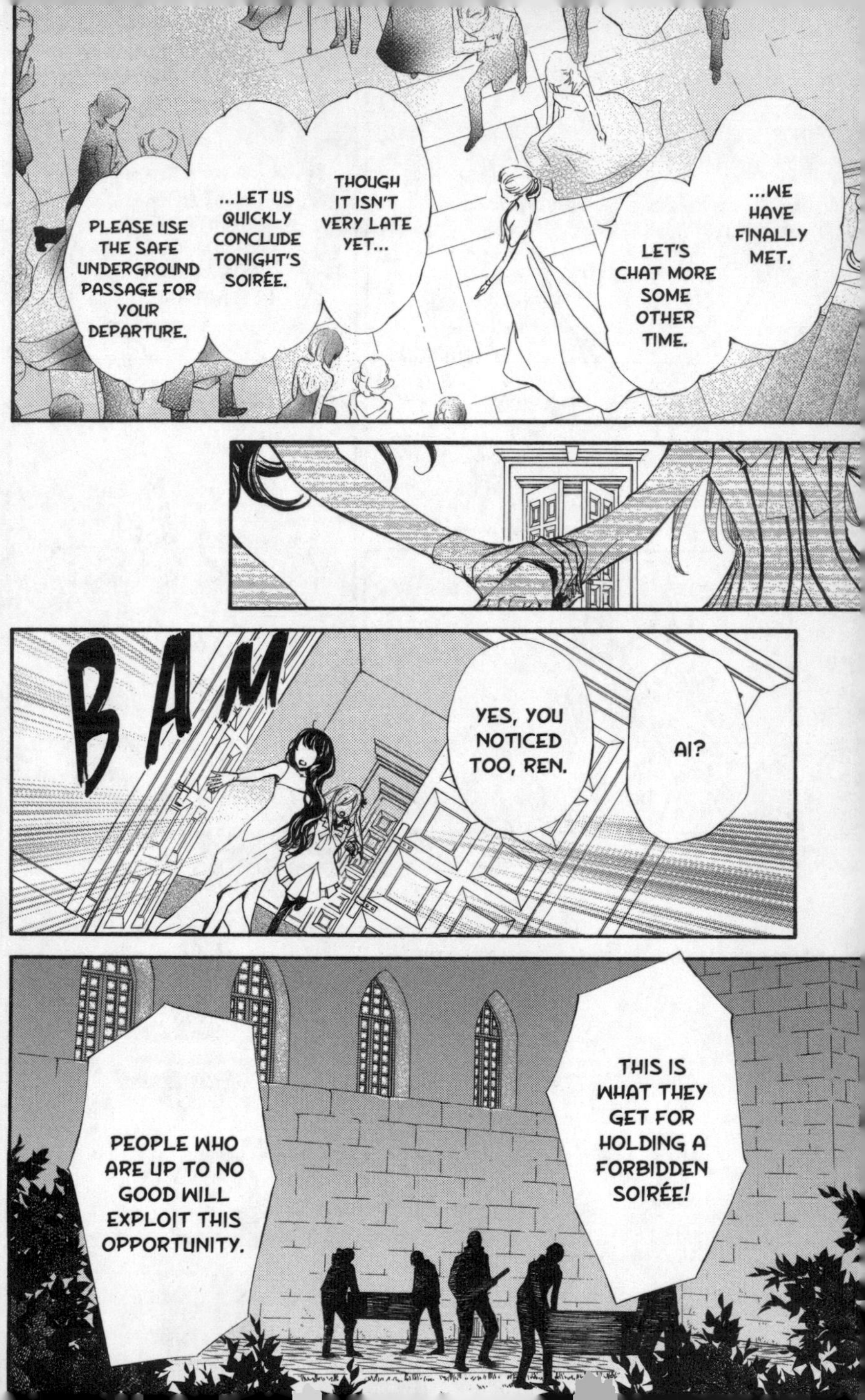
...WE HAVE FINALLY MET.
LET'S CHAT MORE SOME OTHER TIME.
THOUGH IT ISN'T VERY LATE YET...
...LET US QUICKLY CONCLUDE TONIGHT'S SOIRÉE.
PLEASE USE THE SAFE UNDERGROUND PASSAGE FOR YOUR DEPARTURE.
AI?
YES, YOU NOTICED TOO, REN.
BAM
THIS IS WHAT THEY GET FOR HOLDING A FORBIDDEN SOIRÉE!
PEOPLE WHO ARE UP TO NO GOOD WILL EXPLOIT THIS OPPORTUNITY.

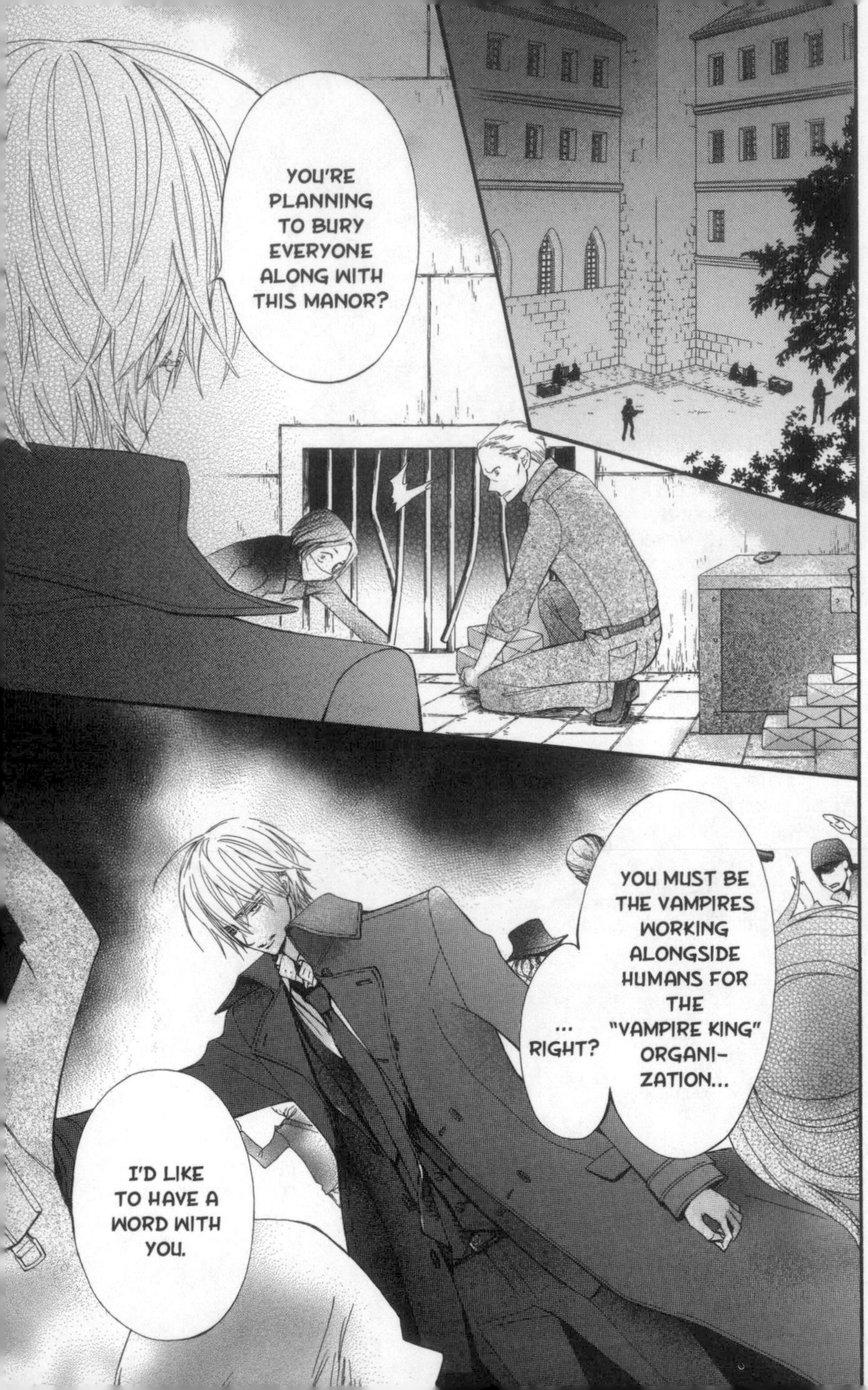
YOU'RE PLANNING TO BURY EVERYONE ALONG WITH THIS MANOR?
YOU MUST BE THE VAMPIRES WORKING ALONGSIDE HUMANS FOR THE "VAMPIRE KING" ORGANI-ZATION...
... RIGHT?
I'D LIKE TO HAVE A WORD WITH YOU.

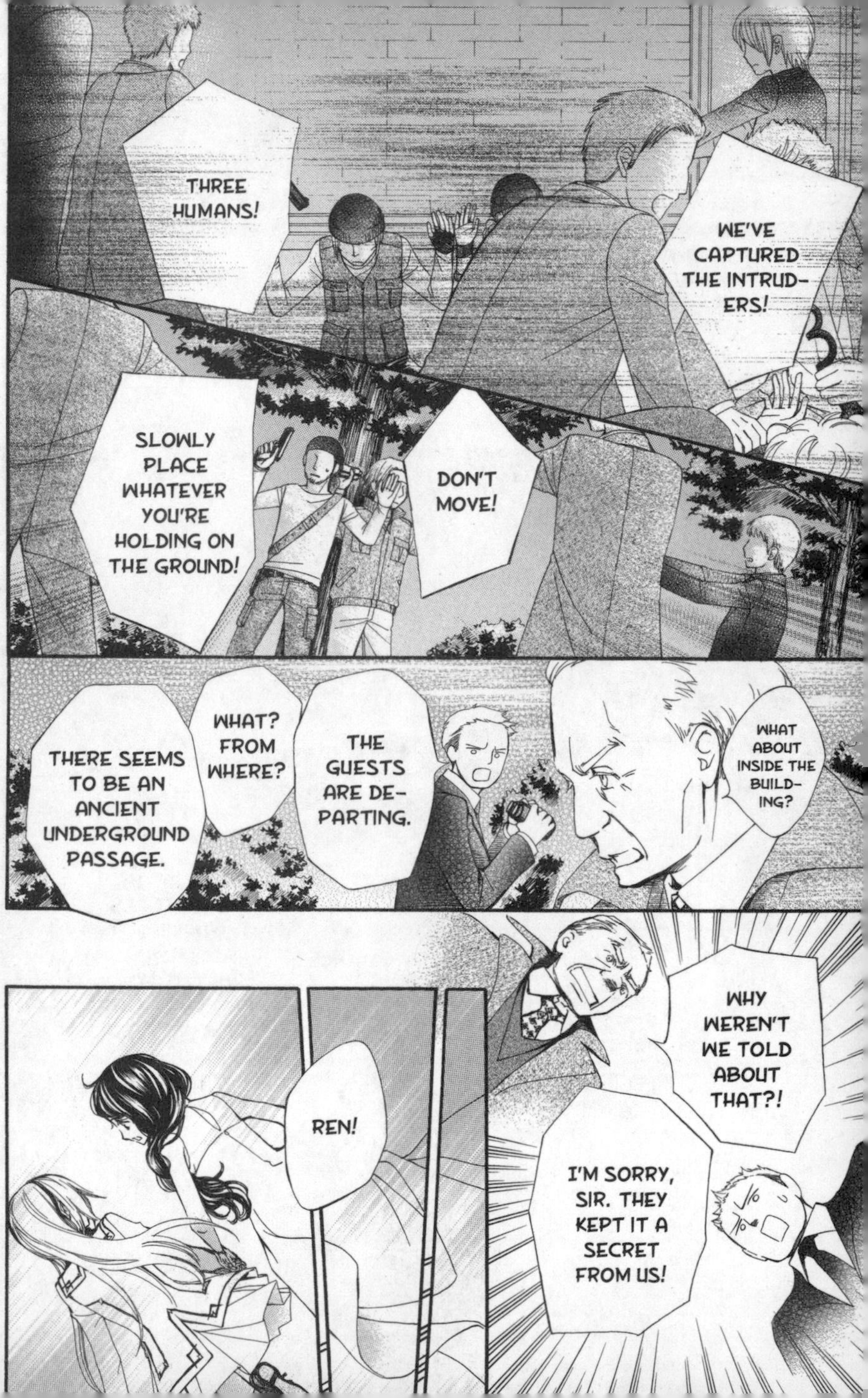
WE'VE CAPTURED THE INTRUD-ERS!
THREE HUMANS!
DON'T MOVE!
SLOWLY PLACE WHATEVER YOU'RE HOLDING ON THE GROUND!
WHAT ABOUT INSIDE THE BUILD-ING?
THE GUESTS ARE DE-PARTING.
WHAT? FROM WHERE?
THERE SEEMS TO BE AN ANCIENT UNDERGROUND PASSAGE.
WHY WEREN'T WE TOLD ABOUT THAT?!
I'M SORRY, SIR. THEY KEPT IT A SECRET FROM US!
REN!

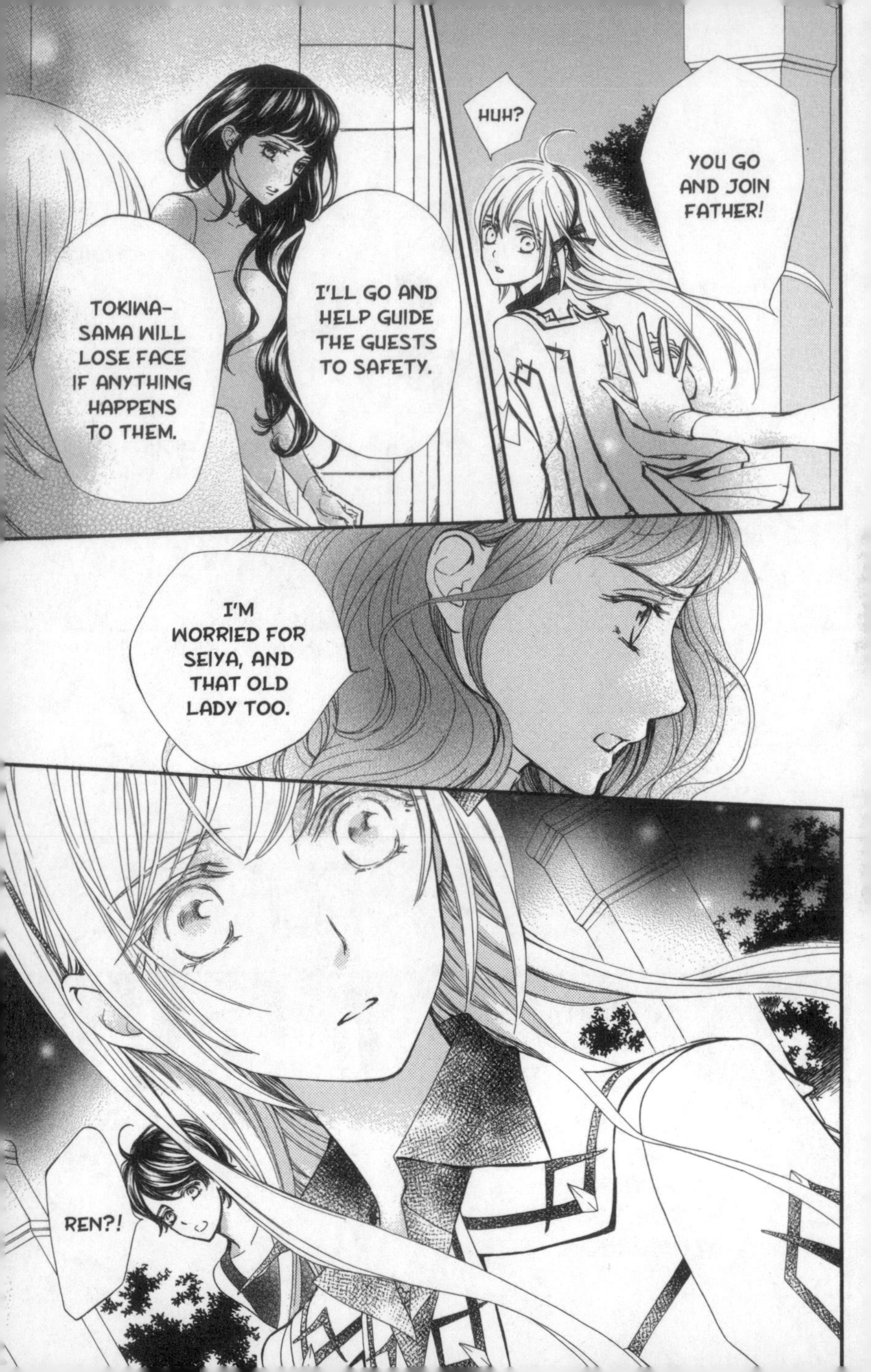
YOU GO AND JOIN FATHER!
HUH?
I'LL GO AND HELP GUIDE THE GUESTS TO SAFETY.
TOKIWA-SAMA WILL LOSE FACE IF ANYTHING HAPPENS TO THEM.
I'M WORRIED FOR SEIYA, AND THAT OLD LADY TOO.
REN?!

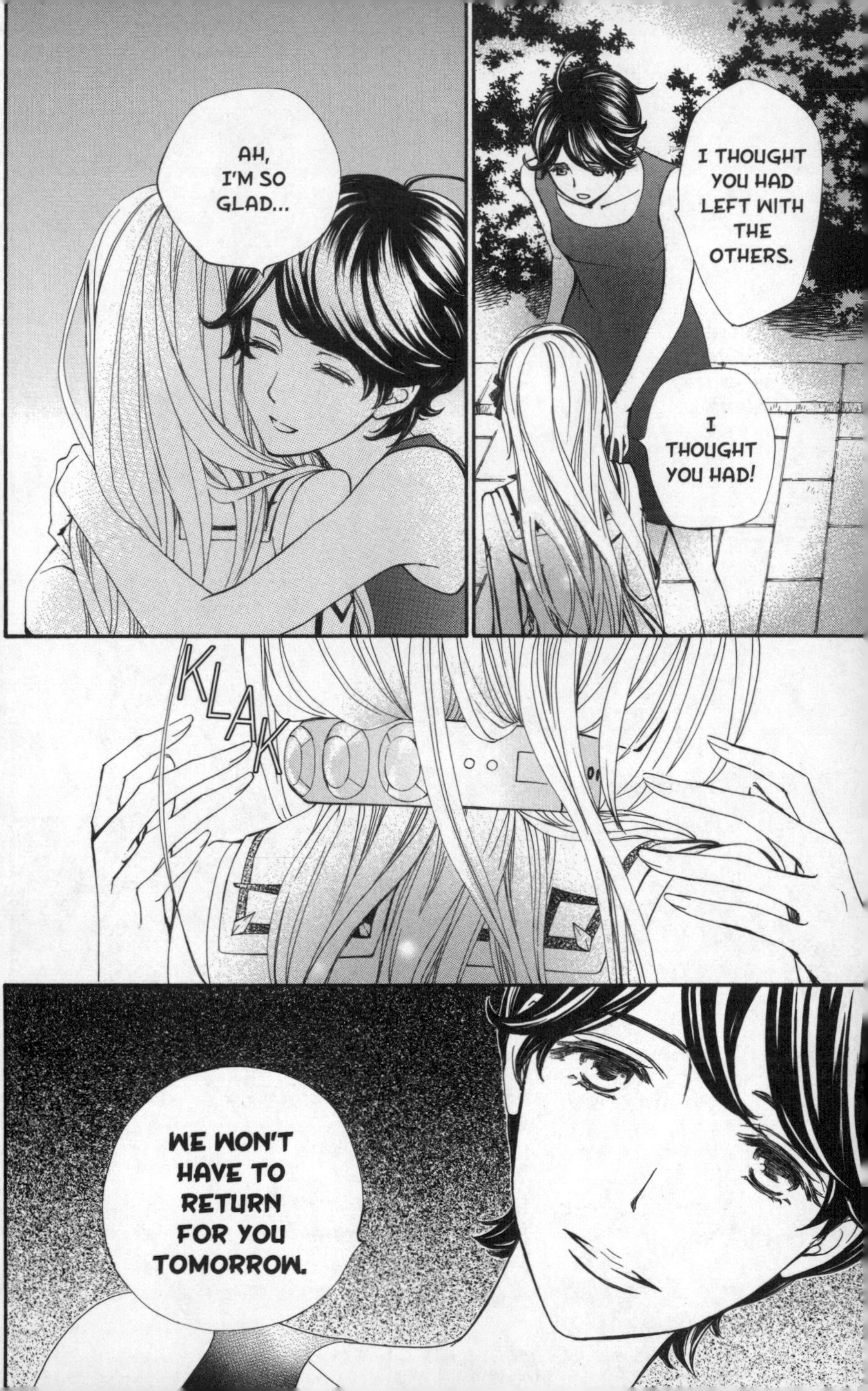
I THOUGHT YOU HAD LEFT WITH THE OTHERS.
I THOUGHT YOU HAD!
AH, I'M SO GLAD...
KLAK
WE WON'T HAVE TO RETURN FOR YOU TOMORROW.

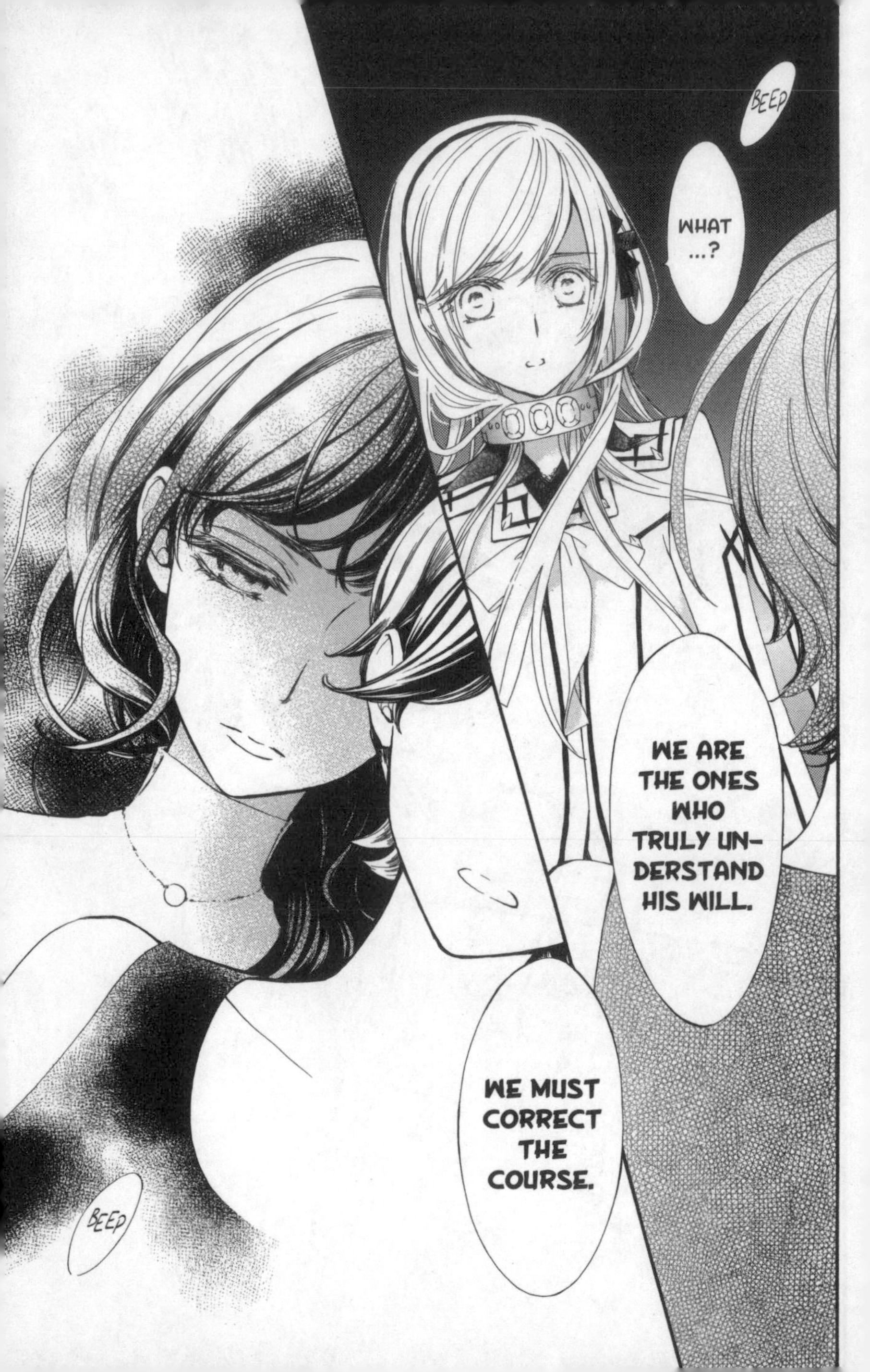
BEEP
WHAT ...?
WE ARE THE ONES WHO TRULY UNDERSTAND HIS WILL.
WE MUST CORRECT THE COURSE.
BEEP

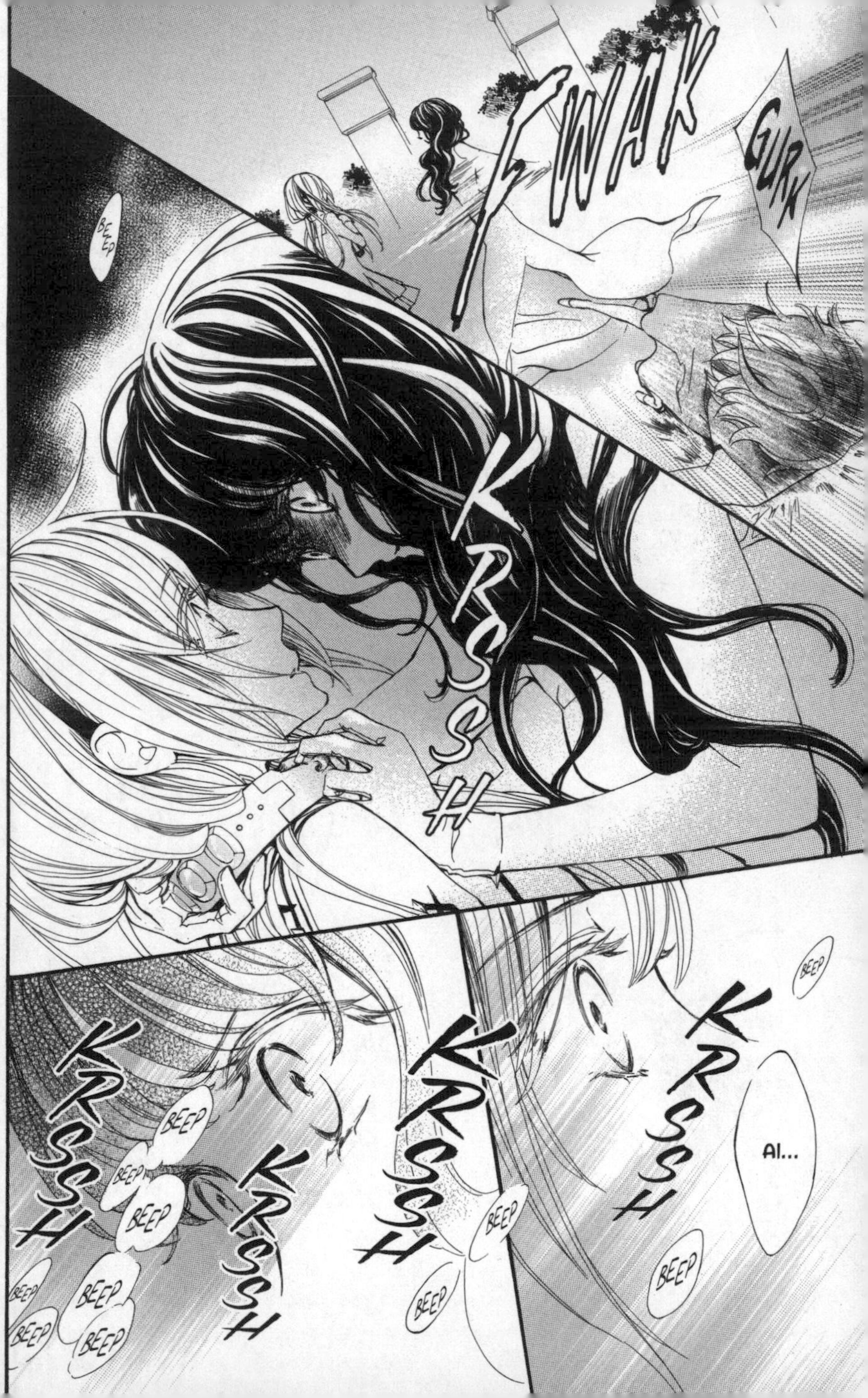

GURK
FWAK
KRSSH
BEEP
BEEP
KRSSH
AI...
BEEP
BEEP
BEEP
KRSSH
KRSSH
BEEP
BEEP
BEEP
KRSSH
BEEP
BEEP
BEEP
BEEP

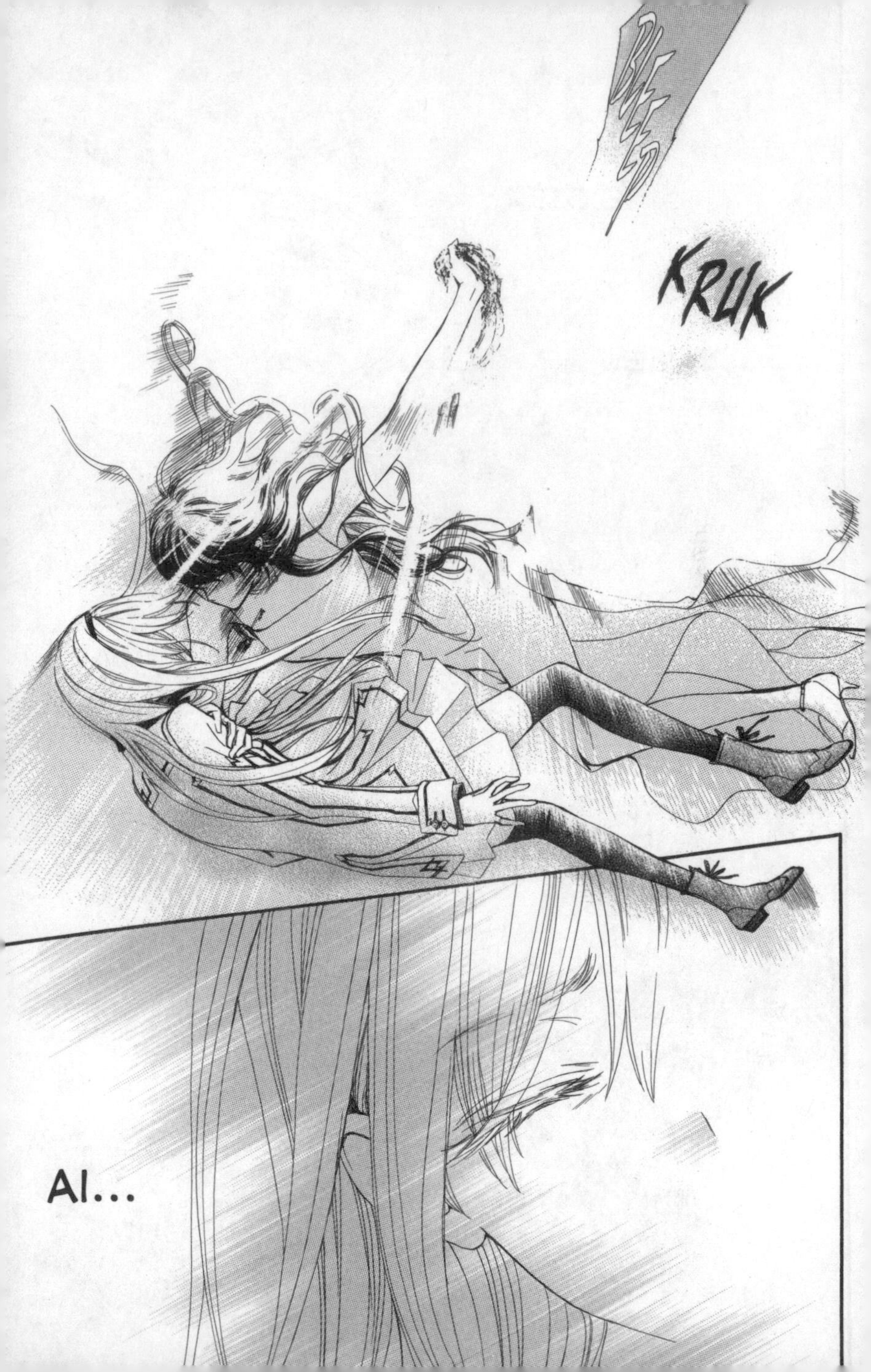
KRUK
AI...

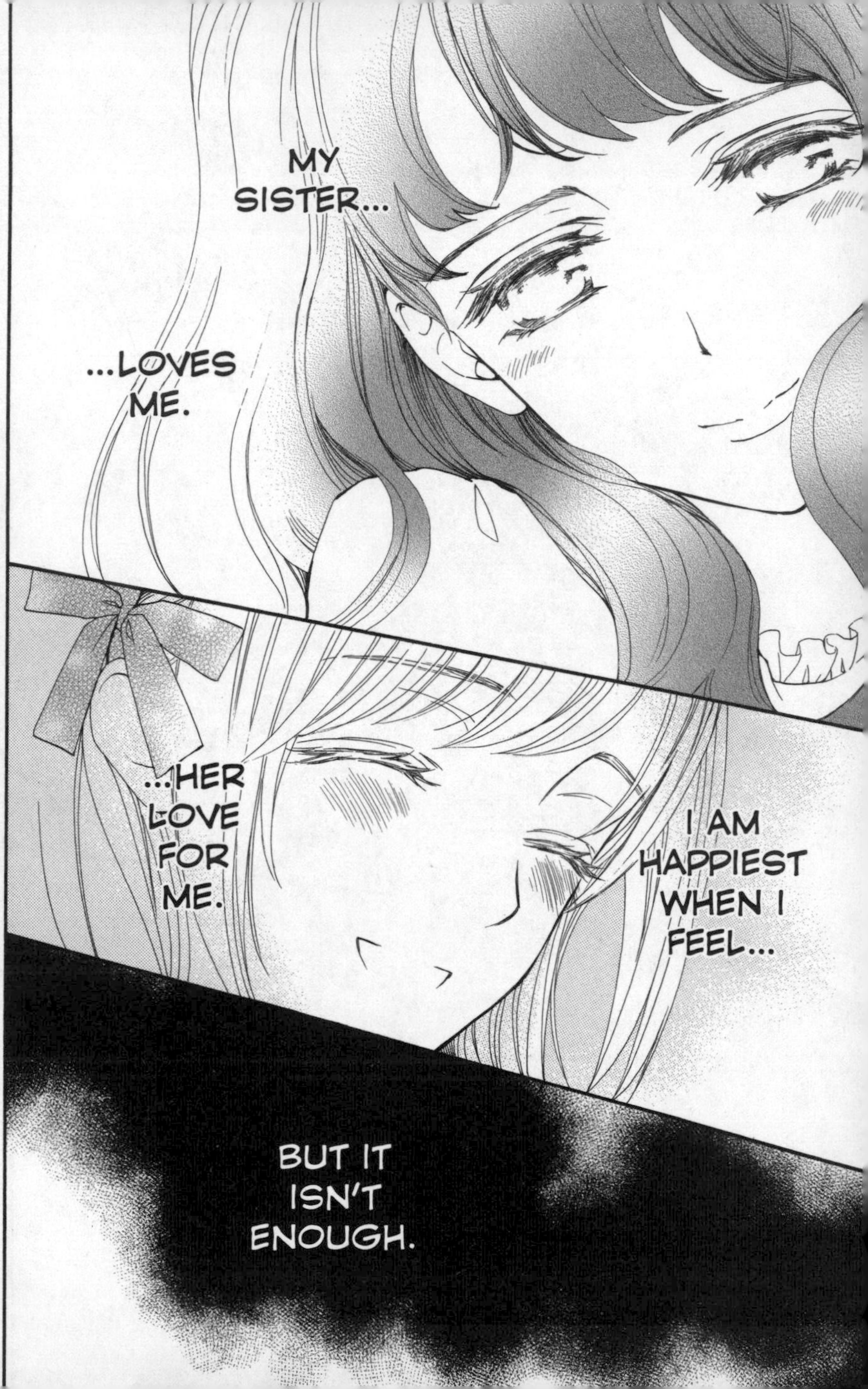
MY SISTER...
...LOVES ME.
I AM HAPPIEST WHEN I FEEL...
...HER LOVE FOR ME.
BUT IT ISN'T ENOUGH.

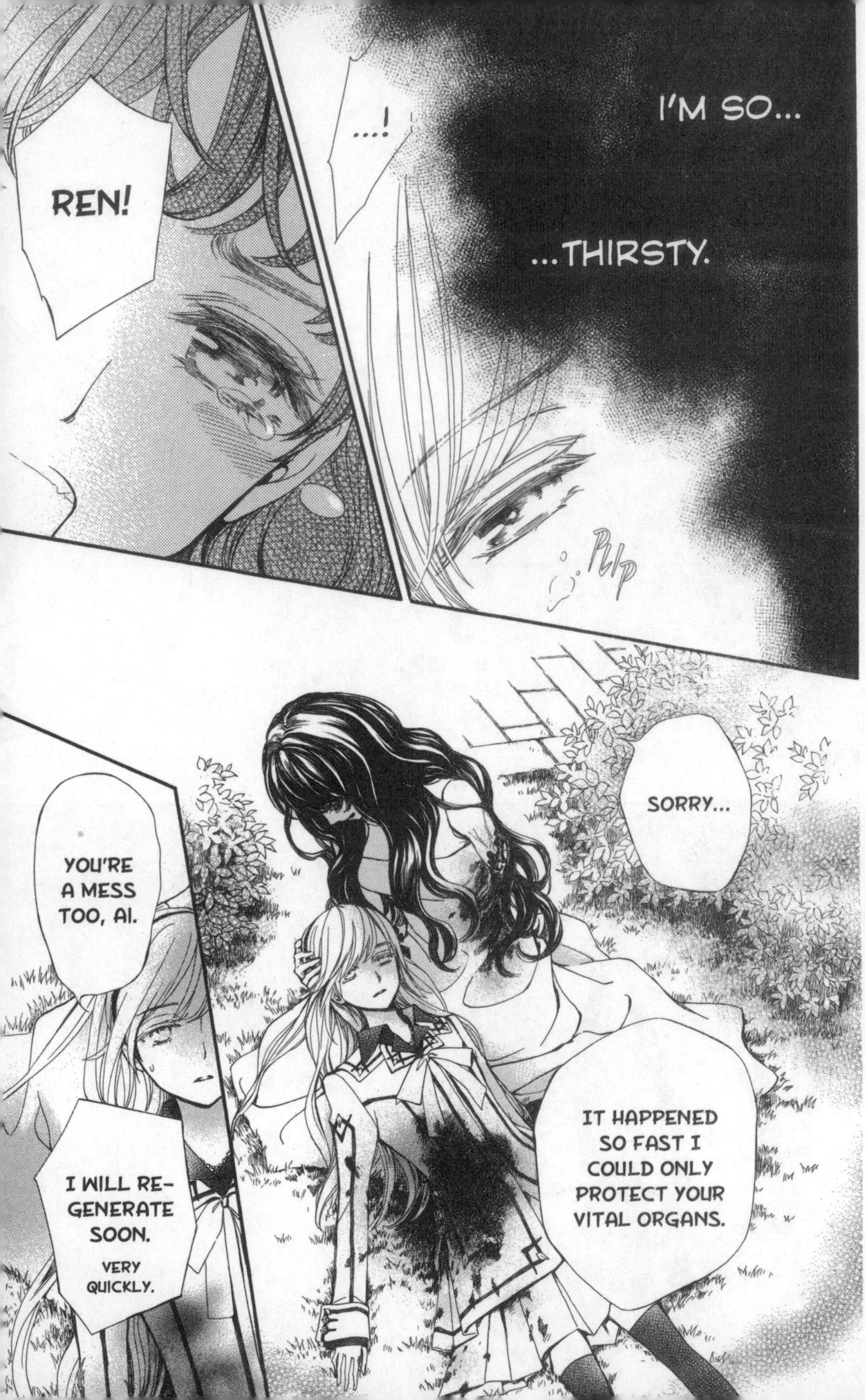

I'M SO...
...THIRSTY.
...!
PLIP
REN!
SORRY...
IT HAPPENED SO FAST I COULD ONLY PROTECT YOUR VITAL ORGANS.
YOU'RE A MESS TOO, AI.
I WILL RE-GENERATE SOON.
VERY QUICKLY.

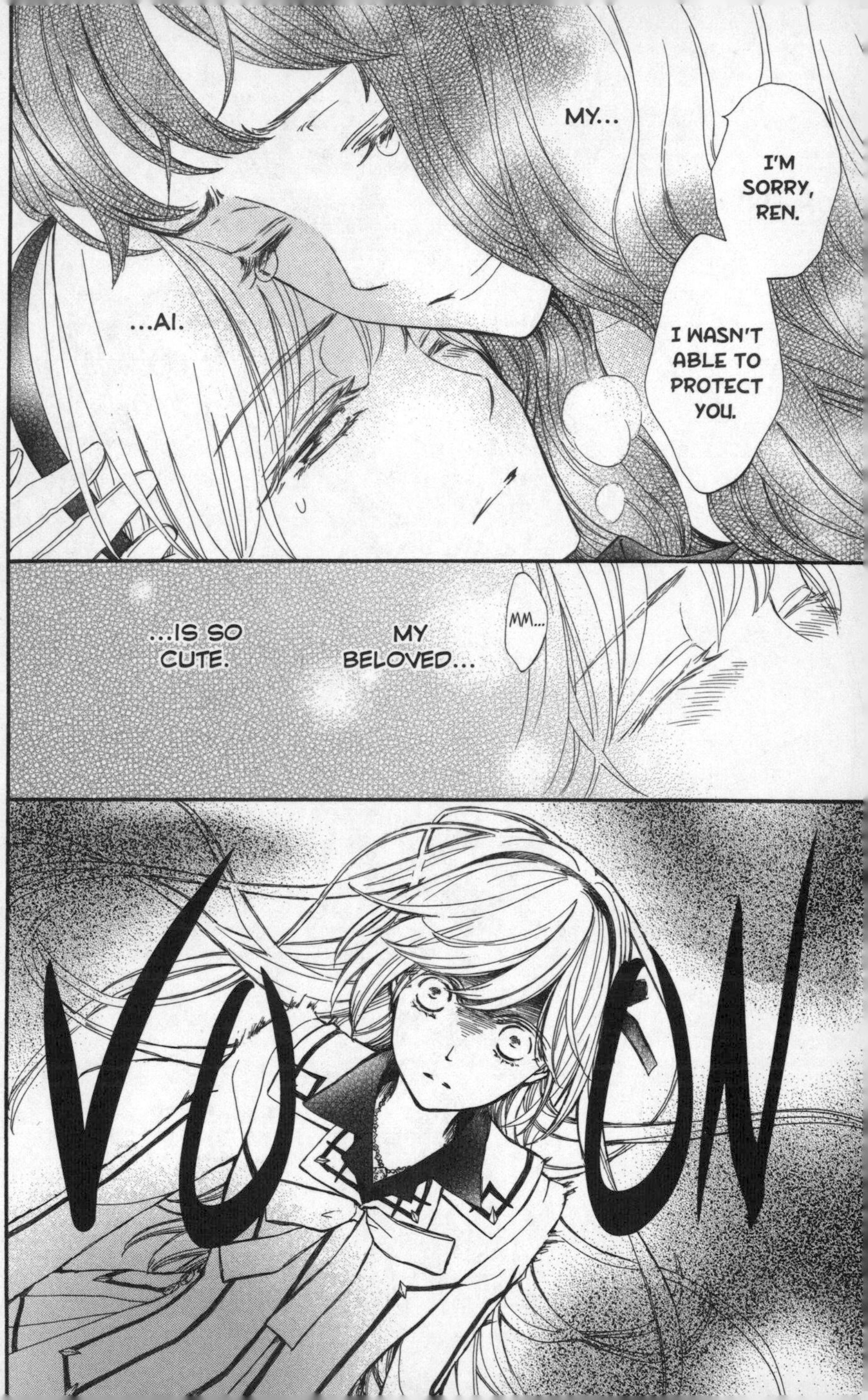
I'M SORRY, REN.
I WASN'T ABLE TO PROTECT YOU.
MY...
...AI.
MM...
MY BELOVED...
...IS SO CUTE.
VOON

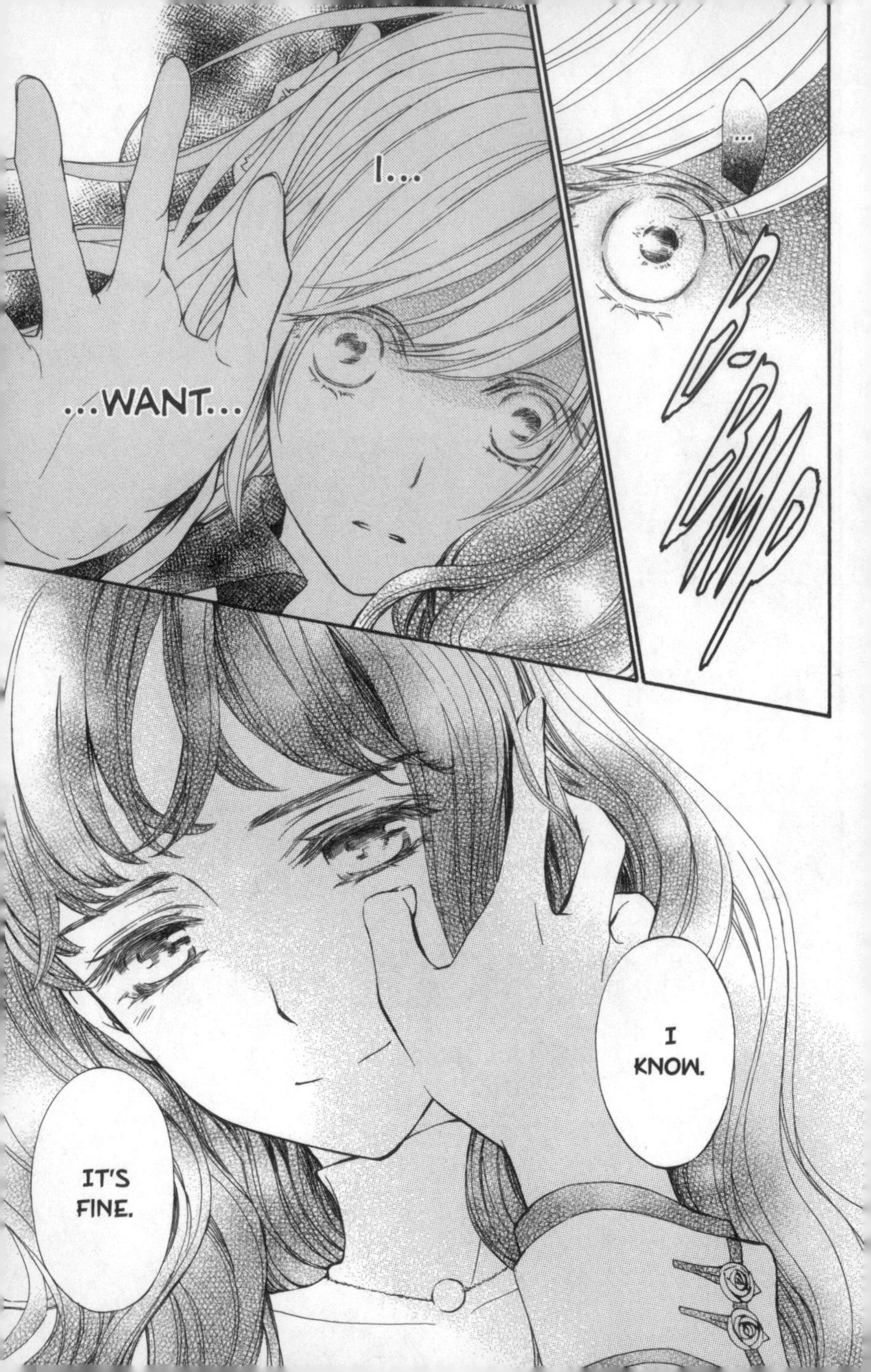
...
I...
...WANT...
I KNOW.
IT'S FINE.

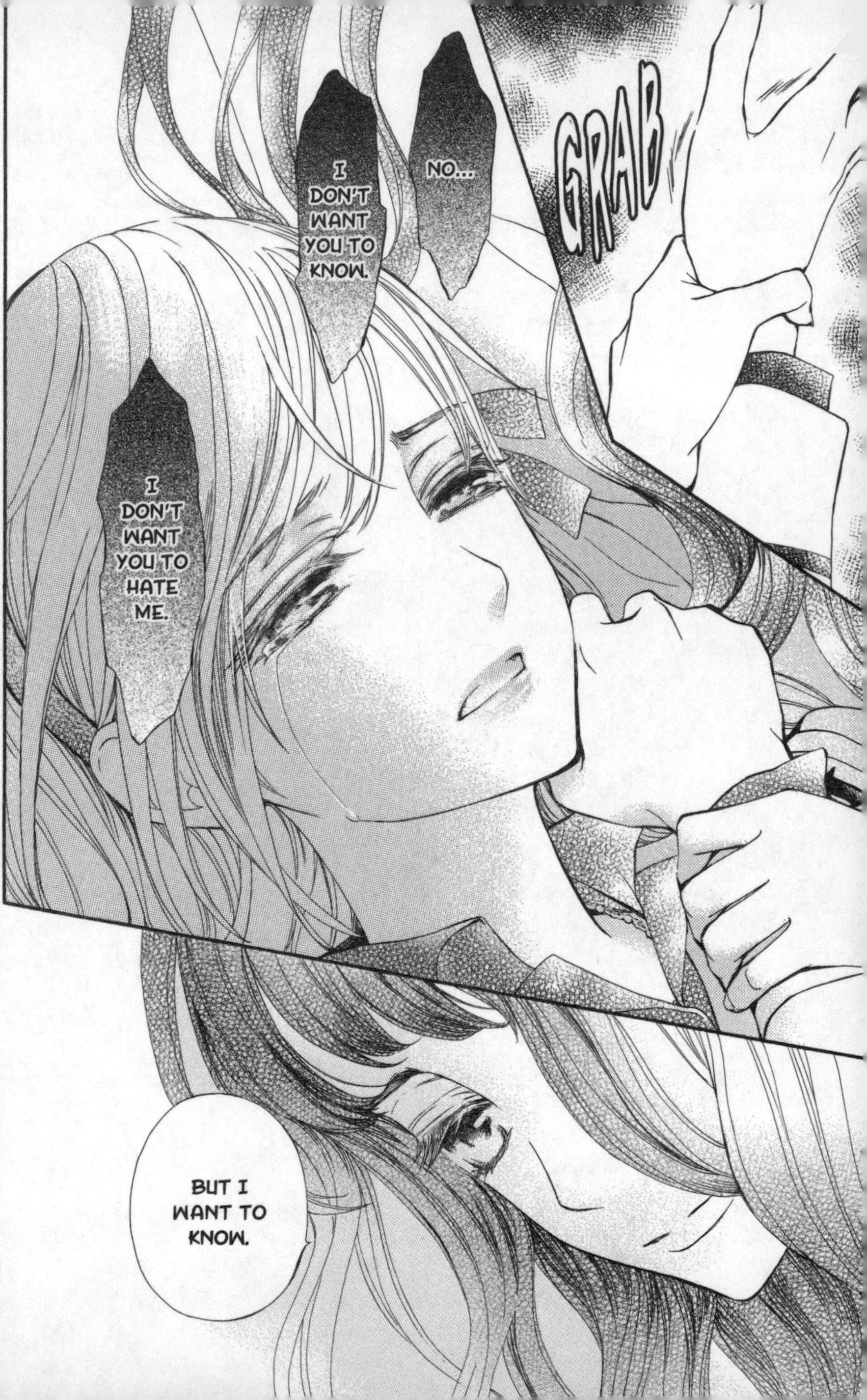
GRAB
NO...
I DON'T WANT YOU TO KNOW.
I DON'T WANT YOU TO HATE ME.
BUT I WANT TO KNOW.

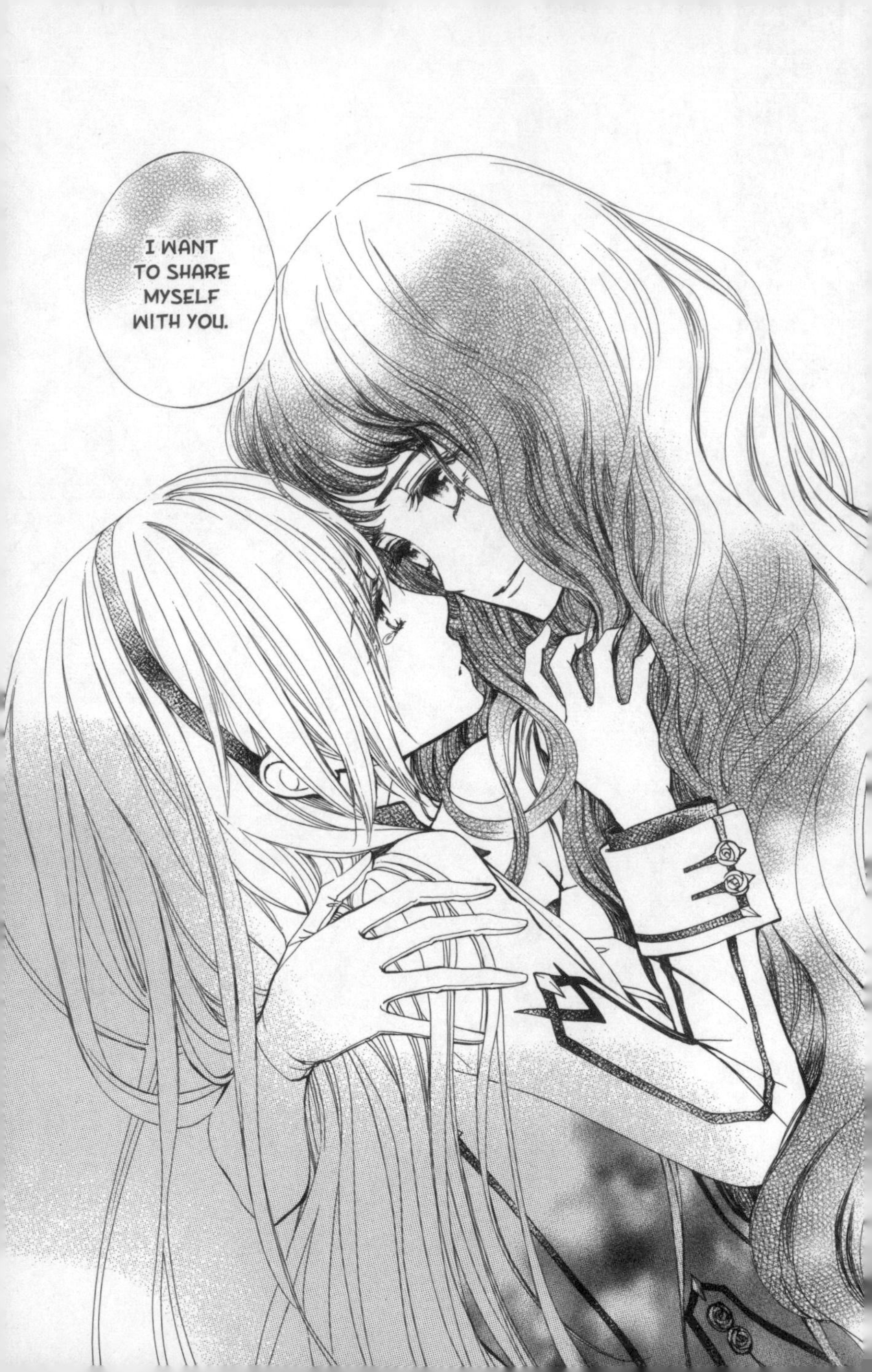
I WANT TO SHARE MYSELF WITH YOU.

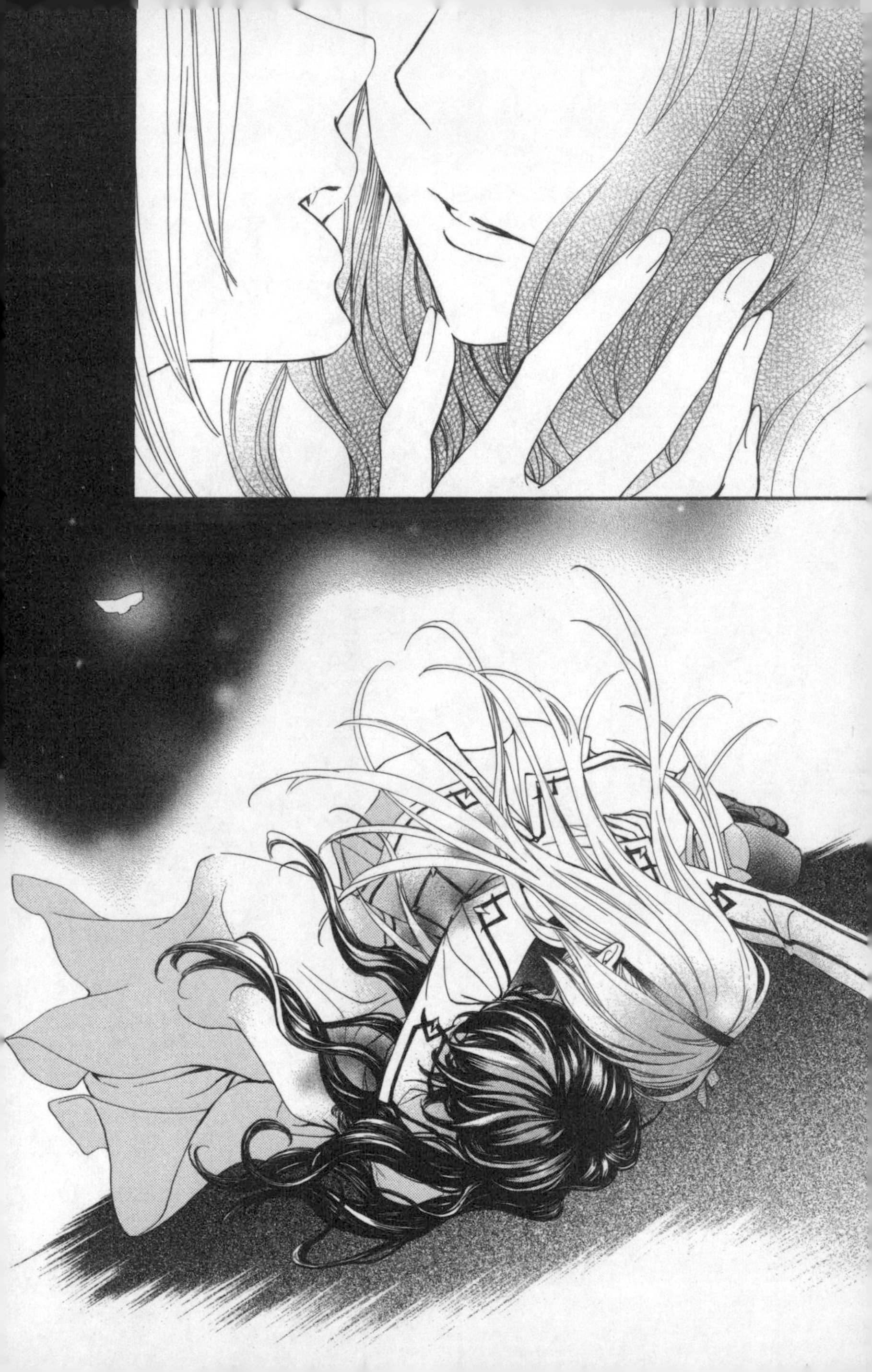

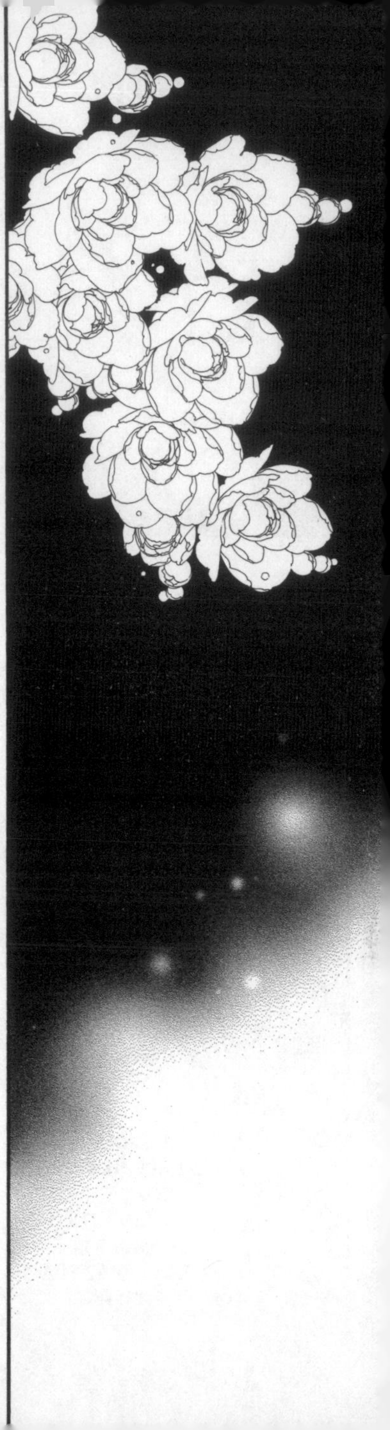

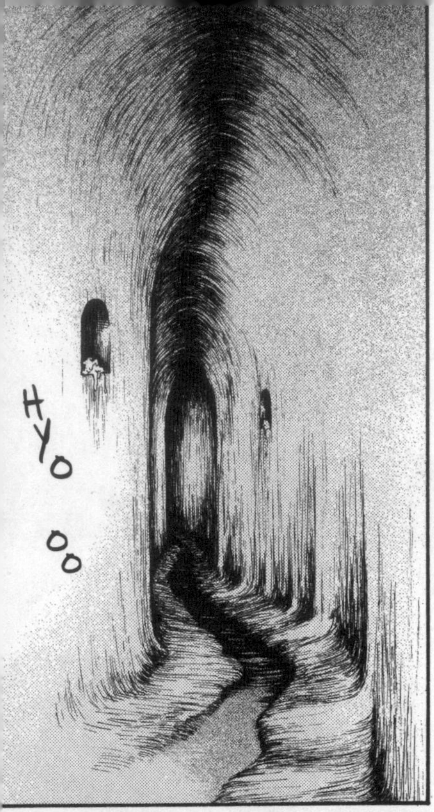
HYO OO

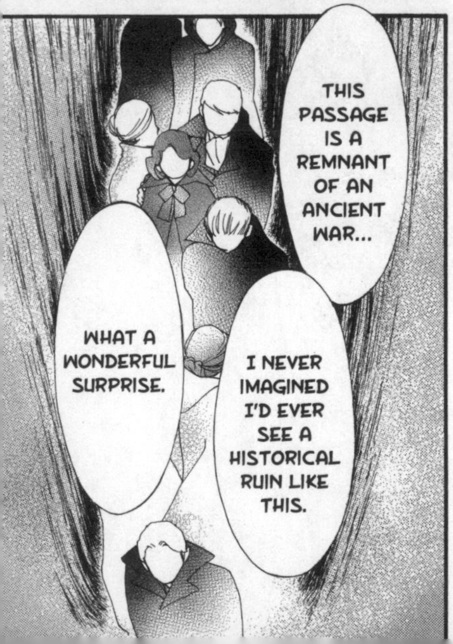
THIS PASSAGE IS A REMNANT OF AN ANCIENT WAR...
I NEVER IMAGINED I'D EVER SEE A HISTORICAL RUIN LIKE THIS.
WHAT A WONDERFUL SURPRISE.

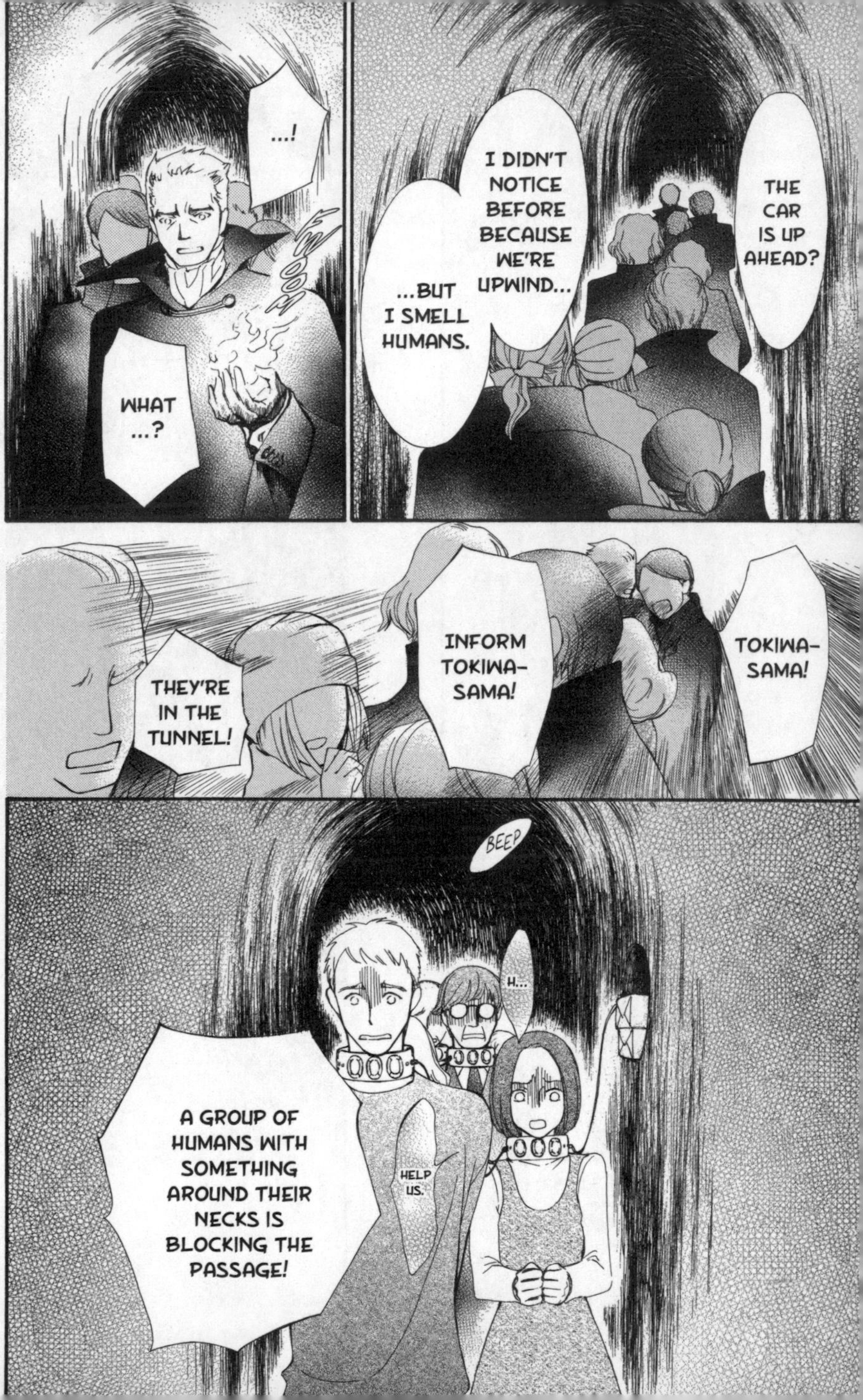
THE CAR IS UP AHEAD?
I DIDN'T NOTICE BEFORE BECAUSE WE'RE UPWIND...
...BUT I SMELL HUMANS.
...!
WHAT ...?
TOKIWA-SAMA!
INFORM TOKIWA-SAMA!
THEY'RE IN THE TUNNEL!
BEEP
H...
HELP US.
A GROUP OF HUMANS WITH SOMETHING AROUND THEIR NECKS IS BLOCKING THE PASSAGE!

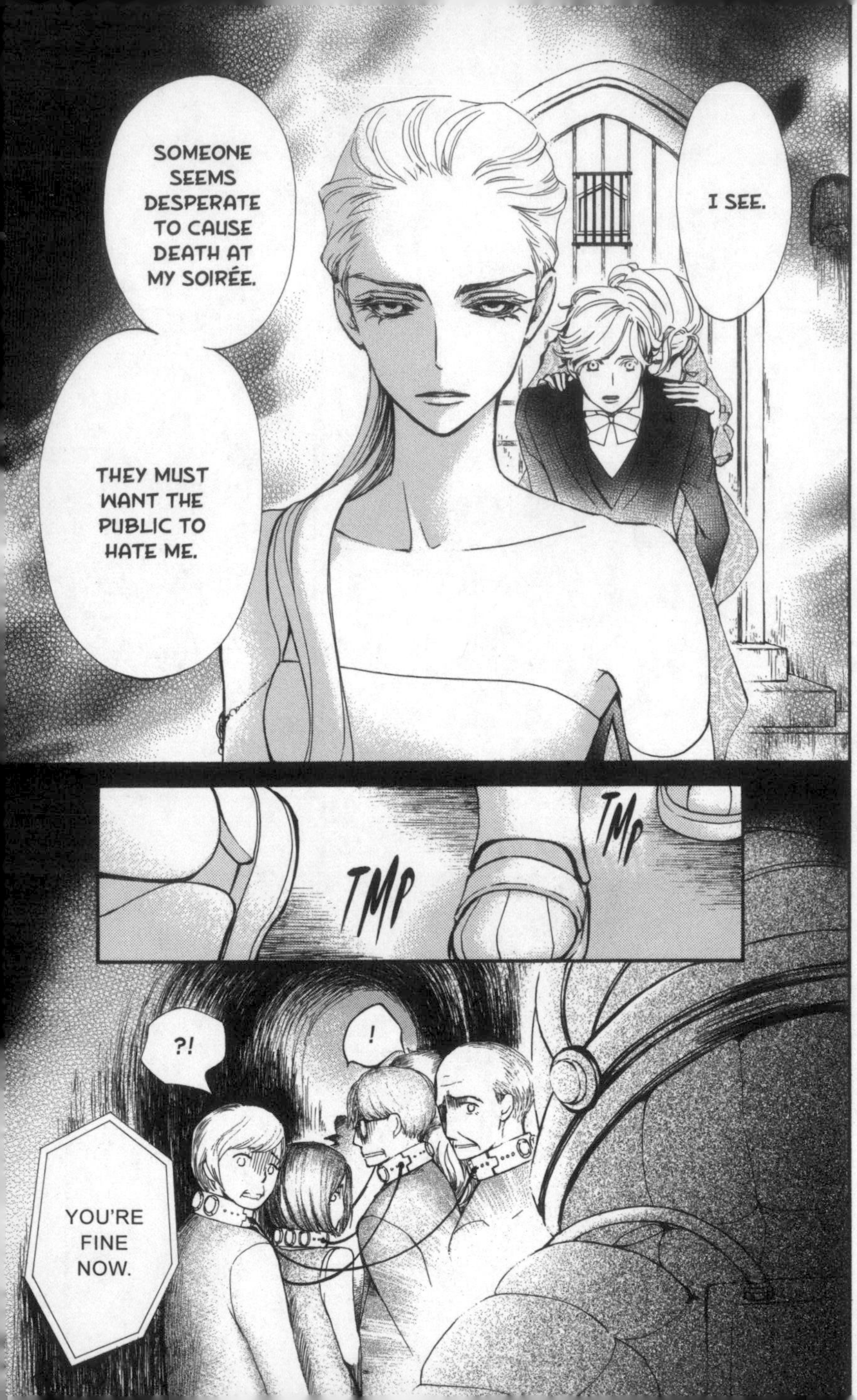
I SEE.
SOMEONE SEEMS DESPERATE TO CAUSE DEATH AT MY SOIRÉE.
THEY MUST WANT THE PUBLIC TO HATE ME.
TMP
TMP
!
?!
YOU'RE FINE NOW.

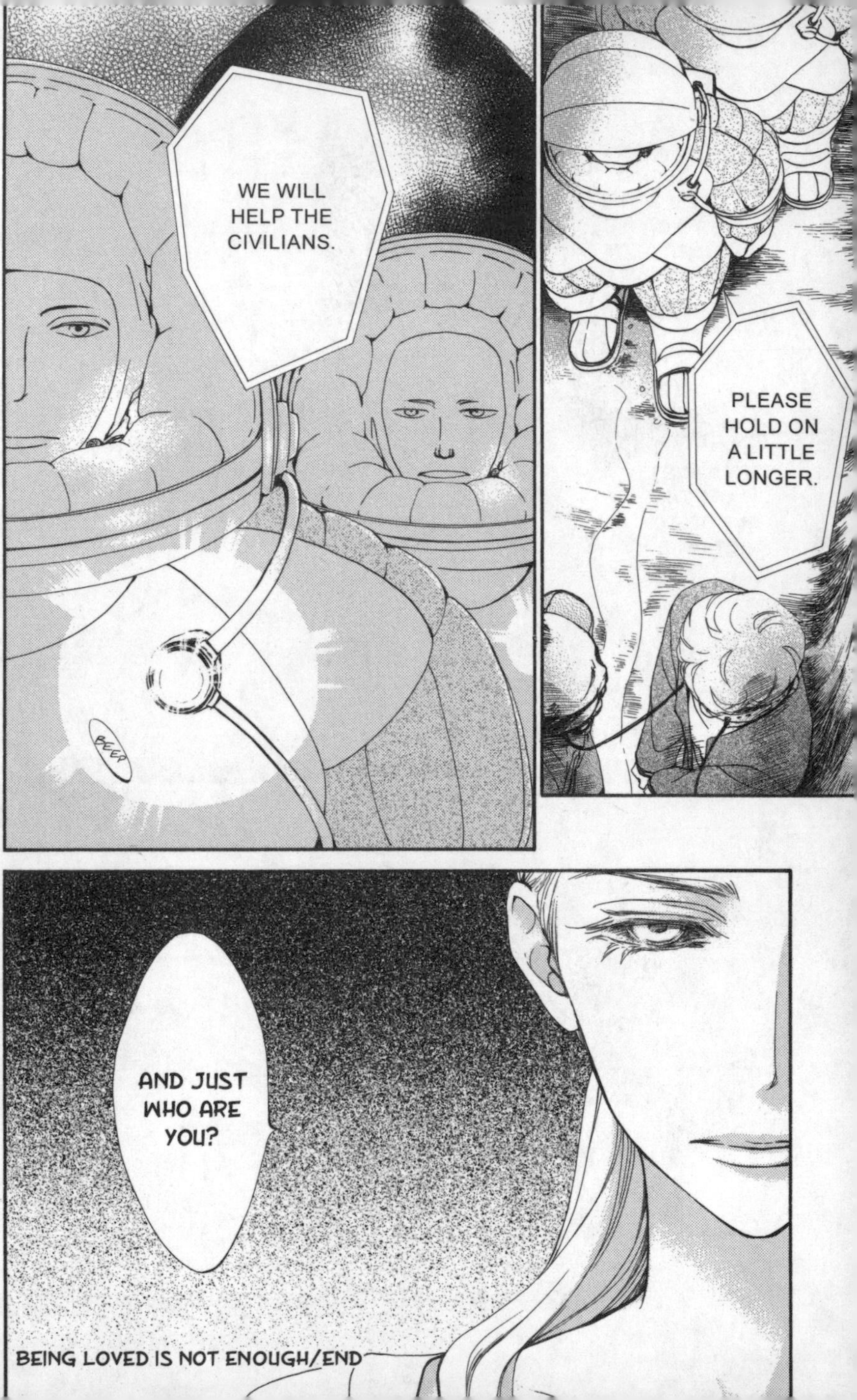
PLEASE HOLD ON A LITTLE LONGER.
WE WILL HELP THE CIVILIANS.
BEEP
AND JUST WHO ARE YOU?
BEING LOVED IS NOT ENOUGH/END

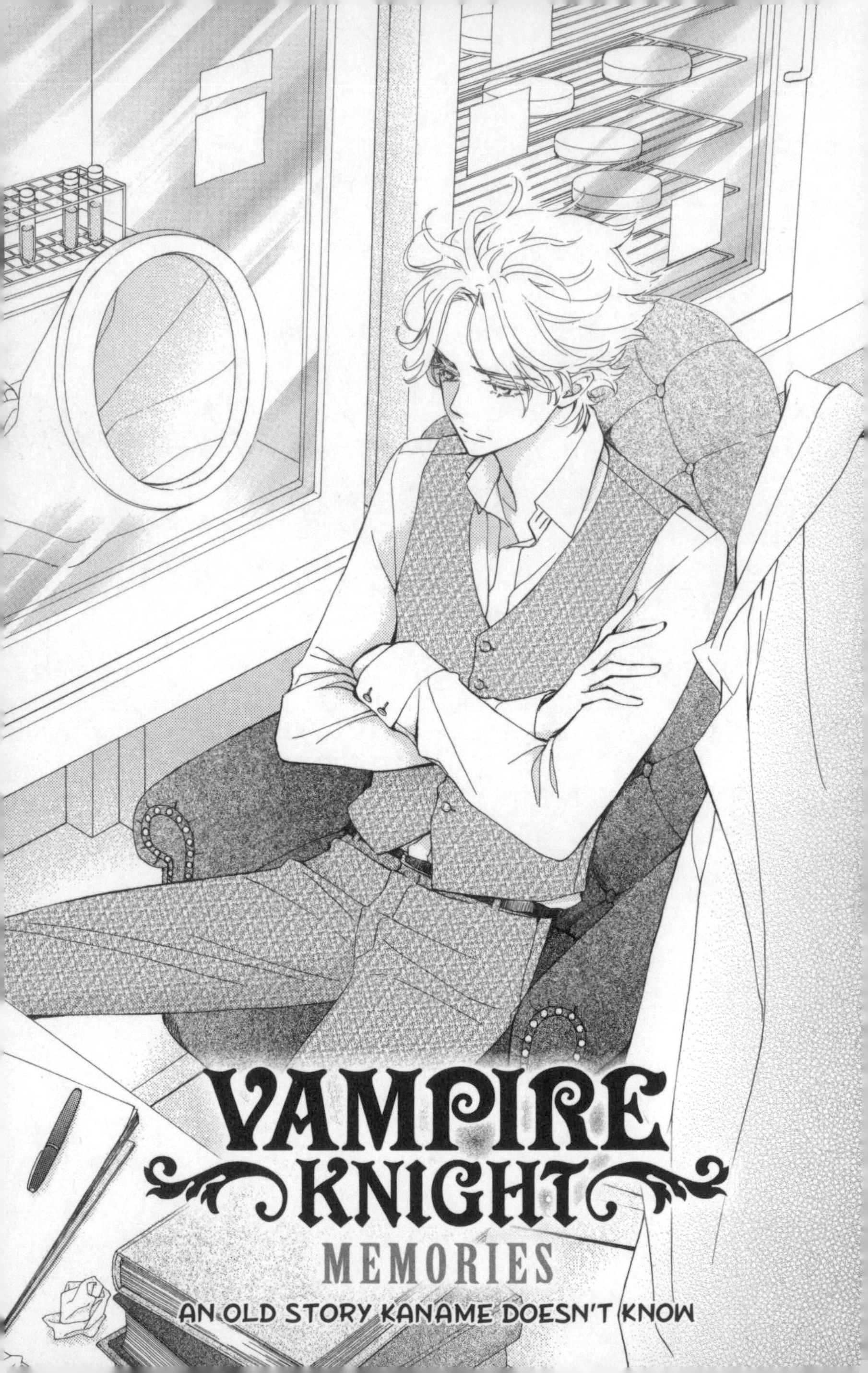
VAMPIRE KNIGHT
MEMORIES
AN OLD STORY KANAME DOESN'T KNOW

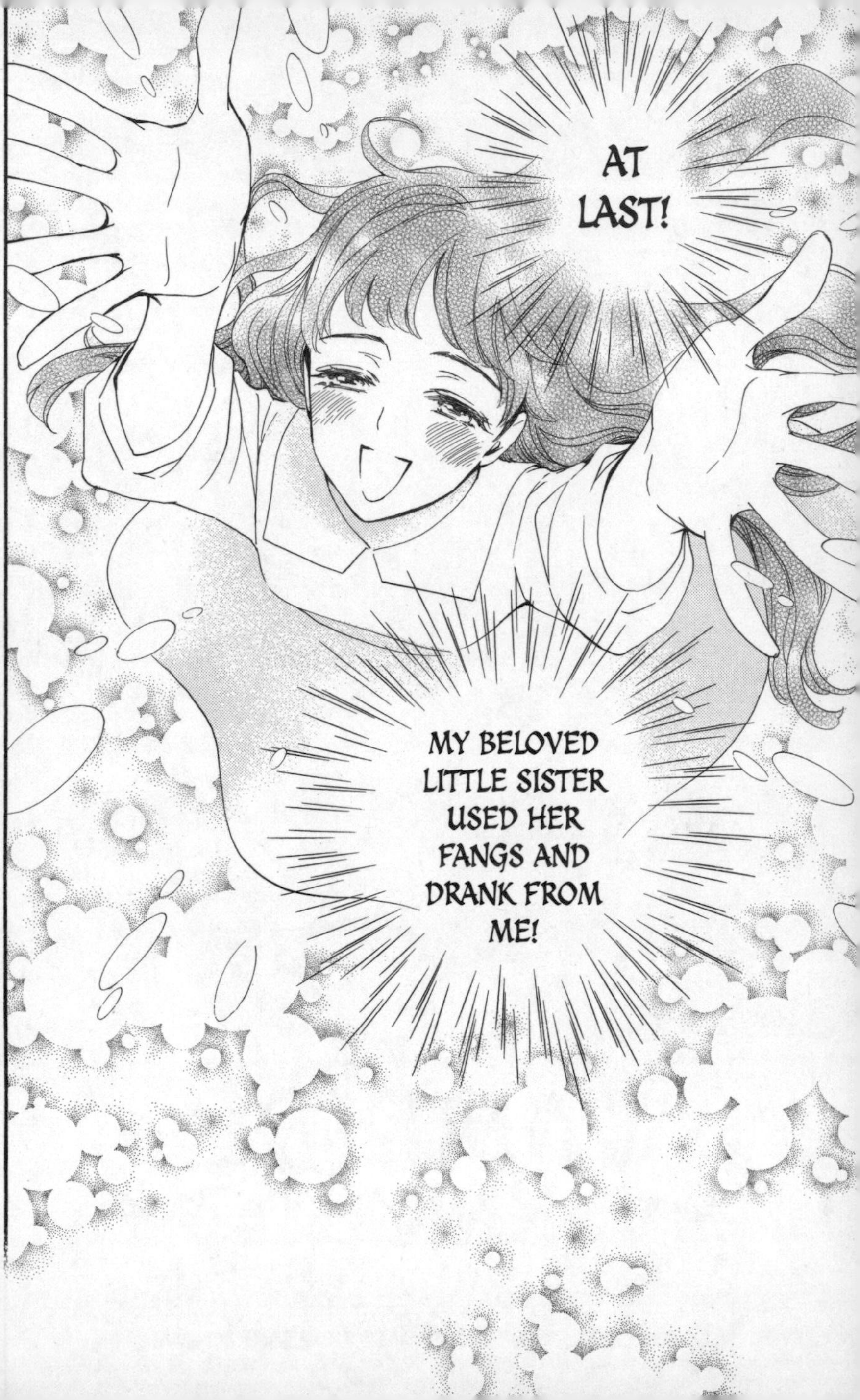
AT LAST!
MY BELOVED LITTLE SISTER USED HER FANGS AND DRANK FROM ME!

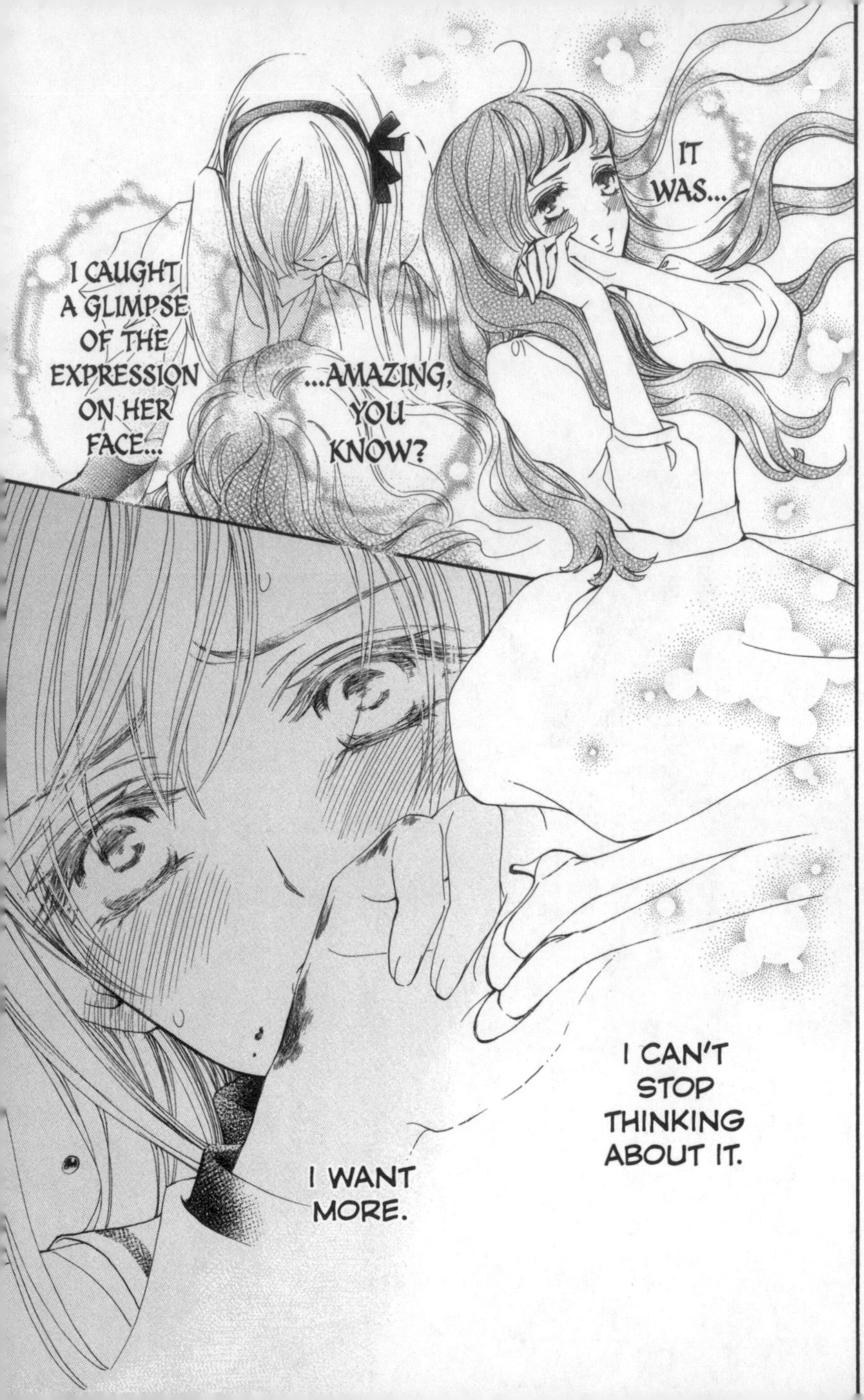
IT WAS...
...AMAZING, YOU KNOW?
I CAUGHT A GLIMPSE OF THE EXPRESSION ON HER FACE...
I CAN'T STOP THINKING ABOUT IT.
I WANT MORE.

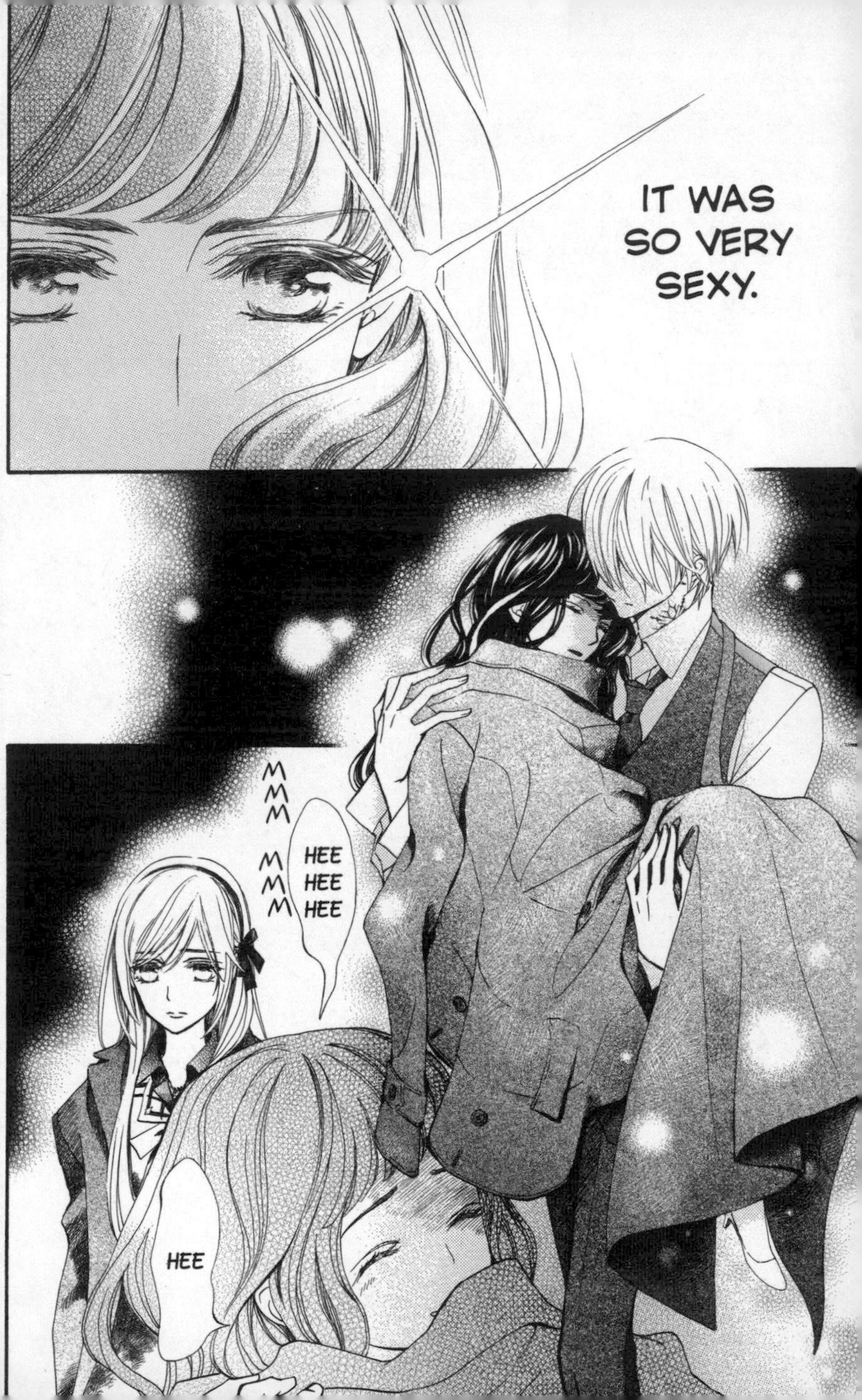
IT WAS SO VERY SEXY.
HEE HEE HEE
MMM MMM
HEE

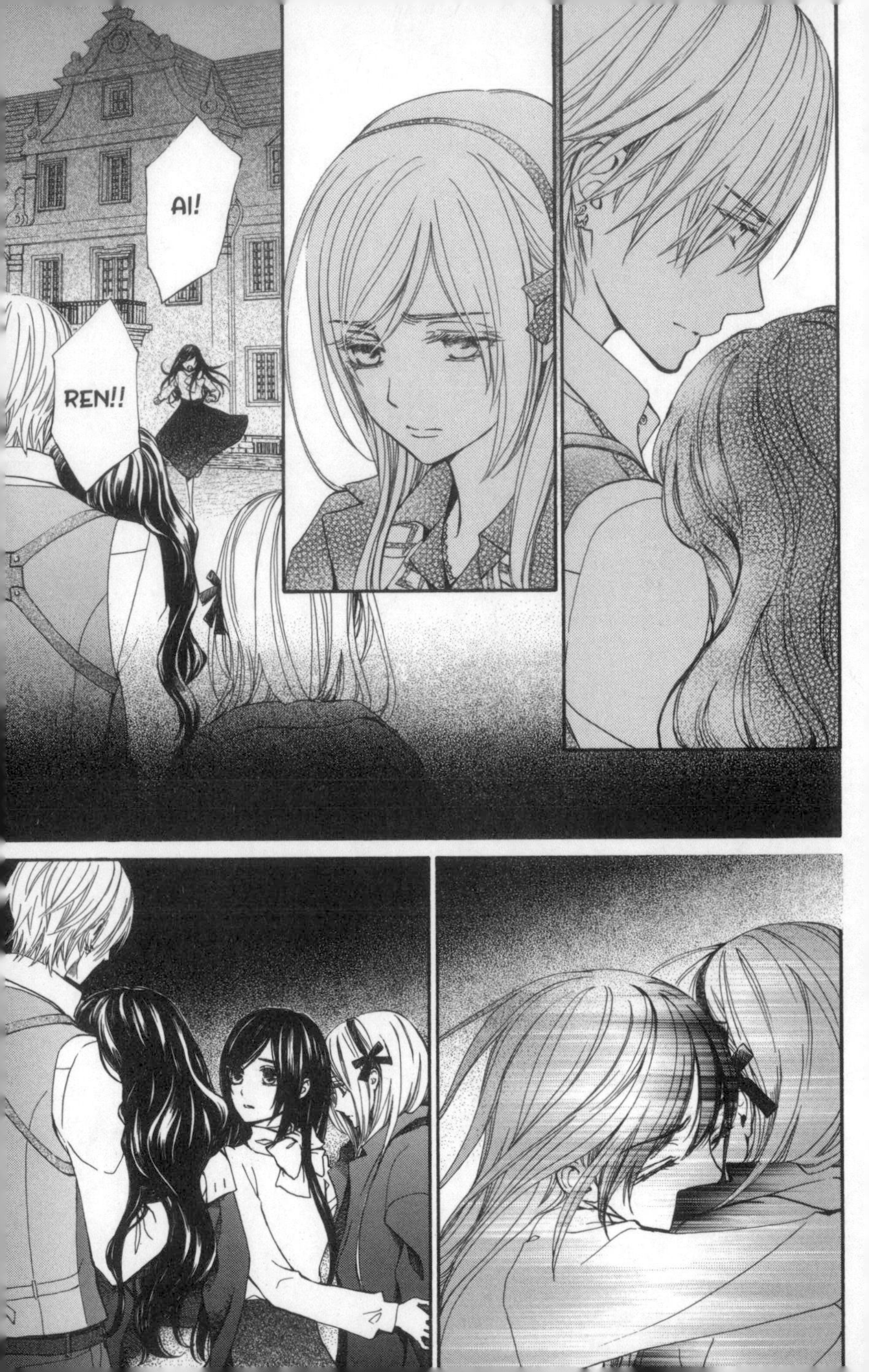
AI!
REN!!

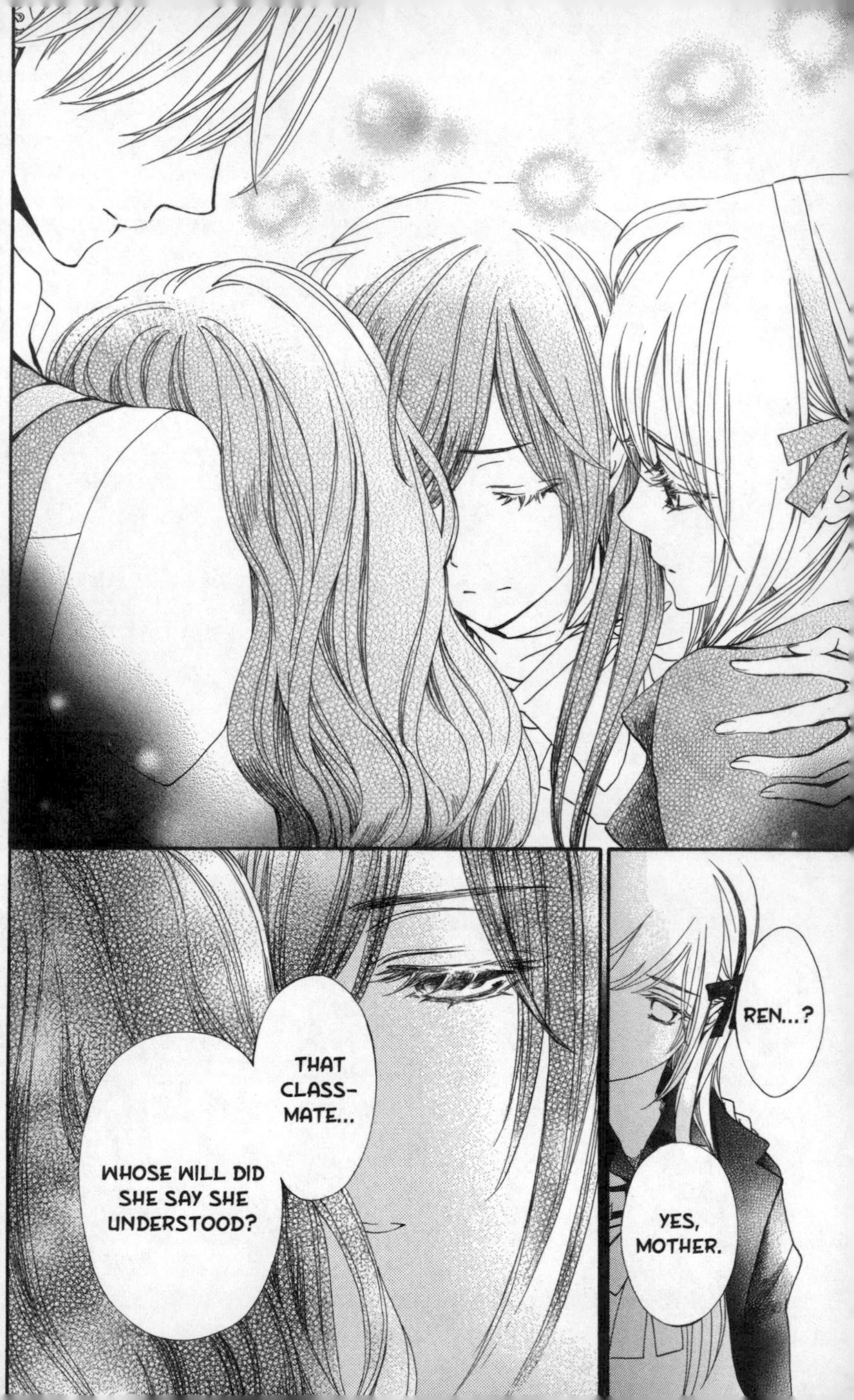
REN...?
YES, MOTHER.
THAT CLASS-MATE...
WHOSE WILL DID SHE SAY SHE UNDERSTOOD?

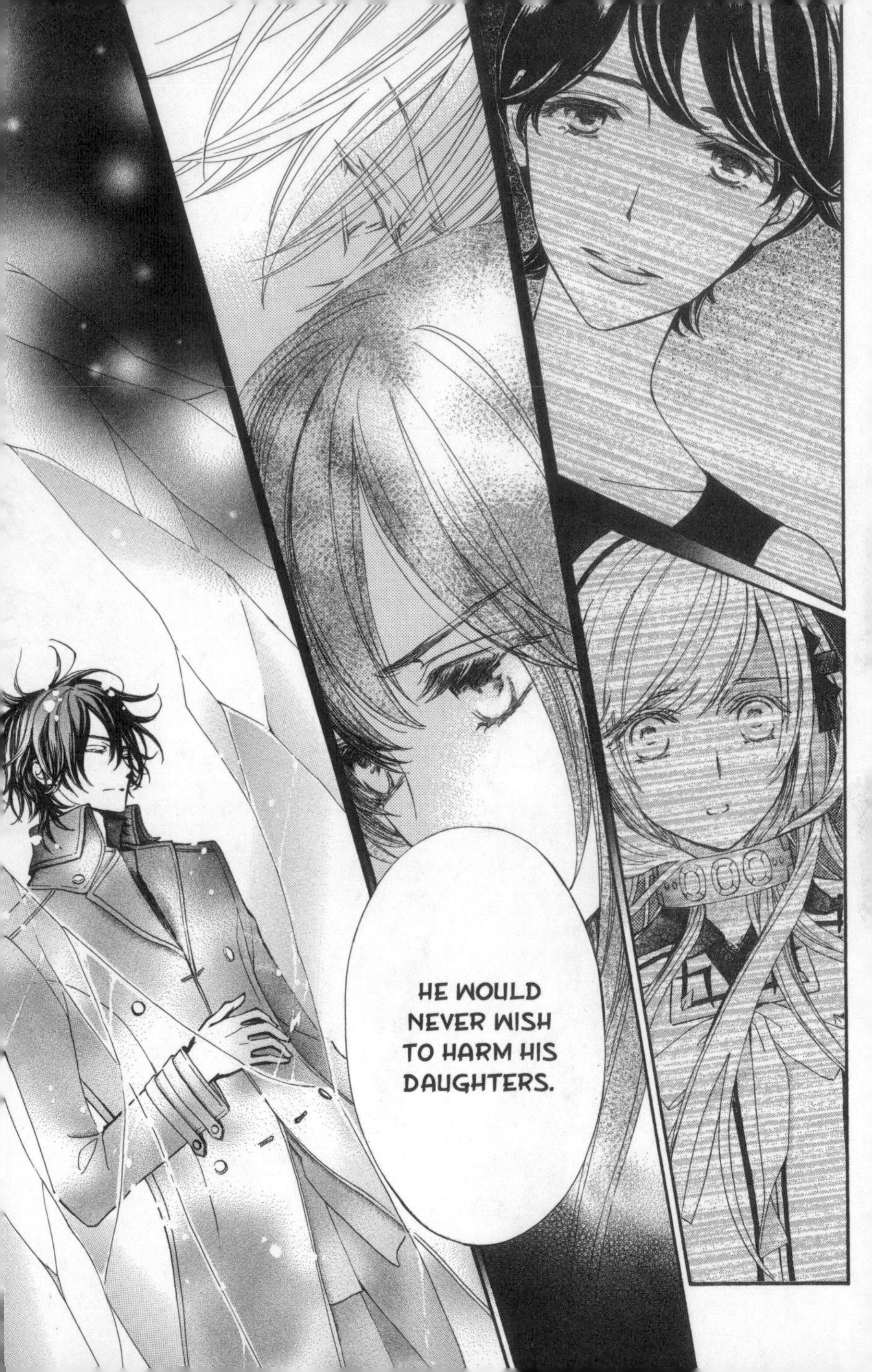
HE WOULD NEVER WISH TO HARM HIS DAUGHTERS.

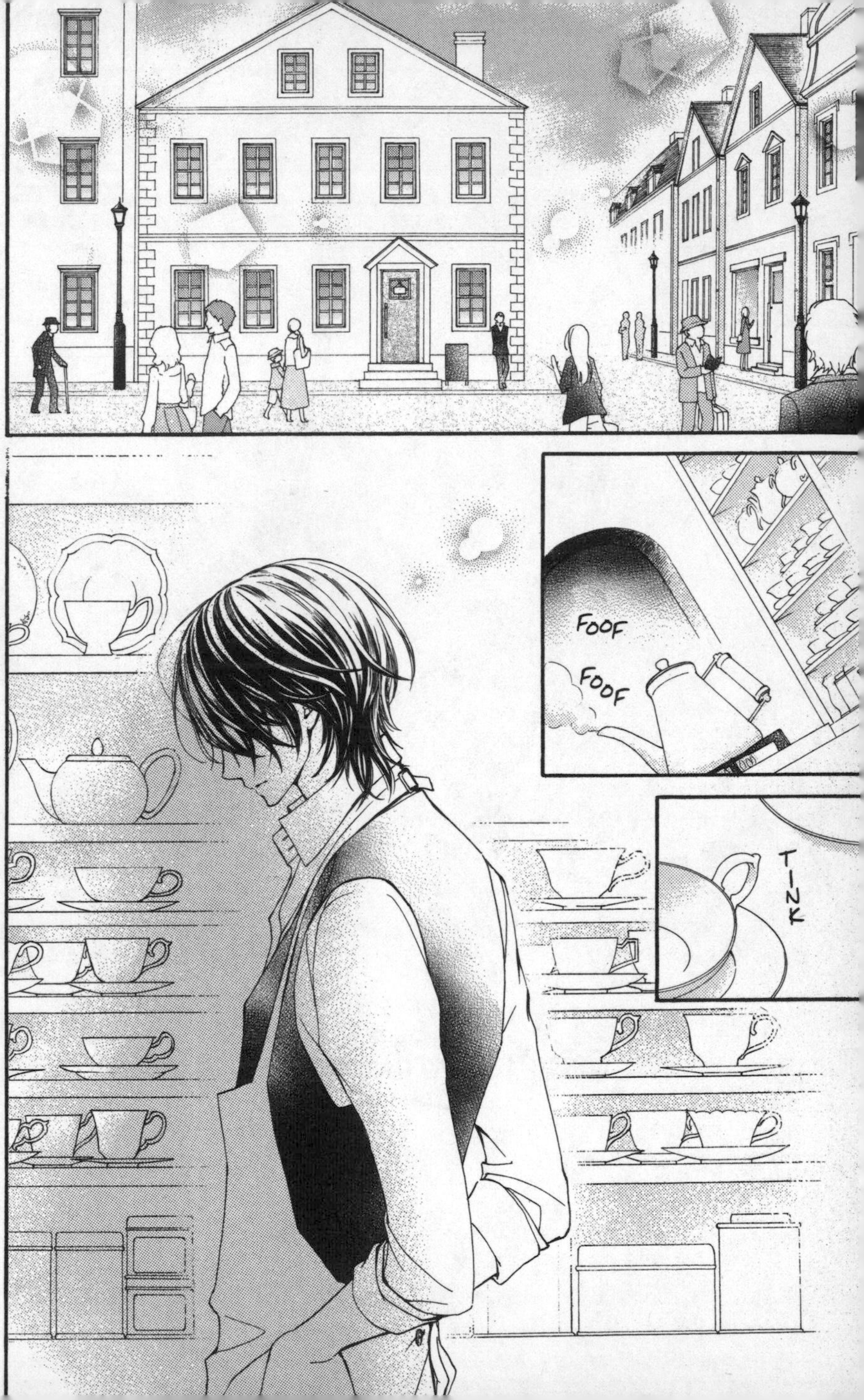
FOOF
FOOF
TINK

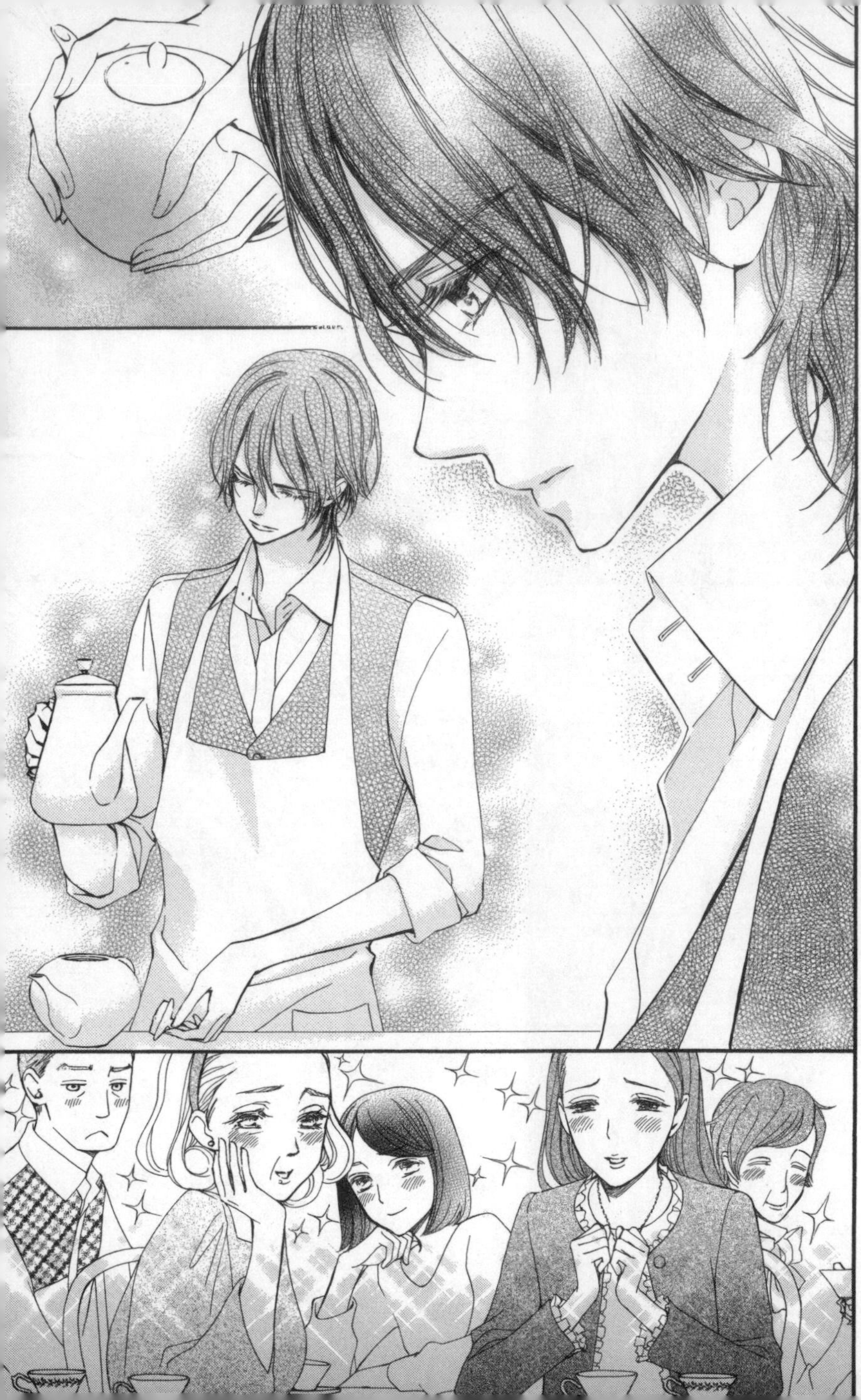

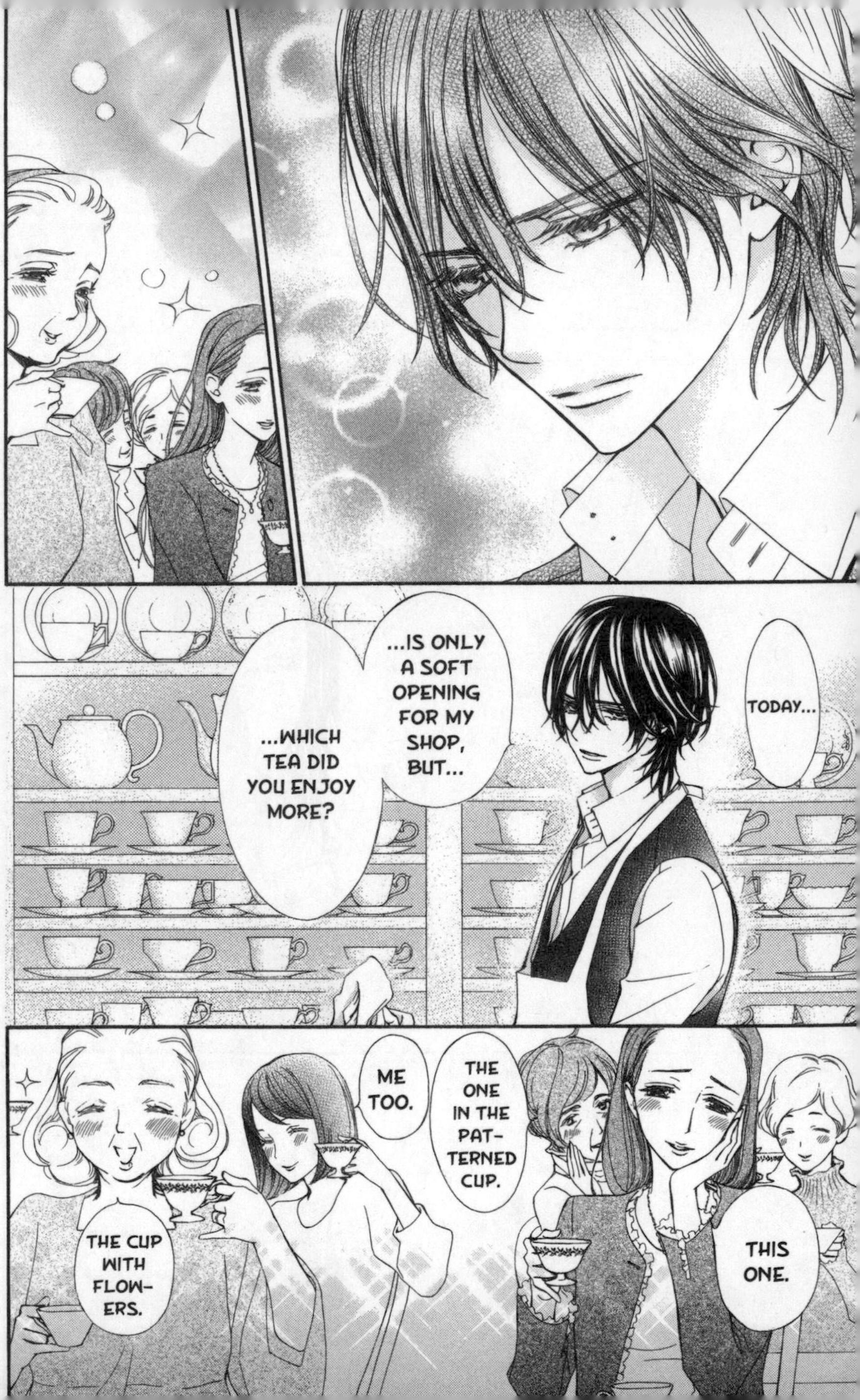
TODAY...
...IS ONLY A SOFT OPENING FOR MY SHOP, BUT...
...WHICH TEA DID YOU ENJOY MORE?
THIS ONE.
THE ONE IN THE PAT-TERNED CUP.
ME TOO.
THE CUP WITH FLOW-ERS.

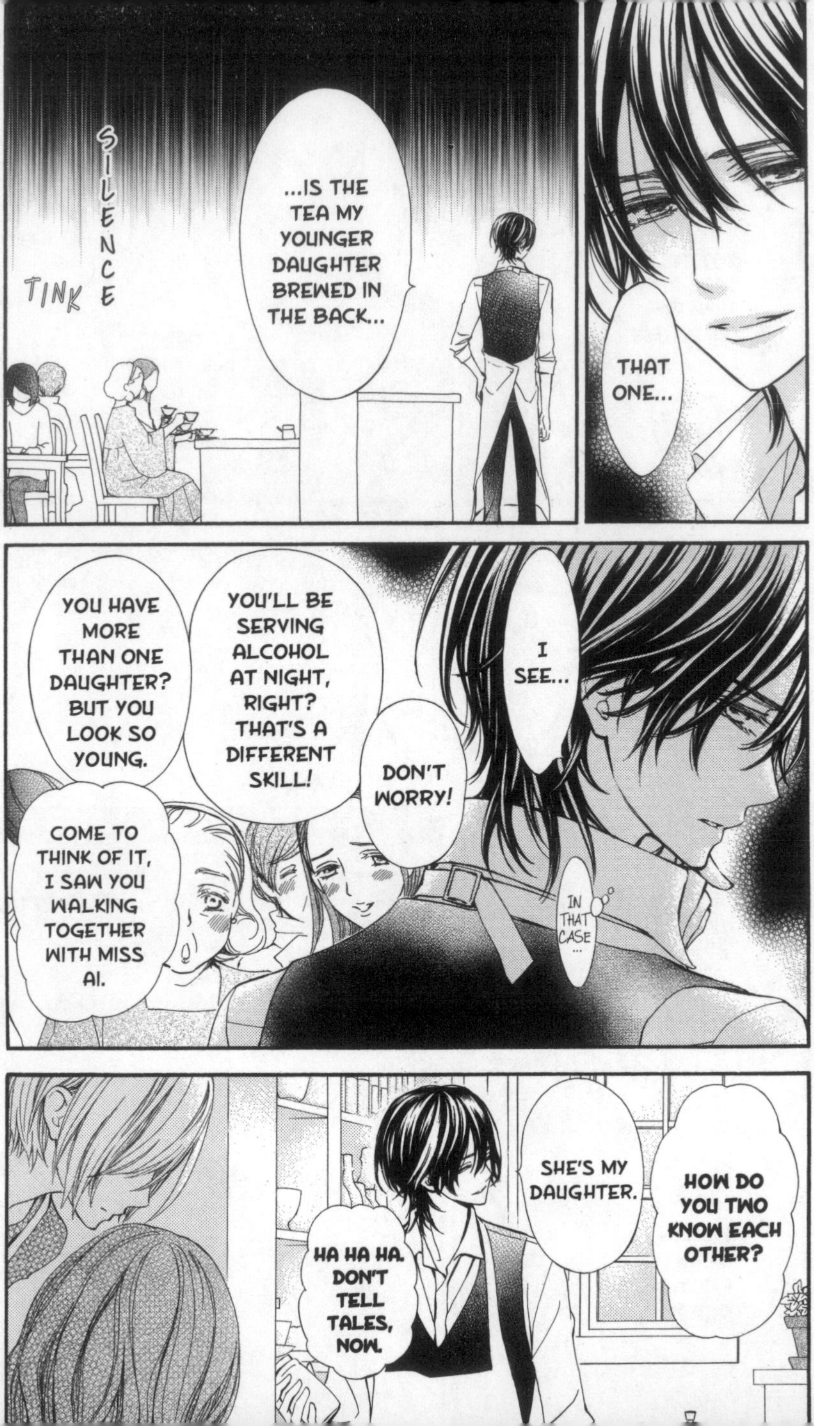
THAT ONE...
...IS THE TEA MY YOUNGER DAUGHTER BREWED IN THE BACK...
SILENCE
TINK
I SEE...
IN THAT CASE...
DON'T WORRY!
YOU'LL BE SERVING ALCOHOL AT NIGHT, RIGHT? THAT'S A DIFFERENT SKILL!
YOU HAVE MORE THAN ONE DAUGHTER? BUT YOU LOOK SO YOUNG.
COME TO THINK OF IT, I SAW YOU WALKING TOGETHER WITH MISS AI.
HOW DO YOU TWO KNOW EACH OTHER?
SHE'S MY DAUGHTER.
HA HA HA. DON'T TELL TALES, NOW.

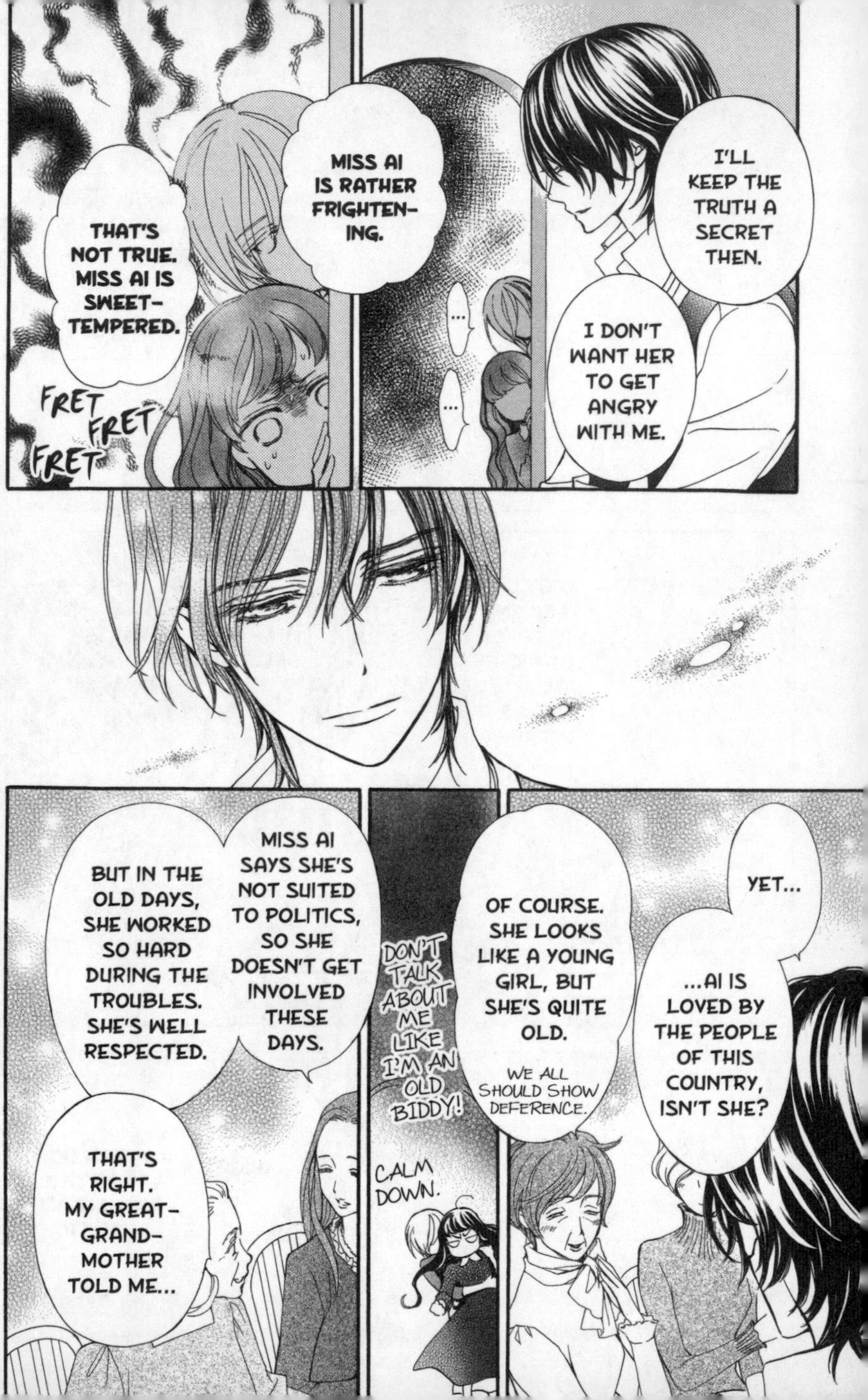
I'LL KEEP THE TRUTH A SECRET THEN.
I DON'T WANT HER TO GET ANGRY WITH ME.
MISS AI IS RATHER FRIGHTEN-ING.
...
...
THAT'S NOT TRUE. MISS AI IS SWEET-TEMPERED.
FRET FRET FRET
YET...
...AI IS LOVED BY THE PEOPLE OF THIS COUNTRY, ISN'T SHE?
OF COURSE. SHE LOOKS LIKE A YOUNG GIRL, BUT SHE'S QUITE OLD.
WE ALL SHOULD SHOW DEFERENCE.
DON'T TALK ABOUT ME LIKE I'M AN OLD BIDDY!
CALM DOWN.
MISS AI SAYS SHE'S NOT SUITED TO POLITICS, SO SHE DOESN'T GET INVOLVED THESE DAYS.
BUT IN THE OLD DAYS, SHE WORKED SO HARD DURING THE TROUBLES. SHE'S WELL RESPECTED.
THAT'S RIGHT. MY GREAT-GRANDMOTHER TOLD ME...

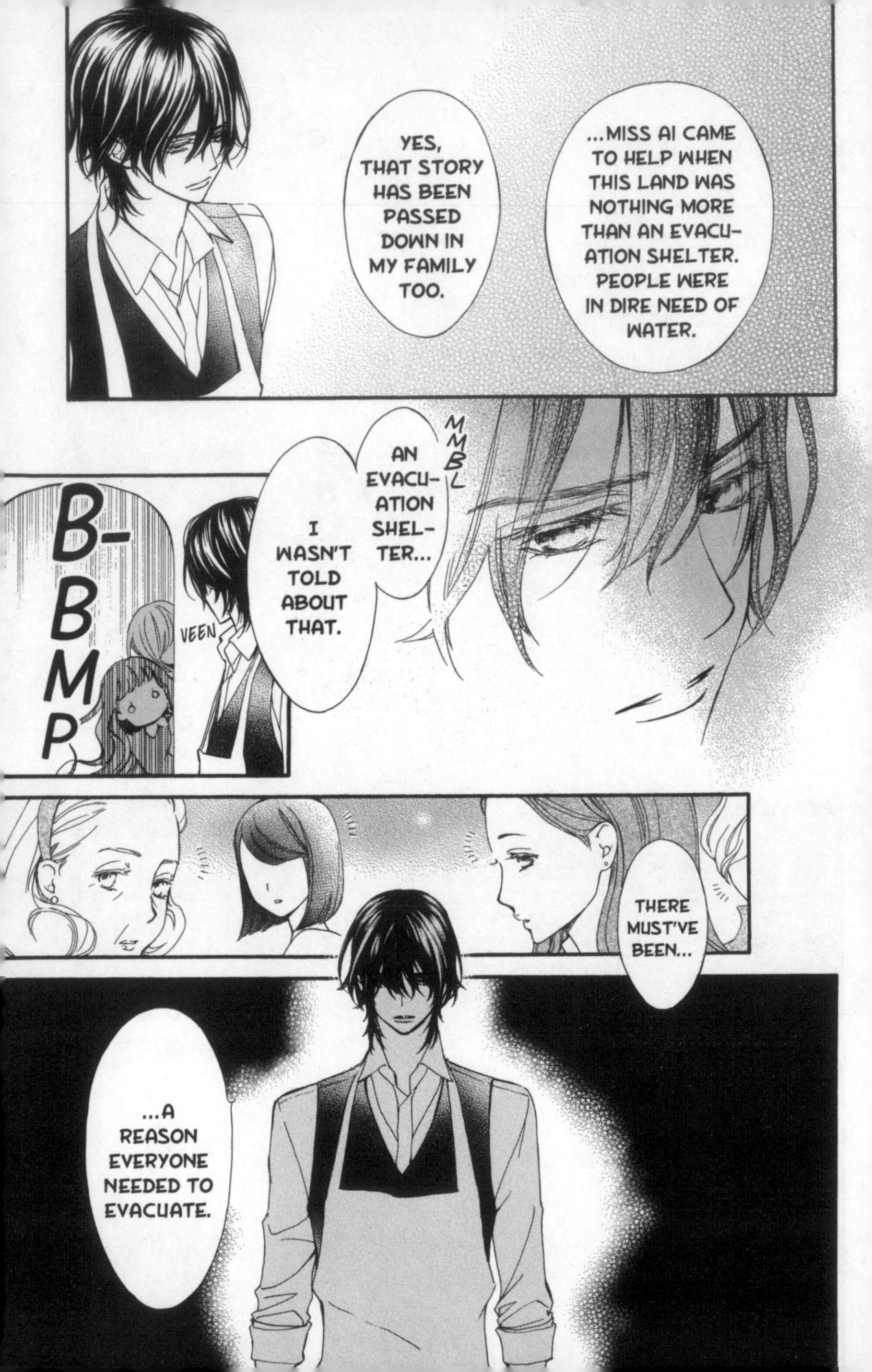
...MISS AI CAME TO HELP WHEN THIS LAND WAS NOTHING MORE THAN AN EVACU-ATION SHELTER. PEOPLE WERE IN DIRE NEED OF WATER.
YES, THAT STORY HAS BEEN PASSED DOWN IN MY FAMILY TOO.
MMBL
AN EVACU-ATION SHEL-TER...
I WASN'T TOLD ABOUT THAT.
VEEN
B-BMP
THERE MUST'VE BEEN...
...A REASON EVERYONE NEEDED TO EVACUATE.

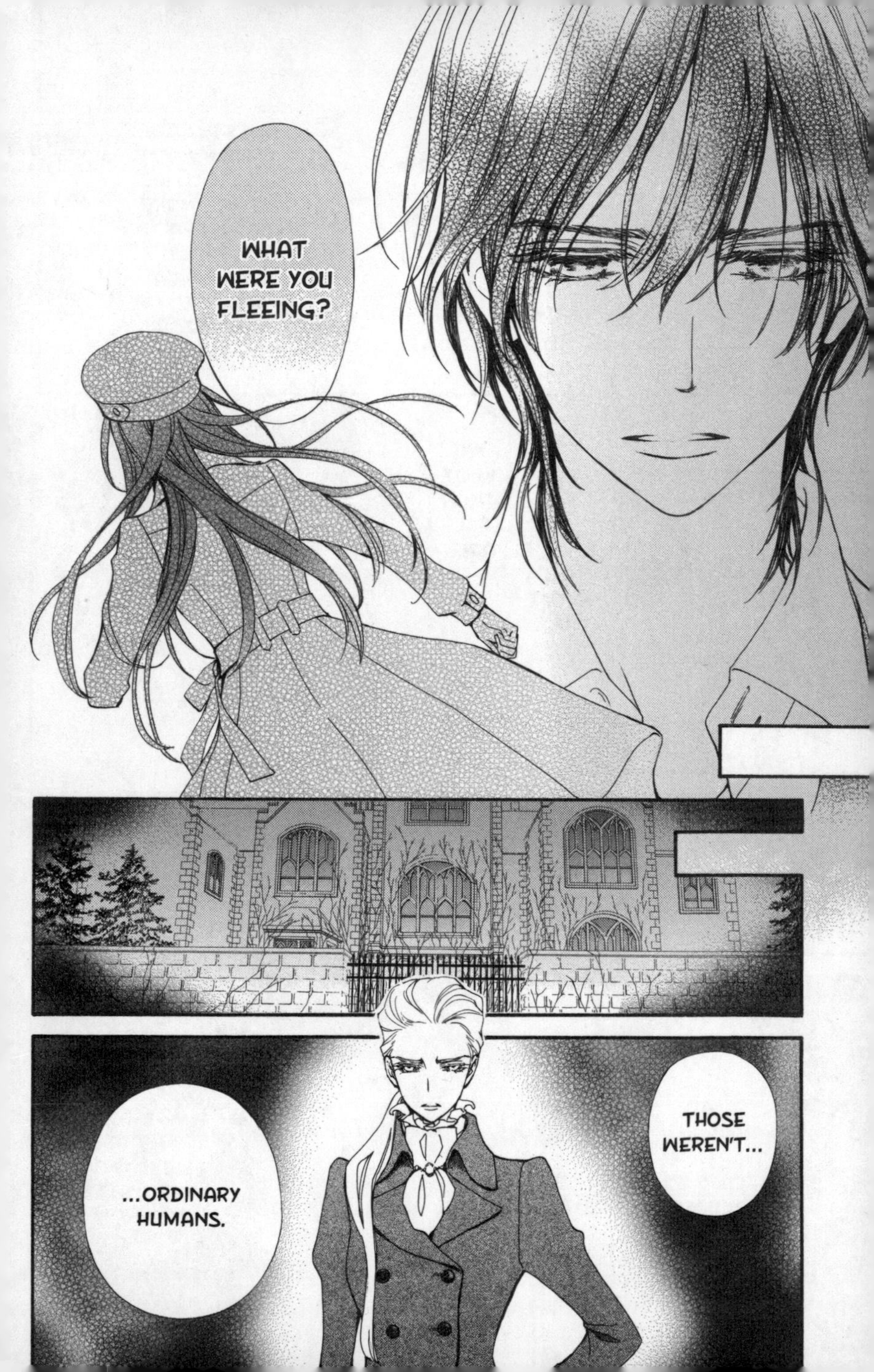
WHAT WERE YOU FLEEING?
THOSE WEREN'T...
...ORDINARY HUMANS.

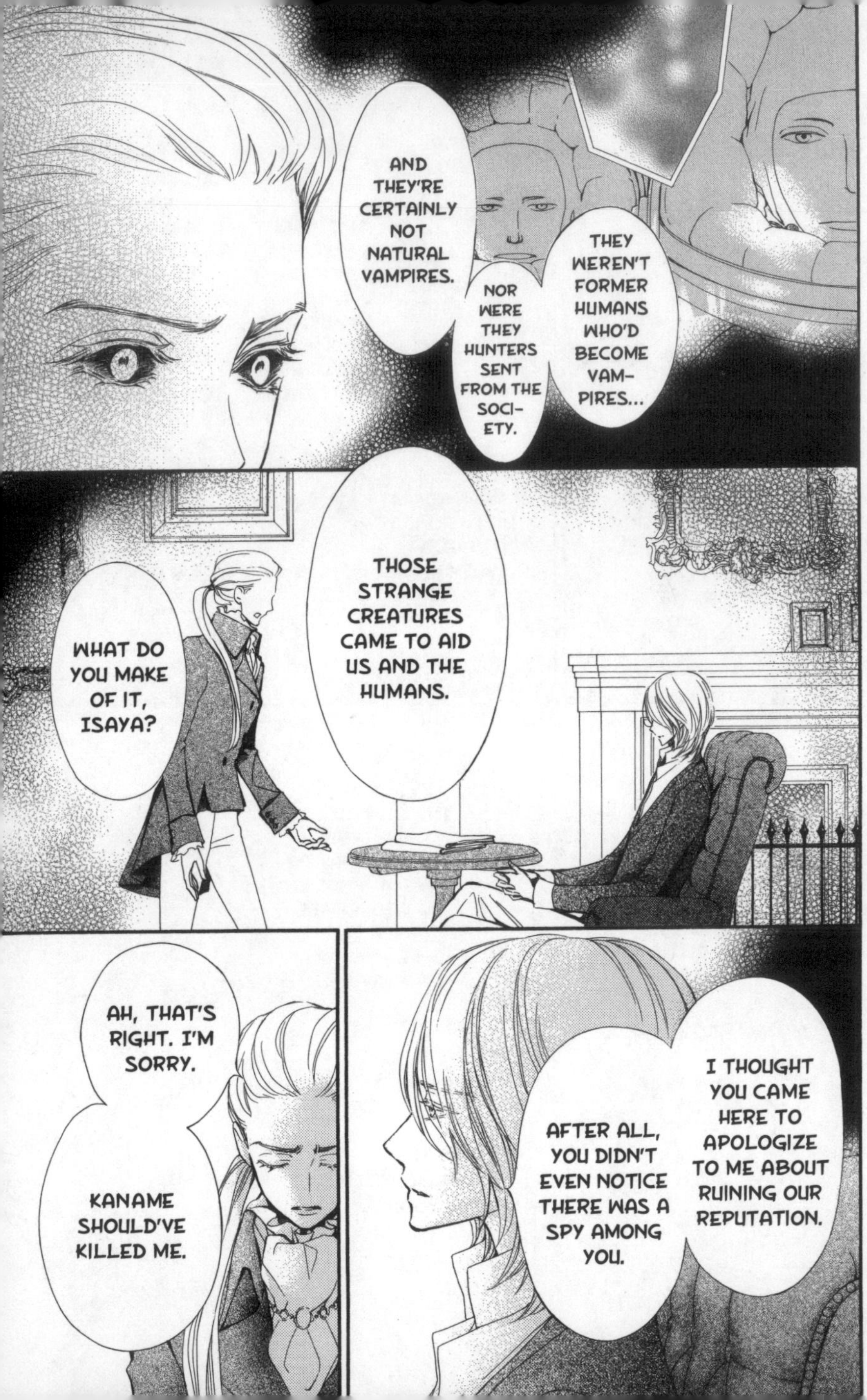
THEY WEREN'T FORMER HUMANS WHO'D BECOME VAM-PIRES...
NOR WERE THEY HUNTERS SENT FROM THE SOCI-ETY.
AND THEY'RE CERTAINLY NOT NATURAL VAMPIRES.
THOSE STRANGE CREATURES CAME TO AID US AND THE HUMANS.
WHAT DO YOU MAKE OF IT, ISAYA?
I THOUGHT YOU CAME HERE TO APOLOGIZE TO ME ABOUT RUINING OUR REPUTATION.
AFTER ALL, YOU DIDN'T EVEN NOTICE THERE WAS A SPY AMONG YOU.
AH, THAT'S RIGHT. I'M SORRY.
KANAME SHOULD'VE KILLED ME.

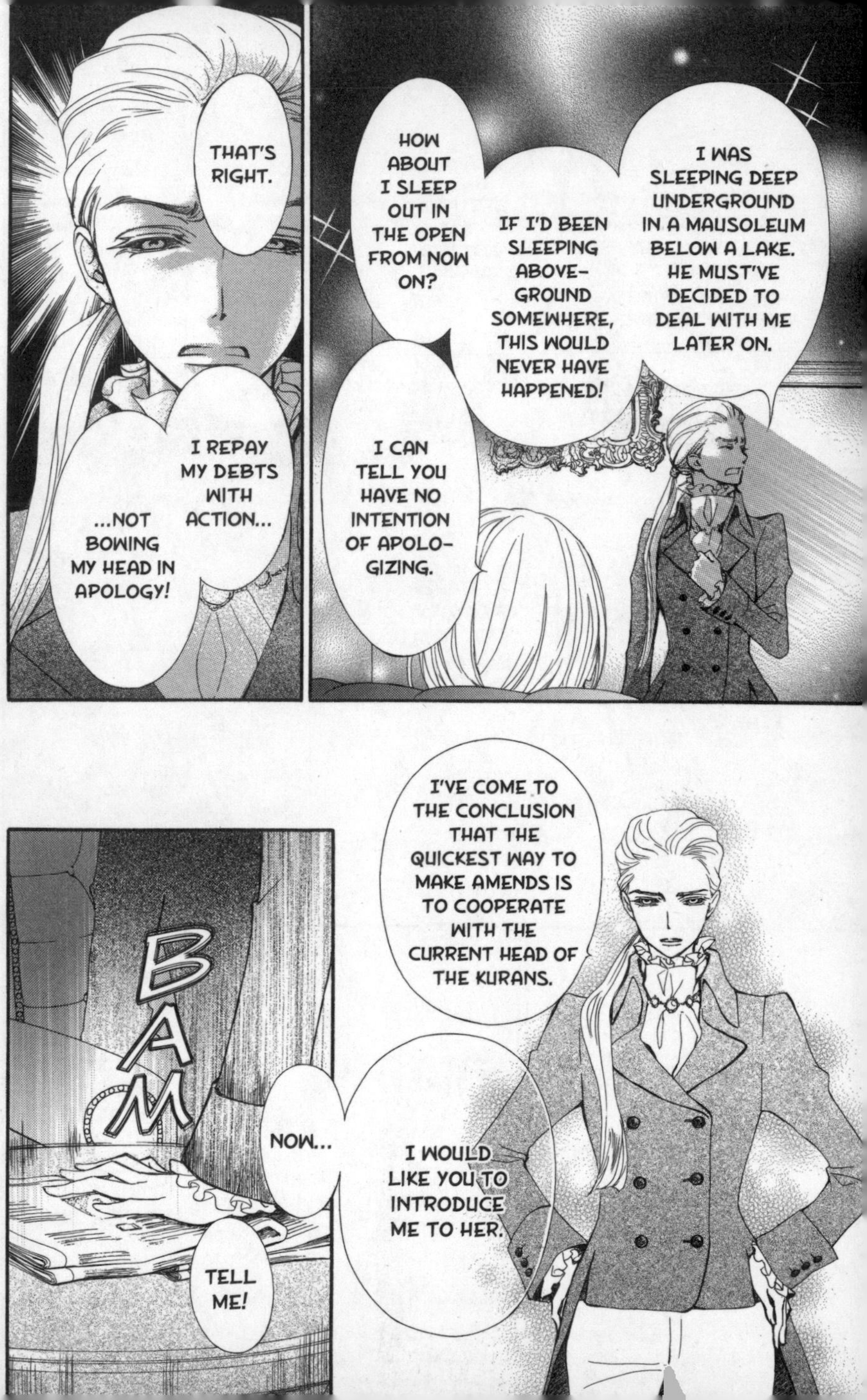
I WAS SLEEPING DEEP UNDERGROUND IN A MAUSOLEUM BELOW A LAKE. HE MUST'VE DECIDED TO DEAL WITH ME LATER ON.
IF I'D BEEN SLEEPING ABOVE-GROUND SOMEWHERE, THIS WOULD NEVER HAVE HAPPENED!
HOW ABOUT I SLEEP OUT IN THE OPEN FROM NOW ON?
I CAN TELL YOU HAVE NO INTENTION OF APOLO-GIZING.
THAT'S RIGHT.
I REPAY MY DEBTS WITH ACTION...
...NOT BOWING MY HEAD IN APOLOGY!
I'VE COME TO THE CONCLUSION THAT THE QUICKEST WAY TO MAKE AMENDS IS TO COOPERATE WITH THE CURRENT HEAD OF THE KURANS.
NOW...
I WOULD LIKE YOU TO INTRODUCE ME TO HER.
BAM
TELL ME!

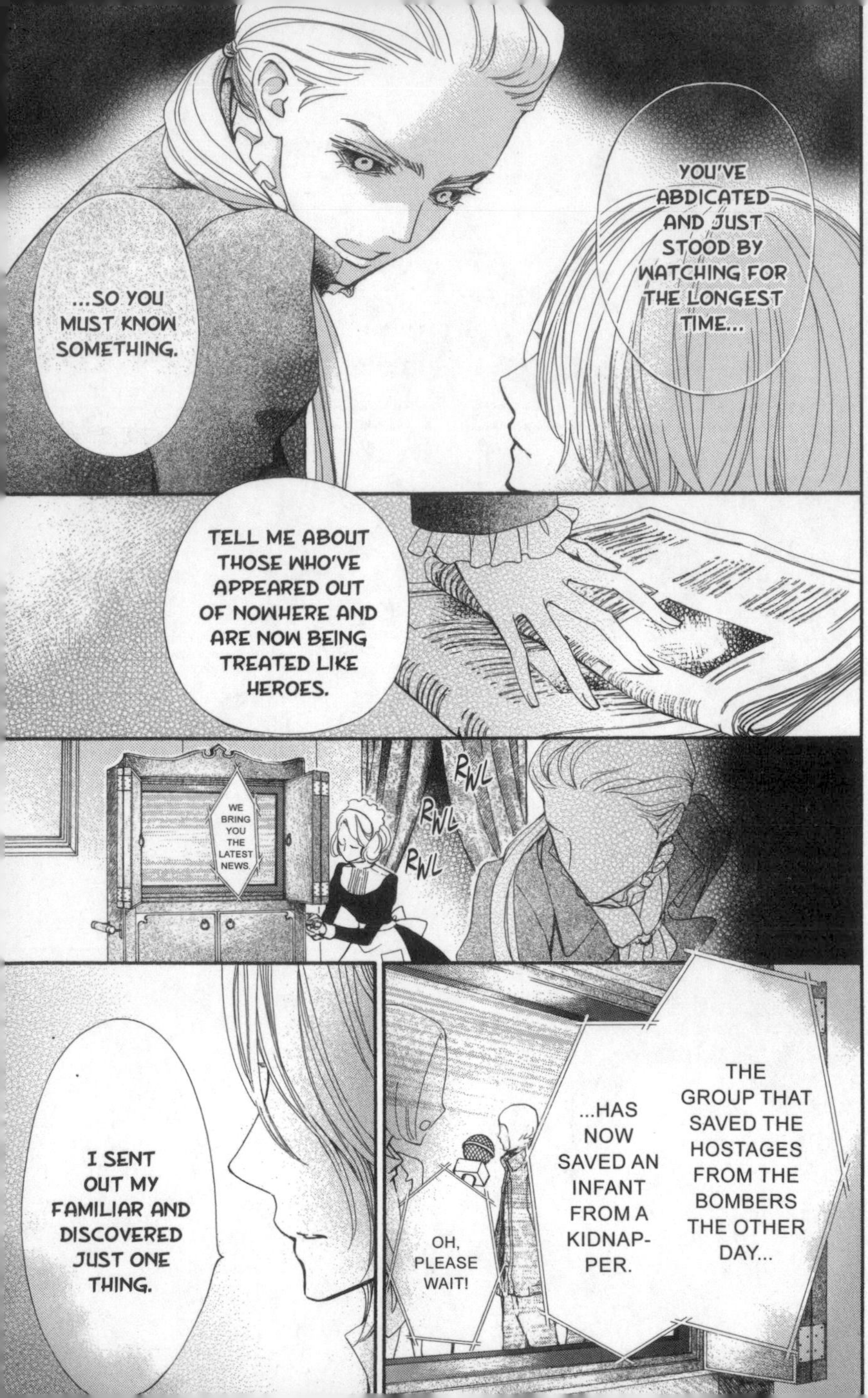
YOU'VE ABDICATED AND JUST STOOD BY WATCHING FOR THE LONGEST TIME...
...SO YOU MUST KNOW SOMETHING.
TELL ME ABOUT THOSE WHO'VE APPEARED OUT OF NOWHERE AND ARE NOW BEING TREATED LIKE HEROES.
RWL
RWL
RWL
WE BRING YOU THE LATEST NEWS.
THE GROUP THAT SAVED THE HOSTAGES FROM THE BOMBERS THE OTHER DAY...
...HAS NOW SAVED AN INFANT FROM A KIDNAP-PER.
OH, PLEASE WAIT!
I SENT OUT MY FAMILIAR AND DISCOVERED JUST ONE THING.

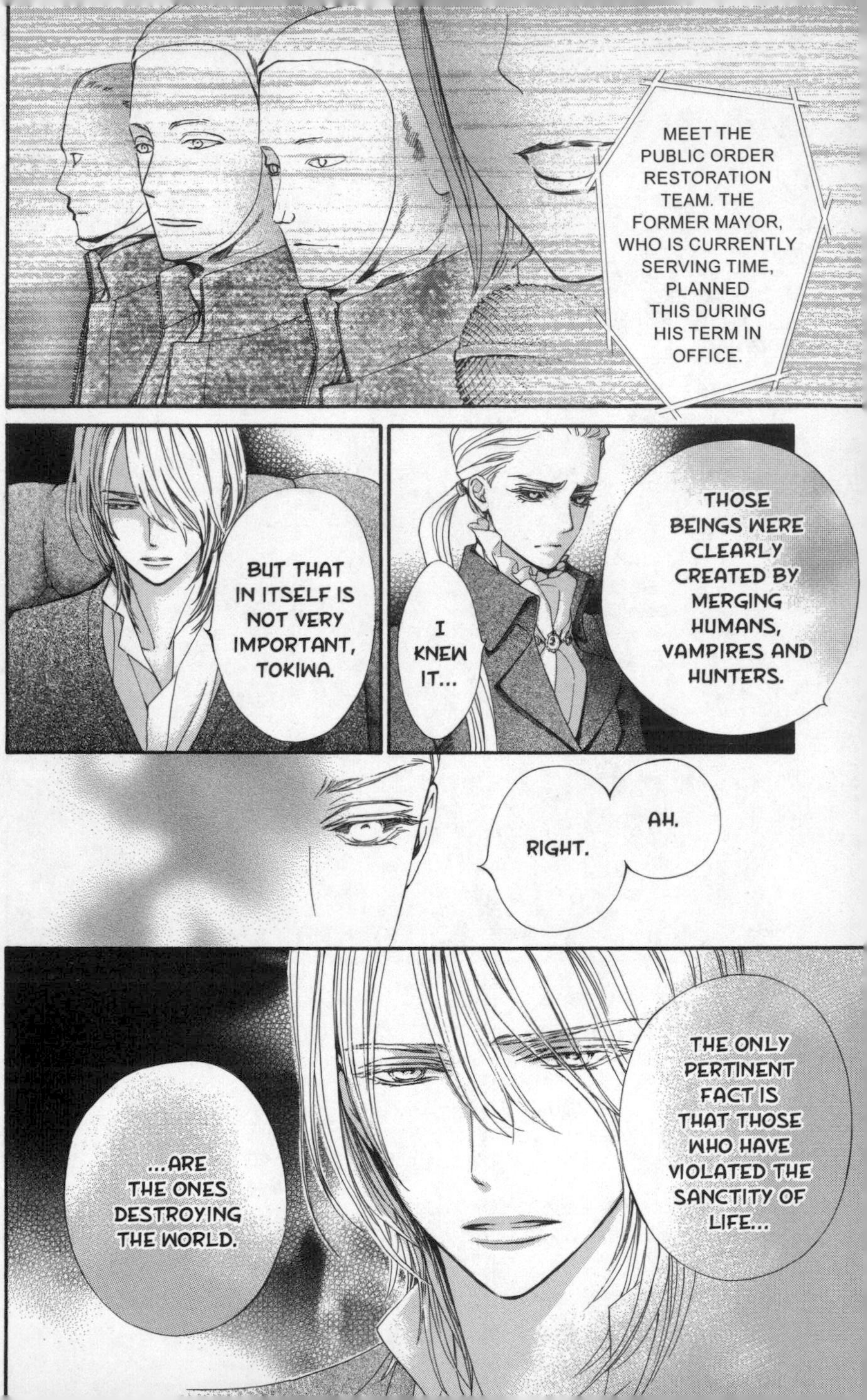
MEET THE PUBLIC ORDER RESTORATION TEAM. THE FORMER MAYOR, WHO IS CURRENTLY SERVING TIME, PLANNED THIS DURING HIS TERM IN OFFICE.
THOSE BEINGS WERE CLEARLY CREATED BY MERGING HUMANS, VAMPIRES AND HUNTERS.
I KNEW IT...
BUT THAT IN ITSELF IS NOT VERY IMPORTANT, TOKIWA.
AH.
RIGHT.
THE ONLY PERTINENT FACT IS THAT THOSE WHO HAVE VIOLATED THE SANCTITY OF LIFE...
...ARE THE ONES DESTROYING THE WORLD.

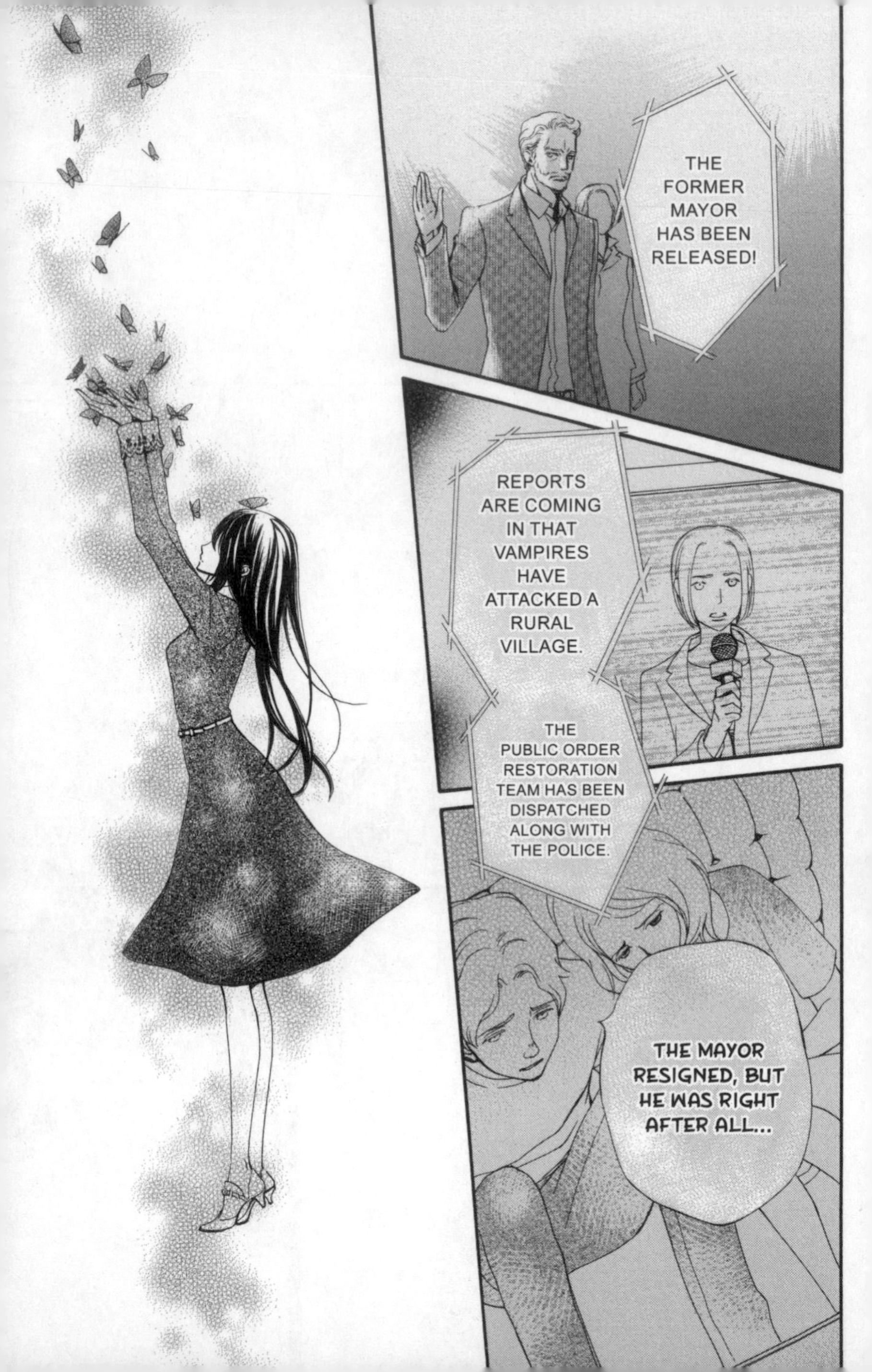
THE FORMER MAYOR HAS BEEN RELEASED!
REPORTS ARE COMING IN THAT VAMPIRES HAVE ATTACKED A RURAL VILLAGE.
THE PUBLIC ORDER RESTORATION TEAM HAS BEEN DISPATCHED ALONG WITH THE POLICE.
THE MAYOR RESIGNED, BUT HE WAS RIGHT AFTER ALL...

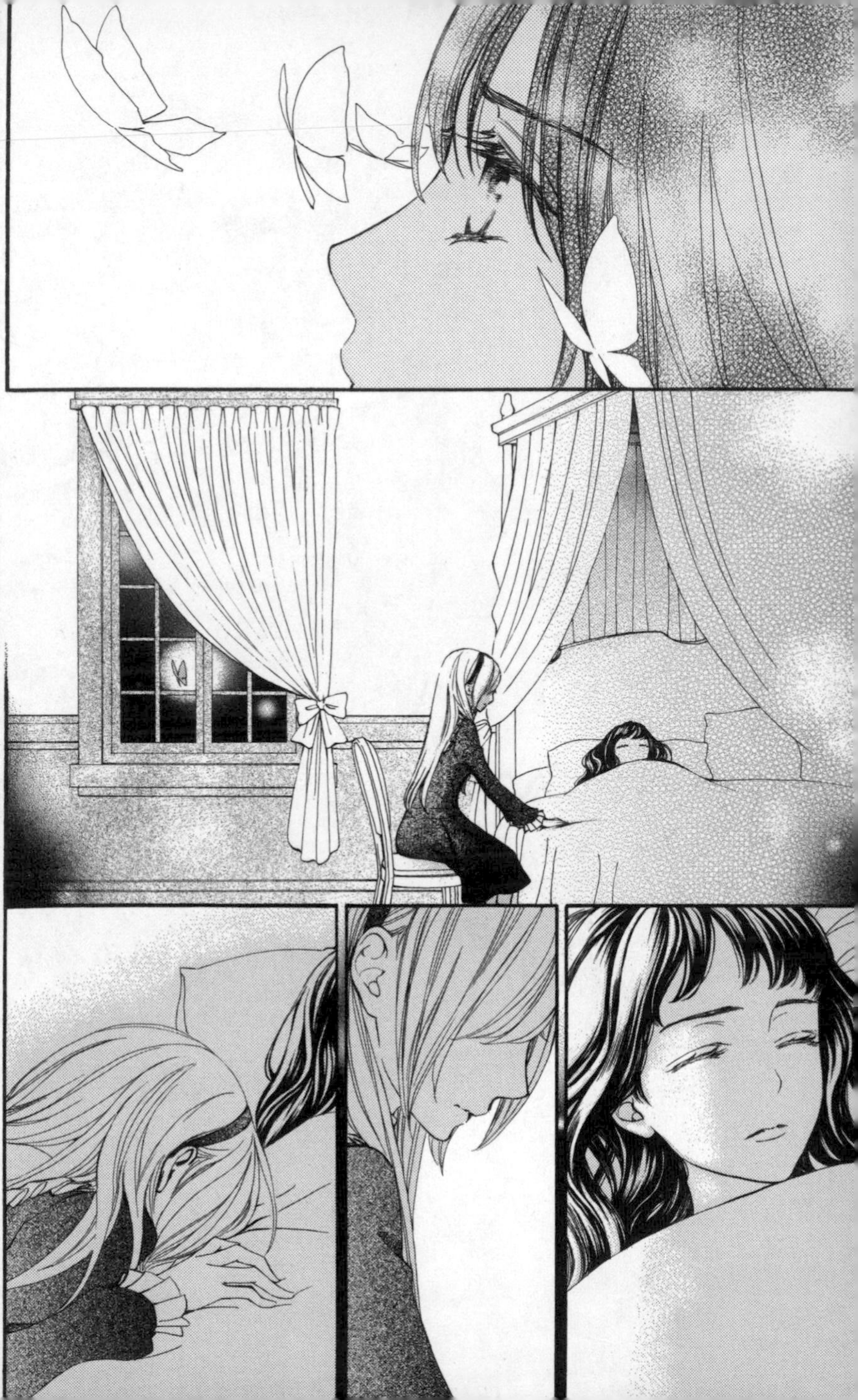

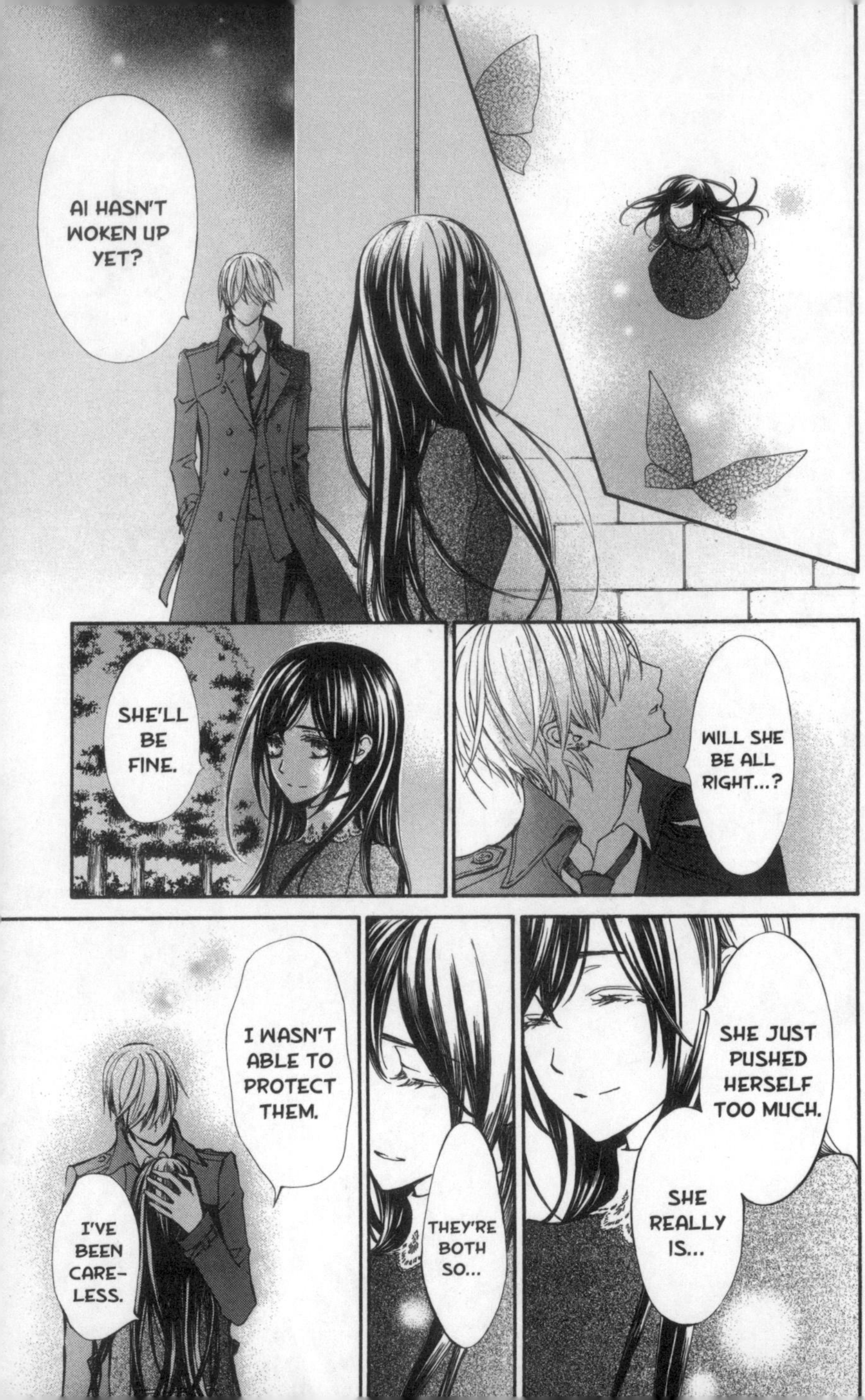
AI HASN'T WOKEN UP YET?
WILL SHE BE ALL RIGHT...?
SHE'LL BE FINE.
SHE JUST PUSHED HERSELF TOO MUCH.
SHE REALLY IS...
THEY'RE BOTH SO...
I WASN'T ABLE TO PROTECT THEM.
I'VE BEEN CARE-LESS.

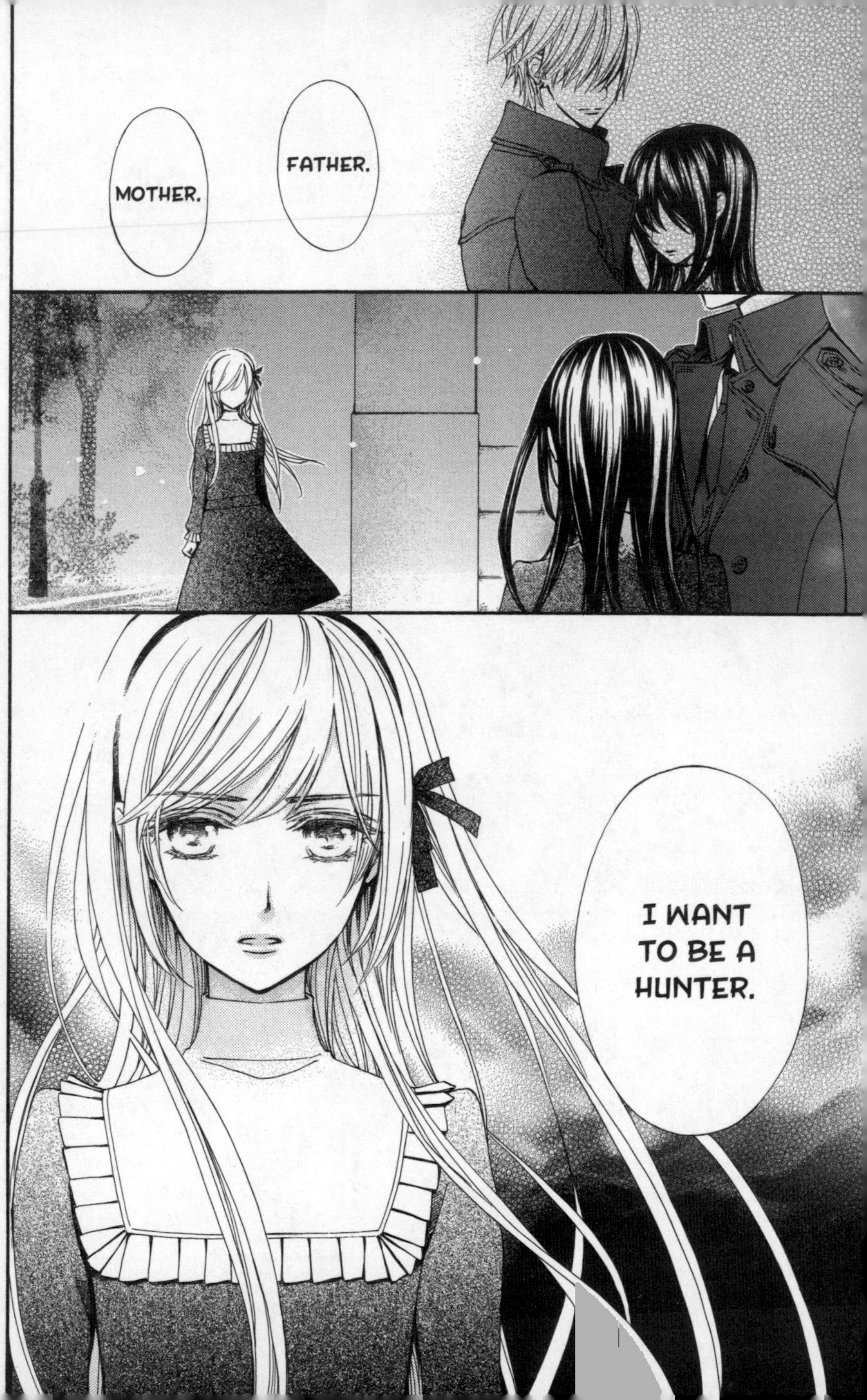
FATHER.
MOTHER.
I WANT TO BE A HUNTER.

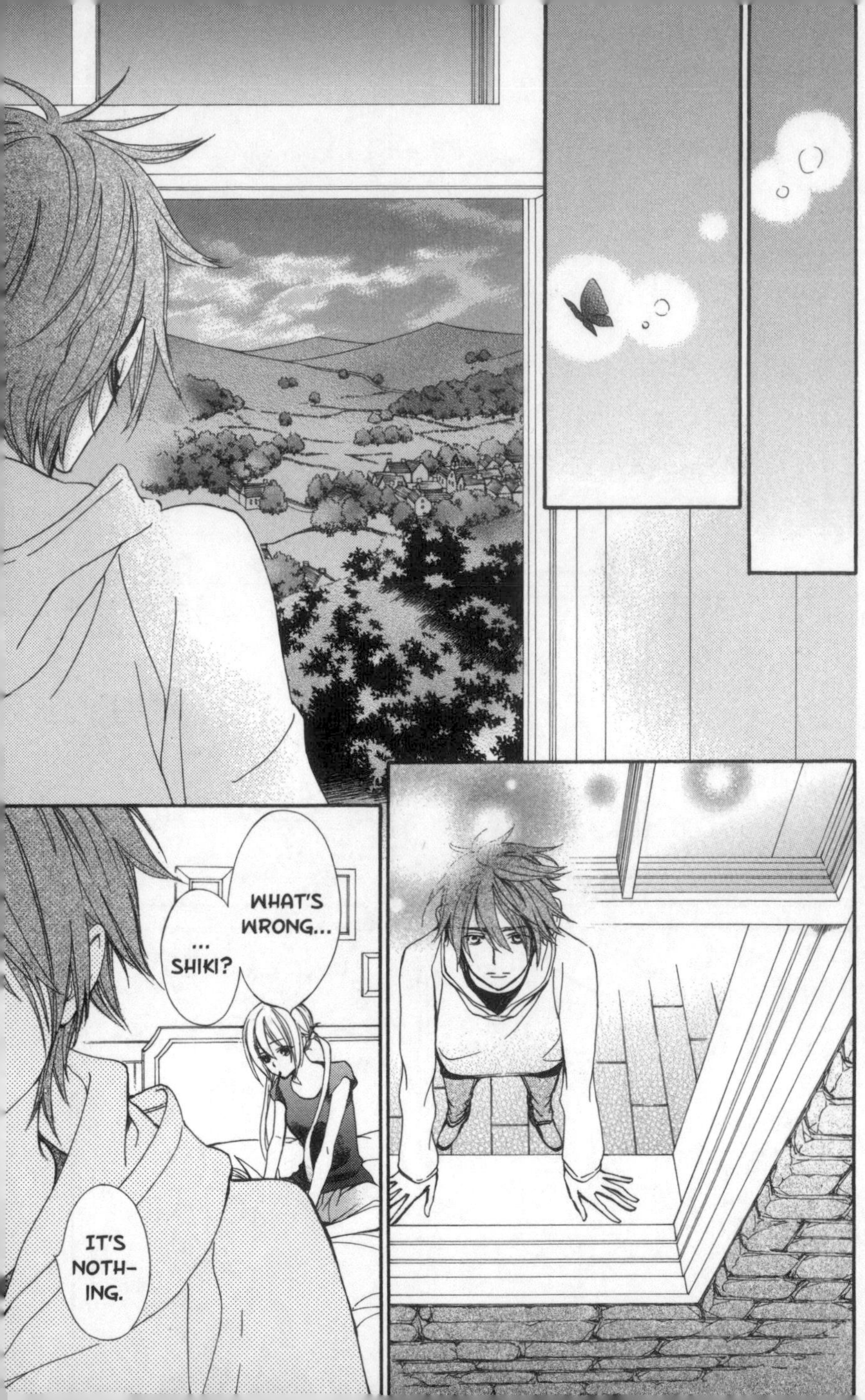
WHAT'S WRONG...
... SHIKI?
IT'S NOTH-ING.

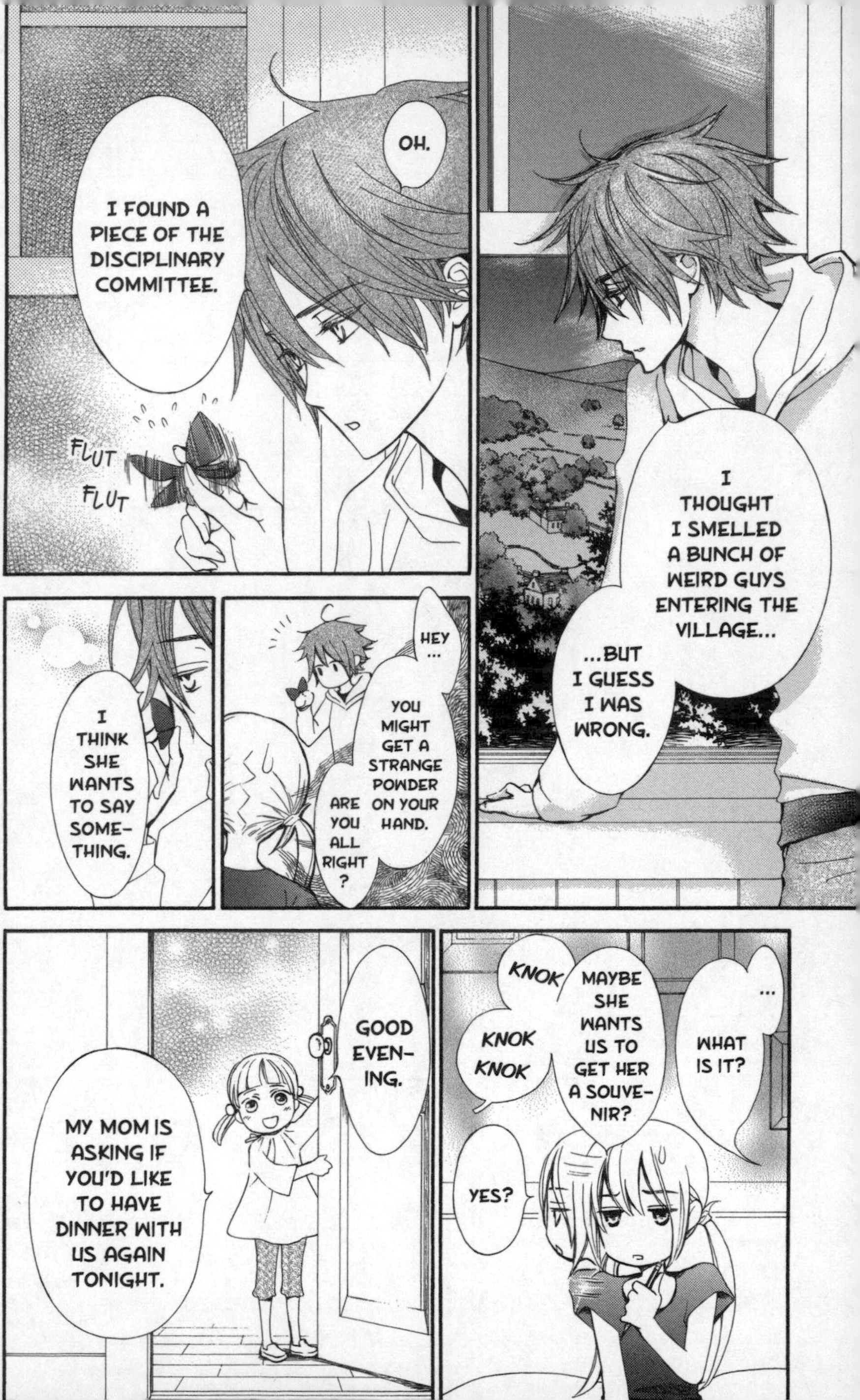
I THOUGHT I SMELLED A BUNCH OF WEIRD GUYS ENTERING THE VILLAGE...
...BUT I GUESS I WAS WRONG.
OH.
I FOUND A PIECE OF THE DISCIPLINARY COMMITTEE.
FLUT
FLUT
HEY...
YOU MIGHT GET A STRANGE POWDER ON YOUR HAND.
ARE YOU ALL RIGHT?
I THINK SHE WANTS TO SAY SOME-THING.
...
WHAT IS IT?
MAYBE SHE WANTS US TO GET HER A SOUVE-NIR?
KNOK
KNOK
KNOK
YES?
GOOD EVEN-ING.
MY MOM IS ASKING IF YOU'D LIKE TO HAVE DINNER WITH US AGAIN TONIGHT.

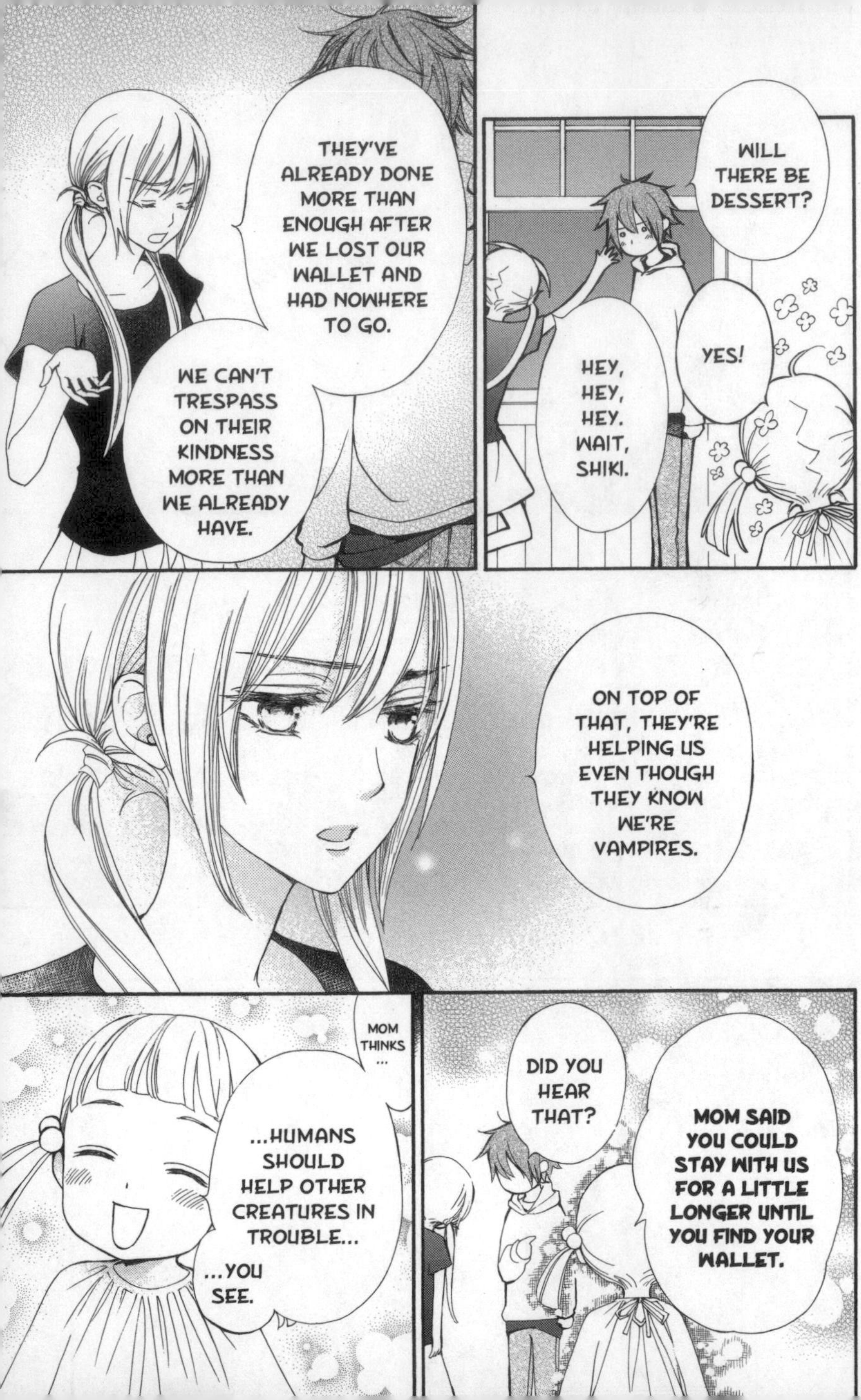
WILL THERE BE DESSERT?
YES!
HEY, HEY, HEY. WAIT, SHIKI.
THEY'VE ALREADY DONE MORE THAN ENOUGH AFTER WE LOST OUR WALLET AND HAD NOWHERE TO GO.
WE CAN'T TRESPASS ON THEIR KINDNESS MORE THAN WE ALREADY HAVE.
ON TOP OF THAT, THEY'RE HELPING US EVEN THOUGH THEY KNOW WE'RE VAMPIRES.
MOM SAID YOU COULD STAY WITH US FOR A LITTLE LONGER UNTIL YOU FIND YOUR WALLET.
DID YOU HEAR THAT?
MOM THINKS...
...HUMANS SHOULD HELP OTHER CREATURES IN TROUBLE...
...YOU SEE.

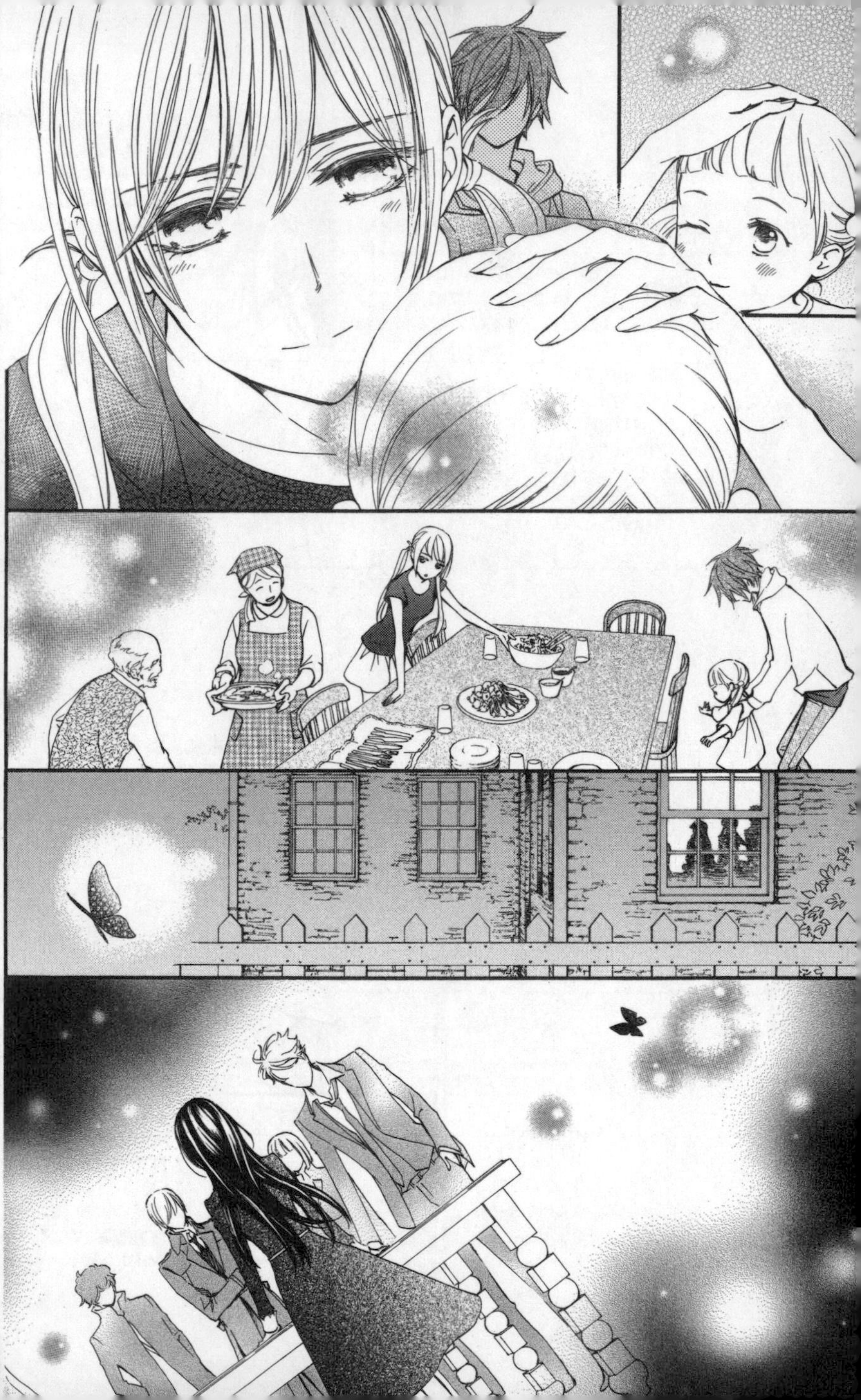

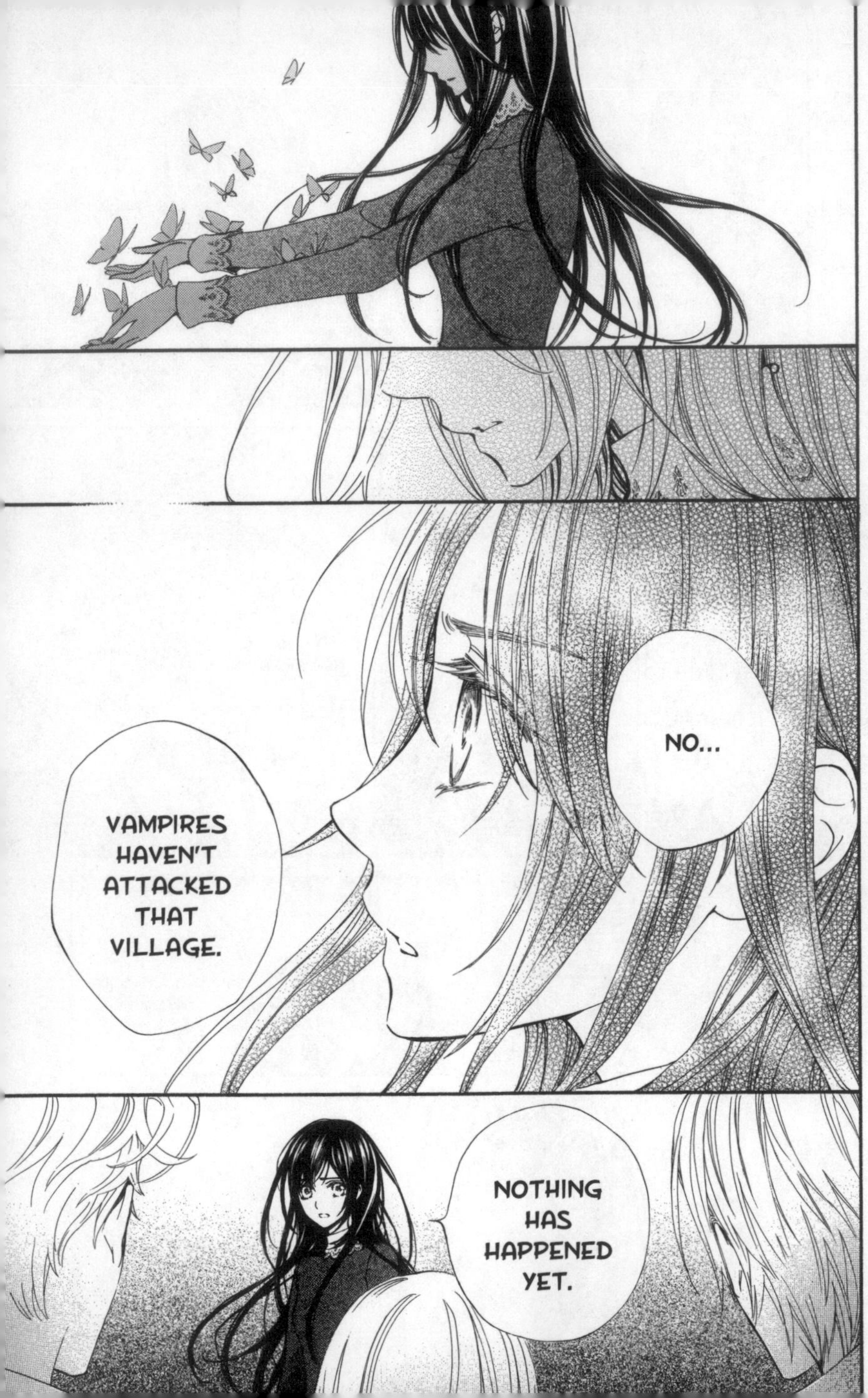
NO...
VAMPIRES HAVEN'T ATTACKED THAT VILLAGE.
NOTHING HAS HAPPENED YET.

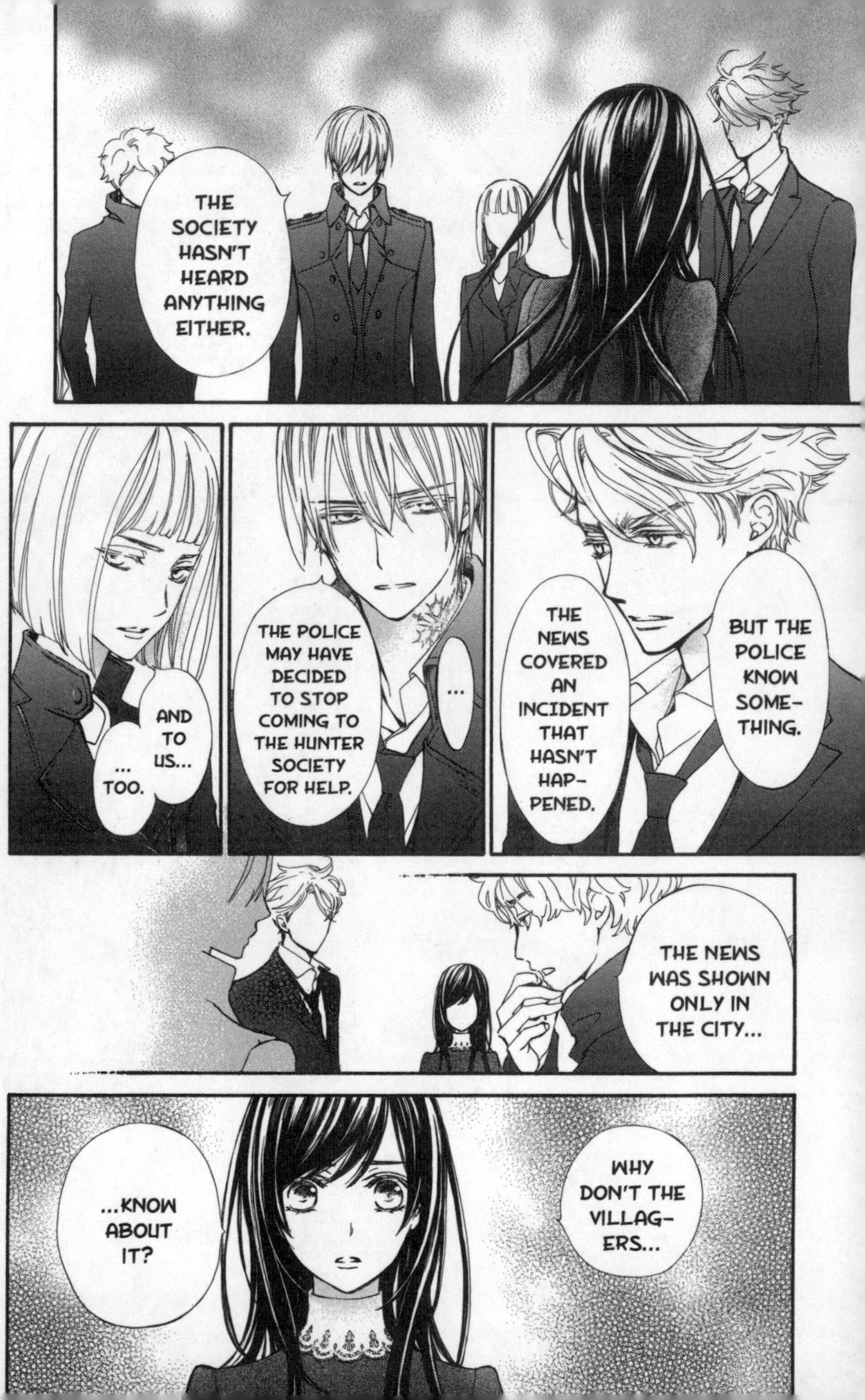
THE SOCIETY HASN'T HEARD ANYTHING EITHER.
BUT THE POLICE KNOW SOME-THING.
THE NEWS COVERED AN INCIDENT THAT HASN'T HAP-PENED.
...
THE POLICE MAY HAVE DECIDED TO STOP COMING TO THE HUNTER SOCIETY FOR HELP.
AND TO US...
...TOO.
THE NEWS WAS SHOWN ONLY IN THE CITY...
WHY DON'T THE VILLAG-ERS...
...KNOW ABOUT IT?

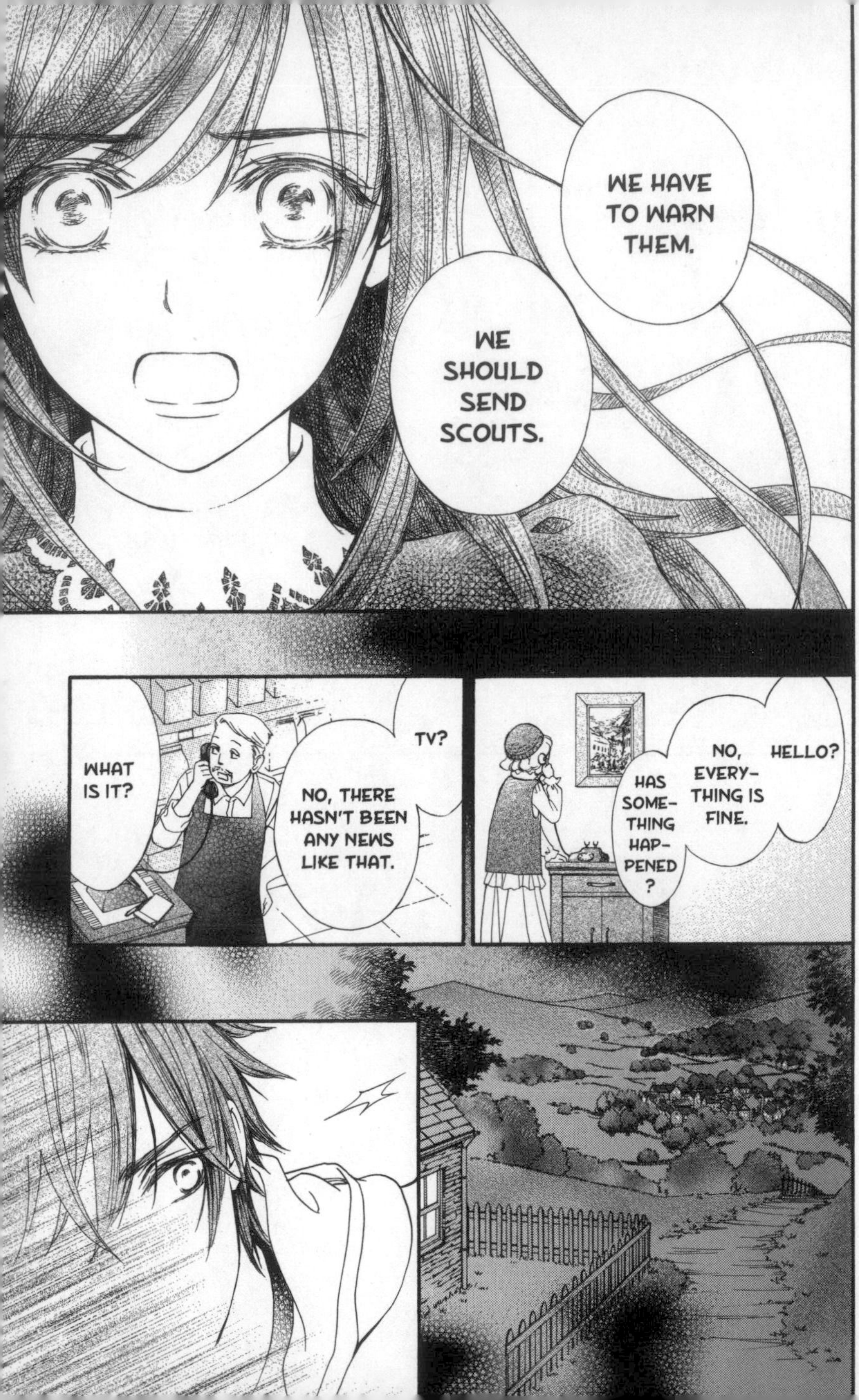
WE HAVE TO WARN THEM.
WE SHOULD SEND SCOUTS.
HELLO?
NO, EVERY-THING IS FINE.
HAS SOME-THING HAP-PENED?
TV?
NO, THERE HASN'T BEEN ANY NEWS LIKE THAT.
WHAT IS IT?

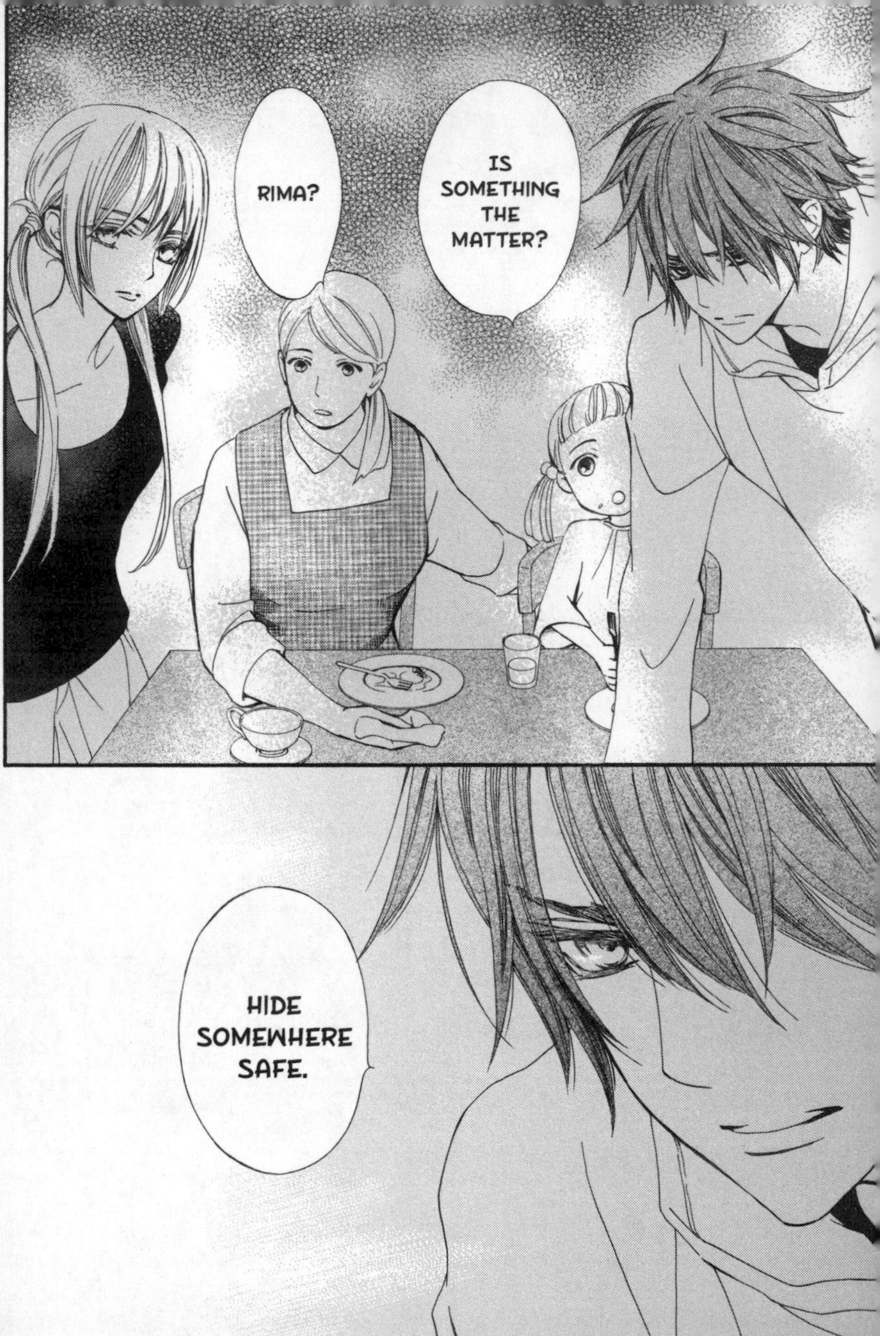
IS SOMETHING THE MATTER?
RIMA?
HIDE SOMEWHERE SAFE.

AN OLD STORY KANAME DOESN'T KNOW/END

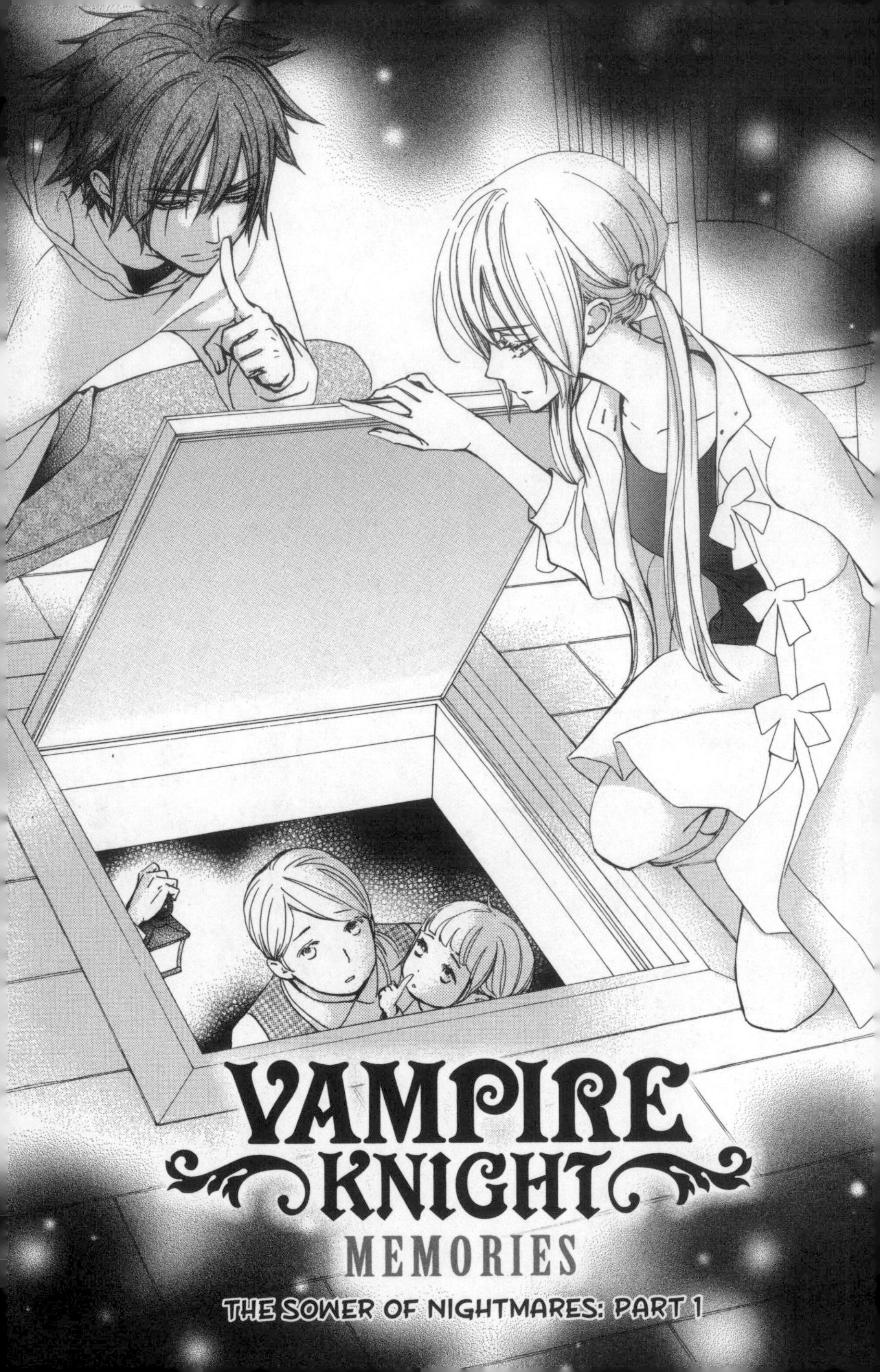
VAMPIRE KNIGHT
MEMORIES
THE SOWER OF NIGHTMARES: PART 1

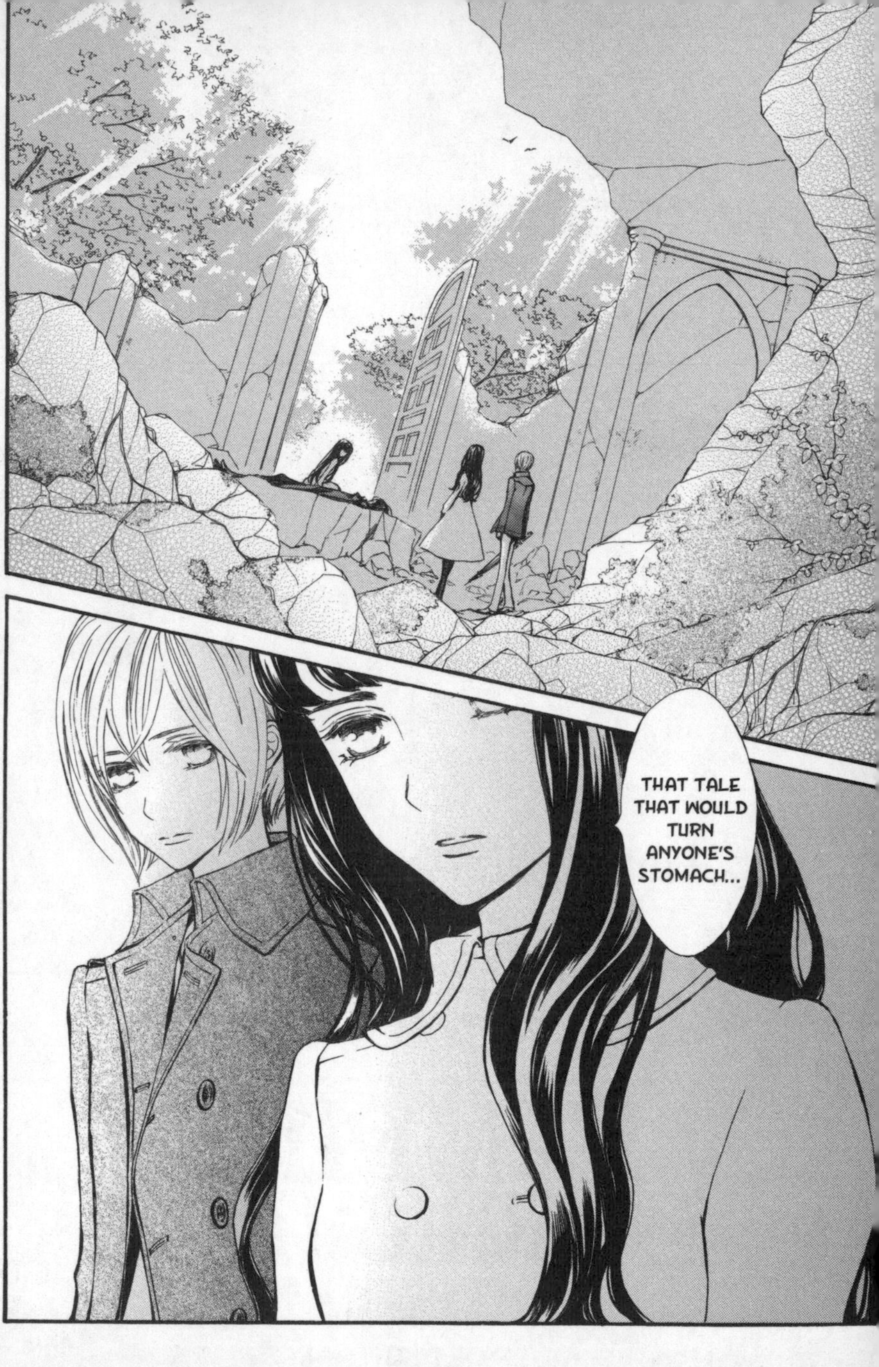
THAT TALE THAT WOULD TURN ANYONE'S STOMACH...

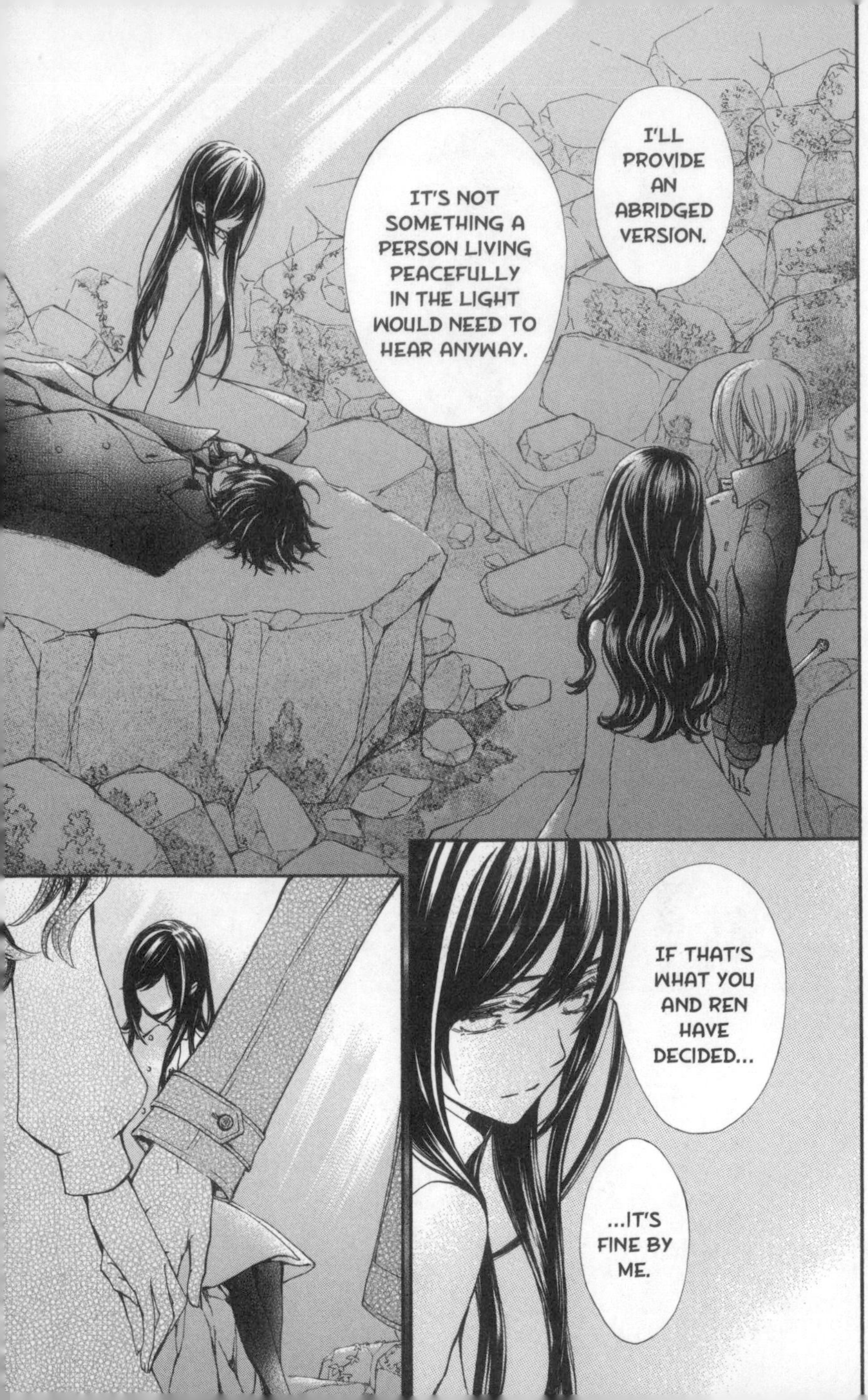
I'LL PROVIDE AN ABRIDGED VERSION.
IT'S NOT SOMETHING A PERSON LIVING PEACEFULLY IN THE LIGHT WOULD NEED TO HEAR ANYWAY.
IF THAT'S WHAT YOU AND REN HAVE DECIDED...
...IT'S FINE BY ME.

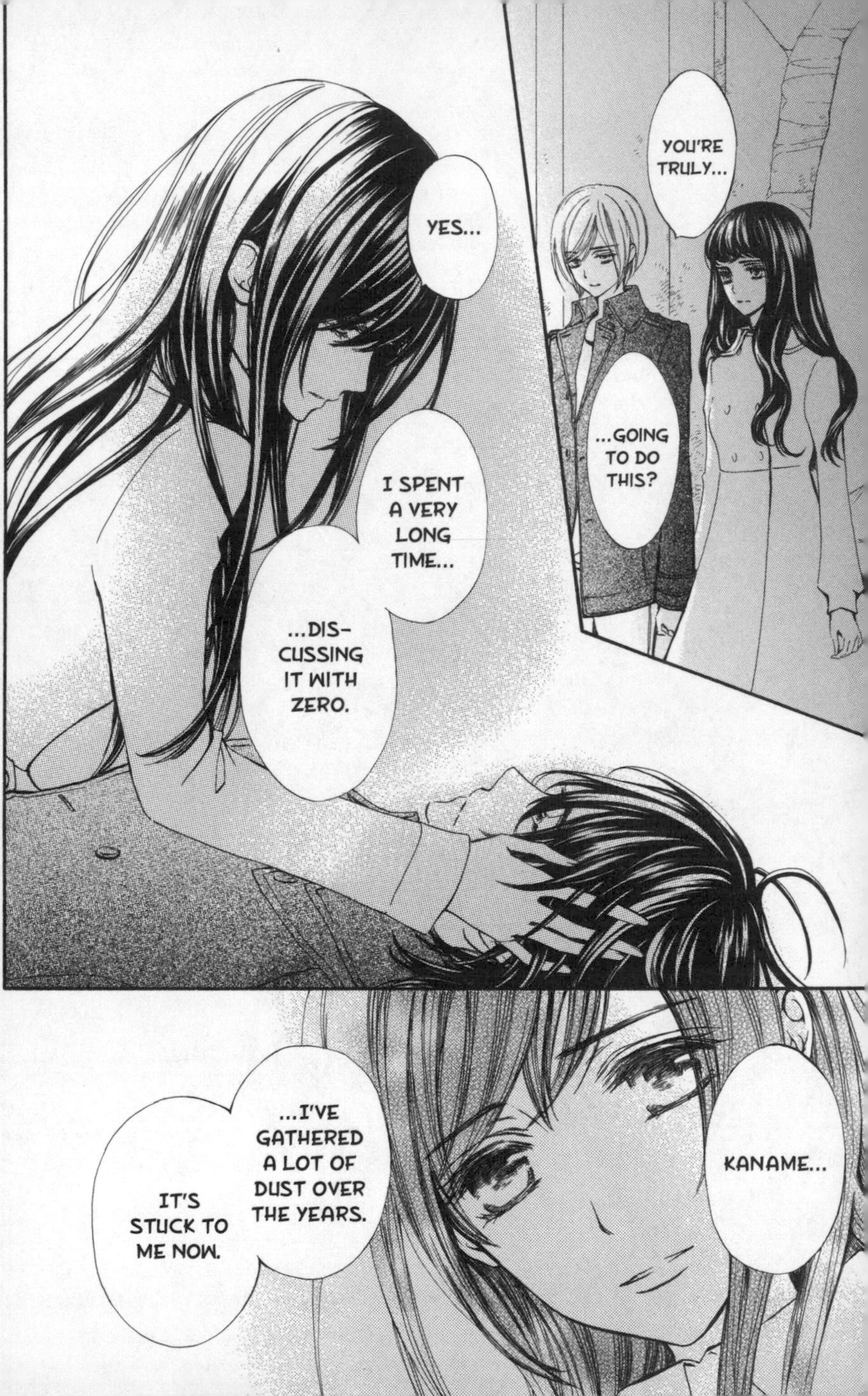
YOU'RE TRULY...
...GOING TO DO THIS?
YES...
I SPENT A VERY LONG TIME...
...DIS-CUSSING IT WITH ZERO.
KANAME...
...I'VE GATHERED A LOT OF DUST OVER THE YEARS.
IT'S STUCK TO ME NOW.

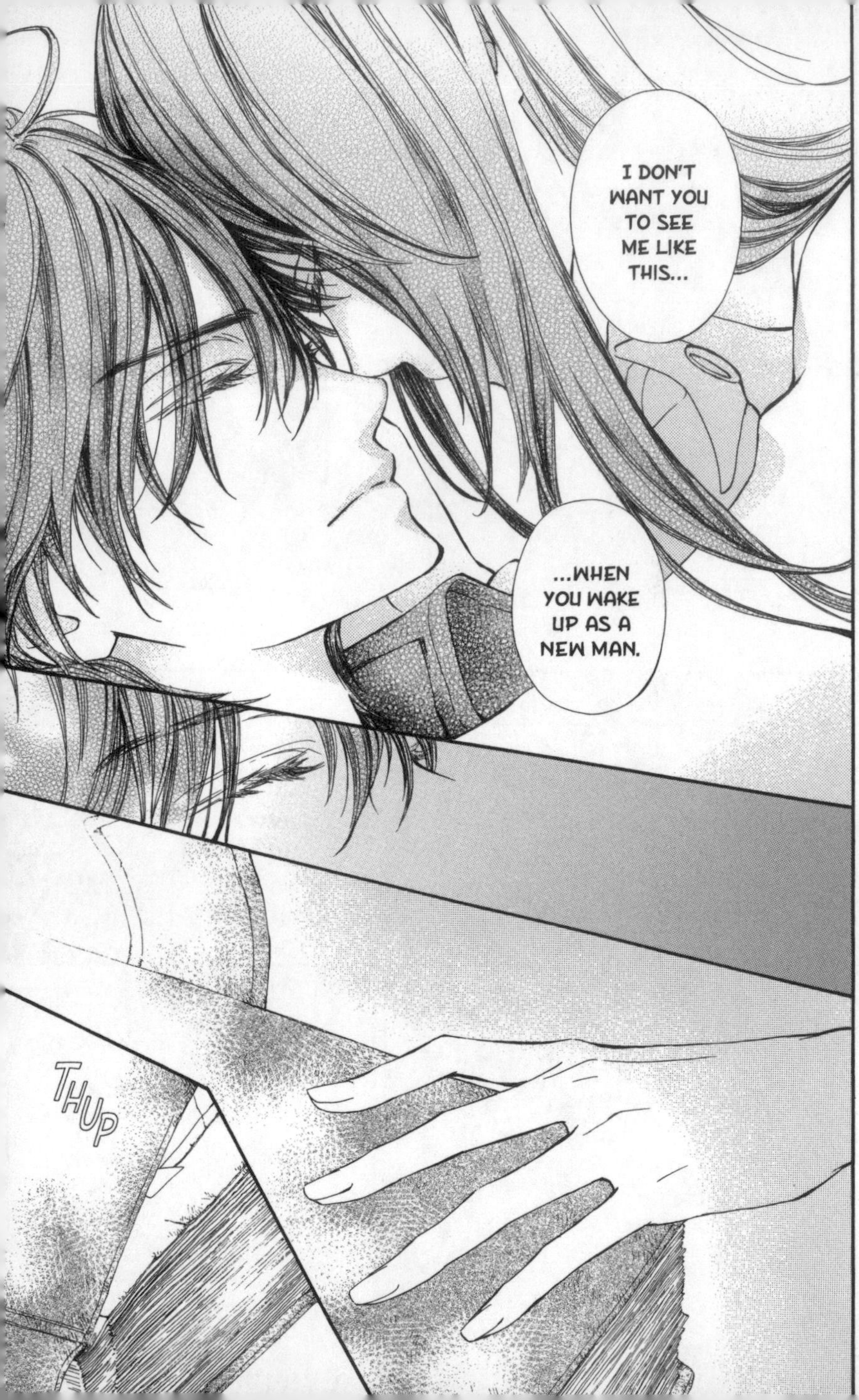
I DON'T WANT YOU TO SEE ME LIKE THIS...
...WHEN YOU WAKE UP AS A NEW MAN.
THUP

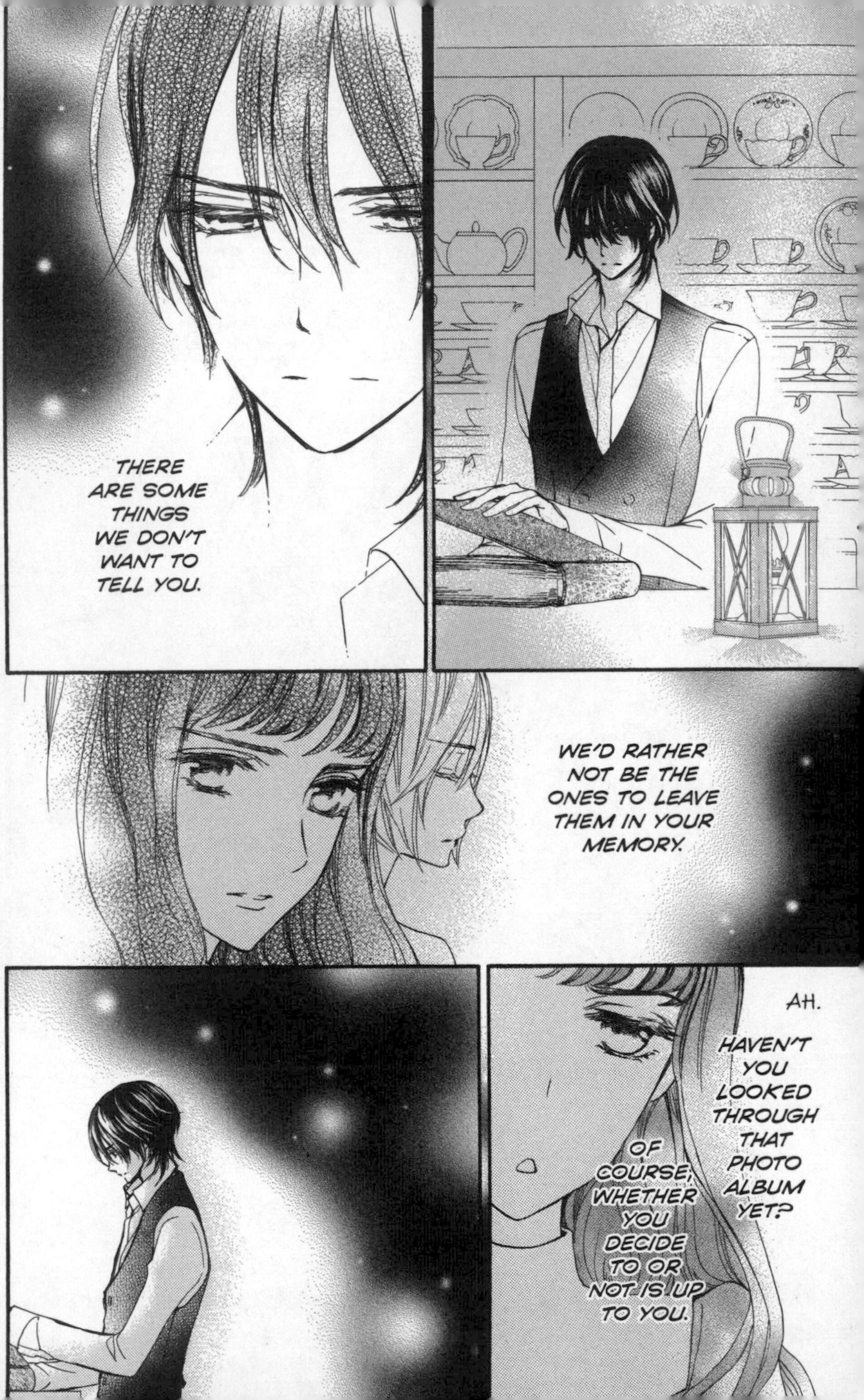
THERE ARE SOME THINGS WE DON'T WANT TO TELL YOU.
WE'D RATHER NOT BE THE ONES TO LEAVE THEM IN YOUR MEMORY.
AH.
HAVEN'T YOU LOOKED THROUGH THAT PHOTO ALBUM YET?
OF COURSE, WHETHER YOU DECIDE TO OR NOT IS UP TO YOU.

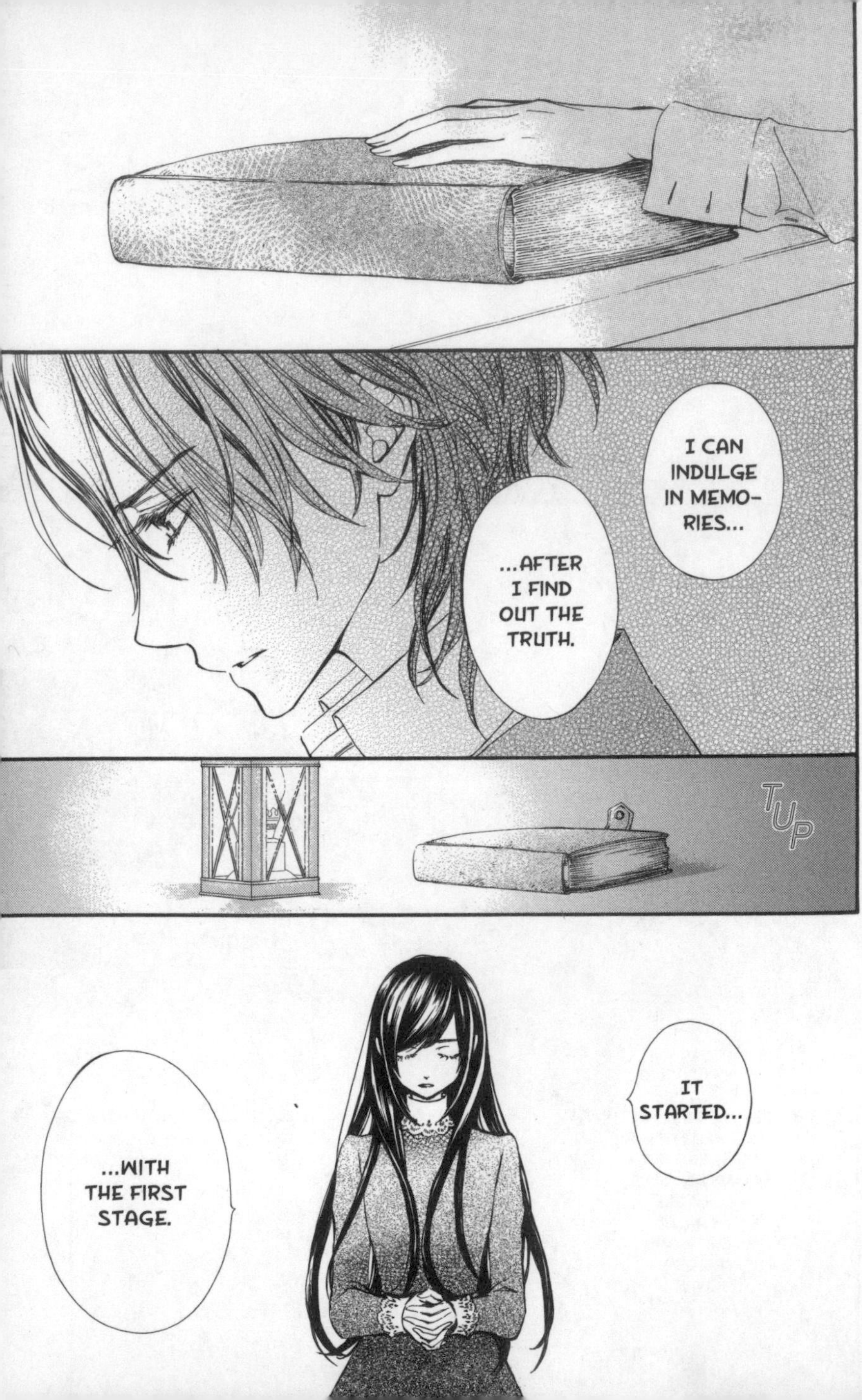
I CAN INDULGE IN MEMO-RIES...
...AFTER I FIND OUT THE TRUTH.
TUP
IT STARTED...
...WITH THE FIRST STAGE.

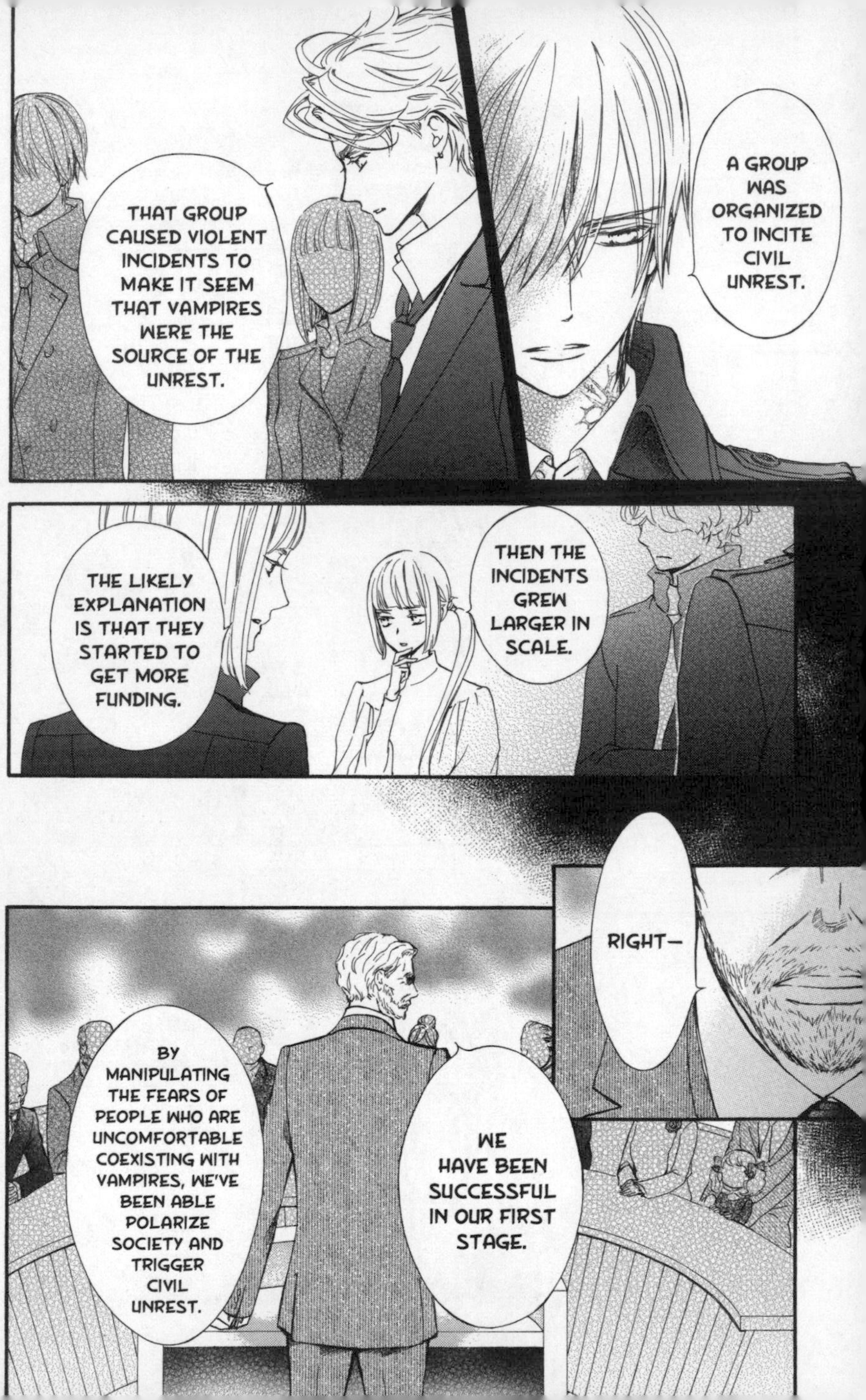
A GROUP WAS ORGANIZED TO INCITE CIVIL UNREST.
THAT GROUP CAUSED VIOLENT INCIDENTS TO MAKE IT SEEM THAT VAMPIRES WERE THE SOURCE OF THE UNREST.
THEN THE INCIDENTS GREW LARGER IN SCALE.
THE LIKELY EXPLANATION IS THAT THEY STARTED TO GET MORE FUNDING.
RIGHT—
WE HAVE BEEN SUCCESSFUL IN OUR FIRST STAGE.
BY MANIPULATING THE FEARS OF PEOPLE WHO ARE UNCOMFORTABLE COEXISTING WITH VAMPIRES, WE'VE BEEN ABLE POLARIZE SOCIETY AND TRIGGER CIVIL UNREST.

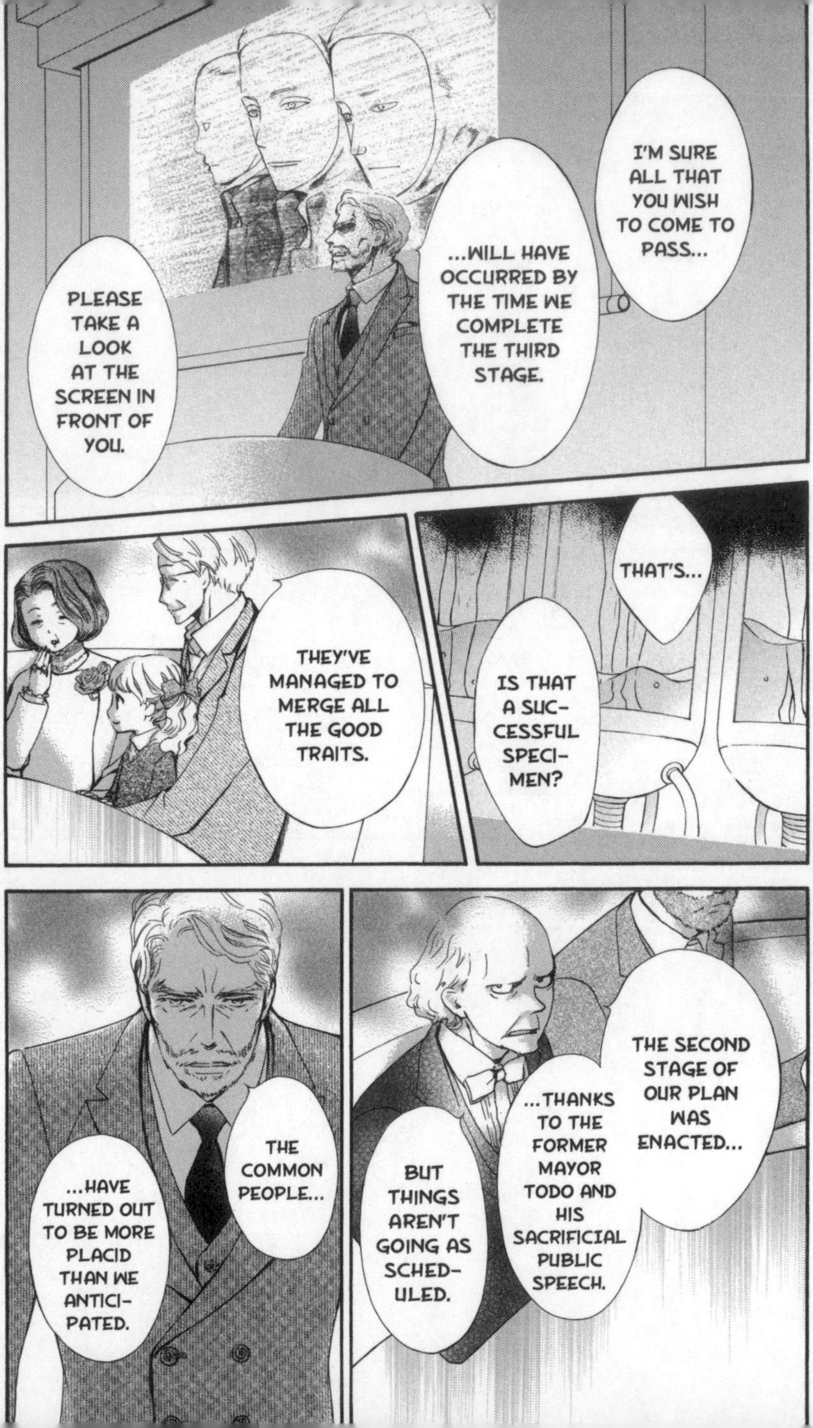
I'M SURE ALL THAT YOU WISH TO COME TO PASS...
...WILL HAVE OCCURRED BY THE TIME WE COMPLETE THE THIRD STAGE.
PLEASE TAKE A LOOK AT THE SCREEN IN FRONT OF YOU.
THAT'S...
IS THAT A SUCCESSFUL SPECIMEN?
THEY'VE MANAGED TO MERGE ALL THE GOOD TRAITS.
THE SECOND STAGE OF OUR PLAN WAS ENACTED...
...THANKS TO THE FORMER MAYOR TODO AND HIS SACRIFICIAL PUBLIC SPEECH.
BUT THINGS AREN'T GOING AS SCHEDULED.
THE COMMON PEOPLE...
...HAVE TURNED OUT TO BE MORE PLACID THAN WE ANTICIPATED.

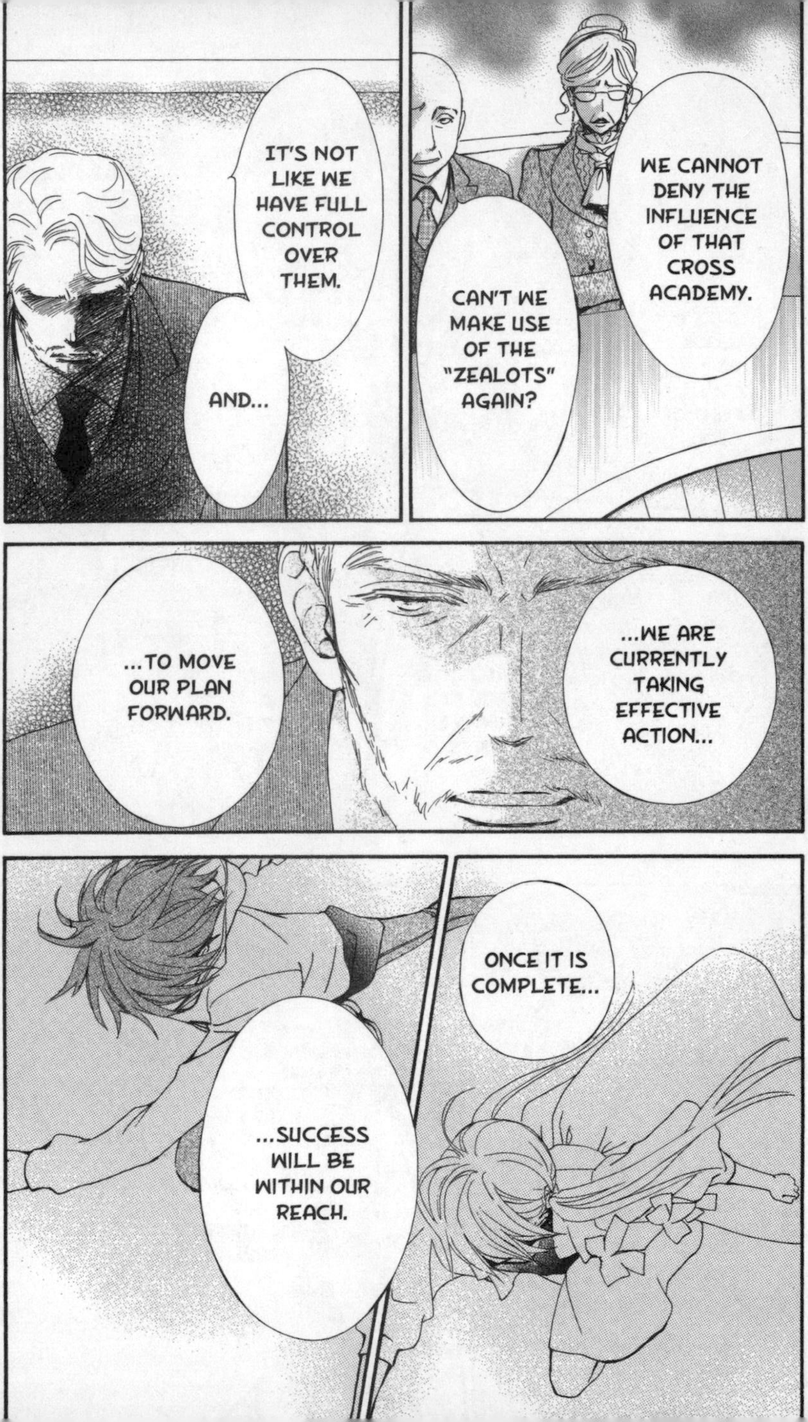
WE CANNOT DENY THE INFLUENCE OF THAT CROSS ACADEMY.
CAN'T WE MAKE USE OF THE "ZEALOTS" AGAIN?
IT'S NOT LIKE WE HAVE FULL CONTROL OVER THEM.
AND...
...WE ARE CURRENTLY TAKING EFFECTIVE ACTION...
...TO MOVE OUR PLAN FORWARD.
ONCE IT IS COMPLETE...
...SUCCESS WILL BE WITHIN OUR REACH.

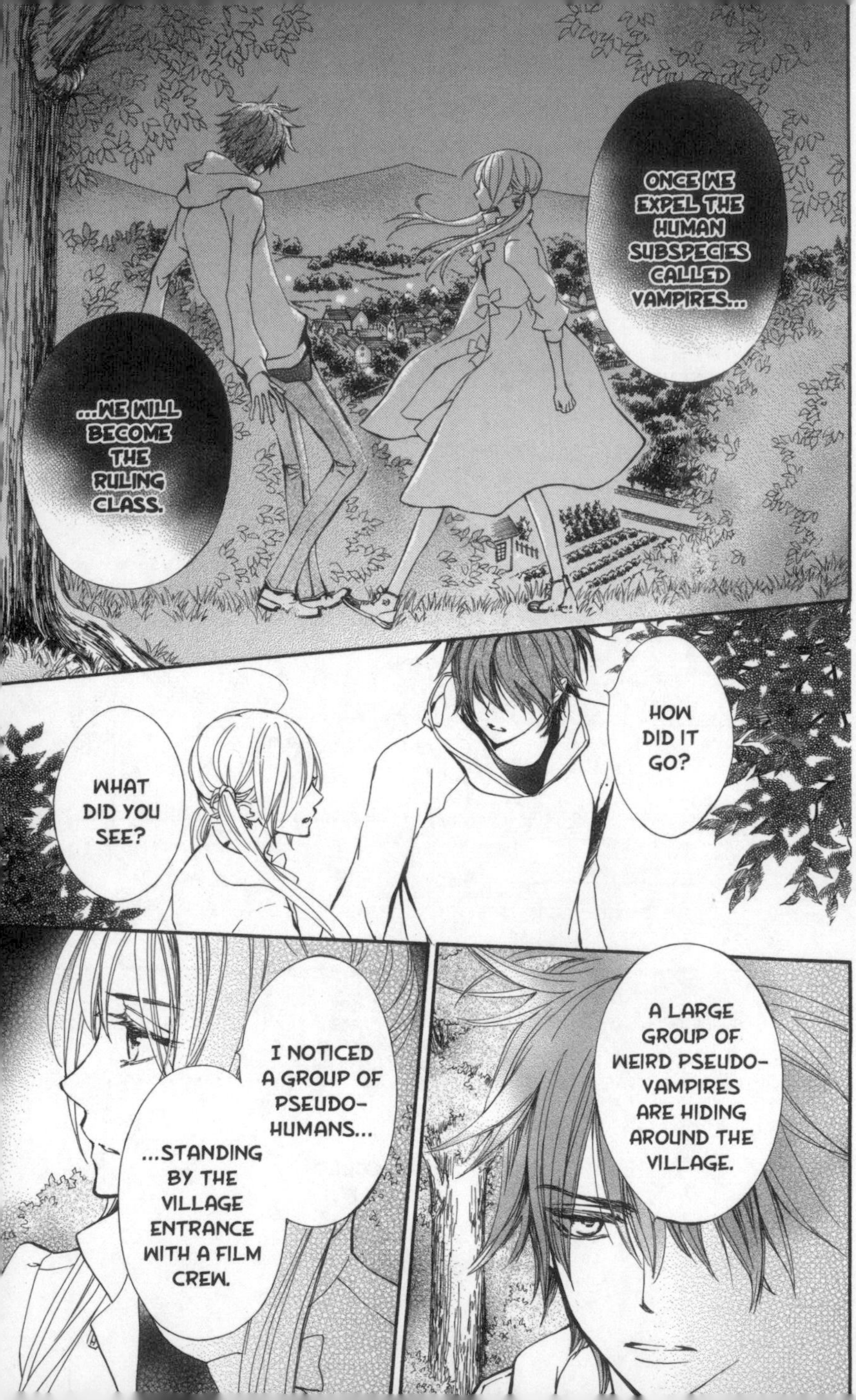
ONCE WE EXPEL THE HUMAN SUBSPECIES CALLED VAMPIRES...
...WE WILL BECOME THE RULING CLASS.
HOW DID IT GO?
WHAT DID YOU SEE?
A LARGE GROUP OF WEIRD PSEUDO-VAMPIRES ARE HIDING AROUND THE VILLAGE.
I NOTICED A GROUP OF PSEUDO-HUMANS...
...STANDING BY THE VILLAGE ENTRANCE WITH A FILM CREW.

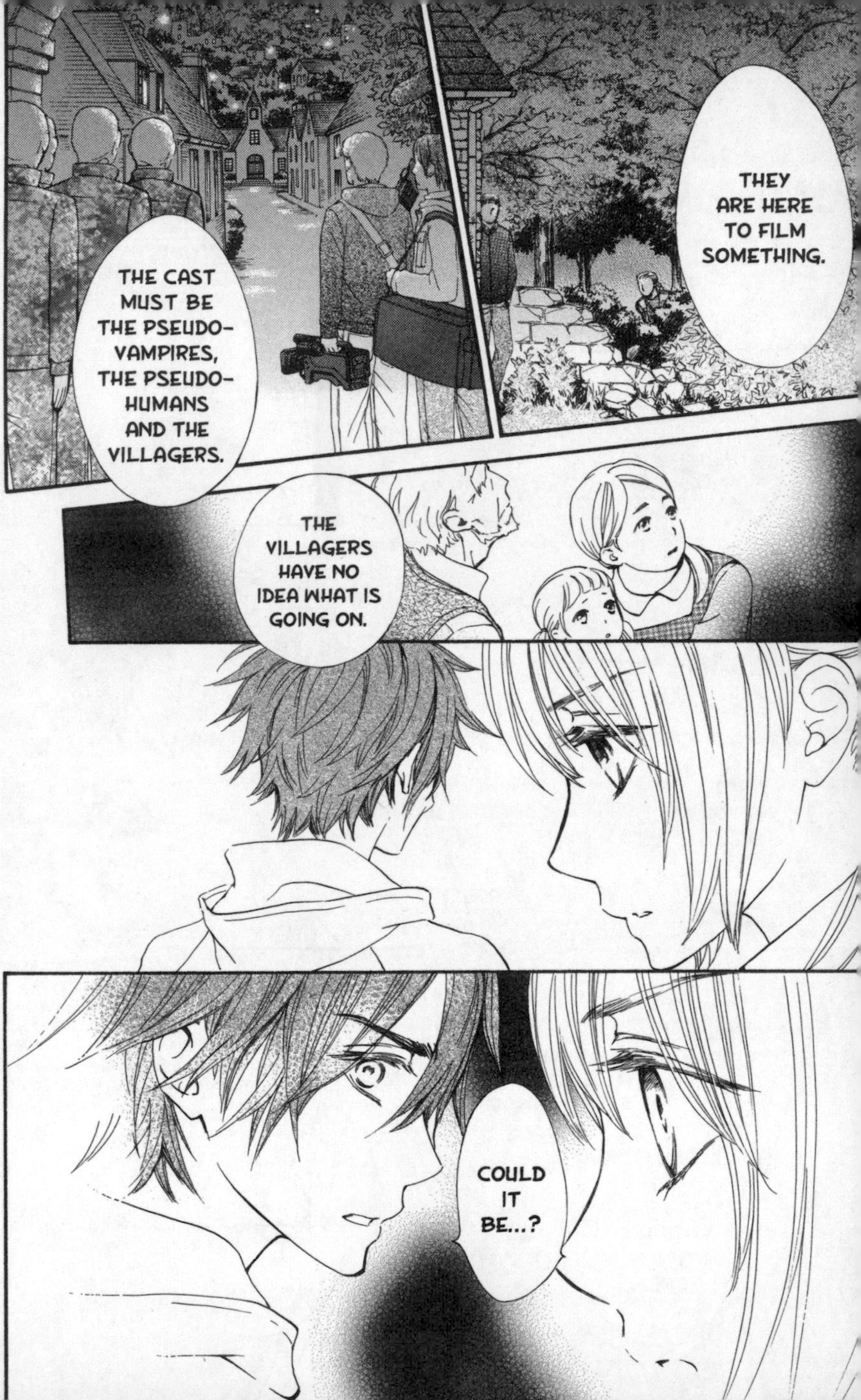
THEY ARE HERE TO FILM SOMETHING.
THE CAST MUST BE THE PSEUDO-VAMPIRES, THE PSEUDO-HUMANS AND THE VILLAGERS.
THE VILLAGERS HAVE NO IDEA WHAT IS GOING ON.
COULD IT BE...?

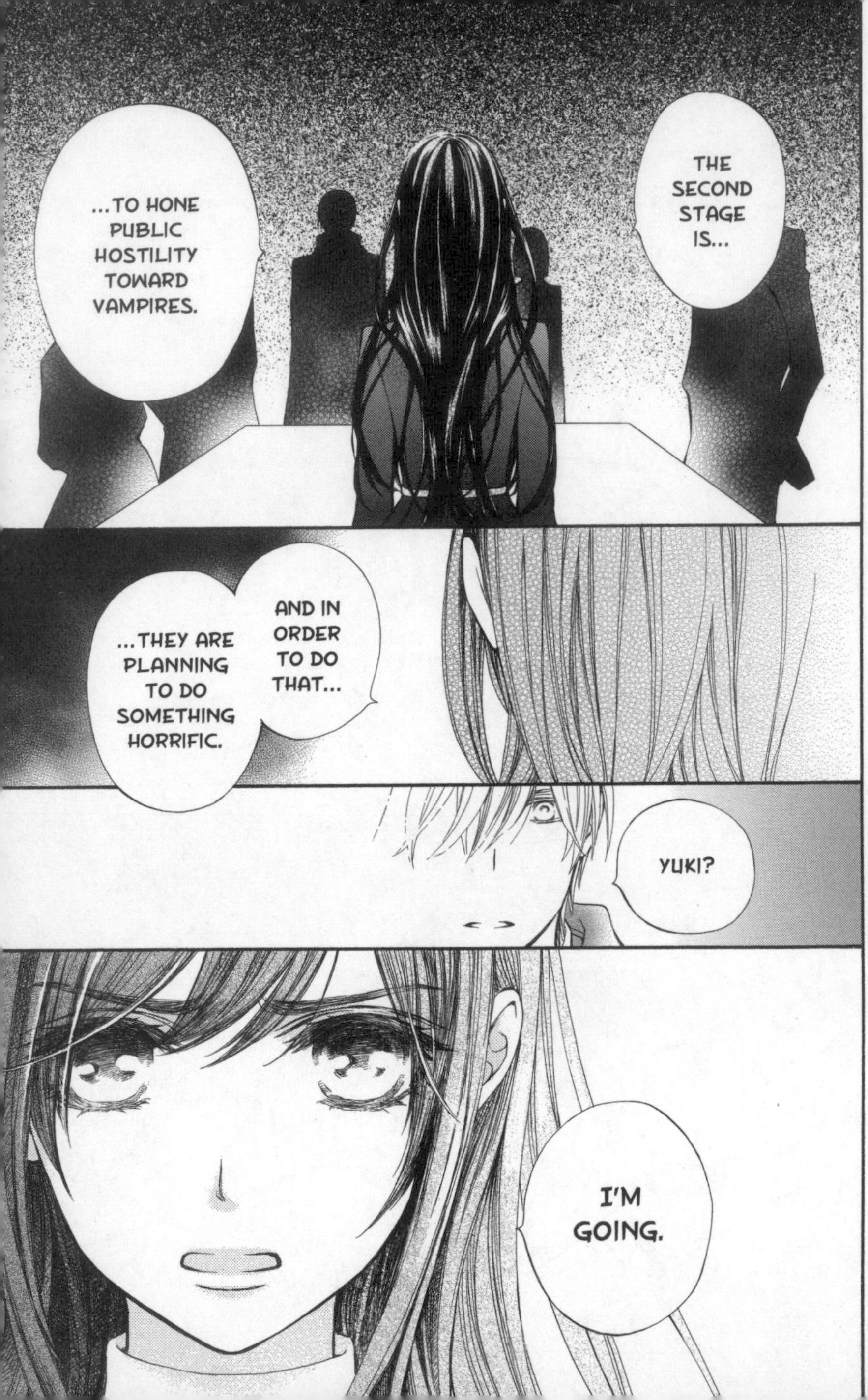
THE SECOND STAGE IS...
...TO HONE PUBLIC HOSTILITY TOWARD VAMPIRES.
AND IN ORDER TO DO THAT...
...THEY ARE PLANNING TO DO SOMETHING HORRIFIC.
YUKI?
I'M GOING.

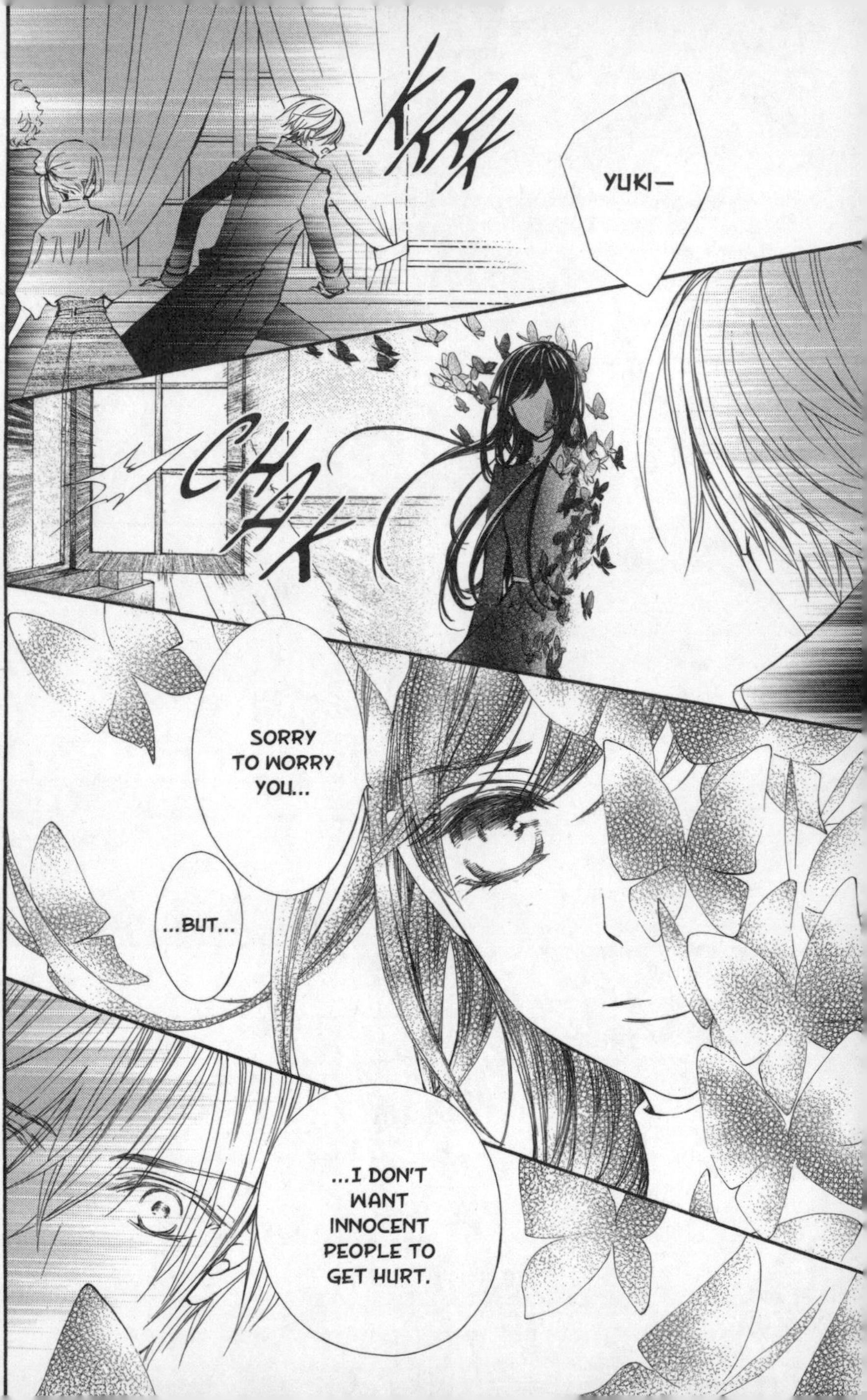
YUKI—
KRRK
CHAK
SORRY TO WORRY YOU...
...BUT...
...I DON'T WANT INNOCENT PEOPLE TO GET HURT.

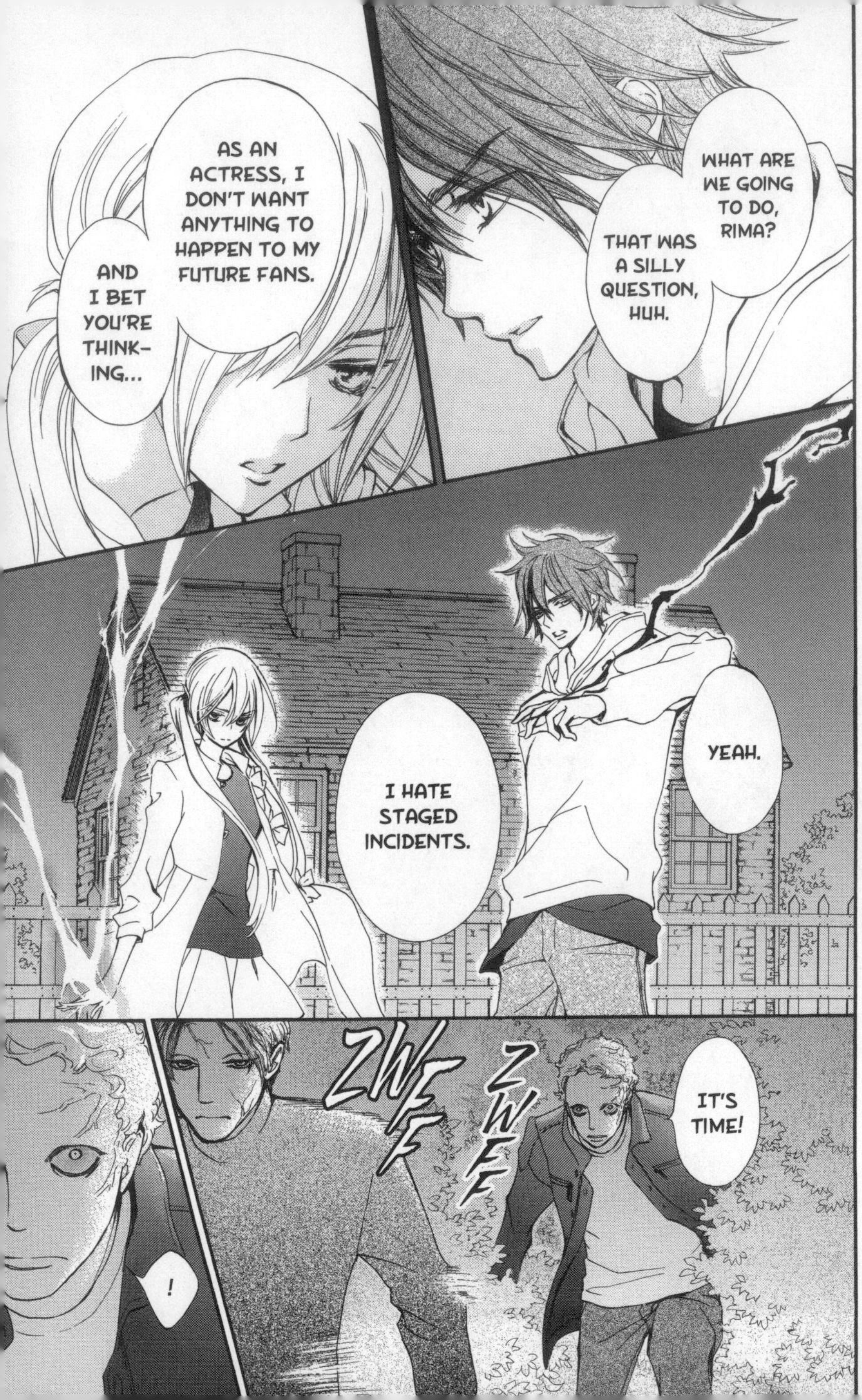
WHAT ARE WE GOING TO DO, RIMA?
THAT WAS A SILLY QUESTION, HUH.
AS AN ACTRESS, I DON'T WANT ANYTHING TO HAPPEN TO MY FUTURE FANS.
AND I BET YOU'RE THINK-ING...
I HATE STAGED INCIDENTS.
YEAH.
IT'S TIME!
ZWEFF
ZWEFF
!

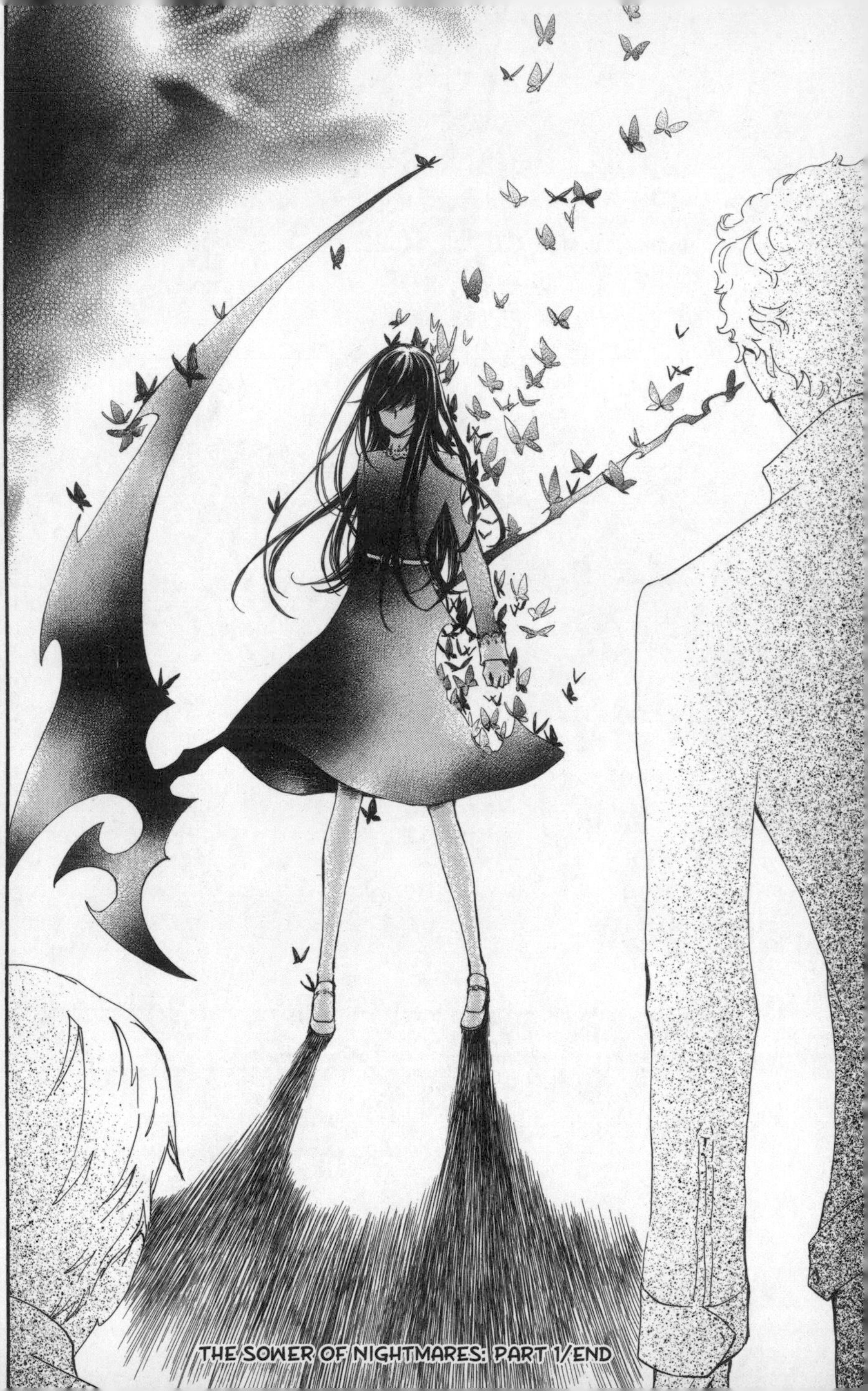
THE SOWER OF NIGHTMARES: PART 1/END

EDITOR'S NOTES

CHARACTERS

Matsuri Hino puts careful thought into the names of her characters in *Vampire Knight*. Below is the collection of characters throughout the manga. Each character's name is presented family name first, per the kanji reading.

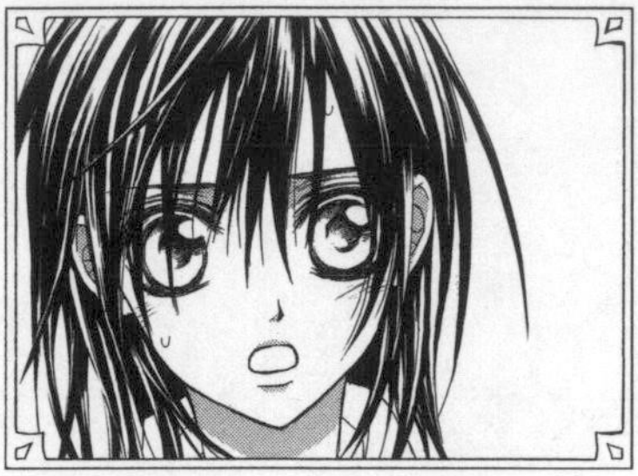

黒主優姫

Cross Yuki

Yuki's last name, *Kurosu*, is the Japanese pronunciation of the English word "cross." However, the kanji has a different meaning—*kuro* means "black" and *su* means "master." Her first name is a combination of *yuu*, meaning "tender" or "kind," and *ki*, meaning "princess."

錐生零

Kiryu Zero

Zero's first name is the kanji for *rei*, meaning "zero." In his last name, *Kiryu*, the *ki* means "auger" or "drill" and the *ryu* means "life."

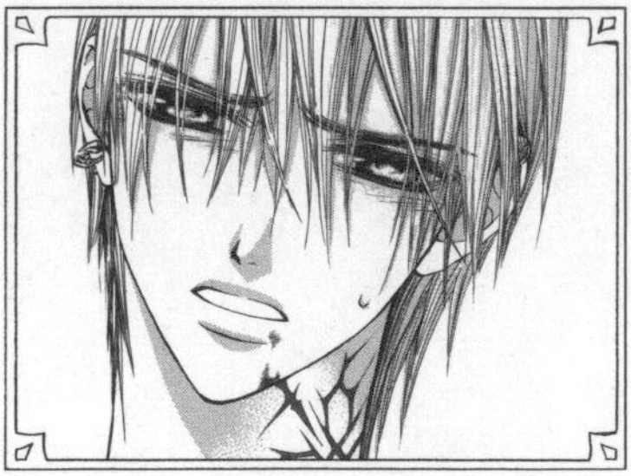

玖蘭枢

Kuran Kaname

Kaname means "hinge" or "door." The kanji for his last name is a combination of the old-fashioned way of writing *ku*, meaning "nine," and *ran*, meaning "orchid": "nine orchids."

藍堂英

Aido Hanabusa

Hanabusa means "petals of a flower." *Aido* means "indigo temple." In Japanese, the pronunciation of *Aido* is very close to the pronunciation of the English word *idol*.

架院暁

Kain Akatsuki

Akatsuki means "dawn" or "daybreak." In *Kain*, *ka* is a base or support, while *in* denotes a building that has high fences around it, such as a temple or school.

早園瑠佳

Souen Ruka

In *Ruka*, the *ru* means "lapis lazuli" while the *ka* means "good-looking" or "beautiful." The *sou* in Ruka's surname, *Souen*, means "early," but this kanji also has an obscure meaning of "strong fragrance." The *en* means "garden."

一条拓麻

Ichijo Takuma

Ichijo can mean a "ray" or "streak." The kanji for *Takuma* is a combination of *taku*, meaning "to cultivate," and *ma*, which is the kanji for *asa*, meaning "hemp" or "flax," a plant with blue flowers.

支葵千里

Shiki Senri

Shiki's last name is a combination of *shi*, meaning "to support," and *ki*, meaning "mallow"—a flowering plant with pink or white blossoms. The *ri* in *Senri* is a traditional Japanese unit of measure for distance, and one *ri* is about 2.44 miles. *Senri* means "1,000 *ri*."

夜刈十牙

Yagari Toga

Yagari is a combination of *ya*, meaning "night," and *gari*, meaning "to harvest." *Toga* means "ten fangs."

一条麻遠，一翁

Ichijo Asato, a.k.a. "Ichio"

Ichijo can mean a "ray" or "streak." Asato's first name is comprised of *asa*, meaning "hemp" or "flax," and *tou*, meaning "far-off." His nickname is *ichi*, or "one," combined with *ou*, which can be used as an honorific when referring to an older man.

若葉沙頼

Wakaba Sayori

Yori's full name is Sayori Wakaba. *Wakaba* means "young leaves." Her given name, *Sayori*, is a combination of *sa*, meaning "sand," and *yori*, meaning "trust."

星煉

Seiren

Sei means "star" and ren means "to smelt" or "to refine." *Ren* is also the same kanji used in *rengoku*, or "purgatory." Her previous name, *Hoshino*, uses the same kanji for "star" (*hoshi*) and *no*, which can mean "from" and is often used at the end of traditional female names.

遠矢莉磨

Toya Rima

Toya means a "far-reaching arrow." Rima's first name is a combination of *ri*, or "jasmine," and *ma*, which signifies enhancement by wearing away, such as by polishing or scouring.

紅まり亜

Kurenai Maria

Kurenai means "crimson." The kanji for the last *a* in Maria's first name is the same that is used in "Asia."

錐生壱縷

Kiryu Ichiru

Ichi is the old-fashioned way of writing "one" and *ru* means "thread." In *Kiryu*, the *ki* means "auger" or "drill" and the *ryu* means "life."

緋桜閑, 狂咲姫

Hio Shizuka, Kuruizaki-hime

Shizuka means "calm and quiet." In Shizuka's family name, *hi* is "scarlet" and *ou* is "cherry blossoms." Shizuka Hio is also referred to as the "Kuruizaki-hime." *Kuruizaki* means "flowers blooming out of season" and *hime* means "princess."

藍堂月子

Aido Tsukiko

Aido means "indigo temple." *Tsukiko* means "moon child."

白蘓更

Shirabuki Sara

Shira is "white" and *buki* is
"butterbur," a plant with white
flowers. *Sara* means "to renew."

黒主灰閻

Cross Kaien

Cross, or *Kurosu*, means "black
master." *Kaien* is a combination of
kai, meaning "ashes," and *en*, meaning
"village gate." The kanji for *en* is
also used for Enma, the ruler of the
underworld in Buddhist mythology.

玖蘭李土

Kuran Rido

Kuran means "nine orchids."
In *Rido*, *ri* means "plum"
and *do* means "earth."

玖蘭樹里

Kuran Juri

Kuran means "nine orchids." In her first name, *ju* means "tree" and a *ri* is a traditional Japanese unit of measure for distance. The kanji for *ri* is the same as in Senri's name.

玖蘭悠

Kuran Haruka

Kuran means "nine orchids." *Haruka* means "distant" or "remote."

鷹宮海斗

Takamiya Kaito

Taka means "hawk" and *miya* means "imperial palace" or "shrine." *Kai* is "sea" and *to* means "to measure" or "grid."

菖藤依砂也

Shoto Isaya

Sho means "Siberian iris" and *to* is "wisteria." The *I* in *Isaya* means "to rely on" while the *sa* means "sand." *Ya* is a suffix used for emphasis.

橙茉

Toma

In the family name *Toma*, *to* means "Seville orange" and *ma* means "jasmine flower."

藍堂永路

Aido Nagamichi

The name *Nagamichi* is a combination of *naga*, which means "long" or "eternal," and *michi*, which is the kanji for "road" or "path." *Aido* means "indigo temple."

縹木

Hanadagi

In this family name, *hanada* means "bright light blue" and *gi* means "tree."

影山霞

Kageyama Kasumi

In the Class Rep's family name, *kage* means "shadow" and *yama* means "mountain." His first name, *Kasumi*, means "haze" or "mist."

愛

Ai

Ai means "love." It is used in terms of unconditional, unending love and affection.

恋

Ren

Ren means "love." It is used in terms of a romantic love or crush.

藍堂星夜

Aido Seiya

Aido means "indigo temple." *Sei* means "star" and *ya* means "night": "starry night."

Terms

-sama: The suffix *-sama* is used in formal address for someone who ranks higher in the social hierarchy. The vampires call their leader "Kaname-sama" only when they are among their own kind.

Matsuri Hino burst onto the manga scene with her title *Kono Yume ga Sametara* (When This Dream Is Over), which was published in *LaLa DX* magazine. Hino was a manga artist a mere nine months after she decided to become one.

With the success of her popular series *Captive Hearts*, *MeruPuri* and *Vampire Knight*, Hino is a major player in the world of shojo manga.

Hino enjoys creative activities and has commented that she would have been either an architect or an apprentice to traditional Japanese craftsmasters if she had not become a manga artist.

VAMPIRE KNIGHT: MEMORIES
Vol. 5
Shojo Beat Manga Edition

STORY AND ART BY
MATSURI HINO

Adaptation/Nancy Thistlethwaite
Translation/Tetsuichiro Miyaki
Touch-Up Art & Lettering/Inori Fukuda Trant
Graphic Design/Alice Lewis
Editor/Nancy Thistlethwaite

Printed in the U.S.A.

Published by VIZ Media, LLC
P.O. Box 77010
San Francisco, CA 94107

10 9 8 7 6 5 4 3 2 1
First printing, December 2020

viz.com

shojobeat.com

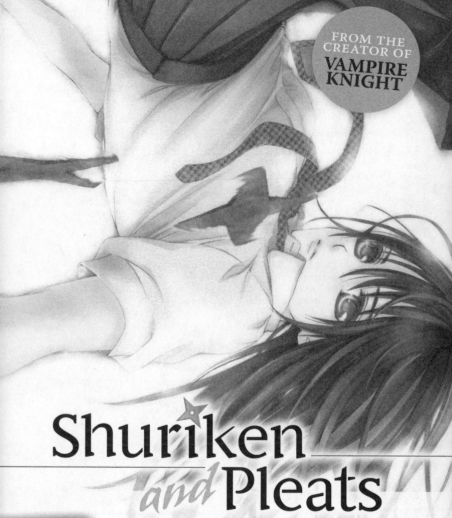

Shuriken
and Pleats

When the master she has sworn to protect is killed, Mikage Kirio,
a skilled ninja, travels to Japan to start a new, peaceful life for
herself. But as soon as she arrives, she finds herself fighting to
protect the life of Mahito Wakashimatsu, a man who is under
attack by a band of ninja. From that time on, Mikage is drawn
deeper into the machinations of his powerful family.

www.viz.com

IDOL dreams

STORY & ART BY ARINA TANEMURA

At age 31, office worker Chikage Deguchi feels she missed her chances at love and success. When word gets out that she's a virgin, Chikage is humiliated and wishes she could turn back time to when she was still young and popular. She takes an experimental drug that changes her appearance back to when she was 15. Now Chikage is determined to pursue everything she missed out on all those years ago—including becoming a star!

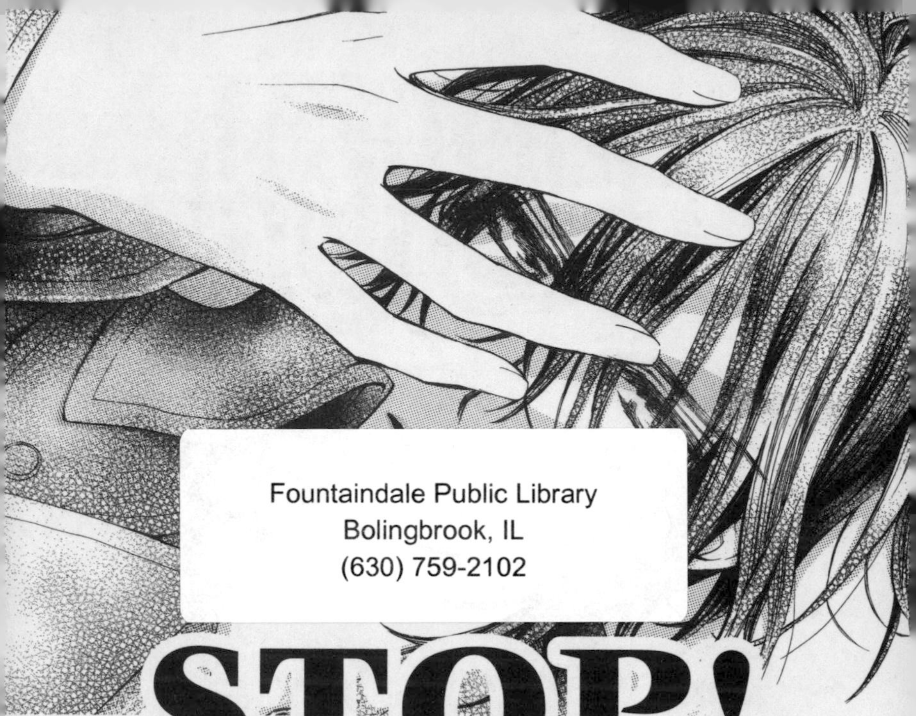

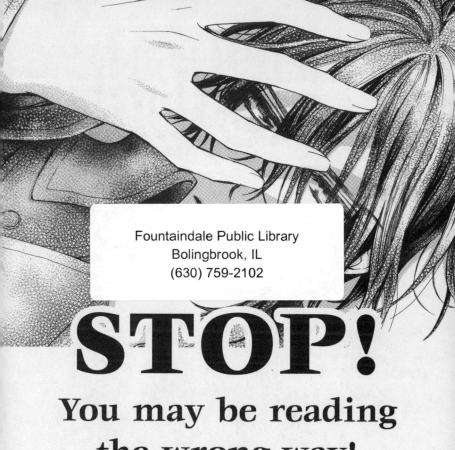

STOP!

You may be reading the wrong way!

In keeping with the original Japanese comic format, this book reads from right to left—so word balloons, action and sound effects and are reversed to preserve the orientation of the original artwork.

Check out the diagram shown here to get the hang of things, and then turn to the other side of the book to get started!

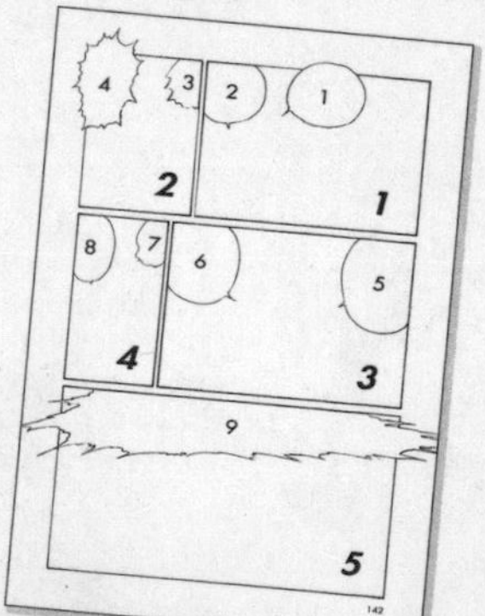
1
2
1
3
4
2
5
6
3
7
8
4
9
5